German-Jewish History
in Modern Times

VOLUME 2
Emancipation and Acculturation
1780–1871

German-Jewish History in Modern Times

VOLUME 1

Tradition and Enlightenment
1600–1780

VOLUME 2

Emancipation and Acculturation
1780–1871

VOLUME 3

Integration in Dispute
1871–1918

VOLUME 4

Renewal and Destruction
1918–1945

Advisory Committee
Jacob Katz, Jürgen Kocka, Werner E. Mosse, Jehuda Reinharz, Reinhard Rürup,
Ismar Schorsch, Fritz Stern, Yosef Hayim Yerushalmi

Coordinator
Fred Grubel

German-Jewish History in Modern Times

Edited by Michael A. Meyer

MICHAEL BRENNER, ASSISTANT EDITOR

VOLUME 2
Emancipation and Acculturation
1780–1871

MICHAEL BRENNER

STEFI JERSCH-WENZEL

MICHAEL A. MEYER

A Project of the Leo Baeck Institute

Columbia University Press

NEW YORK

Columbia University Press
Publishers Since 1893
New York   Chichester, West Sussex
Copyright © 1997 Leo Baeck Institute
All rights reserved

The chapters by Michael Brenner and Stefi Jersch-Wenzel were
translated from the German by Allison Brown

Library of Congress Cataloging-in-Publication Data

Deutsch-jüdische Geschichte in der Neuzeit. English.
  German-Jewish history in modern times / edited by Michael A. Meyer
and Michael Brenner, assistant editor.
    p.   cm.
    "A project of the Leo Baeck Institute."
    Contents: v. 1. Tradition and enlightenment : 1600 –1780 /
Mordechai Breuer, Michael Graetz; translated by William Templer.
    ISBN 0-231-07474-3
    1. Jews—Germany—History. 2. Judaism—Germany—History.
3. Haskalah—Germany—History. 4. Germany—Ethnic relations.
5. Germany—Ethnic relations. I. Meyer, Michael A. II. Brenner,
Michael. III. Breuer, Mordechai, 1918–   . IV. Graetz, Michael.
V. Title.
DS135.G32B48   1996
943'.004924—dc20   96-13900
                                                                    CIP

Casebound editions of Columbia University Press books are printed on
permanent and durable acid-free paper.

Printed in the United States of America
c 10 9 8 7 6 5 4 3 2 1
p 10 9 8 7 6 5 4 3 2 1

Contents

Emancipation and Acculturation
1780–1871

Introduction

The Age of Enlightenment marked the transition to Jewish modernity. Among Enlightenment thinkers—Jews and Gentiles alike—surrounding Moses Mendelssohn and Lessing, the first signs of a new age could already be perceived, yet the influence of these circles was still limited to a small minority, and legal discrimination persisted unchanged. Comprehensive changes did not appear on the horizon until the 1780s. This decade began with theoretical writings and practical measures for the improvement of the Jews' civil status in Prussia and Austria; it ended with the French Revolution, which resulted in France becoming the first European state to grant complete emancipation to its Jews.

Upon the urging of Moses Mendelssohn, Prussian military councillor Christian Wilhelm Dohm wrote his programmatic work, *On the Civil Improvement of the Jews*, in 1781; in the same year, Emperor Joseph II enacted the first, albeit cautious, legal measures aimed at implementing such improvement in parts of the Habsburg Empire. Although independent of one another, these initiatives in Berlin and Vienna were undeniably linked. The signs of the times clearly pointed to an end to the segregation of Jews from their Christian environment, a segregation that still existed in all areas of social life, despite the fact that autonomous Jewish communities were gradually being dismantled. The aim was for Jews to live together with, rather than merely parallel to, the non-Jewish population. Once the privileges of the estates were eliminated and the way was paved toward a new bourgeois society, Jews could not continue to exist as the last remaining "state within a state," a charge they repeatedly heard. In the end the emancipation process was inevitable, due much less to specific needs of the Jewish minority than to vast changes in the emerging modern state, which was in the process of freeing itself from traditional corporative structures.

Only in view of developments in society as a whole can it be explained that France was the first European state to grant comprehensive equality to its Jewish population, although in the German states the first theoretical writings on the emancipation of the Jews had already appeared and practical measures been implemented in the early 1780s. Just as the revolution itself never came to pass in the German states, neither did a revolutionary emancipation of Jews there. Instead, emancipation was achieved over a prolonged period of almost a century and its success was made dependent on whether Jews were willing to reeducate themselves. This process was largely connected with other areas of reform politics, including agrarian reform and the gradual weakening of medieval organizational structures such as the guild system.

The price of emancipation was the relinquishing of all Jewish characteristics that were viewed as national. This did not, however lead to the dissolution of Jewish identity, rather to its being redefined as a religious denomination analogous to Christian denominations. In concrete terms it meant adopting the German language and culture, striving to increase Jewish "productivity" through occupational redistribution, and the modernization of expressions of the Jewish religion. The last was apparent not only in the emergence of the Reform movement, but in two other forms assumed by modern Judaism in nineteenth-century Germany: Conservative Judaism (called "positive-historical") and neo-Orthodoxy.

Recent research does not dispute these important developments, but there is a prevailing trend to consider giving greater weight to aspects of continuity. Until well into the second half of the nineteenth century, most of German Jewry resided in villages and small towns, where Jews felt the ideological and social changes less radically than did their urban coreligionists. Although some progress was made in terms of legal equality in the decades following Moses Mendelssohn's death, total emancipation remained an unfulfilled desire throughout the entire period. The terminology used in recent historical research has also reshaped the image of German Jewry. For example, the concept of *assimilation*, which historians traditionally used in reference to this period, is now employed only with caution. In focusing on the redefinition of Judaism rather than its abandonment the term *acculturation,* which has a less ideological connotation, seems more appropriate with respect to a majority of German Jewry. This term does not imply that Jews merged totally into German society but rather that they attempted to participate in both the Jewish and German spheres. Emancipation and acculturation were thus the basic issues determining the course of German-Jewish history between 1780 and 1871.

The most significant break during this period is the year 1848, not so much on account of actual changes that were implemented as of the hopes that accompanied the revolutionary events. A victory for German liberalism would have brought with it a liberalization of policies toward the Jews; the success of the National Assembly in St. Paul's Church would have meant comprehensive equality for Jewish citizens. But, just as the revolution failed, the hopes of German Jews were also buried. Nevertheless, 1848 initiated a genuine breakthrough. For the first time Jewish politicians appeared at the state and national level, some of them gaining unprecedented prominence. From a negative perspective the events of the year of the revolution brought to the surface what the "Hep Hep" riots of 1819 had already revealed: there was widespread public resistance to the granting of equal rights to the Jewish minority and in times of crisis this could manifest itself in acts of violence.

Although these sharp rebuffs gave some German Jews reason to doubt their total integration, a general feeling of optimism nevertheless prevailed. This outlook was nurtured not only by increasing social integration but especially by the legal equality that was finally granted in the 1860s after a long struggle, first in individual states and then in 1869 in the newly formed North German Confederation.

No other period would transform both German and Jewish society as fundamentally as the nine decades from 1780 to 1870. For most Jewish families economic success, expanding legal equality, and social ascent marked their exodus from the feudal world and their entry into the emergent bourgeois society.

Part One
1780–1847

1 | Legal Status and Emancipation

1. The Conditions of "Protection" and Reforms of the Late Enlightenment

The Enlightenment, the French Revolution, and the Napoleonic conquests, each with its corresponding consequences, led to a reevaluation of the legal status of Jews in Central Europe toward the end of the eighteenth century. Even though the majority of Central European Jews was poor, or at best belonged to the petty bourgeoisie, Christian contemporaries became increasingly aware of the fact that there was a small economic upper-class of Jews and just as small an intellectual elite whose efforts at acculturation could not be overlooked. In the middle classes contact between Christians and Jews continued, as in the past, to occur mainly in the economic sphere. Jewish court factors, wholesalers, and industrial entrepreneurs, however, as well as predominantly self-taught Jewish intellectuals, met together formally and informally with Christian scholars and bureaucrats (most of whom came from aristocratic backgrounds) and members of the bourgeois Enlightenment. An important subject of their discourse was the discrepancy between the legal situation of the Jews and the interest they were showing in integration with the Christian society around them.

Jewish legal status varied greatly from territory to territory in the German Empire in the period from the late eighteenth to the second half of the nineteenth century, and even within a single territory laws were not always uniform. The different categories of territories within the German-speaking realm included major territorial states (*Flächen-staaten*), large and small principalities, free imperial cities, cities under the direct rule of the emperor (*Immediatstädte*), and manorial demesnes. The most heterogeneous of all was the territory ruled by the Habsburg monarchy, although only a portion of the Jewish population resided in the German-speaking region.

Of all the German states, Prussia was without a doubt the most powerful. Originally it had brought together widely dispersed territories and, by the end of the eighteenth century, formed a major state, although it was still in quest of full centralization. Prussia had expanded largely through acquisition of regions with long-standing traditions of their own. Yet its vastness in land and people and its aggressive policies made Prussia a power that was both feared and admired among German rulers. As Prussian rulers took over new territories, they acquired Jewish subjects, who made up a greater percentage of the total population in the new provinces than in the old. These new territories included especially the regions annexed through the partitions of Poland—i.e., West Prussia, South and New East Prussia, and the later grand duchy of Posen—as well as Silesia, which had already been annexed decades earlier.

The legal status of Jews was different in each of the territories that had been inherited, acquired through war, or annexed. In the Brandenburg-Prussian heartland—i.e., Brandenburg, Pomerania, and East Prussia—in Halberstadt, Minden, and Magdeburg, as well as Cleves, Mark, and Ravensberg in the western regions, the basis for their legal status until 1812 was the Revised General Code of 1750. (In Minden, Magdeburg, and Ravensberg its application was interrupted by the civil equality granted from 1807 to 1813 during the period of French rule in the kingdom of Westphalia.) Gradual relaxation of the rigid restrictions of the General Code of 1750 did lead to the suspension of the obligation to pay a body tax (*Leibzoll*) upon crossing borders (1787–1788) and the elimination of collective liability of the Jews in a community or region for payment of individual protection fees (1792) and for damages caused by offenses committed by individual members, such as theft, "fraudulent bankruptcy," etc. (1800–1801). However, Jewish existence was still categorized according to a graduated scale of rights: 1. holders of general privileges, 2. privileged protected Jews, 3. unprivileged protected Jews (i.e., additionally restricted in their employment), 4. Jewish *publique Bediente*, or public employees of the Jewish community, 5. the unprotected (i.e., those with-

1   Dietrich Monten, *The Jew and the Guard*, oil, 1824

out protected status and domestic servants). The structure was similar, though other categories were used, in the province of Silesia, which came under Prussian rule in the 1740s. Until fundamental reforms were initiated by the liberal statesmen vom Stein and Hardenberg, Silesia enjoyed an independent decentralized administration to an extent that Immediatstädte and manorial demesnes did not.

The situation was different in the territories acquired through the partitions of Poland. Here the government applied the General Ordinance Concerning Jews in South and New East Prussia of 1797 wherever it could. Jews desiring to live there were still required to have letters of protection and safe conduct in order to settle and they had to pay numerous fees in addition to those for protection. However, in comparison with the old provinces, the legal situation of Jews here was indeed less restrictive. In view of their significance in trade and industry in this still largely agrarian region, local Jews were subjected to hardly any professional disabilities. Restricting their economic activities would have meant, in the words of a high-ranking official, that "many places would become wastelands and the manorial demesnes would lose most of their income."[1] For this reason, in addition to trade, they were also allowed to work in handicrafts, farming, cattle breeding, and transport as well as performing wage labor. Aside from local needs, the productivity-oriented interests of Enlightenment thinkers probably also played a role here, as they recognized an opportunity to train the Jews to be "more useful" subjects.

Around 1800 written laws and actual practice did not always coincide, even in Prussia, but there was definitely a more systematic administration of the Jewish population in the new provinces. Few other German territories had anything comparable, although Jews elsewhere possessed a similar social stratification: the small upper class, the protected Jews and their families and servants, and the unprotected, often foreign Jews who usually barely managed to squeeze out an existence as peddlers and junk dealers and who could almost be grouped with the Jewish beggars. Common to all the numerous and changing regulations of Jewish life in the individual territories were restrictions imposed upon Jews in the economic sphere in order to favor the working Christian population, the obstruction or prohibition of house sales, and the basic principle of the respective authorities to keep down the size of the Jewish population.

This last principle was greatly relaxed in the final decades of the eighteenth century. However, in 1799 in Hesse-Kassel, specifically with respect to the city of Kassel, it was still the case that "protection may be granted only to the oldest son but by no means to daughters; also Jews may not be allowed to acquire or lease a residence on the most exclusive streets."[2] As regards Baden, which like Hesse and Württemberg had an extensive rural population, it was still the case—also around 1800—that letters of protection could not pass automatically from parent to child. Although, in fact, such passage generally occurred, there was no legal basis to assure it. In the electorate of Trier a letter of protection was supposed to be transferable to a child only in the case of death or if the parents transferred their business to the child.

Letters of protection continued to be issued on an individual basis in the German territories until the period of the French occupation or the beginning of the period of political reform. Also up until this time corporative associations of rural Jewish communities (*Landjudenschaften*) in many areas remained responsible for the collection of the protection fees. Numerous special taxes were also levied, some to be paid in money and some in kind. The latter were especially common on manorial demesnes and in small towns, and they continued far into the nineteenth century.

In the southern German territories that were merged in 1777 to form the electorate of Bavaria Jewish legal status varied from territory to territory. Whereas in the principality of Sulzbach and in the Palatinate Jews required letters of protection but could be certain of the favor of the respective authority, in the region of the old duchy of Bavaria they had been theoretically barred from settling since the passage of the legal code of 1553. It was only because of the court's shortage of funds that court factors and Jews with safe conduct passes were, as an exception, allowed permanent residence starting in 1750. However, gradually, and with apparent tacit acceptance, more and more Jews settled in the area and began to establish themselves despite very restrictive conditions.

In Hamburg and Frankfurt am Main, both free imperial cities with very large Jewish communities, the status of the Jews was affected by conflicts among city authorities, the Jews often becoming an object of dispute. The Ashkenazi Jews in Hamburg (which around 1800 was the largest Jewish community in Germany), Altona, and Wandsbek had merged in 1671 to form a tripartite community. Their legal status was based on the imperial decree of 1710, which bestowed upon "German" and "Portuguese" Jews the same rights and responsibilities. This decree had come as the result of a major conflict between the burghers and the senate about permitted residence for Jews. Here, too, legal status was based on letters of protection, but holders of such protection were assured that, apart from ordinary and extraordinary taxes required of all city residents, no other fees would be levied. Jews in Frankfurt also lived under imperial protection, in accordance with the 1616 ordinance regulating settlement, until 1796, when the ghetto was destroyed by the French. Although the ordinance granted them protection of life and limb, it also introduced rigid segregating regulations that remained in effect for almost two hundred years. Not until the second half of the eighteenth century were Frankfurt Jews, through the support of the emperor, able to attain somewhat more freedom of movement and an easing of restrictions on their economic activities.

Generally, this was the legal status of Jews that the thinkers of the late Enlightenment encountered when, in the final third of the eighteenth century, they began to discuss the improvement of Jewish conditions, though not immediate civil equality. Most held high government service positions and tended to be more pragmatic than concerned with philosophical theory. Their Christian understanding of religion had changed from one of revelation to one of reason, to a rationalization of faith. The resulting critique of the doctrine of divine right of rulers and the demand for a rationalistic foundation of the state, as well as the rapid development of empirical and other sciences, together led to a gradual shift in attitudes toward Jews.

It was characteristic of the most important Enlightenment circles in Berlin that their members connected humanitarian aims based on natural rights with those based on national and estatist law. This was certainly true for the high-ranking Prussian official Christian Wilhelm Dohm (1751–1820; see also volume 1), whose essay on the current situation and future status of the Jews was the most significant work in the ensuing public debate. His book *Über die bürgerliche Verbesserung der Juden* (On the Civil Improvement of the Jews) was published in 1781 (a revised edition appeared in 1783, including responses that he had received up to that point). Dohm's work was by no means directed only to a general educated and scholarly audience; rather, the practical, future-oriented arguments and proposals were also meant especially for decision makers in the Prussian state and in the governments of other German territories. He had written upon the request of his publisher, the writer and journalist Friedrich Nicolai, and Moses Mendelssohn.

Dohm's at that time remarkable demand was to grant Jews the same civil rights as those enjoyed by other subjects in order to make them "happier, better people, more useful members of society,"[3] for he believed that "the once presumed greater depravity of Jews is a necessary and natural consequence of the oppressive situation in which they have lived for so many centuries."[4] To prove this assertion he prepared a brief historical outline analyzing the different living conditions and behaviors of Jews in their respective environments since antiquity. The image of Jews that he conveyed corresponded in part to the dismal reality and in part was colored by the many negative stereotypes common at the time. Later writers—even up to the present day—accused Dohm of being anti-Jewish. But his depiction emphasized that it was unbefitting for the new enlightened age of humanity to allow oppression of the Jews to continue. Corresponding to the Enlightenment principle of equality and the ties between its supporters and the state, he pleaded that Jews be incorporated into the emerging social order, since by nature they had the same abilities as all people. Nevertheless, rights were to be assigned under the protection and control of the state and in a step-by-step educational process. Dohm saw this process as beginning with the necessity to open all branches of the economy to Jews, including farming and the arts and sciences, but to restrict their trading activities, since these were most despised by public opinion.

At the same time the state was obliged to create the necessary conditions for their "moral education" in accordance with the principles of the late Enlightenment. This applied both to the economic sphere and the school system, which—like the entire system of education and socialization—was central to Enlightenment aims. Among the restrictions Dohm initially envisaged in his proposal for granting civil rights to Jews was access to public office, that is, government service, but he favored full freedom of religion, including the building of synagogues and separate jurisdiction for civil suits.

The "educational policy" (*Erziehungspolitik*) pursued in many German states up to the mid-nineteenth century with regard to the Jews mandated granting them rights according to the level of their "improvement," i.e., their acculturation to the surrounding society marked by their overcoming the "depravity" that had resulted from past oppression. The respective authorities had the discretion to decide who was worthy of receiving the full rights of a citizen.

What reactions did Dohm's epoch-making essay elicit from the state, from supporters, from adversaries? Government officials and rulers took note of it—even incorporating some points into their own thinking—but they did not specifically apply his theses and demands. This was not only true in Prussia but also in other German states in which Jews lived, such as the relatively liberal margravate of Baden. The response varied among both supporters and opponents, many of whom either reviewed the work or wrote their own books and brochures, pro or con. It is difficult to distinguish clearly between the two categories, since even supporters criticized Dohm and thoroughgoing critics sometimes agreed with him on certain points. For example, the director of the Berlin chancellery, Heinrich Friedrich von Diez (1750–1817) was one of the few people who took Dohm's demands even further toward emancipation. He rejected any call for assimilation and any restrictions on religious freedom, yet he did agree with Dohm that if Jews were to be treated humanely and like other members of society, one should not doubt that their religious devotion would decrease to the extent to which their civic ties to the state would strengthen.[5] This certainty, that the cohesive strength of the Jewish community would lessen if Jews were given civil rights, was widespread among men of the Enlightenment such as Johann Georg Krünitz (1728–1796), who commented on Dohm: "Certainly the Jews will then stop being the kind of Jews they are now. But why should that concern the state as long as they become good citizens!"[6] Krünitz, publisher of the *Ökonomische Encyklopädie*, one of the most comprehensive reference works of the late eighteenth and early nineteenth centuries, devoted three hundred pages to the article on Jews in the thirty-first volume, published in Berlin in 1784. Fifty of those pages dealt with Dohm's work and commentaries on it. Krünitz could definitely be considered a well-meaning critic of Dohm, who nevertheless wanted a rigid educational phase to precede the granting of equality, including "strict laws" on economic pursuits and just as strict state controls for their enforcement.

Probably the most significant critique of Dohm came from Johann David Michaelis (1717–1791), Orientalist and Protestant theologian in Göttingen. Michaelis had already made a name for himself decades earlier as a scholar and pugnacious journalist. Despite his profession, he based his arguments against Dohm's proposals not primarily on theological explanations but ostensibly on Enlightenment thought, combined with traditional prejudice against Jewish customs and a pronounced xenophobia. Like Dohm, Michaelis explained the "depravity" of the Jews and their supposed tendency to vice and crime as a consequence of the persecutions they suffered throughout history. He too thought it possible to improve the situation for all Jews, not only the wealthy and educated upper class, but he argued that Mosaic law prevented the total integration of Jews within Christian society. Michaelis's evidence, similar to that in many other contemporary polemical tracts, consisted of Jewish religious laws that precluded normal participation in public life. In contrast to Dohm and the reviewer in the *Allgemeine Deutsche Bibliothek* published by Friedrich Nicolai, Michaelis did not think Jews were suited for military service, on account of the commandment to keep the Sabbath. He also argued that "a people that cannot eat and drink with us will always remain a very separate people in its own eyes and in ours as well. There is also the national pride of the Jews, which would make it unbearable, at least for the Germans and the British, to have them as their superiors."[7] As far as their agricultural activities were concerned, he proposed they be allowed to lease land "as colonists in desolate regions, without any disadvantage accruing to the native residents, those German citizens who rightfully hold land and defend it."[8] His approach also induced Michaelis to speak out for a separate Jewish jurisdiction. He concluded that the only solution to the problem would be for Jews to abandon their religion and convert to Christianity.

Because of Michaelis's contrary yet inherently cogent arguments, as well as the high esteem he enjoyed within the scholarly world, Dohm felt obliged to prepare a critical commentary to Michaelis's opinion. He found a comrade-in-arms in Moses Mendelssohn, who, in various writings, supported Dohm's demands for religious tolerance by the state and went even further to speak out against continuation of the rabbinical ban. The two men shared Enlightenment values but differed in their aims: Dohm ultimately hoped to weaken Judaism by granting Jews civil equality, while Mendelssohn sought a state that allowed Jews to lead a religious life and to be loyal citizens at the same time.

All these arguments appeared in the years directly following publication of Dohm's essay. Debate did not end there, however. On the contrary, it continued into the 1790s, though there were no concrete political consequences. Proponents did have the satisfaction that Dohm's work became known beyond Germany's borders. By 1782 a French edition had appeared, which enjoyed a large circulation. The ideas of Abbé Grégoire and the Count Honoré de Mirabeau, staunch advocates of granting civil equality to Jews in France, closely resembled Dohm's proposals. Mirabeau's work, *Sur Moses Mendelssohn, sur la réforme politique des juifs . . .* (1787), adopted virtually all of Dohm's demands. The same was true of Grégoire's *Essai sur la régéneration physique, morale et politique des juifs* (1789). Since both Mirabeau and Grégoire were members of the Estates General in 1789, they were able to introduce Dohm's ideas there as well.

2. Reform-Oriented Policies in the Habsburg Empire

At the time Dohm's work was published, practical reforms that affected the Jews were being introduced in Central Europe through the decrees of Joseph II. When he took power the prevailing policy in almost all parts of the empire was that of his mother, Maria Theresa. It was a policy that aimed at reducing the Jewish population as much as possible. Contemporary opinion held that trade, conducted primarily by Jews, did not contribute to a rise in production that served the interests of the state. In direct succession to the decrees issued by her father, Maria Theresa thus advised the responsible authorities in Bohemia, Moravia, and Lower Austria that only the first-born son in a Jewish family should be allowed to settle, whereas sons born thereafter would be required to leave the country. Similarly, in Galicia, numerous barriers to marriage, including a high tax payment, were intended to serve the same purpose.

The situation of the Jews, which before 1781 was already a topic of debate within government circles throughout the Habsburg Empire, became part of Joseph II's comprehensive politics of tolerance. In that year he had issued a toleration edict (*Toleranzpatent*) for the Christian minorities, with the aim of incorporating them more integrally into the state. Indeed, there were about six million people belonging to Christian minorities, in particular Protestants and Greek Orthodox, who made up almost a third of the total population of the empire.

In October 1781 Joseph issued an imperial decree for the Jews in Bohemia. Until the first partition of Poland, when Galicia became subject to Austrian rule, Bohemian Jewry had been the largest and most self-confident Jewish population within the Habsburg monarchy, resembling Vienna's Jews in their degree of acculturation. Since there was a danger, first of all, that more and more poor Jews from Galicia would attempt to enter Bohemia, and also a noticeable trend of Bohemian and Moravian Jews moving to Vienna, a regulation for this part of the monarchy was enacted before those for Vienna and Lower Austria. However, the legal status of Jews was little changed by this Ordinance for the Furthering of Education and Enlightenment, since special taxes and restrictive marriage requirements were maintained. The number of families in Bohemia was not allowed to exceed 8,300. Conditions were relaxed with regard to economic activities, in which virtually no restrictions were to be retained; Jews were even given the right to be peddlers so that the poorer elements would not move away. The regulations stipulated in the measure aimed at a Germanization of the Jews, as did the later *Toleranzpatente*. It was assumed that within two years the German language would find widespread use in public, especially in the commercial sphere, and lessons in the planned Jewish schools would be conducted in German. If necessary, Jewish children would be sent to Christian schools. This ordinance had the status of a law, and it continued in force until 1797. Though in general clearly more restrictive, it was comparable in a number of points to the Toleration Edict enacted for the Jews in the small part of Silesia that was retained by Austria after the Silesian Wars and the one enacted for Moravian Jewry.

The Toleration Edict for the Jews of Vienna and Lower Austria was issued in January 1782. During the preceding year, there had been an extensive public exchange of ideas in Vienna and Prague and heated debates in state commissions. Men influenced by the Enlightenment faced conservative forces in the court chancellery and the government of Lower Austria, in the Church and professional organizations. The first paragraphs of the law corresponded to a modified form of the Ordinance of 1764 regulating Jewish life. They limited the size of the population, required payment of toleration fees based on degree of wealth, and provided for no automatic transfer of toleration from father to children. The succeeding paragraphs divided the Jewish population of Vienna into two groups: the well-to-do Viennese Jews and the mostly poor, non-Viennese Jews. The former group received freedom in the choice of a vocation and access to schools and universities. They were also permitted to invest in real estate of any kind. However, they were not citizens and they were not allowed to hold government positions. For the latter group the body tax gave way to a less demeaning one. Non-Viennese Jews were permitted to stay in the city only temporarily and their commercial activities were subject to restriction. The Germanizing efforts in the significant area of education aimed at weakening Judaism as a religious community. Indeed, Joseph II prohibited Viennese Jews from founding an official community or building a synagogue in order not to strengthen their cohesion as a group.

This Toleration Edict met with varied reactions within and outside Austria. Viennese Jews supported it wholeheartedly, while the strictly observant Jews in the provinces feared that traditional Jewish education would eventually disappear through the repression of the Hebrew language and the requirement that school instruction take place in German. Hardly any support was shown among the urban and rural Christian populations. The strongest protest came from professional organizations such as trade guilds and merchant associations, from the church, and from the nobility, which feared Jews could assume positions of command in the military. Supporters were most likely to be found among Enlightenment thinkers, who, as in Prussia, were often members of the civil service. The issuance of the edict released a flood of polemical writings, continuing the earlier debate, but these had little political impact.

As Dohm triggered the first extended discourse on emancipation, the toleration policies of Joseph II clearly marked the beginning of movement in the direction of Jewish emancipation in Central Europe. Yet, although both Dohm's tract and the policies of Joseph II served to stir public and government interest, for the most part Dohm and his supporters failed to see their theories turned into practice, and German authorities saw

Austrian policies as neither a model nor a threat. Only in the area of education did some states, like Hesse-Kassel, Electoral Mainz, and Baden,
make the effort to encourage the study of secular subjects by Jewish children. Beyond that, little changed in the 1780s, despite internal government reports, appraisals, and debates.

2   Celebrating the announcement of one of Joseph II's edicts of toleration

3. Policies in German Territories Under French Influence

On the one hand, the 1790s in Germany were marked by revolutionary associations of German Jacobites, who tried to institute radical changes in the wake of the French Revolution, mostly in existing power structures, and lay the groundwork for eliminating social inequality. On the other hand, the governments took advantage of the fear of revolution, which emerged in certain areas of the empire as a result of popular uprisings and rioting, in order to propagate moderate reforms as an antidote to "destructive revolution." German advocates of reform policies regarded the full equality that French Jews had attained in 1791 as contributing to supposedly state-threatening "foreign enthusiasms" (*auswärtigen Schwärmereien*).[9] At first, in the decade following the outbreak of the French Revolution, the struggle against the French, the French occupation of German territories, and the subsequent territorial and administrative reorganization, as well as the German governments' lack of a definite policy line, made it impossible to implement a systematic approach to improving the legal status of Jews. Not until the Napoleonic era was it acknowledged that the German states would fail to survive if they did not introduce basic reforms in the areas of agriculture, free choice of profession, the educational system, general conscription, etc.—and also civil equality for Jews. Despite the groundwork laid earlier by the authorities, progress had come to a standstill. Only the pressure of external events forced the temporary implementation of reforms, though decisions were reversed after the Napoleonic period and restrictions reestablished. This was especially true with respect to legislation pertaining to the Jews.

In Germany, and in Prussia in particular, it was initially the Jews themselves who tried to better their situation by writing petitions and supplications. In 1787, after the death of Frederick II and the beginning of the reign of Frederick William II, the elders of the Jewish community in Berlin declared in a petition to the king, sent in the name of all Jewish communities in Prussia, that they wished to work for the public welfare, but numerous legal restrictions prevented them from being able to do so. In particular, they mentioned the exclusion of Jews from trade guilds and high special taxes. The government then demanded they present their specific ideas, a task undertaken by "general deputies" selected by all the Jewish communities. Upon request of the Jews, the government instituted a Jewish Reform Commission to examine the suggestions, but the general deputies were not allowed to see the commission's report until the end of

1789. The commission's proposals turned out to be so disappointing and, once again, discriminatory that the Jewish representatives felt they had to reject them: "And so, with deeply distressed hearts, we must express our wish—a terrible wish—that Your Royal Majesty see fit to leave us in our former condition."[10]

In 1795 the Jews once again attempted to improve their situation. But the royal council and the justice department rejected their basic requests in 1798 with the explanation that current law served to protect the citizens from the collective hatred of the Jews. Before changes could be introduced, the Jews would have to undergo a "fundamental and general improvement."

These efforts, initiated by those experiencing the discrimination, failed as a result of the bureaucracy's unwillingness to reform and its procrastination, which verged on paralysis. At the same time as the bureaucracy in German states was demonstrating such inflexibility and rigid maintenance of the status quo the legal position of a certain segment of the Jewish population underwent fundamental change. After Napoleonic France annexed the regions west of the Rhine, French law, according to which Jews possessed full rights as citizens, began to be applied there in 1798. The occupation of these areas marked the beginning of a decade of drastic reorganization of the German territories in the interests of French imperialism. As a result, an ever larger number of Jews became subject to French law. Satisfaction at this development was overshadowed, however, by the concomitant ongoing military conflicts. For Jews and non-Jews alike these brought persisting uncertainty regarding the longevity of the new system of rule.

In those territories under French rule Jews could enjoy full civil equality only until Napoleon's *décret infâme* of March 1808, which instituted important new restrictions. This "infamous decree" was originally directed against Alsatian Jews, whom Napoleon had learned were speculating in real estate and charging excessive rates of interest. Instead of determining the guilty parties and holding them responsible, he created legal conditions that drastically worsened the situation for Jews, not only in Alsace, but for all those living within French jurisdiction. These restrictions primarily concerned their freedom of settlement and economic activities. The former were abolished for Jews in territories under French rule, while activity in trade and commerce was made dependent upon special permission given by the responsible prefect. Such permission required annual renewal and submission of a character reference. On the other hand, Jews were required to serve in the army and could not buy an exemption as Christian subjects could. The decree was supposed to remain in effect for ten years. After that time, it was hoped, Jews would have sufficiently adapted their economic conduct to that of Christian citizens; in other words, it was a measure designed to punish and instruct at the same time. On German soil only the Jews in Westphalia were exempt. Here, just two months after the décret infâme was announced, King Jérome, one of Napoleon's brothers, likewise issued a decree in which he assured the Jews that the equality of all citizens continued to apply to them. In parts of the later Prussian Rhine province, however, the Napoleonic decree remained in effect until 1847.

In the last decade of the eighteenth century and the first of the nineteenth a variety of writers in the German lands not under French rule expressed their ideas on the legal status of Jews. Their goals were as diverse as their readerships. In the 1790s intellectuals were already turning away from the cosmopolitan, humanitarian premises of the Enlightenment and moving toward discovery of the cultural characteristics of individual peoples, a trend that later led to Germanocentrism in Germany. Johann Gottlieb Fichte made the most penetrating thrust in this direction. His *Beiträge zur Berichtigung der Urteile des Publikums über die Französische Revolution* (Essays to Correct Public Opinion on the French Revolution), which first appeared anonymously in 1793, enjoyed a very warm reception. Fichte's idea of a homogeneous society without divisive corporations such as the nobility, the military, guilds, and, particularly, Jews, was grounded in the categories of German nation and Christian religion. He felt his purpose was to awaken this—nonexistent—nation through a "mystical experience of the soul" and declared the Jews a "state within a state" on account of the special interests arising from their religion. This state was expanding throughout almost all the countries of Europe in a "powerful" and "hostile" manner. Since Fichte regarded this situation as immutable, he concluded: "I see no other means of giving them civil rights than to chop off all their heads in one night and replace them with new ones that contain not even one Jewish idea. In order to protect ourselves from them, I also see no other means than to conquer their promised land and send them all there."[11]

Here we see the clear rejection of the Enlightenment. In the late eighteenth and early nineteenth centuries it gave way to the newly dominant trends of Idealism and early Romanticism, which contained a latent hostility toward Jews prompted both by religious motives and the desire to defend against the emerging competitive capitalism, of which Jews were considered the forerunners and beneficiaries. In 1791 Karl W. F. Grattenauer (1770–1838), a legal councillor in Berlin, had already published anonymously his pamphlet on the physical and moral constitution of the contemporary Jews (*Über die physische und moralische Verfassung der heutigen Juden*), which was characterized by various obscenities and minimal expertise. The public mood at the time was still sufficiently under the influence of the late Enlightenment to prevent the work from receiving very much attention. But the more frequent appearance of irrational values and the broad approval gained by Fichte encouraged other writers with anti-Jewish attitudes to believe they would find a receptive audience. An early attempt in this direction was made by Christian Ludwig Paalzow (1753–1824), a West Prussian official who wrote *Die Juden* (The Jews) in 1799. In contrast to Grattenauer, whose main source in 1791 was still Johann Andreas Eisenmenger's anti-Jewish classic of 1700, *Entdecktes Judenthum* (Judaism Unmasked), Paalzow made reference to Fichte as a respected intellectual predecessor.

In 1803 a full-scale war of words broke out between enemies of the Jews and those who supported gradually granting them civil equality. The conflict was triggered by a revised edition of Paalzow's 1799 work and Grattenauer's new book, *Wider die Juden* (Against the Jews), the latter, with a printing of thirteen thousand, among the most successful books of the epoch. More than sixty polemical tracts for or against the Jews were published that year. The Prussian government began to fear public unrest. "It is inevitable that if Jews continue to be attacked in public, the lower-class Christians will be stirred up and think it justified to insult Jews on the streets and in public places; excessive behavior on one or the other side will be unavoidable," wrote privy financial councillor August Heinrich von Borgstede to Hardenberg. Chancellor of State Goldbeck also complained to Hardenberg that the hateful work, *Wider die Juden*, never should have been granted an imprimatur, "since it aims only to show the Jewish nation in a spiteful light and to ridicule the Jews, which should by no means be condoned."[12] Public debate on the legal status of the Jews in the Holy Roman Empire finally ended with a decree issued in September 1803 by the Prussian Generaldirektorium banning all publications for or against the Jews. In other words, censorship was introduced, here serving to protect the weaker party.

Only a short time after these written expressions of public opinion, discussion on general reforms resumed in the administrations of almost all German territories. This occurred, first, from the growing realization that traditional administrative structures and mechanisms for economic and social development were no longer adequate to deal with new demands. Early industrialization, secularization—not only of ecclesiastic property but of public mentality—and broader political participation posed major challenges. Second, many princes and leading public officials admired Napoleon and sought to emulate French law. Third, there was a prevailing fear—especially in Prussia—that the modernization trends coming from France and the French-occupied or French-ruled territories of the German Reich could lead to unrest among the population at large. Moderate reforms seemed the best solution.

At the time of the greatest expansion of French rule in Europe, there were three major political blocs in Germany: the Austrian Empire, the Confederation of the Rhine, which existed from 1806 to 1813, and the parts of Prussia that were retained after the Prussian defeats at Jena and Auerstedt (1806) within the borders set by the French victors in the Treaty of Tilsit. Attitudes and actions with regard to improving the Jews' situation, or even granting them equality, varied greatly among these blocs. Austria did not continue with the reforms implemented by Joseph II but rather added a few restrictions. Within the Confederation of the Rhine one can distinguish various categories of action with regard to the question of measures to improve the situation of the Jews.

Only in the kingdom of Westphalia did Jews receive full equality as citizens, despite some intense opposition from the bureaucracy, merchants and artisans (mostly because of increased peddling), the Catholic Church, which feared wealthy Jews would buy expropriated church property, French politicians, who believed equality could go too far, and, finally, even some Westphalian Jews, who felt threatened by the centralizing effect of the Jewish consistory created there and its imposition of religious reforms. Once the décret infâme ceased to be in full force, Jews in the grand duchy of Berg, in Frankfurt am Main, and in the small principalities of Anhalt-Bernburg and Anhalt-Köthen likewise briefly gained equality, though more on paper than in practice.

A different course was taken in the areas west of the Rhine, where special legislation regulating the status of the Jews was again introduced as a result of the 1808 decree. As for Jews in the Hanseatic towns, which were incorporated into the French Empire in 1810, there the French simply took over the laws that were in effect at the time.

The newly constituted states in southern and southwestern Germany formed yet another category. They sought to institute equal rights and a uniform administration in the different territories under their rule. Since this goal could often only be attained over vehement protest from particular interests, or even failed as a result, Jews and the population as a whole lived for years in a state of constant uncertainty with respect to their legal situation. The most progress in standardizing legislation pertaining to Jews was made in the newly formed grand duchy of Baden. The 1807 and 1808 edicts for the founding of the new state explicitly included Jews; in 1808 they were declared "hereditary state citizens," though they lacked local civil rights. The 1809 Constitutional Edict for the Jews, which had been greatly influenced by French law, was intended to educate them. In contrast, the kingdom of Bavaria did not introduce a general regulation until 1813, and it was clearly restrictive. All Jews residing there received Bavarian citizenship, but the intent was definitely not to increase the total number of Jews. Rather, the Jewish population was to be decreased through the *Matrikel*, a registration that replaced the letter of protection. The Matrikel numbers were limited and only transferable to the oldest son. Exceptions to this very restrictive settlement policy were only possible if a Matrikel number became available through death or emigration, if a high sum was paid, or if factory owners, artisans, or Jews willing to do agricultural work obtained royal permission. The governments of other states, such as Nassau, Hesse-Darmstadt, and Württemberg, were not able to institute any comparable general regulation during these years and for a long time merely alleviated restrictions on an ad hoc basis.

The legal situation of the Jews changed the least in certain states lying at the margins of the Confederation of the Rhine, including the kingdom of Saxony and the duchies of Mecklenburg-Strelitz and Mecklenburg-Schwerin. Only very few Jews lived in these areas and, moreover, the impact of French rule here was minimal. In these almost exclusively Protestant territories no territorial changes took place due to expropriation of Church land that would have made administrative reform necessary.

4. The Prussian Edict of 1812

Prussia, the third large political unit in Germany, likewise underwent no territorial expansion. On the contrary, after the military catastrophe in 1806 it had lost all its western territories and those eastern territories annexed during the partitions of Poland—except for West Prussia and Ermeland. The military defeat made it obvious that the decline of the old

Prussian estates system, which had been apparent much earlier, actually meant the collapse of the state. No other German state experienced this fate, which is why the reform debates are of particular significance. An attempt was made to institute the comprehensive reform necessary for the state to survive, but in the end it failed. The reforms encompassed the military and administration, agricultural law, the economy, and municipal authority. The ultimate goal, however, was to break the power of the estates and establish a free society of citizens that would remain politically integrated in the monarchical system.

An integral component of the Prussian reform effort was the question of civil equality for Jews. Similar to debate in other areas, reformers made earlier discourse on the issue their point of departure. Unlike the states in the Confederation of the Rhine, Prussia was not under direct or indirect French influence, although Prussian reformers were informed of the changes implemented there. Even before debate on civil equality began at the Prussian administrative level, Jews were incorporated into the revived municipal self-government according to the urban ordinance of 1808. Protected Jews received the right to vote and hold honorary municipal offices on town and city councils, as long as they could prove that they owned either a home or business, a requirement that also applied to Christian citizens. Limiting these rights to "owners" served to maintain the estatist orientation of the urban population, though it now also included those Jews who satisfied the prerequisites for municipal civil rights.

Only a few days after this ordinance for city government was enacted, State Minister Friedrich Leopold von Schrötter (1743–1815), who administered the remaining Prussian provinces, was commissioned by Frederick William III to draft a proposal for the future legal status of the Jews. Schrötter was considered reform oriented and liberal, and various ministries based their statements on this subject on his ideas. His proposal was clearly an educational law; his liberality was directed toward the small circle of well-to-do Jews who would gradually become eligible for all citizens' rights, depending on their degree of willingness to refrain from forming a "state within a state." A connection with Fichte and those who avidly supported him is obvious. All other Jews were to be subject to the same obligations as the Christian population, but equal rights would be left for future generations. Individual departments in the Ministries of the Interior, Justice, and Finances, as well as the General War Department commented on the proposal.

Three main positions can be distinguished in these comments. The judgment of the Ministry of Finance was the most blunt in its hostility toward the Jews, including demands that they refrain from all forms of trade and from the observance of ritual laws. Only then might they be eligible for full civil equality. This was an unmistakable regression from the status of debate in the Prussian ministerial bureaucracy. A majority of the reviewers approved Schrötter's education-oriented proposals, with minor modifications. They saw Jews as objects for education by the state, the latter to determine when they were worthy to receive full rights of citizenship.

The most progressive statement came from the Department of Religion and Public Instruction in the Ministry of the Interior. Head of the ministry Wilhelm von Humboldt (1767–1835) and his staff favored granting Jews full civil equality immediately. In their view the state was not an instrument of education and it needed "only, by granting and restricting freedom and thus creating a balance of rights, to put the citizens in a position . . . to educate themselves."[13] They considered the separation of church and state to be imperative and believed religious affiliation should be left up to each citizen, as that was the only way to ensure the development of what Humboldt postulated as the "freedom of the individual." However, Humboldt assumed that the Jewish religion was essentially comprised of ceremonial laws and that Jews would thus, "since they are driven by an innate human need for a higher faith, turn of their own free will to the Christian [religion]."[14]

These three positions show how differently the term *reform* could be interpreted among leading Prussian officials when it came to rights for the Jews. Schrötter's proposal and the individual statements did not result in any immediate, practical political consequences since other, more urgent legislation took precedence. Not until Karl August von Hardenberg (1750–1822) became state chancellor in the summer of 1810 did debate revive, spurred on, in part, by pressure from prominent representatives of the Berlin Jewish community. Hardenberg, an enlightened liberal, was open to the idea of full emancipation of the Jews. A member of his staff, the later historian Friedrich von Raumer (1781–1873), drafted an appropriate law, which was then distributed for comment to various ministries. However, the responses contained no new arguments or suggestions. Novel only was that, for the first time, a leading Jewish figure in the earlier efforts for equality, David Friedländer, was asked to submit a brief expressing the Jewish perspective. Finally, Hardenberg was able to submit a progressive proposal to the king, who then made changes in two points, whose later implications were not apparent at the time. The first modification concerned the holding of state offices. Hardenberg had suggested that for the next fifteen years explicit royal permission be required to obtain such offices, but the king's modification read as follows: "We shall reserve the right to set down in law at a future time the extent to which Jews shall be admitted to other public services and state offices" (par. 9). Second, Hardenberg's proposal provided for full inclusion of Jews in military conscription. But the king added: "The way in which this requirement shall be applied to them shall be laid down in detail in an ordinance on military conscription" (par. 16).[15] On March 11, 1812, the "edict concerning the civil status of Jews within the Prussian state" was enacted with the abovementioned changes. Jews legally living in Prussia at that time thus gained the status of "native residents [*Einländer*] and Prussian citizens." In order to be granted civil rights they were obliged to take on fixed official family names within six months, use German or another living language for their business records, contracts, and legally relevant declarations of intent, and sign their name in Gothic or Latin script. There were no other requirements. Despite the noted restrictions, the law can be seen as the most far-reaching of all legislation enacted at the time in German states that were not under French rule. Jewish communities thanked Hardenberg effusively. With the exception of a short-lived emancipation edict issued in 1813 in Mecklenburg-Schwerin according to the Prussian model, no German states made any further efforts in this area during the Napoleonic era.

5. In the Wake of the Congress of Vienna

Although the "Jewish question" was only a peripheral subject of discussion at the Congress of Vienna, the constitution passed there in June 1815 had significant impact on the future legal status of Jews in the states of the German Confederation. The impetus to deal with the issue came from demands raised by the Hanseatic cities of Hamburg, Bremen, and Lübeck, as well as the city of Frankfurt am Main, which all wanted to reverse the equality granted to German Jewry. Since it had been dictated by the French, it was held to be illegal. Austria's foreign minister Clemens von Metternich (1773–1859), Prussia's chancellor Hardenberg, and Wilhelm von Humboldt, who had been serving as the Prussian ambassador in Vienna since 1810, strove to negotiate uniform emancipatory legislation, similar to the Prussian Edict of 1812 for all German states. They wanted it to be incorporated into the constitution of the German Confederation. Their efforts failed, however, because of the particular interests not only of the Hanseatic cities and Frankfurt but also of other smaller states that showed considerable resistance. Article 16 of the Constitution of June 1815 read as follows: "The Diet of the German Confederation shall consider how improvements in the civil status of adherents of the Jewish faith in Germany can be implemented in the most broadly acceptable manner and, specifically, how the enjoyment of civil rights in return for the assumption of civic duties in the states of the Confederation can be provided and assured; nevertheless, until this is done, members of this faith shall receive the same rights already offered by the individual states in the Confederation."[16] In that the original wording of the final sentence, "*in* the individual states in the Confederation" was replaced by "*by* the individual states in the Confederation," French laws were declared null and void in all states where they had become binding, since the French political power that was responsible for these laws was declared illegitimate. The new governments, by contrast, saw themselves as legitimate and assumed authority for all measures determining the status of the Jews. Also, the Diet of the German Confederation never seriously considered holding the agreed upon discussion of standardized legislation pertaining to the Jews. As a result, the "regulation of Jewish life" remained a matter of the individual states, of which there were many.

The German Confederation established in 1815 was made up of almost forty states and free cities. Their territorial boundaries were essentially those laid down at the Congress of Vienna or, as in the case of the free cities, their former rights were confirmed. It is important to distinguish between: 1. the small states, whose situation remained virtually unchanged, 2. the intermediate states, which—except for Saxony—were considerably expanded and thus strengthened: especially Bavaria, but also Baden, Württemberg, Hanover, and Hesse-Darmstadt, and 3. the major powers of Prussia and Austria, the latter having relinquished its possessions in western and southern Germany in favor of reacquiring territories in the Alpine regions and in southern and southeastern Europe, and Prussia having transferred to Russia the territories from the third partition of Poland, while receiving in the west the entire Rhineland north of the Nahe River and Westphalia. This modified territorial landscape led to a new balance of power in Germany that remained intact for decades to come.

The territorial changes roughly outlined here once again brought a period of legal uncertainty for the entire population, although Jewish subjects, who very soon experienced material restrictions on their newly acquired rights, were affected the most. The free cities responded most rapidly. Bremen and Lübeck had repealed the French legislation after their liberation in 1813; in 1816 they expelled the Jews. In 1814 Hamburg had reinstated the ordinance of 1710, and in Frankfurt the 1811 decision that granted civil rights in exchange for a payment of 440,000 guilders was replaced in 1815 by the reinstatement of the 1616 settlement regulations (*Stättigkeit*). In 1814 Hanover had already reintroduced the old protected status. It was followed by Nassau in 1815, and Mecklenburg-Schwerin also revoked the rights Jews had gained there only two years earlier. In Hesse-Kassel, where Joseph II's Toleration Edict had been valid before the period of French rule, a form of selective distribution of civil rights was instituted in 1816 after the French occupation had ended. Peddlers and cattle dealers were reduced once more to the status of "tolerated Jews." Finally, in 1817 Waldeck too reversed its 1814 decision granting the Jews state and local civil rights.

Other territories retained Jewish emancipation as it had existed before 1815, though restrictions were sometimes added. This was especially true in Baden, where Jews were still not granted local civil rights, though they continued to be recognized as citizens in accordance with the constitutional edicts of 1807–1808 and 1809, and where, in 1815, protection fees were abolished. In Brunswick, although the previously valid French legislation was diminished, the setbacks were not major. In Bavaria the Edict of 1813 remained in force with its Matrikel, which prevented Jewish life from developing freely. As a result, many younger children who were not included in the Matrikel decided to emigrate, especially to North America, where Bavarian Jews played a major role in founding Jewish communities. The minor princedoms of Anhalt-Bernburg, Anhalt-Köthen, and Schwarzburg-Sondershausen were exceptional cases. The first two had granted full or at least extensive equality to Jews living in their territories in 1810 and the last mentioned followed in 1815.

The development in Prussia was the most difficult. Because of internal government problems and resistance by the king, it was not possible to realize Hardenberg's idea of extending the sphere of the Edict of 1812 to all provinces within the 1815 borders of a greatly expanded Prussian state. The edict applied only to the provinces that were part of Prussia at the time it was enacted: Brandenburg, Pomerania, East Prussia, and Silesia. All other regions were subject to a September 1817 rescript by the minister of the interior stating that "the principle has been put forward

everywhere to leave the situation of the Jews residing in the new provinces as it had been prior to the occupation, until changes are introduced
by new general regulations."[17] All legal changes pertaining to the Jews
introduced during the French occupation were thereby declared null and
void, with the exception of some areas of Westphalia. The legal situation
before the period of French occupation was once again in effect. Estimates
vary regarding the number of ordinances pertaining to Jews that were
operative in Prussia as a result of this decision. Generally, twenty-one or
twenty-two are mentioned, although, if the smallest territories that
Prussia acquired are included, the number increases to thirty-one. Vague,
often contradictory regulations made it difficult to govern the Jewish
population. For the Jews themselves, each of these meant a wide variety
of restrictions. Since they did not have the right to freely change their
place of residence, they also did not have the option of improving their
living conditions by moving to a region where Jews enjoyed more favorable legal status. The promise of "new general regulations," remained
unfulfilled for over thirty years.

Reform fatigue and unwillingness of the governments to emancipate
the Jews were by no means limited to Prussia. Both problems stand in the
context of the general hostility toward progress that was inherent to the
reactionary goals of the time. The Christian religion was the declared
basis of domestic and foreign policy within the "Holy Alliance" formed in
1815 by the rulers of Prussia, Russia, and Austria. All Christian states in
Europe later joined this alliance, with the exception of England and the
Holy See. Characteristic of this restorative epoch were the maintenance
of the doctrine of divine right for rulers and a renewed strengthening of
the conservative order.

This was reflected in statements by contemporary writers and academicians. In the years of French rule these ideas had already been propagated
in the works of leading representatives of German Romanticism, especially
the theorist on state and society Adam Müller (1779–1829), and the poets
Achim von Arnim (1781–1831) and Clemens Brentano (1778–1842). In
1810–1811 they formed the Christlich-Deutsche Tischgesellschaft, a discussion society that existed for several years, allowing entrance only to
those "born into the Christian religion." Jews, even if they were baptized,
were thus excluded. The members of this society were united, first of all, in
their strict rejection of the aims of Hardenberg's reform policies to considerably reduce if not eliminate privileges of the estates. Second, their basic
attitudes were anticapitalistic and preindustrialist; they vehemently

opposed and felt threatened by modernization trends they believed were embodied in the economic activities of the Jews. Finally, they had common ground in their understanding of Christianity as the state religion. Its successor organization, the Christlich-Germanische Tischgesellschaft, founded in 1816 by Clemens Brentano, was much more politically active. A short time later the works of a frequently read contemporary author, Ernst Moritz Arndt (1769–1860), expressed similar goals in a more popular form. Arndt became the epitome of Germanic patriotism based exclusively on Christianity. The "honest, quiet, and loyal German burgher and peasant," who exerts "all the primal and most natural drives and powers of humanity in vibrant activity" is confronted by the Jew, who does "only the artificial and mechanical exercises" of "merchants, money-changers, and brokers."[18] Arndt felt that only by unconditionally abandoning the Jewish religion in favor of Christianity would the necessary conditions be satisfied, so that this then converted Jew would no longer pose a threat to Germanism.

Whereas the anti-Jewish polemics in these works were only one element in a range of restorative arguments, once the appropriate basic line received the blessings of the three major powers in 1815 anti-Judaism became an independent subject of literary-political polemics. However, the starting position of the Jews was different in this literary battle than it had been at the end of the eighteenth century. They had learned to fight back, at least with the written word. Given that the gap between their legal status and their actual position in the German economy and society was wider now than it had been during the Napoleonic era, numerous factors continued to affect their changing Jewish identity and sense of self: the large number of Jewish volunteers that fought in the Wars of Liberation, the increasing impact of their commercial activities on general economic advance, their involvement—to the extent allowed—in the affairs of local self-government, and the extensive publications they directed toward a denominationally neutral readership.

In the period from 1815 to 1850, approximately 2,500 works by Jewish and non-Jewish authors were published, representing a wide range of opinion as to what rights should be granted the Jewish population. The subject predominated in books, brochures, broadsides, and magazine and newspaper articles published during these decades. For this reason presentation of the debate here must remain fragmentary. It started with two works by Friedrich Christian Rühs (1779–1820), a historian at the University of Berlin. Both were published in 1816: *Über die Ansprüche der Juden an das deutsche Bürgerrecht* (On the Jewish Claim to German Civil

Rights) and *Die Rechte des Christenthums und des deutschen Volks. Vertheidigt gegen die Ansprüche der Juden und ihrer Verfechter* (The Rights of Christianity and the German People: Defended Against the Claims of the Jews and Their Advocates). Rühs was followed by Jakob Friedrich Fries (1773–1843), professor of philosophy in Heidelberg and, beginning in 1816, in Jena.

Like Arndt, Rühs also considered religion to be the most significant divisive factor in the relationship of Christians to Jews, whom he perceived to be foreign and terrifying. He therefore demanded comprehensive special legislation for Jews, which would serve to protect the Christians. He denied Jews any claim to civil rights unless they converted to Christianity and thereby also acknowledged their Germanness. Trade had been considered "unproductive, an activity that sucked the Christians dry" for centuries. Rühs could now supplement this charge from the standard arsenal of anti-Jewish agitation by reference to the activity of Jews as factory owners. Through Jews, he wrote, artisans had lost their honest sources of income and ended up in penury.

Rühs based his antiemancipatory reasoning on Article 16 of the constitution of the German Confederation: since the first section granted the same civil and political rights to all citizens of Christian faith, while the second section assigned to the Diet of the German Confederation the task of determining a standardizing regulation for the status of Jews in its member states, Rühs held that this provided a legitimate basis for special legislation regarding "that foreign people." His interpretation of this article proved most useful to opponents of emancipation. That same year Rühs's colleague, Jakob Friedrich Fries, expressed himself in an even harsher manner—despite the fact that he belonged to the liberal camp. In an extensive review of Rühs's publications, which was titled *Über die Gefährdung des Wohlstandes und Charakters der Deutschen durch die Juden* (On the Threat of the Jews to German Prosperity and Character) and appeared in 1816 as an offprint of the Heidelberg periodical *Jahrbücher für Literatur*, Fries denied that Jews were at all willing to "better" themselves. In order not to inflict even more harm on the German people, he favored marriage restrictions and a ban on immigration in order to reduce the number of these "vermin feeding upon the nation." Their expulsion would be justified if they failed to renounce their religion completely as well as the "dishonorable" behavior based on it, in order to live together with Christians.

The Jewish religion, however, was no longer Fries's main target. Rather, he charged that Jews set themselves apart as a nation, forming, as Fichte had already put it, a "state within a state." For Fries, Christianity was an integral component of being German just as the Jewish religion was a part of being Jewish. The Jews constituted a people unto itself and did not regard themselves as owing allegiance to any state. Thus two main lines of attack—which could not always be clearly distinguished from one another—were apparent in the publications that appeared in these years: the one more religious, the other more nationally oriented. However, in view of the advancing and spreading process of secularization, the anti-Jewish orientation that focused on the unbridgeable disparity between Judaism and the German nation proved to have greater long-term impact.

The flood of writings by opponents to emancipation was countered by statements by those supporting it, such as the 1816 work by Johann Ludwig Ewald (1747–1822), ministerial and church councillor in Karlsruhe, *Ideen über die nötige Organisation der Israeliten in christlichen Staaten* (Ideas on the Necessary Organization of Israelites in Christian States). It was followed in 1817 by *Der Geist des Christentums und des ächten deutschen Volkstums, dargestellt gegen die Feinde der Israeliten* (The Spirit of Christianity and the True German People, Presented Against the Enemies of the Israelites), which directly targeted Rühs. Another example was the work by national economist Alexander Lips of Erlangen, written directly before the beginning of the "Hep Hep" riots in 1819, *Über die künftige Stellung der Juden in den deutschen Bundesstaaten* (On the Future Status of Jews in the States of the German Confederation). Lips intended to "finally bring this important subject back to the simple principles of justice and politics."[19] Rationally and pragmatically, he noted that "every citizen appears in a twofold relationship—first as a member of the state and then also as a member of a religious community, of a church party. As adherent of a religion, he is a matter of total indifference for the state."[20] Similar to almost all supporters of emancipation, Lips qualified this clear, rational statement by demanding that the Jews first go through a process of becoming more productive, which was only possible through "temporary political coercion and intervention." Dohm's principle of education was thus—almost forty years later—still considered the most important prerequisite to Jews receiving full equality.

For the first time Jews themselves were also starting to make public statements in growing numbers and with increasing intensity. Generally, they argued along different lines; some were defensive, but a majority was self-assured and assertive in articulating their deviating opinions.

Four statements may serve as examples. Saul Ascher (1767–1822), a book
dealer in Berlin, took the most clearly political position. A philosophical
and religious as well as a political writer, he rebelled against the increasingly fanatical Germanism in Christian circles, analyzing the phenomenon and attacking its supporters from Fichte to Arndt and Jahn. Immediately after Rühs's work appeared, Ascher published his thoughts in
response to it. In *Die Germanomanie. Skizze zu einem Zeitgemälde* (Germanomania: Sketch for a Contemporary Portrait) Ascher sharply criticized Rühs's demand that Jews give up their religion in order to receive
equal rights. Christianity, he wrote, was not "the absolutely essential condition of Germanness." He held it was not religious affiliation that was
the basic principle of the modern state under the rule of law, but a willingness to obey those laws. Many Jews had already demonstrated that
willingness by serving as volunteers during the Wars of Liberation. In his
1818 work, *Die Wartburgs-Feier* (The Wartburg Festival), he assumed
that the currently popular anti-Judaism would not be victorious but give
way before cosmopolitanism and universal education. Ascher held fast to
this belief even after his *Germanomanie* was one of the first books to go
up in flames when in 1817 nationalistic students burned books at the
Wartburg Festival.

Whereas Ascher's works still emphasized the religious and philosophic
background of Judaism, Ludwig Börne (1786–1837) clearly stressed the
achievement of human rights. He wrote articles and essays "For the
Jews," in which he attacked the half-heartedness or even unwillingness of
various Christian institutions to grant Jews civil equality. His views did
not become absolutely clear, however, until 1821, when he used an extensive review as a forum of indictment:

> That which you call human rights are merely animal rights: the
> right to hunt for one's food, eat it, digest it, sleep, reproduce.... Civil
> rights—these alone are human rights, for a human being only
> becomes a human being within a civil society. He is born into it; he
> is therefore born a citizen. This is the fundamental principle in
> England, France, and every free state.[21]

Ascher's attacks on reactionary currents in Germany and Börne's
appeal to give Jews civil rights were supported by the publications of
Jewish educators. The latter argued with varying degrees of emphasis on
three different levels. They wanted to propagate among Jewish youth a
reformed Judaism with a religious, moral, and humanitarian base that was

open to German culture; they argued for the priority of civil and human rights over religious differences among individual subjects, provided only that they "carry the burdens of the state and follow its laws"; and, finally, they assumed the joint victory of Christians and Jews over France represented a unifying bond that could no longer be broken. Jacob Weil, a teacher at the Frankfurt Philanthropin, saw the resulting consequences for Jewish civil equality to be especially positive. In his 1816 work, *Bemerkungen zu den Schriften der Herren Professoren Rühs und Fries über die Juden und deren Ansprüche auf das deutsche Bürgerrecht* (Comments on the Writings of the Professors Rühs and Fries on the Jews and Their Claims to German Civil Rights), Weil stresses the irrefutable connection between the Jews' deep love of their fatherland, demonstrated through giving their "property and blood and lives," and the termination of their exceptional legal status.

Whereas Weil saw in the writings of Rühs and Fries only an evanescent phenomenon, his colleague at the Philanthropin School, Michael Hess (1782–1860), in an essay published in 1816, regarded them as a serious danger. He noted in them a clear latent hostility toward Jews among the people, the "common herd," that could be granted legitimacy by the presentations of two noted academicians. Ultimately, however, he too was confident that civil and human rights would be granted to the Jews and all other disadvantaged people. Like Weil, he emphasized the fact that Christians and Jews had been comrades-in-arms in the Wars of Liberation and came to the conclusion that Jews are "natives and have no other fatherland than the country in which they live."[22]

Two teachers at the Jewish Free School in Dessau, Joseph Wolf (1762–1826) and Gotthold Salomon (1789–1862), in their essay on the nature of Judaism, *Der Charakter des Judenthums* (1817), used the occasion also to respond to the public attacks on Jews. However, their main aim was to present the basic principles of the Jewish religion and the measures—particularly in the areas of education and instruction—that needed to be taken in order to develop a reformed Judaism, whose followers would be able to accept all civil duties and rights.

These are just a few examples of the many comparable public statements on the "Jewish question" made directly after the Congress of Vienna. Christian contributions tended toward Germanocentrism, declaring everything "foreign" to be beyond the pale. Jewish writers—who had sought to retain an enlightened religious identity even as they became an equal part of the society around them, adopting its norms and patterns—

preferred to look toward the future. Their confidence and optimism regarding progress clearly demonstrated their trust in the governments and in those who shared their view that the wheels of history could not be turned back. That outlook did not, however, correspond to reality.

6. The "Hep Hep" Riots

Persistent hatred of Jews found concrete expression in the "Hep Hep" riots of 1819. There is much uncertainty regarding the causes of this unrest, which was reminiscent of medieval persecutions. Explanations range from the widespread and long-standing notion that anti-Jewish actions served to vent feelings about the generally deplorable socioeconomic and political state of affairs at the time to theories that the Christian population's aggression was directed specifically against Jews, whose progressive emancipation was seen as a threat. Presumably, both factors contributed to the start of the unrest and allowed it to reach a high degree of violence. Economic deprivation certainly played a part, increasing the public's readiness to engage in protests. Serious crop failures in the years 1816 and 1817 caused bread prices to skyrocket, and, once the Continental System was abolished, it became apparent that German goods could no longer compete with British ones. Artisans whose occupations were in a state of crisis continued to hold on to their guild traditions, especially in cities that were not flourishing economically; in general, they regarded occupational freedom as life threatening. Merchants and dealers feared free trade, which had already become commonplace in other countries, considering it an increasingly disturbing threat to their livelihood and to the customary way of doing business. The Jews, subject to a lack of economic security for centuries, forced to seek exceptions and loopholes in the restrictions imposed upon them and to take risks, could be viewed as personifying the new form of business conduct once they gained access to more and more areas of commerce and trade. However, aside from their function as an object for general discontent, there were also specific reasons for the anti-Jewish rioting. In many places, especially in the wake of debates on the issue in the Bavarian Chamber of Deputies, the riots arose as a demonstration of public resistance to emancipation of the Jews. The anti-Jewish literary campaign of a few years earlier played its own role in causing latent aversions to break out in violence. Rühs and Fries spoke to intellectuals and the educated middle class, but pamphlets had also appeared targetting the masses. A play such as *Unser Verkehr* (Our Crowd; see chapter 6), had found a sympathetic audience.

The riots began on August 2, 1819, in Würzburg. They were apparently triggered by a dispute in the local press between the author of a fanatically anti-Jewish book and his reviewer, who insisted upon unrestricted civil rights for Jews. Those who took part in the rapidly spreading protest were individuals who felt themselves harmed by the Jews, including traders, artisans, journeymen and apprentices, and peasants and unemployed people indebted to Jews. Jewish shops were demolished and pillaged; the Jews themselves were abused, one soldier and a "Christian citizen and businessman" were killed. The riot spread to other cities and villages in Bavaria and from there to Württemberg and Baden, especially Heidelberg, to Frankfurt, cities on the Rhine, and to Hamburg. Everywhere the rioting was accompanied by chants of "Hep-Hep, Jud' verreck'!" (Hep! Hep! Jews drop dead!). The meaning of the word *hep* remains in dispute. The most common derivation is an acronym for

Hepp ! Hepp !

3   The "Hep Hep" Riots, based on a contemporary copper engraving
by Johann Michael Voltz, 1819

"Hierosolyma est perdita" (Jerusalem is lost), though others exist as well, such as the explanation that *hep*, a word used to call billy goats, alluded to the beard worn by many Jews.

There was considerable property damage and severe physical abuse, but police and militia were able to quash the riots quickly. In Prussia, which was scarcely touched by this hate-filled violence, the authorities anticipated outbursts with legal measures. The swift intervention by city and state officials did not, however, occur solely for the protection of the Jews. More significant was the fear by governing authorities of conspiratorial activities. Patriotic and liberal pronouncements against political reaction, sometimes combined with an extreme German nationalism as at the student-organized Wartburg Festival near Eisenach in 1817, had already resulted in police actions. The signs that public conflict would spread had increased. August von Kotzebue (1761–1819), a popular author suspected of police espionage for the czar, was murdered by fraternity member Karl Ludwig Sand (1795–1820) only a few months before the outbreak of the "Hep Hep" riots. This was a major reason for the enactment of the Carlsbad Decrees in September 1819, which marked the beginning of the period of "demagogue persecution." The authorities placed the press and universities under surveillance and banned student fraternities.

7. Legal Restrictions

Police state actions against actual or alleged nationalist and liberal "machinations" meant protection for Jews from attacks, but at the same time it created a public mood that left little hope for progress in emancipatory legislation. In Bavaria, where a parliament was established as a result of the new constitution of 1818, the parliamentary debates in 1819 that supposedly triggered the "Hep Hep" riots produced no positive results. Neither did the fundamental principles for new legislation that were drafted in 1828 on the suggestion of King Ludwig I. During the following years only very few states relaxed their restrictions. For example, starting in 1820–1821 individual Jews in Hesse-Darmstadt were able to receive civil rights, though the conditions were not precisely laid down. The regulations were just as elastic in Saxony-Weimar, where Jews were given equal rights in 1823 "to the extent that no present or subsequent law acknowledges or justifies an exception."[23] In Württemberg debate was brought to a close in 1828, after twenty years, with the "law regarding the public status of members of the Israelite faith." This was once again an "educational law," since individual Jews could be granted state and local civil rights only at the discretion of the authorities. After prolonged negotiations, in 1824, the Diet of the German Confederation granted private civil rights with restrictions but not full civil equality to the Jews of Frankfurt.

Such minor advances were offset by striking regressions. This was especially true for Prussia. In the years directly following the end of the Wars of Liberation there was much discussion about the promise made that volunteer soldiers would receive government service positions. Most of the actual requests were turned down. Likewise, applications by Jews to continue working in government service after the period of French rule (this applied mostly to the Rhine province and Westphalia) were rejected and no claims for compensation were considered. On the other hand, Jewish volunteers who had been seriously injured in the war were granted a pension corresponding to their military rank without any major complications. In their case there was no fear that they would aspire to any position of authority.

Unrelated to the exceptional situation of the Wars of Liberation, restrictions in everyday life began to be introduced in 1816 with respect to rights associated with real estate acquisition. Although there were no restrictions on the acquisition of property, Jews who became owners of large estates were, according to the general law code, not allowed to act as church patrons. Nor were they authorized to exercise patrimonial jurisdiction on the estates and were thus forced to commission a qualified Christian for this task. If these restrictions applied only to the small number of extremely well-to-do Jews, other restrictions affected the employment of middle- or lower-middle-class Jews. Within only a few years Jews were banned from all professions that either required state approbation or were connected with the exercise of authority. These actions reveal no consistent policy, only a desire for "defense" against the Jews. Almost all decisions were made on the basis of individual cases that had been brought from the provinces to the government in Berlin. First, in 1820, hiring Jews as surveyors was prohibited, since these were considered "public officials." In 1822, the right of Jews to hold academic and school positions, which was specifically guaranteed by the Edict of 1812, was "repealed because of discrepancies that arose in the process of implementation."[24] Even positions on the auction commissions were made state offices in 1827 that "could not therefore be filled by members of the Jewish faith."[25] In accordance with the city ordinance and the Edict of

1812, Jews had been permitted to hold municipal offices and, in fact, had been holding such positions for almost twenty years. However, this right was restricted by the revised cities ordinance of 1831 so that "only those are eligible" for the office of mayor or lord mayor "who are of the Christian faith." In addition, as of 1833 Jews were no longer permitted to head village councils since "police administration takes place solely under the auspices of the state authorities" and Jews were therefore "viewed as not suitable."[26] They were also excluded from arbitration in 1835 in the belief that "the Jewish citizen" was "legally excluded" from holding judicial office.

All these orders of the Prussian government shared a regressive tendency to allow any and every aspect of the exercise of power, no matter how small, to be carried out only by Christians. This held especially for the police, judicial, and educational functions of the states, cities, and villages. It was also apparent in the reactivation of institutionalized estate structures. Hardenberg's promise immediately before the conclusion of the Congress of Vienna to draft a constitution was rejected by an alliance of the old estates and the ruler. Instead of a national assembly, a Diet of the Provincial Estates was introduced in 1823 as the legitimate political body. Land ownership became the prerequisite for membership in the diet, with the result that the Provincial Estates represented landowners' interests. Since belonging to the Christian faith was a precondition for admission to the estates, Jews were excluded from exercising these political rights at the outset. Although the function of the Provincial Estates was only to debate bills drafted for the respective provinces and issue opinions, it could exercise a considerable informal influence on the government. The debates from 1824–1826 in the first provincial diets on future legislation pertaining to Jews resulted in recommendations in almost every province to enact, at the very least, stringent restrictions for Jews, if not to reestablish the former "laws of protection." The economic conduct of Jews was given as the most significant justification, since damage to Christian traders and craftsmen had supposedly increased once Jews were given access to all branches of the economy. There were demands for state intervention in Jewish religious and educational affairs in order to counter their "self-segregation" and thus approach the goal of "bringing as many [Jews] as possible to the adoption of Christianity."[27] The fact that the government in Berlin took note of these recommendations without developing any corresponding measures was mostly due to the general indecisiveness within the individual ministries and differences among them with respect to the future "general regulation of Jewish life."

Unlike Prussia, Baden, since the adoption of its constitution of 1818, possessed a representative body elected by the people, its Lower Chamber. Its constitution was long regarded as the most progressive within the German states. It guaranteed civil equality for Jews at the state level, though not in their home towns and not in candidacy for government positions, which were reserved for members of the three Christian denominations. The same was true with respect to the right to stand for election to the Lower Chamber, the composition of which was markedly different from that of the Prussian Provincial Estates. Criteria for being elected were considerable wealth, a fixed salary as a civil or a church official, or a lifelong pension from a feudal estate. This made it possible for commoners to become representatives and participate in debates, especially civil servants of all kinds, who for a long time comprised half of all parliamentary representatives. When the great Reform Diet in Baden convened in 1831, the political climate was that which had emerged from the July Revolution a year earlier. In those years Baden developed into a focal point of early German liberalism, its advocates making up a majority in the parliament. Jews hoped in vain that these liberals would speak out for Jewish civil equality. In Baden, as in Prussia, the prevailing attitude was that little had changed since the 1809 Constitutional Edict for the Jews. The economic attitudes of Jews were still considered threatening and they were still thought to see themselves as a separate nation hostile to the state. This attitude was so widespread that not even progressive liberals supported expanding the rights of Jews. On the contrary, the chamber resolved unanimously that a reform of Judaism would have to precede such a step. This reform—in keeping with the tendency in German liberalism to level out differences—was intended to eliminate a number of integral elements of Jewish life: the ritual dietary laws, circumcision, use of the Hebrew language, and the celebration of the Sabbath on Saturday. The Talmud would be subjected to thoroughgoing expurgation.

To be sure, the liberals' reform demands, which aimed at political rationalization, were also directed at the Christian churches, but in this instance they were obviously not a prerequisite for the receipt of more extensive civil rights. Jews ranging from reformers to orthodox protested vehemently, since the price to be paid for full civil equality was ultimately nothing less than abandonment of the Jewish religion. While the Baden Ministry of the Interior accepted the resolutions of the parliament only conditionally and gradually, a majority of representatives in the Lower Chamber maintained their demands until the revolution of 1848. As a result, the existing legal regulations remained in force. This stagnation had a particularly negative impact on the status of Jews on the local level, since here, too, response to the demanded reform of Judaism was intended to determine whether Jews were deserving of improved status. Although the same parliament passed a uniquely progressive law regarding the future status of municipalities and the rights of citizens, which transformed 40 percent of the population from "protected" citizens into local citizens with full political rights, the Jews remained "protected" citizens. And, with few exceptions, Jews were still not allowed to move to towns where no other Jews resided.

8. Conflicts During the Years Before 1848

Thus in the two German states that had granted their Jewish subjects the most comprehensive rights—Baden with the Constitutional Edict of 1809 and Prussia with its Emancipation Edict of 1812—further development stagnated and regression of various sorts made its appearance. This occurred against the background of a renewed campaign of anti-Jewish writings that influenced the parliamentary debates in other German states. The type and levels of argumentation used by those opposing the Jews were essentially the same as those used fifteen years earlier. In this phase of restoration, however, they met with more approval by estate and public assemblies, and by governments as well, than they had in the years marked by uncertainty of orientation directly following the Congress of Vienna. The Heidelberg liberal theologian Heinrich Eberhard Gottlob Paulus (1761–1851) had without a doubt the most lasting impact. His work, *Die jüdische Nationalabsonderung nach Ursprung, Folgen und Besserungsmitteln* (Jewish National Segregation: Origins, Consequences, and Corrective Measures), was read before the Baden Lower Chamber in 1831 and greatly influenced the direction of its resolutions. However, the impact of his writing extended to almost all German states. He did not consider "this nation that segregates itself" to be capable of exercising "state civil rights in any other nation" as long as it maintained its religion in the present form. Other authors followed, including the Berlin public official and writer Karl Streckfuss (1779–1844), who demanded "at least a far-reaching restriction of the rights granted up until now" and recommended dividing Jews into two classes: the "useful," who still practice their religion only to the extent "that it does not hinder civic life" and prove "that they have truly attached themselves to the state to which they belong"; and "the repulsive and burdensome aliens," who "roam from city to city, from village to village."[28] Streckfuss thought rights should be granted on an individual basis and not be heritable. Here was an unmistakable demand to reinstate the old laws of protection, but such a demand had by now become anachronistic, especially in areas of growing economic strength. In the province of Posen, however, the division of Jews into two classes was instituted that very year.

Numerous engaged Jews took issue with the publications of Paulus and Streckfuss, including the major protagonist for Jewish equality, Gabriel Riesser (1806–1863), and the Königsberg physician Johann Jacoby (1805–1877), both of whom used political arguments. In agreement with Ludwig Börne's basic view, though without mentioning him explicitly, Riesser declared, "A person's claim upon the state to which he belongs is his claim to civil rights. But the person that belongs to a state is he who was born in it and not he who has freely chosen it as his residence, he who *must* obey its laws, *must* fulfill the obligations it imposes upon him, *must* defend it with his blood."[29] Like Riesser, Jacoby also spoke out for the separation of church and state, thus opposing the spirit of the times and the prevailing doctrine of the German-Christian state. He demanded that Jews receive "a long denied right, completely and totally," a right for which Jews would fight "until a more humane future [satisfies] our just demands."[30]

Understandably, Riesser and Jacoby adamantly rejected Streckfuss's recommendation to divide Jews into two classes, since this contradicted their notion of equality and religious freedom for all citizens as a foundation of the state. But they were forced to witness the Prussian government's making a move precisely in this direction by issuing the Preliminary Ordinance Pertaining to the Jews in the Grand Duchy of Posen in 1833. The ordinance aimed at providing for parts of the Jewish population there the possibility of becoming naturalized Prussian citizens. The prerequisites were so strict, however, that only very few Jews satisfied them. It was relatively easy to meet the conditions for verification of irreproachable conduct, assurance that the German language was used in all public matters, and adoption of a fixed official family name. More difficult, on the other hand, was the requirement to have had permanent residence in the province of Posen since 1815. (This criterion presumably was instituted with the intent of rejecting undesirable immigrants from the Russian part of Poland.) The economic prerequisites to be fulfilled were flexible; Jews had to show that their livelihood was secured through an occupation in the areas of science and the arts, agriculture, in a fixed form of trade (as opposed to peddling), or through ownership of land worth at least two thousand talers or capital assets of at least five thousand talers. Individuals were also qualified if they had "earned special merit through patriotic deeds." This naturalization edict was instituted from the very beginning as a miserly solution, since it was generally known that a disproportionate number of Jews in this poor province lived in penury. Consequently, ten years after the law was passed, not even a fifth (18.3 percent) of the Jews of Posen had been naturalized. Riesser sharply criticized this ordinance in his *Betrachtungen über die Verhältnisse der jüdischen Unterthanen der preussischen Monarchie* (Reflections on the Conditions of the Jewish Subjects of the Prussian Monarchy, 1834). He considered the division of Jews into two classes to be "a thousand times more troubling than even exclusion itself, with its explicit motive of intolerance."[31] Nevertheless, the Jews of Posen welcomed the law as a major step forward. According to a contemporary report, the legal document was carried through the brightly lit Jewish Quarter, splendidly displayed on a velvet pillow. The "patriotic celebration" took place in the presence of President Eduard Heinrich von Flottwell. Chief Rabbi Akiba Eger (1761–1837) gave "a sermon marking the significance of the day" in which he thanked the king for showing his favor but also insisted upon preservation of the Jewish religion.

The 1833 ordinance for Posen was Frederick William III's last comprehensive legislative measure pertaining to the situation of the Jews. Although it applied to about 40 percent of Prussian Jews, as noted, it affected very few. The remainder still had no freedom of residence, no free choice of trades, and no right to hold public office. In an age of developing industrialization, which was able to exploit the working population's willingness to be geographically, occupationally, and socially mobile, over 30 percent of all Jews living under Prussian rule were excluded from participating in this industrial development if they did not take the path of emigration or—less often—baptism.

In 1833 Electoral Hesse likewise instituted a "two-class law" to "regulate the special conditions of the Israelites," though it imposed different hurdles to overcome in crossing the boundaries between classes. The law basically granted Jews the "same rights as subjects of other faiths," however with conditions and restrictions, among them the exclusion of itinerant peddlers from state civil rights. Based on the statistical average of itinerant peddlers from 1821 (18.15 percent) and 1842 (7.85 percent), about 13 percent of all Jews living in Electoral Hesse around 1833 were thus not eligible to receive civil rights. Even those who had been granted them were informally excluded from government service. According to a 1852 report by the Ministry of the Interior to the Foreign Ministry, although Jews were permitted to practice as physicians or legal advisers, except for a few isolated cases in subordinate services, their placement in actual state offices, and as judges in particular, had "*not* taken place" up to this time.[32]

Problems in the interpretation of the law were resolved in Electoral Hesse, as in Prussia and other German states, for a long time on the basis of individual cases, without the application of any general rule. This pertained in particular to three points of complaint voiced by the Christian population, namely, land acquisition by Jews, their right to the use of communal resources, and the sale of nonkosher meat. The attempt once again to restrict the rights of Jews was thus not tied to the fundamental question of their civil equality but to everyday issues. Jews were accused of acquiring arable land and other larger pieces of real estate not for their own use but to divide them into smaller parcels for further sale. Such accusations, however, had little real impact. That was not the case with regard to Jewish access to common resources, especially gathering wood from the public forest, which was available to all local residents. Old established Christian citizens insisted on the long-standing local civil law based on private law, which had been granted to them alone. As a result, even Jews who had been granted state civil rights were excluded from taking advantage of such common resources. As for the third point, it produced virulent conflict, since the butcher guilds feared Jewish competition. Resting their case on the guild organization that was still binding in Electoral Hesse, Christian butchers protested that Jews admitted to the guilds were allowed to sell the hindquarters of the slaughtered animal—which they did not eat for religious reasons—by the pound and not only in whole quarters, as provided for by the 1749 Jewry Ordinance. All these attempts by traditionally oriented, old established Christian individuals and institutions to protect their vested rights ultimately failed because they were outmoded, even if for the time being they defined the practices of daily life.

A new phase of progress in the emancipation of the Jews appeared close at hand when Frederick William IV ascended the Prussian throne in 1840. Although a strong supporter of "political Romanticism," he was thought

to have fundamentally liberal views. He brought the persecution of the
"demagogues" to an end, relaxed censorship of the press, and rehabil-
itated the reputation of ostracized political opponents. The liberally
minded public, including the Jews, thus gained confidence. They hoped
the new government would keep its promise of 1815 to establish a constitution including the principle of equality for all citizens. However, the
political worldview of the ruler, the basics of which had already been
firmly established and became more concrete once he took power, failed
by far to satisfy high expectations. Both the politically conscious non-
Jewish middle class and, even more, the Jewish population were greatly
disappointed. The lower legal status of the Jews was growing ever more
irreconcilable with their understanding of themselves as loyal Prussian-
German citizens.

Only a year after ascending the throne, Frederick William IV denied
the Jews recognition of this self-understanding. In his order of December
13, 1841, he clearly expressed his ideas on the state, based on the example of his planned policies regarding the Jews. Renouncing the concept
prevalent until then of bringing about the Jews' "civil improvement"
through their education with the intent of integrating them into state
and society, the king declared his goal to be excluding them as a separate
corporation. The predominant notion here was that of a Christian estatist
monarchy according to the medieval conception. It meant tolerating the
"Jewish people" that "represents a unique legal case in which peoplehood
is identical with religion, where this religion can belong only to this people, and where the Jews alone have preserved their national peculiarity
through their religious constitution."[33] Jews would not be allowed to
"merge" into German society by establishing "civic relations with the
Christian population of the land." Instead, they were to organize themselves into corporations and collectively—not individually—look after
their interests in local and interregional bodies, without partaking of the
rights and duties of Prussian citizens. This concept was just as restrictive
and, in the end, just as anti-Jewish as the educational policies. Viewing
and treating Jews as an independent "estate" that should represent its
own interests might have been progressive sixty or seventy years earlier;
in the Vormärz, the period leading up to the 1848 March revolution,
however, when more and more Jews were prepared to be loyal Prussian
citizens and involved in the efforts of the liberal bourgeoisie, these considerations had to be viewed as a discriminatory attempt to segregate a
segment of the population.

The order, drafted only for a small circle of advisers, did not remain secret. Only a few decades earlier the reaction of the Jews would have been disappointment; now it was outrage. Spokesman for the protest was the Magdeburg rabbi Ludwig Philippson (1811–1889), founder of the Jewish newspaper *Allgemeine Zeitung des Judenthums* and its publisher since 1837. He supported political liberalism and was prepared to fight for the emancipation of the Jews. In protest of the planned political changes, he drafted a petition in February 1842 that was supported by more than eighty Jewish communities in Germany. The main point of the protest was the announced exemption of the Jews from regular military service, which was to remain open to them only on a voluntary basis. Jews feared they would thereby lose the basis of their civil and political standing—a legitimate fear given the high status of the military in the Prussian state and society. "And so for us too religious consciousness, which fills our entire person, and patriotism are merged within us. Anything that holds us back from active demonstration of the latter would also violate and oppress the religious individual in us,"[34] argued Philippson.

Almost the entire spectrum of rabbis analyzed and documented the compatibility of the Jewish religion with national defense, which had co-existed from time immemorial. A Jewish organization was planned whose members would all commit themselves to volunteer for military service and that would administer a facility for determining those eligible, much like a state recruitment office. Gabriel Riesser even suggested forming an "association for military service," to demonstrate the massive readiness of Jews to serve in the military. The large-scale protest from all camps of the Jewish population as well as the presence of differing opinions among the ministers and articles in the non-Jewish press that vehemently supported the Jewish position all finally led to the proposed law not being officially publicized and also, therefore, not taking effect.

Nonetheless, this conflict contributed to a revival of debate on legislation pertaining to Jews in other German territories. Thus, for example, in the kingdom of Hanover, where the former laws of protection were reenacted in 1814 following the period of French legislation, Jews received limited civil rights in 1842, though this did not apply to itinerant peddlers. Also, in 1842 Jews in Hamburg were allowed to acquire land and, without restrictions, choose their place of residence "both in the city and in rural areas." In Bavaria Matrikel legislation still existed and represented one of the most severe restrictions on Jewish legal status, but in response to petitions from Jews the parliament drafted a reform of the Edict of 1813 that was approved by the government in 1847. However, the outbreak of revolutionary events only a few months later prevented its implementation.

In Prussia, where about half of all German Jews lived around the middle of the nineteenth century, comprehensive surveys on the legal status and "condition" of the Jewish communities were conducted in 1842 and 1843 in individual Prussian provinces to prepare for a uniform legislation pertaining to the Jews. At the time almost two-fifths of the Jewish population in Prussia—especially in Posen, West Prussia, Westphalia, and the province of Saxony—still lacked civil rights. The old protectoral conditions still applied here, limiting Jews in their freedom of residence and choice of profession. In 1845 general military conscription for Jews was finally introduced, giving them a sense of equality at least in this respect. But relics from the Middle Ages remained: not until 1842 did the Prussian Ministry of the Interior announce that a still extant police ordinance of 1573 in the former imperial county of Wittgenstein, which had been part of Prussia since 1816, should no longer be enforced. It had declared heathens, Jews, and Gypsies to be beyond the pale of the law.

Debates on the long-promised "proposal for legislation on the situation of the Jews" began in June 14, 1847, in the two curias of the first United Prussian Diet. They focused on a small number of significant issues: employment of Jews in government service, estate rights for Jews, access to academic teaching positions, and the introduction of Jewish corporations. At the core of the conflict was the contrast between the Christian, estatist, monarchical system, favored by the state, and the separation of church and state, represented by the liberals. The latter wanted strict implementation of the principle of "equal duties, equal rights" for all subjects, so that a qualified Jew would have the same right to a career as "any Berlin porter." Young Bismarck, on the other hand, clearly supported the opposite view: "If I had to imagine a Jew whom I am supposed to obey, I must admit that I would feel deeply dejected, that all joyfulness and the upright feeling of honor would abandon me."[35] The outcome of the debates, which were supposed to present a brief for the drafted legislation, resulted in the law of July 23, 1847, which ratified a far-reaching standardization of Prussian legislation pertaining to Jews, although Posen retained its two-class distinction. The formation of Jewish corporations was dropped. Jews were still denied rights belonging to the estates, and they were still not permitted to hold public offices that involved judicial, policing, or administrative tasks. Within the academic sphere Jews were only permitted in departments ruled to be ideologically neutral, and restrictions existed even there. Despite these shortcomings, the decisions were regarded by the Jews as distinct progress because they meant greater legal equality for the widely scattered areas of Prussia. The speeches by liberal spokesmen were still quoted long afterward in Jewish weekly newspapers.

In sum, during the 1840s liberal democrats clearly spoke out for complete emancipation of the Jews, which led to a certain improvement in their legal status. Above all, the "Jewish question" was now an integral part of liberal efforts in general. Representatives of these efforts expressed their opposition to divinely sanctioned arbitrary rule. They insisted upon the creation of a constitutional monarchy and demanded equal rights for all citizens, including Jews. At the same time, and in connection with these developments, the economic crises, crop failures, and resulting protest actions by the lower social classes helped to create an unstable atmosphere that finally produced the failed revolution of 1848.

2

Population Shifts and Occupational Structure

1. Demography

Once Jews were again allowed to settle in a growing number of German territories, from the period of Absolutism until well into the nineteenth century, demographic developments were largely determined by their legal status. Whether it was Prussian regulations, which allowed a parent's letter of protection to be transferred only to the first child, or Bavaria's *Matrikel*, which replaced the letters of protection but was by no means less confining, or restrictions in Vienna, Frankfurt, and elsewhere, Jewish population growth was forced to conform to strict legal regulations. These restrictions did not pertain to the size of individual families but to an increase in the number of Jewish households, since permission to settle required official authorization. Freedom of residence within a given state was likewise a significant factor in this regard. Although such freedom was relatively easy to obtain in a territory with uniform laws, even within Prussia severe obstacles had to be overcome, for instance, if Jews from Posen wanted to move to provinces where the Emancipation Edict of 1812 was valid. To move from one state to another proved even more difficult.

For the "prestatistical" period, up to the turn of the nineteenth century, the size of the Jewish population in various regions can be estimated on the basis of numbers of men and women with letters of protection. (A widow could assume the protective rights that had been granted her husband, and fathers could transfer their letters of protection to a daughter, who thereby obtained the right to marry a foreign Jew and start an independent household with him.) Since they paid taxes, their numbers had to be registered, even if the size of the individual families was not always recorded. In the case of territorial changes, the records sometimes provide insight into the increase in number of Jewish subjects. Such is the case for the partitions of Poland, through which Prussia and the Habsburg Empire were confronted with Jewish populations of unprecedented proportions. However, at the start of the period of French rule a few years later, the regional units changed once again, making it virtually impossible to obtain reliable statistics regarding the size of Jewish and non-Jewish populations in the individual territories until after the Congress of Vienna undertook the reconfiguration of Europe.

The total Jewish population in the German states, not including the Habsburg Empire, grew by nearly 54 percent from almost 260,000 in 1816 to about 400,000 in 1848, with these figures including only those officially registered, not those who either temporarily or permanently resided there without authorization. During the same period the total population grew by only 44 percent, from 23.6 million to 34 million. The increase in the number of Jews in the mostly German-speaking regions of the Habsburg Empire, concentrated in Bohemia and Moravia prior to 1848, was just as high. In these two lands the Jewish population grew in the same period from 70,000 to 108,000. According to the 1846 census (which must, however, be used with care), there were only 4,296 Jews living in Lower Austria (including Vienna). Although still a low figure, it is several times greater than the less than 1,000 Jews registered in 1816–1817 who lived among 1.3 million non-Jews. In 1846 no Jews at all resided in Upper Austria, Styria, Carinthia, or Carniola.

Since Europe had been restructured at the Congress of Vienna, statistics for the Jewish populations in the individual German states around 1800 are not comparable with those for the following generation. Two examples make this apparent. Around 1800 about 225,000 Jews lived under Prussian rule (including the territory Prussia gained in the partitions of Poland). This represented 2.3 percent of the 9.8 million total population. In 1815, within a total population of 10.17 million, there were only 124,000 Jews (1.2 percent) registered, since the areas annexed in the second and third partitions of Poland, which possessed large Jewish populations, had been brought almost entirely under Russian rule. Figures available for Baden for the years 1802 and 1825 illustrate a different sort of development. Territorial expansion here led to growth in both Jewish and Gentile populations. In

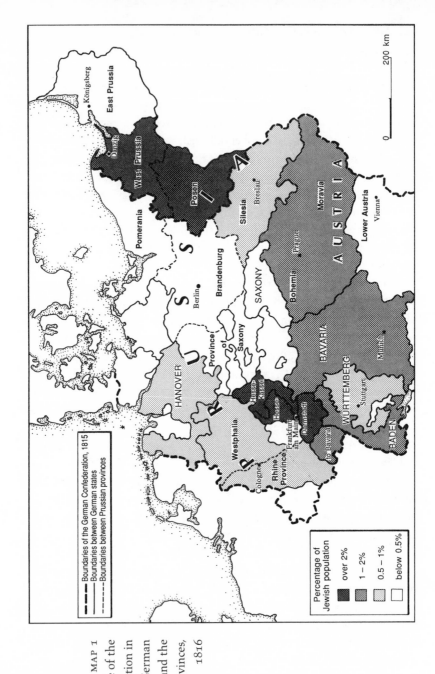

MAP 1
Percentage of the
Jewish Population in
the Largest German
States and the
Prussian Provinces,
1816

Boundaries of the German Confederation, 1815
Boundaries between German states
Boundaries between Prussian provinces

Percentage of
Jewish population

over 2%
1 – 2%
0.5 – 1%
below 0.5%

200 km

0

Königsberg

East Prussia

Danzig

West Prussia

Pomerania

Posen

Silesia

Breslau

Brandenburg

Berlin

SAXONY

Saxony

Bohemia

Prague

AUSTRIA

Moravia

Lower Austria

Vienna

HANOVER

Province
of
Saxony

Westphalia

Hesse-
Kassel

Hesse

BAVARIA

Munich

Cologne

Rhine
Province

Frankfurt
am Main

Hesse-
Darmstadt

to Bavaria

WÜRTTEMBERG

Stuttgart

BADEN

1802 there were 2,300 Jews among 193,000 non-Jews (1.2 percent), and in 1825 there were 17,600 Jews among 1,081,000 non-Jews (1.6 percent).

Because these sets of population figures thus do not lend themselves to comparison, the Congress of Vienna best serves as the starting point for analyzing demographic developments among the Jewish population in the German states up to the middle of the century. The proportion of Jews in the total population of German states in this period ranged from 0.07 percent to 3.4 percent. Although the number of Jews increased more than the non-Jewish population as a result of lower mortality rates, particularly infant mortality, this is not as clearly apparent in relative figures because of the vast difference in size of the two entities. Thus the number of Jews in Prussia in the first half of the nineteenth century increased 77 percent and the total population increased 58 percent, but this represented a rise in the percentage of Jews from 1.2 percent to only 1.34 percent. In Bavaria there was also a growth in the Jewish population (15 percent; the total population increased 21 percent) but here the relative proportion of Jews dropped from 1.45 percent to 1.37 percent as a result of emigration engendered by legal restrictions. The proportion of Jews in the total population likewise decreased in the kingdom of Saxony (from 0.08 percent to 0.07 percent) where Jews were allowed to settle only in Leipzig and Dresden, and even there settlement was authorized only for small numbers and under very severe restrictions. Here change occurred only in the second half of the century as a result of industrialization and the immigration of Eastern European Jews. The greatest increases in the Jewish population relative to the total population were recorded in the comparatively small grand duchy of Hesse (from 3 percent to 3.4 percent) and in the even smaller Electoral Hesse (2.2 percent to 2.5 percent), where there were many rural Jewish settlements. In Baden, Württemberg, and the other German states there was little change in the ratio, even if the absolute figures for Jews rose considerably, especially in Hanover and Württemberg.

The varying inclination of authorities to grant Jews permission to settle, whether on manorial demesnes, in free imperial cities, or territorial states, made the choice of residence in the preemancipation period more dependent on legal factors than on the individual desires of the persons concerned. It was relatively easier to receive permission to settle from manor lords who were directly subject to the emperor and who hoped to benefit financially from the Jews' economic activities. This was true for the rural settlements in western and southern Germany as well

TABLE 2.1

Proportion of Jews in the Total Population of Individual German States
in 1816–17 and ca. 1848 (rounded figures)

State	1816–17		1848	
	Jews	percent of total population	Jews	percent of total population
Prussia (total)	123,800	1.2	218,750	1.3
East Prussia	2,170	0.2	7,530	0.5
West Prussia	12,630	2.3	22,970	2.2
Posen	51,960	6.4	76,910	5.7
Brandenburg	8,050	0.7	19,760	0.9
Pomerania	2,810	0.4	9,640	0.8
Silesia	16,080	0.8	32,340	1.1
Saxony	3,090	0.3	4,940	0.3
Westphalia	9,480	0.9	14,990	1.0
Rhine Province	17,560	0.9	29,670	1.1
Bavaria	53,200	1.4	61,000	1.4
Grand Duchy of Hesse (Hesse-Darmstadt)	20,000	3.0	29,000	3.4
Baden	17,600	1.6	23,500	1.7
Electoral Hesse (Hesse-Kassel)	14,400	2.2	18,500	2.5
Württemberg	8,300	0.6	12,000	0.7
Hanover	6,400	0.5	11,600	0.6
Saxony	1,000	0.08	1,300	0.07
other states	12,300	0.4	19,000	0.4
Total	257,000	1.09	394,650	1.16
Habsburg Empire				
Bohemia	40,000	1.6	70,000	1.6
Moravia	30,000	1.5	8,000	1.8
Lower Austria	1,000	0.08	4,300	0.25
Total	71,000	1.2	112,300	1.37

as for the manorial demesnes east of the Elbe and Oder Rivers. It can be
assumed that, following the expulsion of Jews from major cities in early
modern times, about three quarters of the Jews in Germany around 1800
lived in small towns and rural areas. The respective proportion of Jews
in small, medium-sized, and large cities differed greatly in magnitude,
reflecting in part the authorities' estimate of how much additional
income newly settled merchants could bring in. The impact that a very
high percentage of Jews in the population would have on city life, espe-

cially in regard to the coexistence or conflict of gainfully employed Jews and Gentiles, will be examined below in connection with the Jews' particular economic activities.

The largest Jewish population, in both absolute and relative terms, in a major city of the German-speaking world around 1800 was Prague, with 8,500 Jews (10.6 percent), followed by Hamburg, with 6,300 "German" and 131 "Portuguese" Jews (6 percent), and Frankfurt am Main, with 3,000 Jews (7.5 percent). Although Berlin had a slightly higher absolute number of Jews (3,300) than Frankfurt, they comprised only 2 percent of the total Berlin population (172,000). Breslau and Mannheim both had Jewish populations amounting to approximately 5 percent of the total population. Breslau, however, had a total population of 58,000 (including 2,900 Jews), whereas Mannheim's total population was only 20,000 (with slightly more than 1,000 Jews). The number of Jews in Königsberg and Vienna at that time was low, both in absolute and relative figures. There were 850 Jews in Königsberg compared to approximately 52,000 non-Jews (1.6 percent) and in Vienna, where a Jewish community was not officially allowed until the mid-nineteenth century, there were only 500–600 Jews within a total city population of 200,000 (0.3 percent).

Among middle-sized cities Lissa, in the province of Posen, had approximately 3,700 Jews and 5,300 non-Jews (41 percent) around the year 1800. In Glogau, in Lower Silesia, where the Jews' right to settle, though not uncontested, had been continuous since the Middle Ages, there were 1,500 Jews at that time, comprising 15 percent of the population. A comparably high percentage of Jews lived in the Franconian city of Fürth (2,400 Jews to 13,600 non-Jews), where disputes between the Protestant margrave and the archepiscopal see of Bamberg served to favor settlement by Jews. Within this category of cities a high percentage of Jews (23 percent) lived in the city of Posen.

In the Prussian eastern provinces Jews more often lived in small towns, under the rule of a manor lord, that always had strong ties to the surrounding villages. For the period around 1800 where, as noted, all figures can only be regarded as approximations, we find that in Märkisch-Friedland there were 1,100 Jews and 900 Gentiles (Jews thus made up 55 percent of the town residents); in Zülz, in Upper Silesia, there were approximately 1,100 Jews to 1,000 Gentiles (52.4 percent); in the West Prussian town of Zempelburg, 1,050 residents were Jews and 1,450 Gentiles (42 percent); in Inowraclaw, in Posen, there were 1,100 Jews and 1,800 Gentiles (38 per-

MAP 2   Percentage of the Jewish Population in Selected Cities
and Towns Around 1800

cent). There were also a few southern German villages or towns with a particularly large proportion of Jews or even a Jewish majority, especially in
Württemberg, Baden, Franconia, and Hesse. Even into the 1830s 93 percent
of the Jewish population in Württemberg, and two-thirds in Hesse, lived in
rural areas.

    Already before the middle of the nineteenth century a trend was dis-
cernible with regard to Prussia's Jewish population: the migration from
rural areas and smaller towns to the major cities, which would become
characteristic for all Germany during the second half of the century. This
development was clearly apparent in Zülz and Glogau, long-standing
Jewish communities in Silesia. As mentioned, the 1800 population of Zülz
was slightly over 50 percent Jewish; by the middle of the century, how-

ever, the Jewish share was only about 22.2 percent. In Glogau, a larger city, the proportion of Jews sank from 15 percent to 6.2 percent. Zülz was owned by a manor lord and could offer its residents neither prospects for economic advance nor educational opportunities for the children. Glogau, the capital of Lower Silesia, was dominated by government institutions and the garrison, which made up almost a third of the population; it offered no prospects for significant economic development. The decrease in the Jewish population as a result of emigration was likewise extreme in the small town of Märkisch-Friedland, where it dropped from 55 percent to 22.2 percent.

While many Jews in parts of Prussia east of the Elbe were thus migrating from smaller to larger towns, in southern German states, by contrast, the Jewish population in smaller towns often continued to grow up to the mid-nineteenth century. In Jebenhausen, in Württemberg, for example, the Jewish community grew in the period from 1798 to 1846 from 178 to 496 members, representing a percentage increase relative to the total population from 28.3 percent to 43.5 percent. In nearby Buttenhausen the number of Jews increased from 127 in 1798 to 280 in 1830 and the Jewish

TABLE 2.2

The Jewish Population of Selected Cities Around 1800 and 1848
(estimates)

City	1800		1848	
	Jews	*percent of total population*	*Jews*	*percent of total population*
Märkisch-Friedland	1,100	55.0	500	22.2
Zülz	1,100	52.4	540	22.2
Zempelburg	1,050	42.0	1,360	42.5
Lissa	3,700	41.0	3,110	32.2
Inowraclaw	1,100	38.0	2,100	35.5
Posen	3,700	23.0	7,700	17.1
Fürth	2,400	15.0	3,000	17.6
Glogau	1,500	15.0	950	6.2
Prague	8,500	10.6	11,700	9.0
Frankfurt am Main	3,000	7.5	4,900	8.3
Hamburg/Altona	6,430	6.0	10,000	6.7
Breslau	2,900	5.0	7,380	6.7
Mannheim	1,000	5.0	1,500	6.5
Berlin	3,300	1.9	9,600	2.3
Königsberg	850	1.6	1,950	2.6
Vienna	500–600	0.3	4,000	0.8

population did not reach its peak ratio of 52 percent of the total population until the 1850s. Absolute figures continued to rise until 1870, when there were 400 members in the Jewish community. As a rule the mid-nineteenth century represented the peak in the Jewish populations of these small towns, both in absolute and relative figures.

In most large cities the Jewish population increased considerably during the first half of the nineteenth century. In Breslau, which was attractive especially for the Jews residing further to the east, the Jewish population grew in the first half of the nineteenth century from 2,900 to 7,400 (155 percent), whereas the population as a whole increased only 91 percent (from 58,000 to 110,700). Fürth, according to contemporary sources the "most bustling and flourishing factory city in Bavaria," embraced numerous branches of trade and industry. It experienced a 25 percent rise in its Jewish population, while the non-Jewish population increased by only 6 percent. Mannheim, another up-and-coming commercial and industrial city had, around 1850, 50 percent more Jews than it did half a century earlier, whereas the increase in the general population was only 15 percent. Only in cities with rapid growth in the total population, such as Berlin, and in those that traditionally had the largest Jewish communities—Prague, Hamburg, and Frankfurt am Main—did the proportion of Jews in the population remain fairly constant. In general it can be said that major cities, whether *Residenzen*, free cities, or provincial capitals, attracted Jews and non-Jews alike. Here economic initiatives in industry, trade, and services were in demand, the steadily growing population required essential goods, and the modes of transportation and commerce were continually being improved.

If relative Jewish population growth was due, in part, to new opportunities offered in larger towns and cities, it was also, as noted earlier, influenced by a relatively lower mortality rate. This is apparent from the figures for Prussia:

TABLE 2.3
Mortality Rates, 1822–1866

Period	Births per thousand		Deaths per thousand		Differential per thousand	
	among non-Jews	*among Jews*	*among non-Jews*	*among Jews*	*among non-Jews*	*among Jews*
1822–1840	40.01	35.46	29.61	21.60	10.40	13.85
1841–1866	39.55	34.75	29.05	18.85	10.50	15.90

Even as urbanization swelled, so did the number of German Jews emigrating overseas. Figures can only be approximate, since there was no clear way of distinguishing transmigrants from Eastern Europe via Germany from German-Jewish emigrants. For Prussia, and in particular the province of Posen, there were at least 13,000–14,000 Jewish emigrants before 1848, and outside of Prussia, above all for Bavaria, there were at least 11,000. At first, Jews emigrated primarily because of the restrictive legal status they experienced as well as their hopes of finding better economic opportunities. Following the crop failure of 1846 and the subsequent years of decline and stagnation from 1846 to 1848, however, their motives were primarily economic. For the province of Posen we have specific evidence that 1,915 Jews emigrated from 1834 to 1838; from 1839 to 1843 the figure was 2,490, and from 1844 to 1848 it was 7,315. In Bavaria, where emigration was already underway by 1830, approximately 3,500 Jews went overseas from 1843 to 1848 alone, corresponding to a 5.7 percent decrease in the Jewish population.

In sum, demographic developments within the Jewish population in the German-speaking realm during the first half of the nineteenth century were influenced by a number of factors. In much of the German Empire, and later in the German Confederation, permission to settle was determinative. In this regard authorities in small towns, villages, and rural areas were for economic reasons often more favorably inclined than those in major cities. But by the middle of the nineteenth century the picture had clearly changed. The disproportionate increase of the Jewish population in relation to the non-Jewish and the gradually relaxed restrictions regarding freedom of settlement resulted, as the figures show, in an increase in the number of Jews in medium-sized and larger cities, especially those that became attractive through an upswing in trade and industry. If a move to these areas was not possible or did not promise success, the only way to achieve the hoped for socioeconomic advance was through emigration, a path that in the second half of the century would become particularly characteristic of East European Jews.

2. Economic Activities Around 1800

The economic pursuits of Jews, like the right of settlement, were restricted by law. In theory, once Jews had received permission to settle in a particular location they were free to seek out occupations that had not yet—or only insufficiently—been filled there by non-Jews. Their activities might either satisfy existing needs or create new ones. In practice, however, opportunities for Jews to undertake new economic enterprises were limited, since they remained excluded from the professional associations set up as guilds, which enjoyed monopolylike privileges from medieval times into the nineteenth century. Unlike the immigrant Huguenots and their descendants, Jews were generally unable to develop new and potentially productive trade initiatives. Official restrictions continued until emancipatory reform measures in a number of German states at the beginning of the nineteenth century guaranteed the Jews free choice of profession (though with some retrogression after 1815). By tacit consensus traditional professional associations continued for decades to reject the notion of having Jewish members.

For the period around 1780, when Dohm demanded the "civil improvement" of the Jews, it can be assumed that for the vast majority two factors determined their type of livelihood: their choice of occupation had to be approved by the authorities and it had to fill a need experienced both by the Christian population and by their own group. The economic activities of Jews thus focused on the respective peculiarities and opportunities that were present both locally and regionally. This trend is most obvious for certain variously structured portions of the Prussian state, where we have detailed surveys undertaken at the end of the eighteenth century.

In evaluating the resulting data, it is important to note that the information was normally obtained by questioning the person involved. In other words, the categories "small trade," "petty wares," "street trade," and "second-hand trade" could also include itinerant peddling, a profession met everywhere with suspicion. The sometimes amazingly high numbers of Jewish community employees probably also included people who lacked a long-term residence permit and thus gained protected status by performing the most minor of functions within the community. It is likewise inherently difficult to assign an individual to a specific area of trade since well into the nineteenth century Jews—particularly those in the middle and lower classes—rarely traded in only one product. The reason for this was likely competition within the limited number of accessible occupations, both inside and outside the Jewish community, making it difficult to secure a family's livelihood if the area of economic activity was too specialized. In addition, varied economic activity offered a certain protection against market fluctuations, problems in finding customers, and sudden difficulties in procuring goods for sale.

Thus, in the two districts of the county of Mark around 1800, there were numerous Jews (about 50 percent) who earned their livelihood in part by slaughtering cattle, calves, and lambs. They sold the meat to garrisons and burghers at lower prices than did the few non-Jewish butchers, who were not organized in guilds there and thus not protected. The Prussian king attempted to bring the legal situation with respect to kosher slaughtering into line with regulations in most of the rest of Prussia, where it was allowed only for the Jews' own consumption—except for the hind quarters, which the Jews did not eat on religious grounds. This initiative, however, met with stubborn protest from local officials who insistently and successfully stressed that serious shortages in the meat supply for the entire population would result if Jews were not permitted to slaughter except for their own needs. Since slaughtering was not a daily activity, almost all these slaughterers were also involved in trade, especially pawnbroking. Whether valuables were used as collateral or the anticipated harvest was taken as a security in this predominantly agrarian economy, in either case, it was the Jews who provided financial liquidity for the rural population. Some also traded in old clothing or in horses, peddled small items, mostly foodstuffs sold at outdoor stands, or dealt in used goods of various kinds. There were no large-scale merchants or court factors in the county of Mark. The same was true for nearby Cleves, though it had been the point of origin for the diverse activities of the many-branched Gompertz family of court Jews. In the first half of the eighteenth century they had already moved the center of their economic activities from Cleves, Wesel, and Emmerich to Berlin, and by the turn of the nineteenth century they were no longer active as court factors.

In East Friesland, which became part of Prussia in 1744, it was not the port city of Emden—Prussia's only access to the North Sea—that attracted Jews. Rather, a majority settled in the small towns and especially in the districts outside the cities, where competition from Christian merchants was not as great. Here, too, after some conflict, the Prussian government allowed them to slaughter cattle in keeping with widespread tradition. About two-fifths were active in this trade, some of them only "now and then." The detailed recorded list of various goods, however, certainly conveys a very different picture than that in the districts of the Mark. Many traded in tea, coffee, chocolate, tobacco, or porcelain—that is, essentially colonial products (almost 12 percent), which were accessible due to the proximity of the harbor and apparently found buyers. An even greater number of Jewish traders (almost 14 percent) bought and sold agricultural products such as livestock, timber, grains, honey and wax, feathers, furs, leather, and linseed. The proportion of moneychangers and pawnbrokers was amazingly low (8 percent), perhaps because Jews in other occupations engaged in moneylending secondarily to obtain additional income. The rest of the gainfully employed Jews dealt in products typical of almost all German states, including sundries, locally made textiles of cotton and linen, used clothing, and scrap metal. There were only two instances of itinerant peddlers. Jews in East Friesland were evidently more integrally a part of general economic life than were their coreligionists in the county of Mark, which was not only due to their much greater numbers. The extent of wealth mentioned in estimates for the distribution of taxes also differed greatly. Whereas the amount of 2,700 reichstaler was not surpassed in the Mark, the maximum sums in East Friesland ran to 4,000 and 8,000 reichstaler. Other financial indicators likewise give the impression that there were more large-scale merchants and affluent retailers and slaughterers in East Friesland. Unlike the pre-Prussian period, when the Calman and Beer families served as court factors, there is no indication of similar activity here at the end of the eighteenth century.

A still different picture of Jewish economic activities emerges from a consideration of the figures for the duchy of Magdeburg, above all with respect to the Jewish population in Halle. The closer proximity here to the central authorities, that is, to the king and his officials, served as a hindrance to integrating Jews into a wide range of economic activities. Instead, Jews were concentrated in two main areas favored by the authorities. The first was the trade fair activities, which were traditionally conducted by Jews from Magdeburg and Halle at the Leipzig fairs. About 20 percent of Jewish merchants considered this their main source of income. Another 20 percent sold locally manufactured goods, i.e., silk, cotton, and wool fabrics, as well as lace. Jewish students made up a special group (10 percent); more and more often, they availed themselves of the opportunity to study—medicine, in particular—at the relatively enlightened University of Halle. The remaining occupations were the common ones, such as dealing in money, used clothing, gems, or "whatever petty items they can get hold of."

Jews living east of the Elbe River were involved in yet other economic activities. As in the western region of the state, here too a distinction must be made between those areas in which Jews already resided before Prussian rule, and those where they first received permission to settle from the Prussian government. This is especially apparent with respect to the relevant data for Silesia and the Netze River district lying between

Posen and West Prussia, which Prussia acquired through the partitions of Poland.

In Silesia Jews had for centuries been allowed to settle permanently only in Zülz in Upper Silesia and in Glogau in Lower Silesia. However, the situation had clearly changed in the course of the eighteenth century. Increasingly, Jews settled on manorial demesnes, some of which resembled villages, and in towns. Their main source of income here was leasing distilleries and breweries; approximately half of all Jews in Upper Silesia, outside of Zülz, were in this field. This activity corresponded to their function as mediators between the nobility, who held the rights for the breweries and distilleries, and the burghers and peasants, who consumed the products. Only very few Jews (11 percent) designated themselves traders, sundries retailers, or brokers. There were some workers who supplied everyday or ritual needs, such as butchers, bakers, tailors and lace makers, glaziers, locksmiths, wood-carvers, and—in large numbers— potash producers, who used wood ashes to make fertilizer for agriculture and chemicals for glass production. The proportion of community employees and schoolmasters seems very low at 5 percent. Many religious positions were likely filled informally by individuals living in the respective towns. Whereas in the central and western parts of Prussia itinerant peddling is mentioned only marginally, it is listed by a sixth of the gainfully employed in Upper Silesia, perhaps on account of the immigration of poorer Jews from neighboring Poland.

The largest number of itinerant peddlers and those explicitly referred to as beggars (together 43 percent) was in Zülz, an important center of Jewish life over a long period a time. Here there was only one lessee of a brewery and distillery and relatively few general traders, sundries retailers, and brokers, who also traded in livestock. Instead there were numerous traders providing for the town's local daily needs, either for the general population or for the Jews in particular, with such items as flour, fish, milk, spices, eyeglasses, hardware, notions, etc. Almost 10 percent of the urban Jewish population acted as agents for rural producers in the area of textiles or in buying and selling furs and leather. Among the few manual laborers there were several butchers, gold and silversmiths, seal engravers, and bookbinders. In contrast to the scattered settlements in the rest of Upper Silesia, there was an organized Jewish community in Zülz. It employed about 10 percent of all those working there, who probably also served the surrounding areas.

All in all, of Upper Silesia it can be said that because of the important function Jews served in commerce and trade the Prussian government was forced to adopt structures that evolved over time in response to local needs. The principle of tolerating only wealthy Jews could not be enforced here any more than prohibiting Jews from settling in rural areas. The government was thus faced with a Jewish population, 40 percent of which was rural, another 40 percent of which lived mostly in smaller towns, and the remaining 20 percent in Zülz. Taken together, 25 percent of Upper Silesian Jewry earned their livelihood as itinerant peddlers. Attempts to severely limit their further settlement failed due to the manor lords' independence, which was based on the estates system. In contrast to the old provinces, their power still remained intact.

In Lower Silesia, where Jews made up less than 1 percent of the total population, in comparison to almost 2 percent in Upper Silesia, more than a fifth of working Jews referred to themselves as "trading Jews" or sundries retailers. More than another fifth of the Jewish population worked primarily as lessees of breweries or distilleries, engaging in trade on the side. The large proportion of schoolmasters and community employees (almost 25 percent) seems surprising at first, though it must be assumed that, in view of the numerous small Jewish settlements, the areas they each served were relatively small and that, moreover, in addition to these occupations they most likely also engaged in trade. Noteworthy is the presence of a few mint purveyors (*Münzlieferanten*), though the reference is probably to suppliers of precious metals and not to so-called mint Jews (*Münzjuden*), who actually produced coins. There were also, as in Upper Silesia, producers of potash.

The situation in the city of Breslau, capital of the province of Silesia, was totally different. As a hub of trade with East-Central Europe and the Orient, it had been attracting Jews for centuries. Both the Habsburg and, later, the Prussian governments recognized the significance of Jews in commerce, granting them temporary or long-term permission to settle for that purpose. An important role was played by Polish trading Jews whose agents—known by the Yiddish designation *Schammessen*—had permanent resident status in order to maintain the economic infrastructure for the Polish Jews, provide contacts and information, and represent their interests to the established Breslau merchants, who consistently opposed this undesired competition. Another important group was made up of the "holders of general privileges," of which there were approximately twenty at the end of the eighteenth century. They were granted the hereditary rights of Christian merchants, which they could pass on to their sons. Most were large-scale merchants who traded throughout Prussia and beyond and had established a branch in Breslau, though their business headquarters were usually elsewhere. They performed court factor functions, especially with regard to coinage and in supplying the military. Around 1800 four members of the Ephraim family and two of the Itzig family—both from Berlin—held general privileges in Breslau. The social structure of Breslau Jewry toward the end of the eighteenth century was still primarily defined by the gulf between the elite and the middle and lower classes. On the one side were the few who had been granted privileges and their families (about 30 to 40). Along with hundreds of their employees, who were declared protected and who possibly used this protection to become active in trade themselves, they comprised over one-quarter of the Jewish population. On the other side were three-quarters of the Jews—small-scale traders, itinerant peddlers, money changers, and community employees along with their families. They lived apart from the Christian middle class in Breslau, which had long been organized into various sorts of trade associations. The Jews were most comparable to the "dilettantes" (*Pfuscher*), that is, to craftsmen who worked outside the guilds, their numbers growing steadily, despite massive protests from guild members, since gaining entry to a guild was very expensive. A shift within the social structure of the Jewish population did not take place here until the first few decades of the nineteenth century. As in other major cities, it then resulted in the emergence of a small wealthy upper class and a clearly growing middle class, along with the continuance of a still considerable lower stratum.

In the province of Silesia there were thus three distinct modes of Jewish occupational adaptation to local needs and opportunities. Jews in Upper Silesia had a virtual monopoly on brewery and distillery leases and also worked as itinerant peddlers. In Lower Silesia leasing also played a large role, but more important were small-scale trade in everyday consumer goods, money changing, moneylending, and pawnbroking. In Breslau only the Polish trading Jews and the few holders of special privileges were able to attain a firm and governmentally supported position in the urban economy—especially in trade with Poland and Russia—and in declining activities as court factors.

The regions annexed through the partitions of Poland represent a novel element within Prussian Jewry: the very large number of Jewish artisans. Above all in the Netze district they often lived on manorial demesnes in small towns and villages, along with Jewish merchants, to some extent assuming functions of the middle class, positioned between nobility and peasants. A considerable reservoir of Jewish craftsmen developed in this area while it was still part of Poland. They concentrated on the immediate needs of the local populace and made up about one-third of the total number of working Jews. Minister of State and War Otto Karl Friedrich von Voss (1755–1823) traveled through these regions in the 1790s and reported: "The existence of the Jews in the province is of the utmost importance, since the number of Jews probably amounts to one-eighth or one-ninth of all residents, all commerce is presently in their hands, there is also a mass of artisans of all kinds among them and, all in all, the Jew . . . is a more cultivated person than the burgher in small towns and the peasant in the countryside."[1] Jews in the countryside bought the predominantly homemade notions and fabrics produced in the rural communities and sold them in the cities, in part to the numerous Jewish tailors working there. Most characteristic, then, of the economic activities among Jews in the Netze district, as in all of East-Central Europe, from the time the region belonged to Poland was this widespread activity in the crafts, from which Jews were mostly barred in the German states, along with the purchase and sale of locally produced goods. The function these Jews assumed—and to some extent had developed in the first place—of acting as intermediaries between town and countryside also existed elsewhere, but it was especially noteworthy in this region, which up to that time could boast of no major cities with attractive flourishing economies.

In East Prussia the Baltic seaport of Königsberg exercised a magnetic influence on Jews. Its access to eastern and western sea routes and its proximity to Russia for import and export trade made Königsberg an important trade center in the northeastern German Empire. As in Breslau, Königsberg's middle class was firmly rooted within guilds that had already staked out their spheres in the trades and crafts. Jewish traders were therefore forced to discover new opportunities by selling Silesian canvas, Dutch products, woolen goods, as well as Russian furs, in which about half of all Jewish traders dealt. Moreover, as in Breslau, some Jewish traders and merchants in Königsberg became quite wealthy and received general privileges. Among these was, above all, Joachim Moses Friedländer (ca. 1712–1776), founder of the business firm of the same name, which existed into the twentieth century. Two of Friedländer's sons—one was the pioneering advocate of Jewish emancipation, David Friedländer—married into the Berlin business families, Ephraim and Itzig, thus combining family ties with business interests. Other Jews who were able to accumulate the necessary capital furthered the economic and political aims of the state by establishing factories. But here too this narrow upper stratum contrasted with the much larger population of Jewish poor, who had settled mostly on the outskirts of the city.

Another Baltic seaport, the once rich and relatively independent commercial center of Danzig, promised neither Jews nor Christians any real opportunities for prosperity around 1800 on account of the stagnation it had experienced for decades. Rulership had changed hands several times—Poland, then Prussia, France, and then again Prussia—as had the city's political status, from a free city under Polish sovereignty to a Prussian administrative city, a free state under French rule, and finally a provincial capital in Prussia. These fluctuations had led to a continual decline, which was accelerated by customs barriers and high tribute payments. The guilds had succeeded in expelling Jews from the city in 1723, forcing them to settle in five neighboring communities or on the outskirts of Danzig, where there were few economic opportunities. They worked mostly as petty traders, dealers in used clothing, moneylenders, and sellers of old silver and gold. A permanent, extensive Jewish settlement was not reestablished in the city of Danzig until the early nineteenth century.

Nowhere were the efforts to take advantage of the economic strength of the Jews—and of the Huguenots—as an "imported substitute bourgeoisie" for the promotion and support of innovative, promising business strategies and production methods as persistent as in the "Royal Capital of Berlin." In comparison to Breslau or Königsberg, the economically traditionalist bourgeoisie in Berlin was not very self-confident, its rights having long ago been eviscerated by the central authorities. Before the turn of the nineteenth century the Jewish court factors, bound to the service of the sovereign, had begun to lose significance. The wholesalers and manufacturers—a group that overlapped in part with the court factors—and their offspring, who sought new economic enterprises, submitted several petitions to the relevant authorities in an attempt to eliminate the obstacles that mercantile, state-controlled economic policies posed for the implementation of competitive capitalism. Among them was Moses Mendelssohn, partner in the silk factory of Isaac Bernhard and Sons, and later David Friedländer, as elected representative of Berlin manufacturers and also as the practical expert of the local industrial and commercial association, a position to which he was appointed in 1793.

These developments represented a turning away from the functions of those whom the historian Jacob Toury called Jewish *Adelsbürger*, that is, highly privileged persons whose economic activities were nonetheless dependent on the approval of the authorities, and toward the self-determined economic activities of individual entrepreneurs. They also stimulated the organization of professional associations such as the Berlin stock exchange corporation, established at the beginning of the nineteenth century through a merger of existing trade guilds with merchants and manufacturers, not organized in guilds, who were interested in the stock market. Shortly after the corporation was founded, 170 of the 360 Jews involved in business and trade had already become members. Their broad-based involvement in general economic affairs would have been impossible at the time in those major Prussian cities that had a middle class with long-standing traditions. Even more unthinkable elsewhere was the fact that two of the four principals were Jewish businessmen, namely, sugar factory owner Jacob Herz Beer (1769–1825)—father of banker Wilhelm Beer, composer Giacomo Meyerbeer (Jacob Meyer Beer), and poet Michael Beer—and the banker Ruben Samuel Gumpertz (1769–1851), member of the Gumpertz family that had served the Prussian state and its rulers for five generations in a variety of functions. Gumpertz was also an elder in the Jewish community and a patron of modern Jewish studies. Beer and Gumpertz were leading figures in the movement for Jewish religious reform, active in the city's public life, and, because of their expertise, regarded by other members of their respective professions as equal partners.

However, the great majority of the working Jewish population in Berlin, over 80 percent, could be considered part of the emerging middle class and those involved in small trade. Artisans were represented in very few areas, those in which guild membership was not compulsory. By contrast, 80 percent of the working Christian population were in guilds and only about 20 percent were involved in trade. The result was that approximately one-fourth of all trade in the city was in the hands of Jews, who constituted only 2 percent of the population but were largely dependent on it. A wide range of goods was bought and sold, but products of the textile and clothing industries, which received large state subsidies in Berlin and the Mark Brandenburg, predominated. Another major occupational category consisted of brokerage, commercial activities in general, and financial dealings in particular, trading on commission, and pawnbroking. In a royal residence city in which the traditional guild and middle-class status were practically synonymous, Jews formed a flexible element in the city populace that was open to economic innovation.

All in all, it can be said for the individual regions of Prussia—to the extent that data is available from relevant surveys—that the economic activity of Jews around 1800 was much more dependent on the respective conditions and opportunities at hand within the regions than one would assume from the customary reference back to the occupational fields laid down in the Revised General Code of 1750. Extreme examples are the widespread, although prohibited, activity as slaughterers in the western and northwestern parts of Prussia, the leasing of breweries and distilleries in Silesia, for which prohibition was continually threatened though never carried out, and the extensive activities in the crafts—barred to Jews everywhere else but reluctantly tolerated in those areas acquired through the partitions of Poland.

No other German state at this time was comparable to Prussia, in terms either of its territorial fragmentation or of the number of Jews living there. Although the occupational and settlement patterns of Jews elsewhere also corresponded to respective demand and opportunities available in fulfilling it, the other states were relatively closed territorial units with minimally differentiated economic systems. This was especially true in the western, southwestern, and southern German states of Hesse, Baden, Württemberg, and Bavaria, where Jews resided in hundreds of sometimes extremely small settlements. Even territorial changes that ensued in the course of Napoleonic politics did little to alter these economic structures. Only in a few larger cities were early industrial production facilities established or interregional trade conducted. Other than that, agriculture—performed mostly by peasants—was the prevailing means of subsistence everywhere. Jews in these areas lived in the countryside and maintained a firm position in the rural economy without being greatly involved in farming or breeding livestock. To the extent allowed, they generally bought or leased a piece of land, which they cultivated either alone or with the help of Christian laborers. They often required the land as a "temporary storage" for their trade in livestock, the Jews' main source of income in some areas, which they carried on as a virtual monopoly. Feelings of local peasants toward the Jewish traders were mixed, since on the one hand they were dependent on these intermediaries but, on the other hand, had lived for centuries with the notion that Jews were synonymous with usurers. The fact that, in times of crisis, livestock trading was often combined with moneylending reinforced this image. A contemporary at the beginning of the nineteenth century in Württemberg expressed his hostile attitudes toward Jews by describing the situation as follows:

If they [the Jews] are wealthy, then they use their money for the most contemptible usury; they trade in debts themselves, unload bad livestock on the poor peasants for exorbitant prices on credit, give them money on top of that, and once they totally own such an unlucky soul, they demand their loans be repaid, and once again he must make a major sacrifice. . . . If the Jews are poor, they deceive the ignorant and gullible peasants with their hawking, delivering inferior wares and stealing whenever they have a chance.[2]

This absolutely negative judgment of Jews was firmly rooted in the consciousness of the rural population. But it did not hamper trade between the parties, since there was no alternative. The peasants received hardly any loans from Christian moneylenders in the cities since they were a bad credit risk, while Jews were permitted only these commercial

4   Jewish cattle dealer, lithograph, around 1820

activities. For better or worse, both parties were forced to maintain their dealings with one another. Moreover, the Jewish traders sought out the small farmers in their homes or met them at small local markets, offering them money and goods and buying agricultural products or lending money on the anticipated harvest or livestock production, thus responding quickly and flexibly to the peasants' needs. In all these states petty trade, itinerant peddling, and trading in used goods were carried on in addition to and sometimes together with the livestock trade, surpassing it in terms of volume in some regions. The distinctions between petty trade, peddling, and used goods trading are difficult to determine on the basis of the available evidence, as is the differentiation between such pursuits and earning a livelihood through begging. This is so because the objects bought and sold, especially in peddling and the used goods trade, but also in brokering, could change very quickly and because the prospects of economic success were always uncertain, with the constant danger of impoverishment. According to cautious estimates, up to 90 percent of Jews in Hesse, Baden, Württemberg, and Bavaria can be assumed to have earned their livelihood around 1800 from trade, over half of these from a subsistence peddling that provided only the barest essentials for survival and often fell short of the necessary minimum. Thus Jews were disproportionately poor, as were most of the peasantry, survival being the principal object of their economic activities. The remaining 10 percent of the working Jewish population included a few artisans, the necessary community employees and schoolmasters, and isolated examples of early factory owners.

Court factor activities and wholesale trade were conducted by a few wealthy Jews, primarily in the *Residenzen* and other larger cities such as Darmstadt, Kassel, Karlsruhe, and Mannheim, as well as Stuttgart, Ludwigsburg, and Munich. Because of the prevailing agrarian structures, which delayed industrialization and the urbanization that generally accompanies it, a significant bourgeois middle class among both Jewish and non-Jewish populations did not develop here until decades later. Whereas those Jews who had obtained the right to settle in the major cities soon began to speak out for improved—if not equal—legal status for all Jews and involve themselves in public affairs, rural Jewry retained its tradition-based identity much longer. This not only held true for spheres of life defined strictly by religious belief but was also reflected in an existence largely separate from the Christian population. The respective rulers sought to concentrate Jewish residences on certain streets

5 Jewish uniform dealer, etching, around 1820

or even in entire districts in order to better control or, in the case of attacks, more easily protect them. The Jews too preferred this arrangement since it helped provide a sense of group solidarity and since living in close proximity facilitated their religious observance. Their attitude was that characteristic of almost all minorities that are willing to accept lower status within the surrounding society for the sake of preserving their group identity.

Between southern Germany in the west and the eastern part of Central Europe in the east lay Bohemia and Moravia, the area where most

German-speaking Jews in the Habsburg Empire settled. Whereas only isolated privileged families were tolerated in Vienna and only an insignificant number were living in Lower Austria, Jews made up a considerable portion of the economically active population in Bohemia and Moravia. Protected by the desire of the magnates for an affluent lifestyle on their respective lands, and tolerated—though with interruptions—by the central authorities in Vienna, the Jewish population that became established here was involved in economic activities that differed from those of Jews in southern and southwestern Germany.

The capital of Prague had long held a magnetic appeal for Bohemian Jews, attracting over 40 percent of them. The rest were dispersed throughout hundreds of rural communities and manorial demesnes. In Moravia, on the other hand, where Jews had not been permitted to settle in villages before 1848, they tended to dwell in more compact settlements. Here they lived in about fifty towns, among which the capital city of Brünn (Brno) was especially popular. The general rule was that no Jews should be allowed to settle anywhere above the number already in residence, but this regulation was hardly enforceable in practice. The manor lords did not hold to it, and affluent Jews were able to extend protected status to their employees whose numbers might reach several dozen. The law provided that only homeowners could engage in trade, and it was difficult to acquire a concession to purchase a "Jewish house." One alternative, with obvious limitations, was for a Jew to sell part of a house to other Jews, who could thereupon also receive permission to trade. Those who had leased a distillery, tannery, or potash plant were in principle authorized to live there only for the duration of the lease, though many were able to obtain permission for more extensive commercial activities. For tenants the only option was to engage in some form of petty manual labor, such as mending clothes or shoes, without thereby gaining a permanent residence permit.

These old structures were supposed to be modified by Joseph II's Toleration Edicts, enacted in October 1781 for Bohemia and February 1782 for Moravia. They declared the entry of Jews into crafts and agriculture to be an important political goal. But the efforts that were made proved ineffectual. Christian traders and craftsmen, who continued to be organized in guilds, did their best to oppose such potential competition and the Jews themselves largely preferred to remain in their traditional, though rarely lucrative, activities. As a result, about half of all Jews, both in the towns and the countryside, were engaged in some form of trade. Another 25 percent of urban Jews had occupations in the crafts or as servants, and in rural areas about 15 percent to 17 percent each were involved in crafts, transport, or servants' duties, with the carters and coachmen also usually engaged in trade.

While the relatively high proportion of Jews in the crafts suggests comparison with those parts of Prussia that formerly belonged to Poland, the compulsory or chosen living conditions in Bohemia and Moravia tended more to resemble settlements in southern and southwestern Germany. There, too, Jews were assigned common residential areas, whether individual streets or entire quarters, where they could buy "Jewish houses." The effect, especially in the Jewish section of Prague, was an oppressive closeness. The more affluent tried to escape the congestion by seeking permission to reside in well-regarded Christian portions of the city. This was true, in particular, for the first Jewish manufacturers who, in line with Joseph II's mercantile policies, were explicitly requested to establish such enterprises. These men often simultaneously engaged in interregional wholesaling, an as yet underdeveloped field. Combining the two was often a good formula for success. Other energetically pursued activities were supplying the army (an enterprise that remained relatively immune to crisis), leasing rights to tobacco production, and lending money to the state, somewhat like a state banker.

Jewish manufacturers in Bohemia and Moravia concentrated primarily on textiles and clothes. Some of them possessed factories equipped with machines regarded as advanced for the times and presided over a work force that came out of a well-established, protoindustrial tradition of home labor among the Christian population. Although the first attempts of Bohemian Jews in the linen, woolen, and cloth goods industry proved moderately successful, once permission to import raw cotton was granted in 1779, the principal domain of Jewish industrialists soon became the rapidly flourishing cotton industry. Members of the linen and wool trades, which enjoyed a centuries-old tradition, regarded it as a parvenu industry. In Moravia, too, the first manufacturers came from the ranks of the wholesalers, tobacco lessees, and army suppliers, who possessed the necessary start-up capital. Unlike developments in Bohemia, the clothing industry emerged in Moravia as an independent form of enterprise. It was able to combine the experience Jews had gained in the mending and alteration of military uniforms and old clothing with Jewish and Christian nonguild tailors as the needed work force. An ordered system soon arose in which home workers supplied the necessary fabrics, which were then further processed into clothing. Even fierce protest from the tailors' guilds could not prevent this new, ready-made clothing from quickly finding buyers, especially among the poor, at markets and, ultimately, in regular clothing stores.

These entrepreneurs were exceptional among the masses of Jews, but they required countless "subcontractors" to distribute the products to scattered villages and towns, so that a rather large number of Jews in one way or another earned their livelihood in this emerging clothing industry. In sum, it can be said that although a considerable number of Bohemian and Moravian Jews around 1800 were poor their financial status corresponded on average to that of the lower middle class rather than to those living on the margins of subsistence, as was the case in southern and southwestern Germany and some areas east of the Elbe. Therefore Bohemian and Moravian Jews sought all the more to work with the authorities in order to prevent a threat to their livelihood by Jews "creeping in" from neighboring Galicia, where they lived under incredibly wretched conditions. Such intruders might be gangs of thieves and swindlers, beggars, or temporary itinerant laborers.

Finally, what is most striking in the city-states of Frankfurt and Hamburg is the growing significance of the better situated portion of the Jewish population in banking, the stock exchange, and manufacturing. During the Coalition Wars against France and immediately thereafter, these two cities, having come under French influence, became centers for financial transactions relating to the wars and the French occupation. In these few years the stock exchange proved to be the first arena in the most important European trade centers in which Jews possessed equal status. The situation was similar in Vienna, Amsterdam, London, and Berlin, as well as in smaller capital cities. It was no longer only court factors who raised large sums of money for individual royal courts to cover the costs of war and its aftermath; more and more, Christian and Jewish banking houses that provided official loans to the government were being established. These developments should not, of course, hide the fact that most Jews were not involved or that they benefited from them only peripherally, for example, by serving as agents. In Frankfurt, however, a number of Jews became bankers of this new type even though, at the time, the Rothschild family was only at the beginning of its rise, both in terms of major financial dealings and of setting up its "branches" in five European banking cities. Frankfurt, which had long oriented itself toward Amsterdam, the undisputed European center for financial transactions, began to surpass it in the 1790s. Among the approximately one hundred bankers in Frankfurt around 1800 the most successful, with few exceptions, were Jews. At this time, when twenty war-related government loans had already been transacted in Frankfurt, as yet not a single one had been provided in Berlin.

In Hamburg, too, there were several banking firms that had an impact on the European financial market. Here family connections among Jews often facilitated access to a number of locations of financial importance. For example, Joel von Halle, of the wealthy Hamburg banking family, married a daughter of Salomon Moses Levy, who was influential on the Berlin capital and credit markets. He then moved to Berlin where his in-laws arranged the necessary business connections. At the same time he was able to give his father-in-law's banking house direct access to commerce in Hamburg. The same was true for Joseph Mendelssohn, who opened a banking business in Hamburg in 1801, having followed in the footsteps of his father-in-law Nathan Meyer, who had moved to the Danish city of Altona, near Hamburg, a few years earlier and who had already had business relations with Joseph's father, Moses Mendelssohn. Together with his brother Abraham and their two families, who had also settled in Hamburg, Joseph Mendelssohn successfully ran the Mendelssohn Brothers banking firm, maintaining close ties with the parent company in Berlin until Hamburg's occupation by the French.

In addition to bankers, a number of Jewish manufacturers were able to gain wealth and status in Hamburg. "Certainly everyone knows . . . that our calico cotton factories are largely owned by Jewish residents,"[3] notes the report of a Hamburg senator from the year 1800. Those who did not benefit from this temporary upswing—if they did not earn their bread as itinerant peddlers—generally traded in "all sorts of wares" including colonial products such as coffee, tea, sugar, chocolate, tobacco, and brandy. Although they also occasionally produced goods by hand or in factories, few became affluent. Moreover, the high tribute that had to be paid to the French led to rapidly spreading poverty and, ultimately, to financial stagnation in both cities.

3. Areas of Enterprise Between 1815 and 1848

The free access to all economic areas that some German states granted to the Jews during the French occupation met with fierce, though ultimately futile, opposition by the old established, traditionally organized burghers. Reform discourse in Prussia and elsewhere still stressed the goal of "productivization," which did not prevent the freedom of occupational choice, granted generally in 1810–1811, from being extended to Jews through the Edict of 1812. They now possessed the right to practice occupations that had formerly been reserved for members of guilds, at least in the areas that Prussia had retained in 1806–1807. Existing law remained in force in lands newly acquired or reacquired in 1815: in the western provinces, the French constitution, limited by Napoleon in 1808, and in the grand duchy of Posen, which became the province of Posen, the "guild constitution."

Compared with other German states, Prussia clearly played a pioneering role in the introduction of free occupational choice, despite restrictions that existed there. The era of restoration after 1815, in general, strengthened the legitimacy of established organized forms of trade and commerce until even beyond the revolutionary events at mid-century. Nearly everywhere free choice of occupation was not adopted until the years between 1860 and 1868, and a standardized law had to await the formation of the North German Federation.

Occupational restrictions could not, however, hold up the trend from an estatist feudal society to a bourgeois capitalist one, which eventually gained momentum everywhere. The varied legal status in the individual German territories no longer had the same decisive impact on the economic activities of Jews that it had decades earlier. Thus the overriding theme for the period after 1815 is the development of Jewish participation in multiple branches of the economy.

At the beginning of this period the focus of debate was still on efforts at occupational redistribution from subsistence peddling to the crafts and agriculture. Such a shift was regarded as prerequisite for a productive Jewish community that could be useful to the state and the rest of society. Many German states held it necessary to "educate" Jews in this manner, making it a condition for more extensive rights and, hence, virtually compulsory. Jews actively supported these efforts, in part because they would thereby gain access to fields that were previously barred to them and in part to satisfy the prerequisites for civil equality.

In the 1820s dozens of new associations were formed in the various German states and cities for the purpose of "promoting crafts and agriculture among the Jews." In some cases existing Jewish charitable organizations likewise took on this task. Except for Prussia, where "increased productivity," though also desired, was not an explicit condition for the improvement of Jews' legal status, these organizations received state subsidies to assist them in their quite difficult project. However, the associations, which attempted to assist Christian master craftsmen in search of apprentices, often encountered sustained resistance. The notion of training a Jew to join their trade was still too foreign and there was considerable fear of unnecessarily creating competition. According to a memorandum issued by Bavarian Jews in 1821:

> In some areas it is almost impossible to find training positions for the apprentices; in others, it requires the expenditure of much effort and money. . . . Unprecedented obstinacy is preventing Israelites from receiving the status of master craftsmen. Most masters are as consumed with hatred of Jews and fear of competition as are so many tradesmen, and the former believe they are more entitled to their feelings than are the latter.[4]

On the other hand, the organizations also had to convince their fellow Jews to allow their sons to become apprentices for a craft rather than making early making use of their sons' labor for the family business.

Associations in Baden and the Hessian states, officially subsidized by their governments, seem to have been the most successful. Figures available for Frankfurt am Main show that by the middle of the century the Association for the Promotion of the Crafts had supported over seven hundred apprentices until they completed their training. Good results were also achieved in Karlsruhe and Munich, where emphasis was placed on training in agricultural skills.

The Association for the Training of Elementary School Teachers and Promotion of the Crafts Among Jews, begun in 1825 in Münster, deserves special attention. Its initiator and the founder of the institution associated with it was the physician and philanthropist Alexander Haindorf (1784–1862). His goals were to assure better schooling for children through the proper training of teachers and at the same time to provide training programs for artisans. The latter were intended especially for orphans and the poor whom such associations generally sought to assist in starting a career. The institution, which was originally set up to serve the province of Westphalia, expanded its sphere in 1834 to include the Rhine province. After receiving a large donation from Haindorf's father-in-law, Elias Marks, it became the Marks-Haindorf Foundation and gained prominence in both its fields of endeavor. Although conducted in accordance with Jewish tradition, it soon began accepting Christian students as well. In the first fifty years of its existence it helped approximately 350 apprentices to become trained craftsmen, and it educated hundreds of teachers and prayer leaders for the Jewish communities until well into the twentieth century.

It is difficult to estimate the precise number of Jews who started a lasting career in the crafts or agriculture either on their own or as a result of the efforts of such associations. Official statistics did not distinguish between those who completed training in a particular occupation and those who actually practiced it. Consequently, Jews would often identify themselves as trained craftsmen, since the authorities looked upon practicing a craft more favorably than upon commercial activities. This must have been the case in Bavaria and other southern German states, where the right to settle or the marriage age among Jews was generally dependent upon the practice of a "productive" occupation. Legal pressures led many Jews to obtain training in agriculture or the crafts, as weavers, tailors, or butchers, but they frequently practiced these occupations on the side, combining them with trade in the same area in order to secure a sufficient income to live on.

According to official statistics, the proportion of Jews involved in trade went from between 70 and 80 percent of the total Jewish population in the German states at the beginning of the century down to about 50 percent at mid-century. The ratio of Jews in agriculture and the crafts increased correspondingly. In Bavaria, where permission to settle was dependent on occupation, the number of trained Jewish artisans and farmers increased from 7.7 percent in 1822 to more than one-third of the total working Jewish population twenty years later. In Prussia the proportion of trained craftsmen rose from 4.6 percent (excluding Posen) in 1813 to 19.3 percent in 1843, although it is important to note that almost half of those included in the latter figure lived in Posen, where Jews had long been active in the crafts. On the other hand, in Prussia, where Jews had not been allowed to settle outside the cities, only about 1 percent of the working Jewish population was involved in agriculture during the first half of the nineteenth century. About 40 percent of this small number lived in the province of Silesia, where Prussian rulers had been forced to accept existing rural Jewish settlements when they gained possession of the area.

According to official statistics, the number of Jews who entered the crafts leveled off around the middle of the century, and the figures soon began to decline. Three factors were responsible. First, governments no longer enforced their "education" policies as strictly as they had in the 1820s and 1830s; second, guilds continued to make life difficult for Jewish craftsmen so that it can be assumed—although no statistics are available—that many of the trained Jewish artisans emigrated. The third and, for the long term, decisive factor was the declining importance of the crafts—as well as agriculture—for general economic development. Competitive capitalism, which accompanied emerging industrialization, technological innovation in methods of production, and the flexibility and mobility that were becoming imperative for survival all contradicted the basic characteristics associated with craftsmanship: a settled form of existence, traditional ties, and a sense of social cohesion with one's own group. An entire social class was coming increasingly under prolonged threat. The process generally progressed more rapidly in the major cities than in small and middle-sized towns, and it took place faster in the consciousness of Jews, who had been living with less security for centuries, than among many non-Jews, who relied upon the security of the traditional established rights to which they were accustomed. As a consequence of this conflict between assertive and cautious economic behaviors, Jews in increased numbers returned (to the extent that they had left it at all) to the economic field that had earlier been imposed upon them and that they had developed as their own, that is, to commercial activity. Or they turned to new ways of earning a living in industry.

Jewish families of private means, and those in academic professions, as well as wholesalers, bankers, and industrialists still made up only a small group in numerical terms, but one suited to the new age. Banking firms were replacing the countless petty moneylenders and changers, assuming their tasks while incorporating the rational methods of modern finance. And there was already a considerable number of people who could support themselves "from the profits of their investments in rented or leased real estate."[5]

Until the middle of the nineteenth century there was a definite decline in the number of Jewish traders who earned their livelihood by selling commissioned goods, brokering, taking pawns, or as itinerant peddlers. On the other hand, there was a sharp increase in those selling their wares from "open shops," that is, from a permanent address. To be sure, of all Jews active in trade, between 30 percent and 50 percent, depending on the region, still supported themselves from petty transactions as hucksters, itinerant peddlers, and used goods dealers, but their unmistakable goal was to rise from a marginal existence to that of a "proper" respected merchant. It is doubtful that this trend resulted from governmental "education policies" alone. In all likelihood, far more significant for the process were changing consumer needs, new classes of consumers that emerged in the wake of urbanization and industrialization, improved transportation and commercial conditions resulting from the construction of highways, canals, and the first railroads (which all facilitated procurement of goods), as well as uncomplicated credit procedures to acquire start-up capital and similar innovations.

The shift to a bourgeois capitalist society, however, did not become dominant until the 1830s. At first a lengthy period of economic scarcity followed in the aftermath of the Napoleonic Wars. The immense growth in population accompanied by agricultural crisis forced the nonpropertied peasantry to move to the cities in search of employment, which did not exist to the degree hoped for. Thus the process of social change extended over decades.

For urban Jewish traders this crisis-driven phenomenon meant potential growth in their circle of customers, although the impoverished peasants arriving from the countryside possessed little purchasing power. They did force a change in the commodities offered, however, since certain everyday items were no longer as frequently produced at home. This was especially true for clothing, food, and luxury items, as well as furniture, and—in view of the spreading poverty—for inexpensive and used wares, including scrap metal products. Consumers with better resources were also offered spices, colonial goods, lace, and jewelry. Jews experienced the trend toward becoming middle-class merchants equally whether they lived in towns or cities. It was strongest in those places where no traditionally established Christian bourgeoisie existed, as it did in Hamburg, Breslau, or Frankfurt, and where it continued to oppose Jews entering its ranks. Hamburg's city council tried repeatedly to break the popular resistance to admitting Jews as members in the Honorable Merchants Society, representing all Hamburg merchants, but was unsuccessful until the middle of the century. Not until a new chamber of commerce was founded in Breslau, in 1849, were all merchants, including Jews, represented in a common organization.

In Berlin which, by contrast, lacked countervailing traditions, Jews were accepted early on into the professional organizations. As early as 1796 the king had pressured the cloth and silk merchants' guild to accept David Friedländer into its ranks. When, after prolonged negotiations, a Berlin commercial organization was formed in 1820 from a loose association of Christian guild merchants and Jewish nonguild merchants, Joseph Mendelssohn (1770–1848), the oldest son of Moses Mendelssohn and the only one to remain faithful to Judaism, became its vice president and, in 1834, its president.

Karlsruhe and Mannheim, where Jews participated fully in the chambers of commerce, showed a similar willingness to view economic activities as the basis for a common representative body and joint activities between Gentiles and Jews. Proposed statutes of 1827 and 1835 for the Karlsruhe chamber of commerce provided, respectively, for six Christian and two Jewish and four Christian and two Jewish representatives on the governing board. As early as 1819, and again in 1830 and 1833, banker Jacob Kusel was elected to the chamber's executive. In Cologne Simon Oppenheim headed the chamber of commerce there starting in 1834. To be sure, this form of respect was extended only to individual outstanding Jewish business personalities, but the cooperation between Christian and Jewish merchants in professional organizations suggests a broader mutual acceptance. New business structures made it necessary to work together, at the very least giving relatively more importance to "achievements," even though earlier prejudiced attitudes toward Jewish economic activity certainly remained present as well.

From the perspective of these fundamental changes in economic relationships we can now view the truly spectacular and often recounted successes of a number of Jewish banking families, which for many reasons made an unprecedented public impact in the first few decades of the nineteenth century. Incredible sums of money were needed to fight the Coalition Wars, and again during the Napoleonic campaigns and the following period of French rule, or French occupation, in major portions of the German Empire. The reconsolidation of state finances in the subsequent years of general poverty made it necessary to create an entire system of extensive loans on German and European financial markets. This phase was then followed by the takeoff of the industrial age in the 1830s and 1840s, which did not yet have any far-reaching repercussions on production and consumer demand but required large amounts of capital.

Jewish and Christian bankers, wholesalers, and industrialists—whose fields were not yet clearly distinguishable from one another—often formed loose associations, either temporarily to fill single orders or to create early forms of regular stock companies, in order to cope with diverse and sometimes very complex loan operations. This required cooperation with both domestic and foreign banking houses. Extended family connections established by the Jews proved helpful for them in securing business contacts quickly and easily. The most impressive and at the same time most envy-inducing example was the Rothschild family, with their parent company in Frankfurt and branches in London,

Vienna, Naples, and Paris. However, the sons of banker Jonas Hirsch, who had moved from Bohemia to Fürth in the eighteenth century, also opened banks in Amsterdam, Frankfurt, Vienna, and Paris, and the banking house of Salomon Oppenheim, founded in Cologne in 1801, was represented by a commercial company in London through his son Simon. Hermann Oppenheim, another son of Salomon, was a partner in commercial enterprises in Paris, Constantinople, and Alexandria. Marriages with sons and daughters of other banking families created connections, for example, between the Oppenheims in Cologne, the Habers in Karlsruhe, and the Beyfuses in Frankfurt.

Major and minor banking companies found such connections through family relations were imperative for exchanging information, refinancing, and various degrees of participation in financial transactions. In times of crisis, however, or with regard to very risky endeavors, they could also lead to great difficulties, since a loss of credit by one branch would threaten all the others. That was one reason why the Rothschild family sought firmer control by marrying almost exclusively within their own—very extensive—family.

It is impossible to estimate the extent to which Jewish bankers helped raise the capital needed by German states. Amounts required varied from

6   The marriage of Anselm and Charlotte von Rothschild in Frankfurt, 1826

state to state and city to city. Assets of the respective Jewish or non-Jewish creditors also varied over the years. In the first two decades of the nineteenth century state bonds in Baden amounted to almost 24 million florins, and more than half was provided by Jewish banking firms; the Haber family in Karlsruhe alone provided 8.4 million florins, or about 35 percent. In Berlin in 1812, by contrast, it required eighteen Jewish bankers—more than half the bankers in the city—to raise about 60 percent of the capital for a loan of about 500,000 taler. Liepmann Meyer Wulff in this case provided almost 10 percent, or 45,000 taler, clearly more than anyone else. Here, then, we have a number of bankers of moderate or quite limited financial means who had to think in far more modest terms than their colleagues in Berlin a generation later. The Mendelssohn family success was then only beginning and Samuel Bleichröder's money changing business did not evolve into a banking house until the 1820s.

What remains certain is that from the beginning of the nineteenth century business methods and the extent of transferred capital in German banks and stock exchanges experienced greatly accelerated development. Jewish bankers who were involved were able to benefit more from it than were Christian competitors on account of their longer experience in finance. Although only very few grew really wealthy at this time, since interest payments and even repayment of principal dragged on very slowly, the Jewish bankers did noticeably strengthen their economic position.

Of the areas Jewish capitalists chose for investment the one that was particularly noted by contemporaries and looked most toward the future was financing the first railroad companies. These new enterprises had considerable initial impact not only on branches of industry that were directly affected such as transportation, commerce and the capital markets but also on the structure of the economy as a whole. The major Jewish banking houses considered railroad construction to be a highly profitable investment opportunity for the future. The first railroad lines in the Rhine and Ruhr valleys are thus inextricably tied to the financial efforts of Abraham Oppenheim, the construction of the Berlin-Stettin railroad in 1836 to the Mendelssohns, along with other private Jewish banks. The Rothschilds of Frankfurt financed several railroads in Germany, including the Taunus line in Hesse and the Rhine-Nahe line. Even more significant was the four-hundred-kilometer-long railroad line from Vienna to Galicia that was financed by Salomon Rothschild in Vienna. The construction, which began in 1837, required over fourteen thousand workers.

Another, albeit rare, investment opportunity for bankers was to provide extensive credit to industrialists. Here the Haber banking firm of Karlsruhe played a major role. In 1836 its investments led to the founding of the three largest industrial firms in Baden: a sugar factory in Waghäusel, a textile plant in Ettlingen, and a machine factory in Karlsruhe.

More often than providing credit for the industrial enterprises of others, Jews set up their own factories with capital they had accumulated through trade. Although there were already isolated Jewish master craftsmen who tried to expand their workshops into production facilities with hired employees, most Jewish industrialists were merchants who shifted within their field from commerce to production. Almost all such factories or factorylike enterprises were newly established, since most of the manufactories initiated and subsidized by the state in the eighteenth century had, before the turn of the century, already closed or changed hands. Fresh opportunities created a new type of entrepreneur who differed from the earlier Adelsbürger. This new class, which included

7 Festive opening of the Brünn (Brno) train station on the
Kaiser-Ferdinand-Nordbahn, built by the Rothschilds

numerous Jews, was guided by individual initiative and a willingness to take risks.

As was generally the case in the early industrial age, most Jewish manufacturers, too, produced goods in the textile and clothing industry for which home labor and domestic raw materials, wool and linen, were readily available and that, in contrast to the metalworking or engineering works industries required no expensive machinery.

Calico cloth production and processing, however, proved more forward-looking and lucrative than the manufacture of woolen and linen fabrics. The light cottons were inexpensive and found more buyers, both on the domestic market and as an export. New dyeing processes and drum printers were developed in the 1820s and 1830s in Berlin especially for calico printing. The Wallach and Nauen cotton commercial firm financed these inventions and then began producing calico. The owners of the company were among the first Jews in Berlin to receive municipal civil rights there in 1809. Two Jewish families, the Liebermanns and the Reichenheims, who were connected by both business and marriage ties, became leaders in the calico printing industry. Once they began manufacturing, individual family members assumed a variety of functions in production and sales. Joseph Liebermann (1783–1860), grandfather of the painter Max Liebermann, introduced himself to King Frederick William IV as the man who forced English calico printers from the continent. In 1843 he was named *Kommerzienrat,* a title conferred on distinguished businessmen; other members of his family later received this honor as well. His sons expanded the company to produce the necessary machinery and built it up into an enterprise with hundreds of employees, plus additional hundreds of home workers.

A few years later, between 1839 and 1847, Nathanael Reichenheim (1776–1852) and five of his sons moved to Berlin from Anhalt-Bernburg. Like the Liebermanns, their business soon made the transition from merely the sale of manufactured goods to the entire process of calico production. The N. Reichenheim and Son Company soon moved most of its production to Silesia, where it had purchased extensive wool and yarn spinning and weaving works in Wüstegiersdorf. Along with a number of similar enterprises, it had been founded by the Prussian state bank in order to create work for needy Silesian weavers. When the Reichenheims bought the plant toward the end of the 1840s, there were approximately 1,800 workers there (600 in the factory, 1,200 home laborers). Within several years the number of workers, including home laborers, had grown to around 5,000, forming a small town. Leonor Reichenheim (1814–1868)—son of the company founder and later active in politics—built a school, orphanage, Sunday school, and other public facilities for the employees.

In Bavaria and Württemberg Jews were only beginning to set up true factories by the middle of the century in Fürth and Munich as well as some smaller cities in Württemberg. Stuttgart and Cannstadt did not significantly attract Jewish businessmen until later. By contrast, in Bohemia and Moravia the extensive early factory production started by Jewish entrepreneurs around 1800 and described earlier grew so dramatically that by mid-century it employed tens of thousands of workers. Some of these large companies were outgrowths of existing ones, but numerous new ones, small and large, made up the majority. The center of gravity everywhere lay in the diverse branches of the textile industry.

As industrialists in textiles provided thread, fabrics, ribbons, lace, and other accessories, factories in Berlin, Hamburg, and elsewhere began processing these articles into standard-sized clothing using serial production methods. In the course of the nineteenth century Jews became leaders in this new industry, especially in Berlin. In the 1840s, in Hamburg, it was primarily Jewish master tailors who, outside the rigid tailors' guild, created a specialized division of labor in cutting and sewing as well as specialization in men's or women's clothing. Almost half of these tailors came from the Prussian or Russian sections of Poland, where there was a long tailoring tradition. There was a similar long tradition in the Habsburg portions of the empire, where ready-made clothing production had been growing since the eighteenth century.

Jewish entrepreneurial activities in the textile and clothing industries comprised about 40 percent to 50 percent of all Jewish industrial initiatives. Other important areas were the production of leather goods, the foodstuff and allied industries—from sugar to tobacco processing—the production of luxury goods and jewelry, and the wood processing industry, particularly the production of paper and wallpaper. The chemical industry, which would later become a domain of Jewish entrepreneurs, was then still a new branch, only in its beginnings. Until the middle of the nineteenth century it was essentially limited to soap production, medicines produced by apothecaries, dyeing processes, and candle production. Seen from this perspective, the extensive chemical factory of Samuel Heinrich (formerly Hirsch) Kunheim (1781–1848) was a revolutionary innovation.

It is difficult to determine the percentage of Jewish employees in all these enterprises. Contemporary statistics had categories for "day laborers" and "servants," but it is not possible to determine clearly whether they worked in industrial enterprises. It is also difficult to recognize who were self-employed artisans and who were skilled workers in factories. A list for Hamburg in 1837, although certainly not representative, can provide some guidance with respect to the various occupations. According to these figures, there were only one hundred Jews working as factory laborers and sorters, one hundred as cigar workers, sixty as simple laborers and porters. An additional seven hundred people were paid as servants, that is, for personal services not involving factory work. It therefore seems reasonable to assume that Jewish entrepreneurs were dependent to a very large extent on the labor of Christian employees.

Given the increasing number of Christian women who were officially registered as employees, most of them coming to the cities from poverty-stricken rural regions and working as domestic servants, it would be of interest to know if and how the horizons of Jewish women changed in these times from their focus on the concerns of the family and assistance in the occupation of the husband. Only very little data is available on gainful employment of Jewish women in the first half of the nineteenth century. Around 1800 primarily widows or unmarried women earned their own livelihood by sewing linens, making lace, or simply "working with their hands." Scattered figures indicate that up to the middle of the century a majority of single and widowed Jewish women were dealers in apparel, millinery, or clothing accessories. There were also women who sold manufactured and dry goods as well as used items or who were owners of pawn brokerages, midwives, proprietors of guest houses—and, in one case, an art dealer. Others lived on inherited property, supported from their family's assets. There is no information regarding female servants, who certainly existed, or Jewish women who worked in the factories. Generally, a woman's gainful employment was not considered desirable, arising only from economic necessity. There was no established vocational training for Jewish girls—for Christian girls, too, it was only very rudimentary—and women tied to a family generally did not want to part with their role as an "assisting family member."

With regard to the economic activities of the Jews, the first half of the nineteenth century, then, contained contradictions. On the one hand, the state supported measures to make Jews more "productive," redirecting them into occupations in the crafts and agriculture. On the other hand, it did not want to dispense with the Jews' acumen in money matters when it came to floating state loans. Most of the Jewish population, however, was involved neither in productivization efforts nor in major financial transactions. They were much more affected by the trend from petty and itinerant trading to activities of middle-class merchants with an "open shop" and a permanent address. As for industrial production, certainly its beginnings were marked by more innovation and experimentation on the part of Jews than by non-Jewish enterprises, so that in some areas Jews assumed a kind of pioneering role that was to bear rich fruits in the decades after 1848.

3

Jewish Communities in Transition

1. The Persistence of Tradition

Although German Jewry during the late eighteenth century and the first half of the nineteenth underwent changes in its religious and cultural life not less striking than those in the political and economic sphere, the values and practices characteristic of earlier generations only gradually gave way before the forces of modernization. Jews raised in the traditional Jewish ambience, and especially their religious leaders, accustomed as they were to the world of the traditional Jewish community, did not willingly surrender the sanctified ways of their ancestors, however much the modernists emerging from their midst might find them incongruous with the changed reality of advancing emancipation and acculturation. If for an ever increasing portion of German Jewry this was a period of profound reorientation, it was also a time when most of that Jewry, though not unaffected by change, remained attached to the beliefs and practices of earlier times. Even as the Jewish enlightenment (the Haskalah), sparked by the Jewish philosopher Moses Mendelssohn (1729–1786) in the second third of the eighteenth century, spread in Berlin and Königsberg, and from there to other German cities, the mass of German Jewry, especially in the countryside, remained resistant to its influence. Until about the middle of the nineteenth century the tradition-oriented Jews in Germany remained the majority.

Although, as we shall see, the governments of German states altered the structure of the Jewish community in various ways and removed or greatly diminished its authority over individual members, in most respects it remained possible to live the traditional Jewish life as it had been lived in previous generations. The rhythms of this life remained clearly at variance with their surroundings, even as the latter began to impinge upon them. The Jewish calendar served as a religious and cultural barrier. Numerous holidays, each with its own particular symbols, provided sensory experiences, first absorbed in childhood, that left a deep imprint, even upon those Jews who later abandoned their strict observance. Surplus wealth, to the extent that traditional Jews possessed it, was invested in the sphere of the sacred. Religious occasions were marked by a higher quality of food and finer utensils. The aesthetic sense was indulged in the purchase of ritual objects: a silver spice box for the ceremony marking the conclusion of the Sabbath, a decorated container for the citron (*etrog*) used on the festival of Tabernacles (Sukkot), an embroidered curtain donated for the synagogue ark, which contained the scrolls of the Torah.

Sabbath observance continued to set traditional Jews apart from non-Jews, regularly withdrawing them from the workday environment in which they interacted with the non-Jewish world. Jewish peddlers might be forced to remain away from home for most of the week, but they returned before nightfall on Friday evening. The biblical commandment to rest on the Sabbath and do no manner of work, expanded by the Rabbis into a complex pattern of prohibitions, continued to be meticulously observed. It was, in part, the prohibition against writing on Saturday that made observant parents unwilling to send their children to Christian schools when that opportunity became available.

Within the traditional Jewish home role expectations were clearly defined. Fathers passed on to sons the acceptance of those religious obligations, such as regular prayer, that devolved upon Jewish males alone. Mothers imbued daughters with knowledge of the particular religious responsibilities that fell upon women, such as preparing for the Sabbath, lighting the Sabbath candles, and maintaining sexual purity. Each generation took the place of its predecessor without disruption. Religious piety and familial piety were inextricably linked. Only where religious doubt emerged in acculturated circles were these severed and the more durable relations to family then become, in some instances, the sole remaining reason for continued Jewish identification.

Their various origins and local religious customs (minhagim) distinguished traditional German Jews by regions and communities. Thus the

Jews of Posen, who until the late eighteenth century were part of Polish
Jewry, retained some of the attributes of that larger community, especially its devotion to the dialectical method of talmudic learning known as
pilpul. In southern Germany, by contrast, Jewish learning was more
focused on the details of practical observance. Although religious services
all followed a standard basic liturgy, particular melodies, liturgical sup-
plements, and modes of holiday observance differed from place to place.
Frankfurt am Main, for example, possessed its own unique and renowned
rite, which it had preserved from medieval times. Jews distinguished the
more authoritative category of law (Halacha) from custom, allowing for
variance only in the latter, but their attachment to minhagim was no less
fervent—to the point that, under pressure of acculturation, they were
often as reluctant to depart from them as from the theoretically more significant Halacha.

Among the more striking and persistent of the customs particular to
Jews of southern and western Germany was the ceremony of *Holekrash*,
whereby a month-old Jewish infant was given a vernacular name as cradle

8 *Holekrash*, naming ceremony for a Jewish infant

and infant were thrice lifted into the air. Although it has no roots in classical Judaism and was probably taken over in some form from the non-Jewish environment, this ceremony became a quasi-religious rite of passage, tenaciously observed, with local variations, into the twentieth century.

Jewish traditions survived with the least opposition in the small towns and villages where most German Jews continued to live until the last decades of the nineteenth century. Here religious skepticism gained little entry. Even patently superstitious practices, such as the use of amulets to protect against harmful angels or demons, were not quickly given up. In rural Germany Jews were not directly confronted with a high literary or artistic culture whose values could call their own into question. Here too the pressures for religious conformity, exercised by family and the religious leadership of the community, were more effective than in the city. A powerful milieu-sustained piety encompassed even those Jews who possessed little formal Jewish learning. Rural Jews effectively insulated themselves from competing influences even, in some instances, to the point of not reading newspapers. When *Landjuden* did move to the city, local customs were left behind as inappropriate in the new context and a broad disregard of tradition often followed.

Among traditional Jews peculiarities of language continued to provide a mark of distinction long after Moses Mendelssohn's Bible translation introduced its readers to High German usage. Only very slowly did Western Yiddish (Judeo-German), the peculiar language of German Jews, give way to a common speech—either local dialect or High German— fully shared by Jew and non-Jew. With regard to written language, there was an intermediate step along the way: the printing of High German in Hebrew characters, as Mendelssohn himself had done in the first edition of his translation. The Hebrew characters apparently continued to be more familiar than the German Fraktur and made the adoption of a language still regarded as foreign more acceptable. In some places Jewish children continued to be taught German in such Hebrew garb as late as the second half of the nineteenth century.

The persistence of spoken Yiddish was not limited to the countryside or the Jewish lower class. The prominent Hamburg banker Solomon Heine (1767–1844), despite his multiple business connections with non-Jews, had difficulty speaking proper German. The two rabbis of the Berlin community in the middle of the nineteenth century had similar problems. Even when Yiddish began to be displaced in the public sphere, where enemies of Jewish emancipation pointed to it as a sign of the Jews' inabil-

9   Rural Jews in their living room, watercolor by
Mathias Christoph Hartmann, 1817

ity to fully assimilate, it lingered on in the sphere of private discourse, longer among women than among men. In the German Jews' spoken language, Yiddish terms, especially those used in typically Jewish rural occupations, like the sale of livestock (viz. *beheme*: a cow), and in home ritual (viz. *berches*: Sabbath bread), persisted into the twentieth century.

The Hebrew language, likewise, did not fully disappear among German Jews. To be sure, in Germany itself there was no successor to the Haskalah Hebrew periodical, *Ha-Me'asef* that had been the pride of Mendelssohn's disciples during the last two decades of the eighteenth century. However, in Vienna, at the Hebrew printing press of the non-Jew Anton Schmidt, Shalom Cohen (1772–1845), the last editor of *Ha-Me'asef*, in 1820 inaugurated an influential Hebrew literary journal, *Bikure ha-itim* (First Fruits), that lasted for a dozen years. It was followed by *Kerem ḥemed* (A Delightful Vineyard), published successively in Vienna and Prague and briefly resurrected in Berlin. In Frankfurt am Main two teachers at the modern Jewish school, Michael Creizenach (1789–1842) and Isaac Marcus Jost (1793–1860), still published a scholarly religious periodical in Hebrew, called *Zion*, from 1840 to 1842. In Rödelheim, just outside Frankfurt, the traditionally inclined Jewish scholar Wolf Heidenheim (1757–1832) established a Hebrew press in 1799 that for decades produced meticulously accurate Hebrew prayerbooks with German translations, along with other liturgical books, Hebrew classics, and his own works on Hebrew grammar. Although the readership for Hebrew works among German Jews was surely diminishing in the first part of the nineteenth century, it had not fully disappeared. And in all community synagogues Hebrew remained exclusively or almost exclusively the language of prayer.

Nor had the link with Jewish settlements in Palestine been severed. To be sure, governments did not welcome the export of funds to support traditional Jewish scholars in Jerusalem and the other holy cities, and in Bavaria an attempt was made to prohibit it. Also, acculturating Jews were embarrassed by the poorly dressed, sometimes arrogant visitors. But in the nineteenth century these emissaries still made their way to various parts of Germany, receiving donations along with an attentive ear to their stories and the respect they felt was due them as Jews who had fulfilled the important commandment of dwelling in the Land of Israel.

The traditional form of Jewish education likewise persisted, although, of course, its influence diminished. In the late eighteenth century nearly all Jewish boys in German lands were educated almost exclusively in Jewish religious texts, beginning with the Pentateuch and graduating to the Talmud and its commentaries. Neither Hebrew grammar nor principles of faith occupied any role in the curriculum. Generally, less than half a dozen hours per week were devoted to secular subjects such as basic German and arithmetic. Wealthier families, usually in the larger towns, were able to employ private tutors in their homes; poorer families sent their children to a classroom (*ḥeder*) often located in the teacher's house. In rote fashion the children learned to translate the texts from Hebrew or Aramaic into Yiddish, which was the language of instruction. Boys studied until the age of thirteen; girls were often left without any formal education, simply learning from their mothers to read Yiddish and to perform the tasks of a Jewish housewife. Even as this form of Jewish education came under attack, both by German governments and by enlightened Jews, some parents remained committed to it, resisting change as best they could. In Posen, for example, *ḥadarim* were still to be found well into the nineteenth century.

Although some of the old-style teachers were doubtless men devoted to their task, many were not. To be a teacher of small children, a melamed, was never an occupation of high status in the Jewish community. It seems often to have been a career of second choice. Accounts from Germany around the beginning of the nineteenth century describe men who had either failed in a business career or had proven themselves insufficiently talented to complete studies for the rabbinate. Few of them possessed any but the most rudimentary secular knowledge. Especially among impoverished village Jews, they were paid poorly and had to seek other sources of income. It was usual for them to serve also as prayer leader in the local synagogue and often, as well, as ritual slaughterers (shoḥatim). In the absence of a local rabbi they sometimes became the resident religious authority to whom householders addressed questions of religious practice. They were hired only for short terms, which might be as little as six months. In places where the number of permitted Jewish marriages was limited, they were unable to establish a family. After German states began to require that Jewish teachers possess secular knowledge and pedagogical skills, these melamdim had either to quickly master the needed elements that were missing from their education or to find some other source of income.

At the beginning of the nineteenth century Jews who sought a higher Jewish education of the traditional type could still find the requisite institutions in German lands. In Berlin a school of higher talmudic studies, a yeshiva, still functioned. It drew some forty students who came to study with the three rabbis of the city and received modest stipends from community funds. Despite the Austrian regulation of 1797, which required that rabbinical candidates undertake philosophical studies, the yeshiva in Prague continued in its accustomed manner. Jews and Christians referred to it as the "talmudic university" and it possessed an international reputation. The most famous yeshiva in Germany still operating in the early nineteenth century was located in Fürth, then the largest Jewish community in Bavaria. It attracted students from a wide area, some simply seeking an advanced traditional Jewish education, others planning a career in the rabbinate. As in Berlin, the students in Fürth were supported by the local community. In 1826 the Bavarian king issued a rescript that sought to turn the yeshiva into a modern seminary under government supervision whose curriculum would include advanced secular studies. However, the effort was unsuccessful and the Munich government closed this last prominent institution of the old learning in Germany three years later. At the end of the eighteenth century and during the first decades of the nineteenth the German rabbinate consisted almost exclusively of men trained in the yeshivot and lacking formal secular education. Those in the larger cities were men of profound learning, who contributed important Hebrew works to the corpus of rabbinic commentary and responsa literature. Scholars of more modest accomplishments were scattered among the smaller towns. In Württemberg in 1828 there were fifty-one rabbis serving sixty-nine communities. They defined their role as experts in Jewish law, not as preachers or pastors. Their principal domain was the study chamber and the Jewish court, not the synagogue, where services were led by prayer leaders who were not themselves rabbis.

The most prominent and respected of the rabbis serving a German community during this period was Akiba Eger (1761–1837) of Posen. Born in Hungary, he early showed extraordinary proficiency in the Talmud, becoming the leading casuist of his day. His ingenious talmudic

10   Rabbi Akiba Eger and two escorts at the Posen marketplace, detail of a painting by Julian Knorr, around 1835

novellae and glosses on a variety of rabbinic texts, though generally far removed from practical issues, brought him international fame for their brilliance. So did his responsa, his vigorous charitable activities, and his legendary modesty. Eger vigorously opposed even the most minute changes in law or custom, fearing that removal of so much as a single brick from the structure of Judaism might eventually bring about its collapse. His own knowledge of German was severely limited and he made every effort to minimize the scope and extent of secular study in Jewish schools. However, this opposition to what other Jews regarded as progress did not make him a lonely figure. Until his death Eger enjoyed respect and support not only from his large circle of disciples but also from a sizable majority of Posen Jewry.

Men of the traditional type continued in other rabbinates as well. In the south of Germany the old style of rabbinical leadership maintained itself the longest. Here the central figure was Seligmann Baer Bamberger (1807–1878). Born in a Bavarian village, Bamberger studied at the Fürth yeshiva to the exclusion of a university education. In 1840, when he became the rabbi of Würzburg, the government was forced to exempt him from a satisfactory performance on the generally required examination in secular disciplines. In Würzburg Bamberger presided over his own yeshiva and in 1864 established a long-lived seminar to train teachers for traditional Jewish schools. His scholarship was mainly devoted to issues of practical Halacha, reflecting the concerns of the pious but less learned village Jews of the south.

These premodern rabbis believed themselves the chief guardians of Jewish tradition and generally rejected any changes in Jewish education or religious practice, whether proposed by Gentiles or by reform-minded Jews. They resented the efforts increasingly made by governments to interfere with the inner life of the Jewish community and looked back longingly to earlier times when rabbinical authority had been unchallenged by external forces. In secular studies they perceived a wedge that would eventually crack open and destroy the sacred world of Jewish tradition that had been successfully preserved in and through its isolation. They were especially concerned for the Jewish masses, who they feared would be unable to integrate new values with old ones. In opposing ritual changes they not only championed the Halacha but also sought to protect those peculiar customs that set Jews apart from non-Jews, maintaining their distinctiveness. Unlike equally orthodox younger colleagues, these representatives of "Old Orthodoxy" opposed even cosmetic reforms in the synagogue that in no manner violated Jewish law, simply because all departure from tradition was both irreverent and likely to pave the way for more fundamental change.

Traditional rabbis and their adherents were fervently loyal to constituted political authority. It had long been customary in Judaism for special occasions in the lives of monarchs and nobles to be celebrated in the synagogue with prayer and oratory. Reciprocally, members of the nobility would sometimes attend the ceremony dedicating a new synagogue building. A regular part of the worship service on Sabbaths and festivals was a prayer for the ruler. But these were occasional links between two realms that traditional Jews desired to keep separate. Necessarily they favored the economic benefits that emancipation offered; they were grateful for the removal of discriminatory laws and the expansion of such rights as freedom of domicile and occupation. But they were deeply ambivalent about political emancipation and especially about the efforts to make them over culturally and religiously that were part and parcel of the *Erziehungspolitik* (the politics of education) often linked to emancipation. In Baden and in Bavaria strictly orthodox Jews as late as the 1840s believed that emancipation would bury Judaism, since it would necessarily entail cultural and social integration, and with integration would come the inability to maintain an all-encompassing Jewish life. Culture would be severed from religion and the sphere of the latter ever more reduced. With social integration would come abandonment of the ritual commandments, such as observance of the Sabbath and the dietary laws. To become increasingly German would entail becoming decreasingly Jewish. Hence traditional Jews tended to be politically conservative, fearing the likely consequences of political reforms that were allegedly instituted for their benefit and espoused by their liberal coreligionists. They resisted them as best they could.

Thus inwardly focused premodern Judaism was not quickly destroyed by government edicts intended to integrate the Jews into German society and culture. In most instances the movement for religious reform, even in its more moderate proposals, did not deeply penetrate the southern countryside. Indeed, internal migration from town to city in the second half of the century often removed those elements of the Jewish population most open to religious and cultural integration, returning rural areas to the undisputed authority of the traditionalists. Even in Berlin, in an atmosphere of renewed political conservatism during the 1820s and 1830s, Orthodox Jews regained official leadership of the community. If the inner history of the German Jews in the first half of the nineteenth century is characterized by an expanding breakdown of tradition and a reaching out to the world of European and German culture, it is marked also by a less often noted persistence of the old ways, which in the number of those who held fast to them, if not in portent for the future, remained significant. It is against this often insufficiently noted background of persistence and resistance that new departures by governments and by the Jews themselves must be seen.

2. External Pressure and Internal Division

Even as some German Jews managed to maintain customs and practices nearly unchanged for generations after the Enlightenment, forces inimical to continuity were manifesting themselves with increasing intensity. German states that centralized their administrations could no longer tolerate the independent status of Jewish corporations. Liberal German political writers who advocated the Jews' emancipation required, in return, their abandonment of the privilege of self-rule. Sensing a profound change in their environment, the Jews themselves were divided in their response. Whereas some sought to reduce the impact of the new demands, others saw in them the beginning of a new and better time for the Jews as they learned to live side by side with Christians—indeed, a messianic fulfillment in Europe, not Palestine.

At first it remained unclear which of the old institutions would survive into the new age and in what form. Was Judaism itself capable of adjusting to the new situation or was it inextricably tied to the insular life of the ghetto? Beginning in the last decades of the eighteenth century, and especially for those Jews closest to the intellectual and political centers in the larger cities, confusion and division now spread. To an increasing number there seemed an unbridgeable gap between the old Jewish life and the new circumstances being imposed upon them. They were uncertain whether that hiatus could at all be bridged and, if so, how to go about it.

Medieval states had been content to allow Jews to run their own affairs according to Jewish law. As recognized corporate bodies, Jewish communities enjoyed the right to levy taxes upon their members. They possessed their own law courts and were able to exercise strict social and religious control through the imposition of fines, public penance, and the ban. Earlier political authorities were not concerned with the nature of Jewish worship so long as it did not include any aspersions upon Gentiles.

Similarly, they left it up to the Jewish communities to educate their young as they pleased—or not to educate them at all. Their interest was limited to the economic advantages to be gained by Jewish residence, to the taxes that were levied collectively upon the Jewish communities, and to reducing, as much as possible, Christian social contact with non-Jews.

In the eighteenth century that attitude changed, and by the early nineteenth century government intervention in internal Jewish affairs had become the norm. The shift was, of course, part of a more general change in policy that affected not only Jews but all other hitherto semi-independent elements within German society—the old estates, the churches, and other minority groups. The emerging absolute state could not tolerate independent sources of power. But for the Jews this intrusion had particularly serious results. The earliest significant government encroachment upon the internal Jewish sphere was the limitation or abolition of the right of Jews to settle civil disputes in their own courts and to enforce religious conformity. The removal of the judicial function to secular courts with regard to nearly all matters, excepting only specifically religious issues like divorce and other questions of personal status, meant a great diminution of communal and rabbinical authority. The prohibition against applying the ban in cases of religious infraction had the most significant long-term impact of all. It meant that Jews could now violate religious law with impunity and freely choose which observances they would retain and which ones they would abandon.

In Prussia the process of infringement upon Jewish legal autonomy began with a limited reduction as early as Frederick the Great's Revised General Code of 1750. From there it expanded as secular courts assumed virtually all of the judicial functions. The 1797 General Regulation for Jews in South and New Eastern Prussia specifically denied rabbis judicial authority in civil and religious matters and stated that no Jew could be called to account or punished for any offense he might commit against Jewish belief or ritual law within the confines of his own home. Paragraph 30 of the Emancipation Edict of 1812 once again stated the prohibition against Jewish communal authorities, rabbis, or community elders assuming any form of legal jurisdiction.

In Austria Jewish judicial functions were abolished in 1784, two years after the Edict of Toleration. In Bavaria Jewish corporations were dissolved in 1806 and an end put to rabbinical jurisdiction; the Bavarian *Judenedikt* of 1813 incorporated these provisions and made the Jewish communities into private religious societies. In Baden judicial autonomy was abolished in 1809, though here Jews were allowed to exercise the same ecclesiastical discipline that was permitted Christian religious authorities. In some places limited autonomy lasted a bit longer. Thus in Württemberg an 1812 ordinance still allowed Jews judicial authority to settle their own disputes. Most exceptional was the situation in Altona, then still under Danish rule, where Rabbi Jacob Ettlinger (1798–1871) was allowed to serve as a judge in civil matters among Jews until 1863.

The loss of rabbinical and communal power was accompanied by a decline in the rabbinate itself. When rabbinical positions fell vacant, major Jewish communities, such as Frankfurt am Main, Berlin, Hamburg, and Prague, were content to allow rabbinical functions to be carried on by men of secondary rank and prestige. Perhaps the extreme example of deprecating the rabbinate as of little relevance in a new age of political integration and individual autonomy is the oral memorandum supplied by the elder of the Berlin community, Ruben Gumpertz, to a Prussian official in 1820. Gumpertz denied that rabbis were at all comparable to Christian clergy. With the end of rabbinical jurisdiction, their activities had shrunk to the administration of ritual regulations. They were, he held, nothing more than *Kauscherwächter* (supervisers of dietary observance).

No less significant in its impact than the demise of rabbinical authority was the loss of the right to enforce payment of community taxes. In Prussia, as a result of the Emancipation Edict of 1812 (and until new legislation in 1847), the Jewish communities were reduced to the status of private associations. As such, they could no longer require their members to pay the sums that were levied upon them. Their only recourse was the lengthy and expensive procedure of suing for payment in the regular courts. In Glogau not only did some local Jews refuse to pay but others took advantage of their right to settle elsewhere, leaving the community strapped to pay its debts and sustain its institutions; by 1837 the yearly tax there was being paid by only a small minority of the members. In Bavaria the Jews Edict of 1813, which removed rabbinical jurisdiction in civil law, likewise took away the right of taxation.

The effect of weakened communal authority upon individual Jews was intensified by the seductions of emancipation and integration, offered conditionally if Jews would give up most of their distinguishing characteristics. Already in the eighteenth century the more tolerant Christian writers had raised Jewish hopes by portraying virtuous Jews in literature and on the stage more as they imagined they might be once they had cast aside Jewish customs and mannerisms than they were in fact. In the debates over emancipation it was nearly always assumed that the Jews would undergo a metamorphosis that would transform them into Germans at the expense of most of their Jewish traits. Similarly, Jewish social acceptability was made dependent on the willingness to give up most Jewish observance. Moses Mendelssohn could still welcome inquisitive and admiring non-Jews to his observant home. In the next generation an increasing number of city Jews came to regard observance of ritual law as a hindrance to social intercourse.

Especially in Berlin, but also in other centers of Jewish enlightenment such as Königsberg and Breslau, regular synagogue attendance declined, Sabbath prohibitions were partially or completely ignored, and dietary laws were violated. By the first decades of the nineteenth century, under the influence of a French occupation whose values called into question the entire old order, Jewish disregard for the traditional life spread to Hamburg and the Rhineland. Lacking any means to control individual religious behavior, the champions of tradition could hope for no more than to maintain the old ways within the institutions of the community, especially the synagogue. The home and the street were now beyond their sphere of authority.

During the reign of Frederick William II (1786–1797), an atmosphere of libertinage reigned in Berlin that was inspired by the court. It was reflected in the Jewish community by an increased divorce rate, the birth of numerous illegitimate children, and a sharp rise in the number of Jewish conversions to Christianity. Offspring of the upper stratum of the community, especially, which had become immensely wealthy during the Seven Years War (1756–1763), now increasingly threw off religious restraints and took on the cultural attributes of the age. The community, which during the first half of the eighteenth century had uniformly been as pious as any other in Germany, by the first decades of the nineteenth was sharply divided. Perhaps as few as one half of the Jews in Berlin still purchased kosher meat.

One writer, Sabattia Joseph Wolff (1757–1832), himself among the acculturated Jews of Berlin and an advocate of educational and religious reform, detected the presence of four classes among his coreligionists around the year 1812. The first consisted of the learned and pious traditional Jews who had, until recently, made up the leadership stratum of the community. The second class, which greatly admired the first, was composed of the unlearned traditionalists, whose religious orientation was grounded mainly in force of habit. The third, and smallest group—with which Wolff himself apparently identified—consisted of the enlightened, who had liberated themselves from prejudice in favor of their own faith and now refused to regard any one religion as inherently superior to another. Alienated from the traditional religious services, they had abandoned the synagogue to the first two classes. The fourth class that Wolff described paralleled the second, in that it too consisted of ignorant imitators, but in this case imitators of the educated enlightened. Its claim to enlightenment lacked a principled foundation and its practice was marked by confusion and contradiction. Nearly every person in this group had his own set of laws that he observed while he guiltlessly violated others.

This division had severe social consequences. Jews who differed in their attitudes to secular culture and their religious practices no longer formed a single society with shared values and a shared way of life. Being simply a Jew was no longer a sufficient common denominator for social intercourse. Alongside the divisions between wealthy and poor, learned and ignorant, that had always existed, there was now the additional cultural and religious divide. Jews of the various categories defined by Wolff associated predominantly with each other, shunning the company of those with whom they differed. Division existed even within the same families, especially between the older and younger generation, but also sometimes between husband and wife. What one would regard as sacred became the butt of ridicule for the other. Parents were unable to eat at the tables of their adult children, while the children were embarrassed to visit their parents. The most difficult relationships resulted where part of a family had converted to Christianity. The converts no longer felt at home among Jews, and their families who had remained Jews were fearful of the influence of their example. Yet, unlike in earlier ages, contact was not always completely severed. By the beginning of the nineteenth century divisions between the generations were apparent also in cities other than Berlin, such as Hamburg and Frankfurt am Main.

For a significant number of city Jews in these years the future of Judaism had become uncertain. Their communal institutions had been deprived of coercive authority; rabbinical leadership and the learning upon which it was based had ceased to enjoy their earlier prestige. The unique revelation of Judaism, which Mendelssohn had declared to be limited to the ceremonial law, no longer commanded all Jews' acknowledgment or obedience. Drawn to a universalism that subsumed Jew and Christian under the category of human being, the more acculturated Jews lost their sense of being God's particular chosen people, which had, through the centuries, served to maintain their strong feeling of difference from others. What emerged from the confusion and uncertainty were efforts to reconstitute the basic institutions of Judaism in a new manner. In the process of transforming community organization, education, and religious leadership and practice, initiatives by governments and by Jews themselves each played a role.

3. New Forms of Jewish Community Organization

With the abolition of autonomy and corporate privileges German governments, to varying degrees and in different ways, began to reshape the structure and nature of their Jewish communities. Whereas in Prussia the government was content to play a minimal role in reconstructing the communities, in French-dominated Westphalia and in southern Germany the part played by non-Jewish authorities was much greater. For this reason Jewish communal institutions began to differ from state to state to a larger degree than had been true earlier.

With the demise of corporate status, Jewish communities in the Kingdom of Prussia became, in the language of the edict of 1812, "private associations permitted for particular purposes." The state ceased to play a role in the selection of the "elders," who continued to govern the Jewish communities. It regarded community employees—rabbis, cantors, and others—as private, not public officials. Hence it set no qualifications for their employment and required only that such persons not be suspected of moral or criminal offense. Unlike Christian clergy, rabbis were not recognized as spiritual leaders; unlike the churches, the Jewish communities received no state support. Except in the Rhine Province, where Prussia retained the consistorial system inherited from the French, it did not foster organized relations among various communities. Rather than use its influence to reform religious practice, Prussia predicated its policy on the assumption that if the Jewish communities were denied official recognition and assistance they would eventually disintegrate and Jews would increasingly convert to Christianity. As an 1818 regulation put it, the Jews were not at all to be regarded as a religious party but simply as "the rubble of a ruined people."[1] Only when the state sensed some danger to its own interests, as occurred when a segment of the Berlin community undertook to create a reformed religious service, did it step in. In this instance, fearing that sectarianism among Jews might engender its equivalent among Gentiles and that a modernized Judaism would inhibit conversion, the Prussian king himself in 1823 issued an edict that forbade any deviation from accepted Jewish custom.

Bavaria was like Prussia in that it too treated the Jewish communities as only private organizations. It did not grant them equality by supporting their institutions or by extending official status to their functionaries. But it did play a more activist role, for example introducing a regional organization of the communities into districts, each with its own district rabbi. It authorized the rabbis, in some instances in conjunction with laymen, not only to exercise all religious functions but also to take responsibility for financial administration and education. This important role given to rabbis went hand in hand with the Bavarian state's effort to change the character of its rabbinate. The *Judenedikt* of 1813 instituted state examination of rabbis and required that they be not only free of moral blemish but also "fluent in the German language and, in general, academically educated."[2] The rabbi was to become more like the Catholic priest and Protestant pastor. The Bavarian government retained final authority regarding matters of religious reform, at first favoring it, later reversing its policy.

Most clearly distinguishable from Prussian policy on the relation of the state to the Jewish community and most activist in character was the approach of the Kingdom of Westphalia, which was based originally upon the model of Napoleonic France. After the Paris Sanhedrin, in 1807, had avowed the complete political loyalty of Jews in the French Empire, the French government established a nationwide Jewish hierarchy, centered in Paris, that was henceforth responsible for all matters pertaining to the French communities. In 1808, a few months after granting full equality to the Jews, Napoleon's brother Jerome established a similar Jewish consistory in the Kingdom of Westphalia, whose structure was determined by an assembly of Jewish deputies he had called together in Kassel. The head of the consistory was Israel Jacobson (1768–1828), a wealthy and energetic court factor with a rabbinical education, who had taken a special interest in improving the political and economic situation of his fellow Jews. He was joined by the three most enlightened rabbis that Jacobson could find and by two laymen, both educators. The Jewish consistory was meant to parallel similar structures among Christians. It bore principal responsibility for regulating Jewish religious life in Westphalia and was, in turn, directly responsible to the Westphalian government.

The Jewish consistory sought to exercise effective centralized control, assure a maximum of religious uniformity among the various communities, and propagate a more decorous, aesthetically attractive religious ser-

11   Israel Jacobson, court banker and president of the
Israelite Consistory in Westphalia

vice. It controlled the appointment of the local rabbis, who, unlike their colleagues in Prussia, enjoyed the status of state officials. It paid their salaries, and those of other Jewish employees, out of taxes that it was entitled to levy from the communities. In return, the rabbis were required to render it regular reports and to conduct their activities in a uniform prescribed manner.

Jacobson and his colleagues were not content merely to administer the religious affairs of Westphalian Jewry. They sought to make it a model of Jewish religious modernization by reshaping Jewish institutions to be formally as similar as possible to their Christian counterparts. Although avoiding obvious violation of Jewish law, they used their government-given authority to introduce such changes in custom and practice as they believed would bring Judaism up-to-date in its forms of expression. A regulation specifying the duties of rabbis, which it issued in 1809, contained provisions that would make the rabbi much more closely the equivalent of Christian clergy. The Westphalian rabbis—many of whom were not trained or prepared for the new role—were now expected to give regular, morally edifying sermons in the German language. Like Christian clergy, they were also required to act as pastors, visiting the sick and comforting mourners. As teachers of the Jewish religion, their task was to instruct the young in the principles of Judaism, preparing them to accept the faith at a formal confirmation ceremony.

A fervent desire of the consistory was to extract from Jewish ceremonies the superstitious and boisterous elements that had become the butt of ridicule among Gentiles and enlightened Jews alike. The synagogue, traditionally a comfortable place where serious prayer was combined with informal conversation on secular topics, was to become wholly a sacred space, devoted exclusively to worship and religious edification. The consistory was persuaded that this transformation would draw back to the religious services individuals whose exposure to religious and aesthetic values among Christians had made practices in the synagogue odious to them. In 1810 it issued a "synagogue regulation" to assure properly dignified conduct within each house of worship. This was the first of such regulations, which in succeeding years would be issued with similar provisions for other communities in Germany.

Although some Westphalian Jews supported the consistory's decrees, others resented their imposition from above and rejected some of the provisions as violating practices hallowed by generations of pious ancestors. To the extent possible they sought to evade the regulations either by ignoring them in the main synagogues or by retreat to illegal private prayer circles (minyanim). Moreover, the taxes required to support the consistory and its institutions sometimes went unpaid, and soon it proved difficult to provide the rabbis with their salaries. Thus this first example in Germany of a new centralized Jewish community structure, whose leadership sought to bring Judaism into as direct a parallel with Christianity as the religion allowed, proved to be of only limited effectiveness, though it might have had greater success if political circumstances had not brought its activity to an end. With the fall of the Kingdom of Westphalia, in September 1813, the consistory ceased to operate and in Prussian Westphalia community affairs reverted mostly to what they had been before 1808.

In Frankfurt am Main the government's participation in the administration of the Jewish community was more direct. Beginning in 1813, during the period of the Grand Duchy, and until 1848, a non-Jewish commissioner was charged with state supervision of Jewish affairs. The Frankfurt Senate appointed members of the executive from lists of candidates provided to it by the community leadership and decisions made by the executive on even strictly religious matters possessed no validity unless approved by the commissioner. Although the executive did not institute reforms in the community synagogue, its composition gradually shifted toward the less traditional elements in the community.

In the southwestern German states the reorganization of the Jewish communities resulted in structures closely resembling those of the Christian denominations. Here governments employed specially devised organizational forms to integrate the Jewish communities into the apparatus of the state. In Baden, as early as 1807, an edict made rabbis into "spiritual state officials," the same as Christian clergy. The provisions of the Jews Edict of 1809, which, in addition to providing a high degree of legal equality, also established a statewide ecclesiastical structure, were the envy of those Jews elsewhere in Germany who favored giving Judaism a status equivalent to that of Christianity. The government divided the Jews into local synagogues under the supervision of three provincial synagogues headed by a regional rabbi and two regional elders. At the top of the hierarchy was a Supreme Jewish Council, composed of nine rabbis and laymen, all appointed by the grand duke, and with its seat in the state capital of Karlsruhe. The duties of the council included assessment of financial support, the appointment of regional rabbis and elders, the examination of rabbis, supervision of religious instruction, and advising the government on Jewish affairs. The extent of this authority vested in the new Jewish communal structure aroused concern in some government circles that it represented a "separated Jewish state within a Christian state." In order to maintain more effective state control, a Christian ministerial commissioner was appointed to chair the sessions of the council, beginning in 1812, and his signature was required on all its decisions. As in Westphalia, some local Jewish communities resented the authority imposed on them from above and the cost of supporting the structure. Traditionalists were unwilling or unable to implement its quite moderate initiatives to modernize Jewish practices and institutions. Although supported by both traditional and reform-minded factions, an ordinance of the council in the year 1824, which sought, in part, to abolish disruptions in the synagogue, introduce confirmations, boys' choirs, and German sermons, and to regulate the training of rabbis and teachers, was not easily or fully instituted. Ten years later the council was still waging a battle to extirpate the Yiddish expressions, "so detrimental to moral and civil culture," from the vocabulary of the younger generation.[3] However, the system itself, with occasional modifications, continued to function into the twentieth century. In 1833 the Jewish communities achieved yet fuller equality with Protestants and Catholics when the estates for the first time granted a state subsidy for Jewish worship and the following year the Jewish school fund likewise received a small allocation from the government.

In Württemberg a new communal structure came into existence much later, almost two decades after Baden, but it too was admired and regarded as exemplary by Jews favoring change. Here even the terminology used clearly revealed the state's intention to organize its Jews religiously in the same manner as its Christian denominations. In 1828 the government gave its Jewish communities legally recognized corporative status and by royal decree created the Israelite Supreme Ecclesiastical Authority, modeled on its Evangelical equivalent, to direct their affairs. As in Baden, this highest body was headed by a non-Jewish government commissioner, to whom were added, in this instance, a rabbi, three lay members, and a secretary, all appointed by the state. It had its own office in Stuttgart, where it met for the first time in 1832, and it was directly responsible to the Ministry of the Interior. Beginning in 1835 it received annual contributions from the state. Under the new system Württemberg Jews were required to belong to a Jewish community and to pay community taxes. Functioning rabbis and cantors had to pass examinations or leave their positions. Those who passed or were newly employed became state officials, paid out of a central treasury and responsible to the central authority rather than to the lay leadership of the local community. They were assigned clerical garb appropriate to their position. Joseph Maier (1797–1873), who was the rabbinical representative in the central authority in 1837, received the title of ecclesiastical councilor and enjoyed the status of non-Jewish clergy in equivalent positions. Like the consistory in Westphalia, the Supreme Ecclesiastical Authority issued regulations both for the synagogue (1838) and for the duties of the rabbis (1841). As in Baden, the system in Württemberg enjoyed a very long life, continuing unchanged until 1912.

Thus, by the end of the fourth decade of nineteenth century, the status and organizational structure of the Jewish communities in Germany varied widely, depending mostly on whether the states in which Jews lived had chosen to ignore their religious lives or to reshape them. But regardless of where the communities were located, both within and outside the sphere of their formal governance an impressive array of voluntary associations drew local Jews to join in secular as well as religious activities. Some of these *Vereine* were taken over from the medieval community. They administered community funds or raised private ones with the intent of providing—if not always adequately—for the ill and the itinerant. They cared for Jewish orphans, supplied food, clothing, and fuel for the local poor, dowered brides, nursed the sick, and buried the dead. Novel were the proliferation of women's charitable societies and those that supported apprenticed Jewish artisans, farmers, and the increasing number of university students. To Jews entering the German bourgeoisie these societies could both fulfill traditional Jewish values and emulate the proliferation of similar associations among the German bourgeoisie, the class to which most Jews aspired to belong. Thus, even as the old Jewish community lost much of its earlier authority, its variegated modern version still served as magnet and milieu for an ongoing Jewish desire to join with and assist fellow Jews.

4. The Transformation of Jewish Education

No single factor played a larger role in the acculturation of German Jewry than the transformation of their children's education. The earliest Jews to

12   Hospital of the Jewish community in Hamburg, built 1841

break out of the spiritual confines of the medieval Jewish cultural world—
Moses Mendelssohn, some of his contemporaries, and his disciples—were
autodidacts in secular studies. They had to piece together a knowledge of
Judaism gained in the old institutions, the ḥeder and the yeshiva, with a
sometimes furtive and always unsystematic study of the sciences, languages, secular philosophy, and literature. Jewish studies necessarily came
first, from early childhood. Then, at some point, there followed an exposure to "external" books, which frequently produced an inner conflict as
to how to reconcile the conflicting systems of value. Often the study of
postbiblical Jewish texts was left behind, representative of a childhood
personally outgrown and, more broadly, of a culture that advancing civilization had left behind. The new Jewish schools that came into existence,
beginning with the last decades of the eighteenth century (see volume 1),
were intended to broaden the education of Jewish children but also to
afford them a knowledge of Judaism that would not seem in basic conflict
with the world revealed to them by their secular studies. Jewish education
became the religious component of a broader training for useful citizenship. This transformation required new institutions, a new curriculum,
and teachers committed to new educational ideals. It was accomplished
through a combination of Jewish initiative and the intervention of states,
which had their own interest in reorganizing the educational system of
their Jewish subjects. By the middle of the nineteenth century nearly all
Jewish children in German-speaking lands were studying either in Jewish
schools that included secular subjects or, if in non-Jewish ones, generally
supplementing these disciplines with Jewish religious instruction. The
result was the gradual formation of a Jewry far more similar to its
Christian counterpart, usually with a rudimentary knowledge of Jewish
beliefs and values, but in its identity reflecting the shift in the curriculum
of its early education: from immersion in a self-sufficient Jewish totality
to an awareness of basic religious tenets that composed a smaller sphere
alongside a broader identification as Europeans and Germans.

      At first, rabbis and traditional parents, fearful of the effect of secular
studies, sought to resist the curricular expansion of Jewish education.
However, governments deemed that equality of rights was appropriate
only for Jews who were educated to be at home in the non-Jewish world,
and gradually even traditional Jews became at least acquiescent to their
children receiving a basic secular education. Already in 1786 the Austrian
government had made the privilege to marry dependent upon graduation
from a public school, in effect forcing secular education upon its Jewish

community. It went even further in 1810 when its demands spread beyond insistence upon secular education to assuring that Jews would learn a version of their faith that made it most compatible with loyalty to the state and most accepting of non-Jews. Until 1848 it insisted that no Jewish man or woman could be married who had not passed an examination on the religious textbook *Bne-Zion* authored by Herz Homberg (1749–1841), the increasingly radical disciple of Moses Mendelssohn and a teacher at the new Jewish school that had been established in Prague in 1782. Although *Bne-Zion*, a "religious and moral textbook for the youth of the Israelite nation," did not contradict Jewish teachings and even gained the formal approval of the highly respected Rabbi Mordecai Banet (1753–1829) of Moravia, it was hardly a textbook of traditional Judaism. Written in German, it was divided into 419 numbered paragraphs, each making a particular point, often accompanied by a biblical, and occasionally a talmudic proof text. Its focal biblical text was the Ten Commandments and it paid no attention to those biblical or talmudic injunctions presenting the particulars of Sabbath observance, diet, and ritual that set Jews apart from non-Jews. Not surprisingly, it concluded with a section on the religious foundations of good citizenship.

Elsewhere in German-speaking Europe the initial efforts at Jewish educational reform were not prompted by state edicts but by Jews themselves. The intent of the Jewish enlighteners who founded modernized schools in Berlin, Dessau, and elsewhere beginning in 1778 was not only to broaden the child's intellectual horizon by integrating secular and Jewish learning in the curriculum but also to integrate the Jewish children themselves into their environment. Thus a number of the new schools eagerly welcomed Christian children. Although they studied their individual religious traditions separately, the two groups could join together easily for all other studies and even for common religious devotions. A contemporary account of the Berlin Jewish Free School relates: "Children of both denominations, the Jewish and the Christian, stand intermingled, amicably praying together, the former with covered heads, the latter without, to our common Creator and Father in Heaven. They do their assigned work and exercises diligently in a spirit of friendly competition."[4] Although for a time governments approved this learning together under Jewish auspices (and with Jewish financial support), during the period of political reaction after 1815 one after another prohibited the practice.

Just as the schoolmasters attempted to bring in Christian children, they also sought to expand the Jewish educational system to include schools for girls as well as boys. In Prague a public school for girls was opened in 1785, only three years after the boys' school; in Hamburg a Jewish philanthropic society opened a free school for poor girls in 1798. Other schools followed. As in the case of the boys' schools, however, they were attended mostly by the poor, while wealthier daughters received private instruction or, especially later, attended non-Jewish schools. In the Jewish elementary schools, established during the 1820s and 1830s in small communities, often with only a single teacher, boys and girls necessarily studied together.

With the growth of compulsory schooling for all children in Germany during the first third of the nineteenth century, various German states, with differing degrees of success, began to take their own initiatives in creating new Jewish educational institutions. A broadened and modernized education would prepare Jewish children for citizenship. Invariably, the Jewish elementary schools that were established included secular subjects within the curriculum, though the proportion of time devoted to Jewish and non-Jewish studies varied. In the community school established in Cologne, for example, it was almost exactly half and half. Most schools were also strongly oriented toward teaching the boys a more "productive" occupation than the petty trade that, in most instances, was the occupation of their fathers. Nearly everywhere the financial burden of supporting the schools, which some governments regarded as simply private schools, was borne by the Jewish communities themselves, although subsidies were forthcoming from some states and municipalities beginning in the 1830s. Whereas the old ḥadarim were generally prohibited, parents were given the option of sending their children to a Jewish school of the new type, to a non-Jewish one, or, in some places, were allowed to continue educating them privately with a teacher approved by the state. In Bavaria those communities that could afford it created Jewish elementary schools after the edict of 1813 required that their children attend a public school. The number of such schools grew during the first half of the century and then began to decline. There were 48 of them in Baden in 1850; in Bavaria there were 150.

Almost invariably, governments, either directly or through the Jewish institutional hierarchy under their control, maintained careful supervision over the new Jewish schools. Since elementary education was still closely associated with the church, this supervision was generally delegated to the local clergy. In the smaller towns in Baden and in Württemberg the supervising officials were either Catholic or Protestant, depending on which confession was locally dominant. In Württemberg the local Christian pastor examined students even in the Jewish religion. Elsewhere, as in Bavaria, this responsibility rested with the rabbi. In Prussian Westphalia the policy of ignoring Jewish institutions prevented the government from giving any rabbi official status as an inspector of the Jewish schools and also, until 1847, from appointing Protestant supervisors.

The first teachers who instructed in the new Jewish schools were men who had themselves received a traditional Jewish education but had managed to supplement it with secular studies gained mostly on their own. In general, they remained observant in their religious practice, but especially those who taught in the cities had often broken away from traditional Jewish conceptions that set the Jews apart from others. Sometimes the teachers were older men who had earlier been melamdim and who, only with great difficulty and late in life, had managed to gain sufficient secular knowledge themselves to be able to teach their pupils. Others were young maskilim—increasingly with a university education—for whom teaching in a Jewish school was the only academic career available. In most instances the lot of a Jewish teacher was not enviable. "I would never have dreamed of becoming a schoolteacher, since that job among Jews brings neither money nor honor" was the way one young Jew put it.[5] Especially in the small towns teachers were ill paid and required supplementary income. Parents treated them little better than they had the melamdim. Their situation was best where they were given official status by the state and received the same salary as Gentile teachers, as in Württemberg, worst in Prussia where their work was not acknowledged and they remained subject to parental whims. In Posen younger, better educated teachers forced older, less capable colleagues to seek work in the smallest villages where conditions of employment remained no better than they had been in earlier times.

Those states that took firmer control of their Jewish communities also imposed qualifications on Jewish teachers, insisting upon proper preparation for their task and subjecting them to examinations in the disciplines they taught as well as in pedagogical skills. In Bavaria both classroom and private teachers had to take examinations; in Baden and Württemberg the teachers were examined by non-Jews in general areas, in religious subjects by rabbis. Even in the various provinces of Prussia Jewish teachers were forced to pass qualifying examinations given by local clergy or other school officials. In one instance in 1828 a private instructor in Posen was required to pass a three-day oral and written examination in order to obtain a certificate attesting to his possessing "sufficient qualifications for an elementary school teaching position."[6] Although in Bavaria traditionally oriented Jewish teacher training institutions were founded around the middle of the century, Jewish teachers at first were forced to gain professional training on their own or in non-Jewish teachers' seminars. In Prussia, where the authorities did not encourage Jewish schools, a small seminar, directed by the scholarly Leopold Zunz, was established in 1840 without government recognition or support. It lasted for only a decade.

With the notable exception of the Jewish Philanthropin in Frankfurt am Main, the early schools established by the maskilim (the Jewish enlighteners) did not survive more than a generation or lost their Jewish character. Increasingly, Jewish parents preferred to send their children to the Christian schools. In Austria the Toleration Edict of 1782 had already specifically allowed them to do so. As there were very few Jewish secondary schools, those Jewish children who wanted to continue their secular studies in nearly every case had no choice but a Christian school. If they planned to enter university, they necessarily attended a *Gymnasium* even when they had gained their elementary learning in a Jewish school. Among city Jews, as in the new and less tradition-bound community of Stuttgart, it was not unusual to send Jewish children to the "German school," although in the Bavarian villages there was great reluctance to do so. Jewish children who attended a non-Jewish school were exposed to teacher prejudices and to Christian elements in the curriculum. In Lemgo teachers at the public schools needed to be enjoined to teach in a manner that would not be "offensive" to their Jewish students. In the small town of Kirchen, where Jewish children were forced to attend the local Evangelical school, the textbook for reading instruction was the Protestant catechism and the students all learned to sing Lutheran songs. Although they were usually freed from writing on the Jewish Sabbath, children in such schools had no choice but to attend classes on that day. Nonetheless, in some places, Cologne and Glogau for example, community leaders, in part out of the desire that Jewish and Christian children study together but mostly in order to save the cost of supporting a Jewish community school, asked parents to send their children to the local Christian school instead. Although in most cases Jewish children attending non-Jewish schools received supplementary religious instruction in Judaism from a Jewish teacher or from their parents outside the school, such learning was necessarily relegated to after-school or Sunday hours, when the children were less ready to concentrate. For their part, the governments of German states were not of a single mind about the entry of Jewish children into non-Jewish schools. Prussian policy was distinctly inconsistent: on the one hand, it sought to assimilate the younger generation of German Jews by bringing the children at an early age into a non-Jewish environment; yet, on the other, it was concerned, in Westphalia for example, about the effect of too many unkempt Jewish children upon their Christian class-mates. Despite all the problems, however, the number of Jewish parents willing to send their children to Christian schools increased steadily, and by the middle of the century Jewish schools were in decline. In Prussia as early as 1847 only one half of the Jewish children were studying in Jewish schools; in Bavaria participation was down to 56 percent in 1870.

Believing that religion was important for civic virtue, German states required that Jewish children, whether studying in Jewish or non-Jewish schools, have religious instruction. In Bavaria it was obligatory for all students up to the age of eighteen; in Württemberg there were special classes on Saturdays or Sundays for older children who were no longer in school. Even in the Prussian province of Posen—though not yet in the rest of Prussia—it was required beginning in 1833. For both Jewish children studying in a modern Jewish school and those attending a non-Jewish one, their study of Judaism, either within the school or outside it, as-sumed a new form. Instead of learning the biblical and talmudic texts in sequence, they studied the principles of the Jewish faith, just as Christian children learned the fundamentals of their religion. Those among their teachers who had been most influenced by the Enlightenment and its pos-tulate of an underlying universal and rational religion common to all civ-ilized peoples stressed that Judaism and Christianity were but variations of that same fundamental religion. The journal *Sulamith*, which served as the organ of the enlightened educators, stressed repeatedly that the im-plantation of this faith was the principal concern of the teacher of Jewish religion. The most important value of Judaism was morality, without which there could be no religion. Rituals were only means to instill moral and religious values, husks that enabled the kernel to grow within. Since in many instances the parents of the children no longer uniformly or completely observed the ritual commandments, the teachers, for the most part, left instruction in these matters to the home. A varying amount of Hebrew was also taught, but usually only sufficient for understanding the basic prayers and some of the narrative portions of the Bible.

The educational tool for studying Judaism as a religion was the textbook rather than the sacred text. During the early decades of the nineteenth century a number of such textbooks appeared, and they were widely used both in Jewish schools and in religion classes arranged for students studying in non-Jewish ones. Like the Christian books of religious instruction on which they were modeled, these textbooks were often in the form of a catechism, using the question-and-answer method to impress upon the children the most fundamental theological and moral truths of their faith. They stressed the duties owed to God, to one's self, to fellow human beings, and, of course, to the state. In most cases their purpose was not to differentiate Judaism from other religions or to stress its uniqueness, but to impress upon the child that his or her religion was one of the legitimate historical expressions of a larger faith shared by Jews and Christians. Religion as such, in whatever historical form it was inherited, had as its chief purpose the attainment of blissful happiness, the goal of every individual life, whether Jewish or Christian. Children who had studied their religion from a catechism, the educators hoped, would be able to distinguish the essence of their faith from peripheral doctrines and customs. On the one hand, they would learn that Judaism did not conflict with German cultural values, or with political loyalties, and that it was different from Christianity only as a species is different within a single genus; that, like Protestantism or Catholicism, it was a denomination. On the other hand, they would be able to feel secure that their religion was not doomed along with the intellectually secluded existence of the ghetto, that it could be taught and affirmed within the larger educational context of the German society to which, increasingly, their parents and teachers wished them to belong.

The goal of the specifically Jewish component in the education of Jewish children, as reflected in the catechisms, was to instill a new identity: no longer that of the medieval "Jew," whose Judaism was rooted as much in Talmud and in rabbinic ordinances as in the Hebrew Bible. The textbooks sought to create instead the "Israelite" or the person of "Mosaic" religion. Aside from their pedagogic usage, these "Old Testament" terms, less laden with negative associations, later in the century also became frequent (though not exclusive) coinage for the names of Jewish organizations and periodicals. They pointed to the Jews' new status, not as a segregated corporate entity, but as a religious denomination. Thus not only did Jewish subjects gradually make way for secular ones but the Jewish element that remained was transmitted to the youth and embedded in Jewish life through a public self-conception more suited to a Jewry

that wanted increasingly to emphasize the distance from its own immediate past and the goal of acceptability in its non-Jewish surroundings.

5. The First Religious Reforms

A close relationship prevailed between educational and religious reform.
It was thought that, whereas the present generation of Jews, whose ideas
and habits had already been shaped, might not easily accept changes in
the synagogue, for the younger generation, raised under conditions of
advancing emancipation, a new style of worship would be more appropriate. Thus the early decades of the nineteenth century witnessed the first
efforts among Jews in Germany to create a modernized religious service.
They occurred initially in schools and in circles of like-minded individuals. Although they encountered opposition in the broader community,
some of the traditionalists themselves eventually made some concessions
to the new age. Increasingly, during the first half of the nineteenth century, the synagogue took on some of the complexion of its German and
Christian environment.

It is difficult to estimate the importance of external political and assim-
ilatory motivations in prompting religious reforms. The first practical
proposals were put forward and the first reformed services instituted in
the wake of newly achieved emancipation. Israel Jacobson's efforts in
Westphalia came immediately after the Jews there attained civil equality;
Moses Mendelssohn's disciple David Friedländer (1750–1834) (see volume 1) made proposals for fundamental religious reform just after the
Prussian Emancipation Edict of 1812. The new situation of the Jews as citizens certainly prompted some Jews to believe that their religion too
should be made less foreign to its milieu. Furthermore, as Jews became
more closely acquainted with Christian practice, some of them came to
see it as a model for all religions in a modern cultural setting. They concluded that certain practices characteristic of contemporary Christianity
but not of contemporary Judaism, such as decorum, the German sermon,
confirmation, and instrumental music, were, in fact, not so much Christian as emblematic of modern religion in general. If Judaism was to survive as a religion in Germany alongside Christianity and Jews be deterred
from conversion to the dominant faith, then, they felt, it had to adopt
those of its external features that were not specifically Christian in character. However, there is no reason to doubt that sincerely felt religious
motivations also played a role. As Jews became more familiar with their

religious and cultural environment, they internalized its values. It was not only to please governments or Gentiles or to make Judaism as inconspicuous as possible that the reformers favored change. It was also because their own religious sensibilities had been altered. Some of the old ways no longer possessed religious significance for them. In the desire to preserve Judaism they sought to give it new forms that would enable it to survive and flourish within, rather than apart from, its environment.

During the early years of the nineteenth century there was not yet a self-conscious Jewish Reform movement in Germany and certainly no clearly defined Reform Judaism. Rather, in the larger communities contemporaries had begun to speak of certain Jews as modernists (*die Neuen*) and others as traditionalists (*die Alten*). The former tended to be more acculturated, less meticulously observant, and in favor of religious reform of the synagogue; the latter clung to ancestral custom. However, the lines were not yet sharply drawn. Even later, when Reform and Orthodoxy became more readily differentiable parties, certain innovations, especially those involving no violation of Jewish law, gained widening support.

There was nothing contrary to Jewish law or specifically Christian about decorum in the worship service. Yet it clearly represented a cultural value that was lacking in the traditional Ashkenazi service, which was characterized by loud shouting, the toleration of disorder, and the presence of clearly profane elements, such as interruption of the service in order to auction off synagogue honors to the highest bidder. Such practices made the synagogue seem not so much unlike the church as simply inappropriate in a society that associated significance with solemnity. One Jewish community after another now adopted synagogue regulations. Although in some places they were more radical, introducing liturgical as well as atmospheric changes, in one form or another they were adopted by more traditional no less than by more reform-minded communities. In fact it was the more decorous character of the Jewish services in German congregations, generally, that made Eastern European Jews see such restraint in worship as characteristic of German Jewry as a whole.

Introduction of the German sermon was more controversial for a number of reasons. First, it meant bringing the German language formally into the synagogue, which implied giving it a certain sanctity alongside Hebrew. Second, it represented an innovation in both content and form. There was a tradition of Jewish homiletics, but it was borne mainly by local and itinerant preachers (*magidim*) whose pride it was to draw fanciful interpretations from biblical texts, to the delight of their listeners. These preachers of the old style usually held forth on Saturday afternoons and their language was Yiddish. Rabbis spoke in the synagogue less frequently, delivering discourses on points of Jewish law or urging full obedience to God's commandments. They had no experience in preparing the morally and theologically oriented sermon characteristic of the Christian service nor did they have sufficient knowledge of German to use the language for a formal purpose. Thus the new sermons were controversial also for a third reason: they were at first delivered by young lay preachers whose traditionalism was subject to doubt and whose role in the synagogue—which now, in the absence of Jewish legal jurisdiction and with the decline of the talmudic study house, was more central to Judaism than ever before—challenged the primacy of the rabbis. Finally, as the traditional Sabbath morning service was already two hours long, the addition of a sermon would either prove burdensome or prompt divisive efforts to delete portions of the liturgy.

Nonetheless, the German sermon spread to the larger communities and eventually to the smaller ones as well. It had first appeared to mark patriotic occasions, as when Mendelssohn himself wrote sermons of thankfulness for the Berlin synagogue to mark victories of the Prussian army during the Seven Years' War. The first regular weekly sermons in German were delivered, beginning in 1808, by the enlightened educator Joseph Wolf in Dessau and two years later by members of the Westphalian consistory for students of its model school in Kassel. Thereafter German sermons became an integral part of every experiment aimed at modernizing Jewish worship. The young preachers who delivered the sermons drew freely upon Christian models. They were familiar with the homiletics of Schleiermacher and the other prominent Christian preachers of the day and employed the formal structures they had learned from them. Their intent was not interpretation of Jewish law but spiritual edification. Gradually, rabbis as well began to give German sermons. The first to do so, during the second decade of the nineteenth century, was Samson Wolf Rosenfeld (1780–1862), who served in the Bavarian town of Markt Uhlfeld and was also the first rabbi in Germany to favor a variety of other religious reforms. When Isaac Bernays (1792–1849) was appointed as spiritual leader of the Jewish community in Hamburg, partly to counter the influence of the local Jewish reformers, one of his principal tasks was to deliver regular sermons. In Vienna the German sermon, along with a high level of musical performance by the cantor and strict decorum, became characteristic of the "Vienna rite," which spread from the capital to certain synagogues in Bohemia and Galicia. To be sure, some rabbis remained reluctant or incapable of assuming the new role. In Bavaria it was necessary to issue a ministerial order in 1835 that required rabbis to preach at least occasionally, apparently in the belief that such sermons would instill moral conduct. However, by the second half of the nineteenth century the German sermon had established itself in most of the larger communities in German-speaking Europe not so much as a mark of religious reform as of Germanization.

Other innovations were more controversial on account of their closer link to Christianity or their problematic character in terms of Jewish law. With the transformation of Jewish identity in Germany from association with an encompassing and unself-conscious cultural, ethnic, and religious whole into a strictly religious affiliation, some Jews began to sense the need for a formal avowal of their faith by Jewish children in the same way that Christian boys and girls affirmed the tenets of their religion through the ceremony of confirmation. Such a solemn commitment, following upon study of the articles of the Jewish faith with the aid of a catechism, might also serve to diminish the likelihood of conversion to Christianity. The ceremony of confirmation among German Jews had its origins in the home and the modern Jewish school from which it spread also to the synagogue. The first time a Jewish confirmation was conducted seems to have been in the modern Jewish school in Dessau in 1803. Initially, it was an individual ceremony upon the child's reaching his thirteenth birthday, the age of Jewish maturity. Later it became a collective occasion for the members of an entire class that had received religious instruction together. As Judaism, unlike Christianity, did not require formal acceptance of a creed, the confirmation ceremony soon assumed the character of a broader affirmation of Jewish teachings, especially in the moral realm, than of specific doctrines. Although borrowed directly from Christianity, it gained acceptance in circles extending beyond those of the outright religious reformers. There did continue to be opposition to the ceremony, especially to its taking place in the synagogue, and it did not spread as widely as the German sermon. Still, as it represented no violation of Jewish law, a few otherwise traditional rabbis were willing to institute it in their synagogues.

Less widely acceptable was the introduction of German prayers and hymns into the religious service. Although Jewish law did not forbid use of the vernacular, its insertion into the recitation of the liturgy was more intrusive than the German sermon. Opponents also argued that it would diminish the need for learning Hebrew, the importance of which for Jewish life was recognized by all but the most radical reformers. The employment of a musical instrument to accompany the worship represented a yet more fundamental violation of accepted Jewish norms. For a Jew to play an instrument on the Sabbath was forbidden by Jewish law. For a Gentile to do so in the synagogue, as was the practice initially adopted, removed the legal objection but still left the atmosphere of worship so fundamentally altered that traditionalists regarded it as nothing less than revolutionary. The use of the organ in Jewish worship remained limited to a handful of German synagogues during the first half of the nineteenth century. Later, however, it came to be the hallmark of difference between Liberal synagogues on the one side, Conservative or Orthodox ones on the other.

One of the purposes of Jewish religious reform from its beginnings in Germany was to bring Jewish women into public religious life together with Jewish men. Unlike the traditional Bar Mitzvah, which was limited to boys, the confirmation ceremony soon included girls as well. Whereas in traditional Judaism women, and especially unmarried girls, did not regularly attend the synagogue, the early religious reformers encouraged them to do so. The vernacular prayers and hymns were in large measure intended for the women, whose knowledge of Hebrew was insufficient to understand the standard liturgy. The sermons, concentrating on personal morality, were directed to them no less than to the men. The organ music and the choral singing were to appeal to their aesthetic taste. In keeping with Christian practice in Germany at the time, the sexes continued to sit separately, and in most cases women remained in the balcony. However, the reformers built synagogues with a larger percentage of seats intended for women and soon removed the barriers that hid them from the men. In certain Baden communities the mothers of confirmands were allowed to sit together with the men during the confirmation ceremony, which followed the regular service.

The initial wave of Jewish religious reforms in Germany in the second decade of the nineteenth century was not motivated principally by ideological concerns. The goal was simply to modernize Judaism, to bring it up-to-date by introducing such formal innovations as would make it fit naturally into a religious landscape whose main features were determined by the Christian denominations. However, the political and social integration of the Jews and their own shifting sentiments with regard to their place in Europe and Germany seemed even at this early stage to require

13   Boys and girls being confirmed together

some adjustments of content as well as form. Thus it was characteristic of
the early reformers to remove or alter liturgical passages that set Israel
sharply apart from the nations of the earth. The Hamburg Temple prayerbook of 1818, the first complete Hebrew and German nonorthodox Jewish
prayerbook issued in Germany, went further, by excising passages of the
traditional liturgy that expressed the hope that all Jews would return to
the ancient Land of Israel with the coming of the messiah. Although the
prayerbook did not exclude mention of Zion and the rebuilding of the
ancient temple in Jerusalem entirely, it reflected the belief that Germany
was the homeland of the Jews who lived there and that they did not desire
another. For those who used the prayerbook, the "pouring out of our
hearts" had become a permanent replacement for the sacrificial service
that traditional Jews still hoped the messiah would reestablish in Zion.

The first distinctly reformed service in Germany was instituted, beginning in 1810, by Israel Jacobson in the newly built chapel of the school he

had established earlier for poor Jewish boys in the town of Seesen. Intended primarily for the students, this "temple" possessed not only an organ but also a bell that chimed the hour of worship. Its interior design departed from Jewish tradition by moving the reader's platform (*bimah*) from the center of the room into the area in front of the ark, where it could more conveniently be used for the delivery of sermons. The very building itself declared that Jews worshipped in a manner not formally different from Christians. For the dedication ceremony Jacobson invited Christian as well as Jewish notables from all over the Kingdom of West-phalia. His sermon on that occasion was a paean to the new spirit of tol-eration destined to bring Jews and Gentiles together as brothers and sis-ters on the ground of their common reason and devotion to God—with-out either group thereby doing violence to its faith. Jews would simply need to remove certain elements from the ritual that were offensive to Christians while the latter needed to overcome their prejudices against Jews. Neither religion required reform of its fundamental beliefs.

After the demise of the Westphalian kingdom and its Jewish consis-tory, Jacobson settled in Berlin, where in 1815 he instituted regular mod-ernized services in his home. Since these services were not a community enterprise and did not impinge upon the community synagogue, where the worship remained strictly traditional, Jacobson's venture did not ini-tially arouse protest from the orthodox. He instituted a decorous service, using the Sephardi pronunciation of Hebrew, which was thought more classical and was associated with a tradition of greater cultural integration among Sephardi Jews. Young preachers, university students, delivered German sermons; there was an organ and a choir to provide the music. On account of its novelty and also because for many Berlin Jews it filled a religious void, the number of those attending on Sabbath mornings grew steadily, sometimes exceeding four hundred. In order to accommodate the large numbers—many of them Jews who for years had not attended ser-vices regularly in the community synagogue—the wealthy sugar refiner Jacob Herz Beer (1769–1825) established a more spacious temple in his palatial home. An 1818 list indicates that close to one thousand Berlin Jews associated themselves with these services, about one-quarter of the Jewish community. They tended to be the wealthier and younger Berlin Jews, although the ranks of the traditionalists likewise included some wealthy individuals, and some adherents of the reformed services were Jews of modest means. Although there were tensions between the young preachers and the older, more established but less educated men who paid their salaries, the services would have continued to play a role in Berlin were it not for the sharp opposition of a Prussian government fearful of religious, no less than political, change. It first ordered the suspension of the services and then, after the Orthodox too had expressed anxiety, put an end to them entirely.

In Hamburg, where the city authorities were less interested in suppressing innovation, the reformers were more enduringly successful. There a group of laymen was able to create a "temple association" in 1817 that would continue without interruption until the Nazi period. But it was also in Hamburg that the new form of service aroused German traditionalists to the first major confrontation between the two factions. The three local rabbinical judges were able to gather twenty-two Hebrew responsa, signed by forty rabbis, that all condemned the use of the vernacular and the organ in the service as well as every alteration in the liturgy. Among the respondents was Moses Sofer (1763–1839), the rabbi of Pressburg in Hungary and among the leading halachic authorities of his day. Believing that changes even in relatively minor externals could undermine full commitment to Judaism, Sofer declared that all innovation in Jewish life was prohibited by the Torah. His influence among traditionalists in Germany was considerable, helping to transform some of them into an unyielding self-conscious Orthodoxy that, ironically, was itself a departure from the more adaptive traditional Judaism of earlier times. Yet the characteristic Orthodoxy of German Jews increasingly differed from that of Sofer's school. It would soon prove more flexible in adopting forms and values from its environment, even as it assumed a no less militant position in its defense of Jewish law and traditional theology.

For a time Orthodoxy, in some instances supported by conservative governments, managed to slow the course of religious reform. During the 1820s and most of the 1830s the Hamburg Temple, with its unique nonorthodox prayerbook, its two preachers, pipe organ, and classes preparing children for confirmation, represented the only regular synagogue in Germany that differed sharply from others in its liturgy and ceremonies. Marked religious innovation continued, however, in some of the Jewish schools. Despite the Prussian prohibition, Jewish teachers delivered German sermons and a boys' choir sang Hebrew psalms on Sabbaths and holidays in the Berlin community school. Although intended primarily for the students, these devotions attracted parents and other adults of both sexes in large numbers. By the 1830s some of the more traditional Berlin Jews were also gathering every other week in the old, privately financed Bet Ha-Midrash to hear the teacher of religion, Solomon Plessner, give inspirational sermons, and they were calling on Plessner to confirm their sons and daughters. The situation in Frankfurt was roughly analogous. There the advocates of a modernized service were content to leave the community synagogue in the hands of the traditionalists. For those dissatisfied with its service, they organized a more acceptable alternative in the Jewish Philanthropin. Especially after it began to take place in its own auditorium in 1828, this "devotional hour," conducted in the German language and centering upon an inspirational sermon, served the religious needs of the more acculturated members of the Frankfurt Jewish community, especially the women, until the moderate Leopold Stein became rabbi of the community in 1844 and began reform of the community synagogue.

These experiments with the introduction of new forms into the religious service were the practical reflections of a desire to make Judaism more indigenous to the German religious context while still preserving some of its distinguishing features. How much differentiation needed to be maintained was the point of difference dividing those who sought to preserve as much as possible of the traditional ambience from those who, in varying measure, sought to depart from it. In the early decades of the nineteenth century such differences were only beginning to crystallize into permanent factions within each community. As yet there were no fully developed ideologies that could be called Orthodox and Reform. Only beginning in the 1830s did a university-trained rabbinical leadership set before the Jewish public new theoretical justifications for the persistence of Judaism—and hence also of Jewish communities.

4 | Jewish Self-Understanding

The broadening of education and the initial reform of Jewish worship were practical adaptations to the non-Jewish context. The first was intended to prepare the younger generation for a life within rather than outside the larger society, the second, to reflect the values of that society within the synagogue, the principal sphere that would remain specifically and exclusively Jewish. Although in the early decades of the nineteenth century the changes wrought in school and synagogue were the most apparent instances of Jewish transformation, they were accompanied by changes in the realm of thought and reflection, at first limited to small circles but eventually broadening into well defined and influential interpretations of Judaism. Acculturation served as the impetus for efforts to conceptualize Judaism—or, more broadly, Jewish identity—in new ways related to the shifting political situation of the Jews and their non-Jewish intellectual environment.

Intellectual response had begun in Germany with the Haskalah (see volume 1), when Mendelssohn proposed a Judaism that, on account of its inherent rationality and lack of dogmas, was wholly in accord with the principles of the *Aufklärung*. However, Aufklärung rationalism came under severe attack during the last decades of the eighteenth century and by the beginning of the nineteenth was widely deemed to be a superficial and inadequate approach to understanding reality. Moreover, Mendelssohn had claimed that the specific difference between Judaism and natural religion lay only in its ritual law, which many enlightened Jews of the following generation no longer regarded as the binding commandments of divine revelation. Those German Jews who attended universities in the third and fourth decades of the nineteenth century were exposed to new systems and values—to philosophical idealism, Romanticism, and historical criticism. Some found them irreconcilable with Judaism and hence, for intellectual as well as for social and professional reasons, either abandoned Judaism or neglected it. Others, however, applied the new intellectual approaches and cultural values to Judaism, thereby giving it new shape. Thus the counterpart of educational and religious reform in the intellectual sphere was reflection upon the nature of Jewish existence and the Jewish religion in the intellectual context of early nineteenth-century Europe. The Haskalah had been a Jewish acculturation to the Aufklärung; the new historical consciousness was a reacculturation to the values of its critics. Although this renewed effort at adaptation was initially problematic for Jewish survival, the eventual result was a deepened Jewish self-understanding that found ongoing expression in historical study and religious ideology. By the late 1830s the significance of the intellectual developments for Jewish institutional life, as well, becomes apparent.

1. History

For the Haskalah, as for the Aufklärung, philosophy rather than history was the principal channel for understanding the world and the self. Reason, self-contained and without reference to a past, could overcome the prejudices from which Jews had suffered and the superstitions that had crept into their faith. The Aufklärung offered them hope of a new beginning. Yet, despite its focus upon eternal verities, which Mendelssohn shared, the eighteenth century did give some attention to history. In the hands of writers as diverse as Voltaire in France and August von Schlözer in Germany, it served the purpose of moral exemplification. It liberated from narrow views and expanded possibilities for the future. Some of the maskilim, the Jewish enlighteners, likewise employed history for didactic illustration, mostly in the form of brief biographical studies. In their journal, *Ha-Me'asef*, they held up as exemplary the lives and accomplishments of Sephardi Jews such as Moses Maimonides and Menasseh ben Israel, who had lived productively within a larger cultural sphere while remaining loyal to their faith. These men were, in the writers' view, the maskilim of earlier times and could serve as worthy models for the present.

More radical maskilim used the study of Jewish history for the purpose of undermining the authority of Jewish norms. The lack of historical consciousness among Jews had created a frame of mind in which customs and beliefs were undifferentiated by origin or degree of centrality.
There was little awareness that some points of doctrine or practice had
once been controversial or had entered the religion very late. Judaism as
it existed in the present was viewed as divinely sanctioned and essentially
unchanged since ancient times. Peter Beer (1758–1838), a teacher at the
new Jewish school in Prague, was determined to use Jewish history for
the purpose of shattering this perceived uniformity of Jewish tradition
and thereby justifying diversity of Jewish identity in the present. In 1822
he published a history not of Judaism but of "religious sects" among the
Jews. By calling attention to Samaritans, Hellenizers, Essenes, Sadducees,
and Karaites, Beer put the Pharisaism and rabbinism upon which contemporary Judaism was built into a broader perspective and laid siege to
the absoluteness of its claims. Since there was historical precedent for being a nonrabbinic Jew, giving up rabbinic laws for the sake of acculturation did not imply giving up Judaism. For Beer himself the consequence
was to reach back to the "pure Mosaic faith" that preceded sectarian division, an earlier and, he believed, religiously higher common ground.
Although, unlike Beer, later religious reformers did not base their Judaism on the Bible to the exclusion of subsequent developments, they frequently used historical study to demonstrate variety and to show that
certain norms of the present were by no means always and everywhere
accepted. When they found contradictions among sacred texts, they did
not, in the traditional manner, seek to reconcile them but chose to account
for them instead as genuine differences explicable by contradictory views
and practices that reflected historical variation and development. The
consequence of historicization was relativization, which opened the way
for reform.

Although the young men who formed the Verein für Cultur und
Wissenschaft der Juden (Association for Culture and the Scholarly Study
of the Jews) in Berlin in 1819 did not lose sight of the practical purposes
of historical study, their motivation for engaging in it was more complex.
This small circle, whose most active members were university educated
and who regarded themselves as "the Jewish intelligentsia,"[1] turned to
the study of the Jewish past with the personal intent of isolating an
essence of Judaism with which they could identify. Influenced by the prevailing intellectual shift from nonhistorical Aufklärung rationalism to

Hegelian philosophy and scientific method, they examined the Jewish past in the hope of gaining a collective Jewish self-understanding within the intellectual context of the early nineteenth century. The Verein's goal was nothing less than "to bring Judaism . . . to self-awareness, to make the Jewish world known to itself."[2]

Formed in the wake of the "Hep Hep" riots, which demonstrated popular resistance to the economic advances Jews had begun to make in Germany, the Verein brought together young, highly acculturated Jews who were not certain of their future in this resurgently hostile environment. Having lost faith in the insular Judaism that was transmitted to them, they were casting about, almost desperately, for a Jewish identity worth preserving despite the persistence of external enmity. One of the leading members, Leopold Zunz (1794–1886), had earlier flirted with the idea of conversion; others, Eduard Gans (1798–1839) and Heinrich Heine (1797–1856), accepted baptism shortly after the Verein's collapse in 1824. Yet collectively they hoped, for a time, to bring Judaism into the perspective of world history and hence to justify its continuance in their own lives. In the words of the Verein's statutes, the times imposed on them the responsibility of leading their fellow Jews to "that point of view which the rest of the European world has attained."[3]

It is not surprising that this effort should have been undertaken under the aegis of Hegelian philosophy. Most members of the Verein were directly or indirectly students of Hegel who, beginning in 1818, taught at the University of Berlin. Thus, unlike Mendelssohn, the members of the Verein did not associate Judaism with the affirmation of natural religion. Instead, they tried to define it as an ongoing force in history, a component of the World Spirit. This endeavor, however, produced a dilemma: they could not, without contradicting Hegel, clearly isolate the Jewish component of the present spiritual reality that, in the Hegelian view, had been absorbed into the whole. According to Hegel, Judaism had ceased to possess independent world-historical significance. But if they could not differentiate Judaism, then there was no intellectually justifiable reason for separate Jewish survival. As long as Judaism was itself exclusive and Jews were excluded by non-Jews, Jewish history ran parallel to world history. But what would the hoped for inclusion of the Jews in European society mean for the place of Judaism within the collective spirit of Europe? The Verein determined that the idea of Judaism was "the idea of unconditioned unity within totality," a formulation which, while associating Judaism with the most significant and embracing truth, implied

14   Eduard Gans, president of the Association for Culture and
the Scholarly Study of the Jews and later professor of law
at the University of Berlin

that the very idea of Judaism required its own absorption. Some Verein
members tried to argue that the Jews would retain their "pure nationality" or their "ethnicity" (*Volkstümlichkeit*) but they were at a loss as to
how to define it.

   The notion that Jewish history had come to an end was an element
likewise in the initial work of Wissenschaft des Judentums (scholarly
study of Judaism) the most significant concept to emerge from the circle
of the Verein. In his programmatic *Etwas über die rabbinische Litteratur*
(On Rabbinic Literature, 1818) Leopold Zunz had written: "Just because
we see the Jews in our day—to consider only the German ones—reaching for the German language and German culture with greater seriousness and so—perhaps often without wanting it or suspecting it—carrying
postbiblical Hebrew literature to its grave, for that very reason scholar-

ship appears and demands an accounting of that which is closed."[4] Zunz assumed that the literature produced by the Jews in a language being rapidly forgotten and on the basis of religious assumptions that were being abandoned could find no continuation. Its creative power was exhausted. However, what Zunz did not note, and probably did not yet realize, was that the critical study of this literature, which he claimed had reached the end of its journey, could itself evolve into a new Jewish literature sustaining both Jewish culture and Jewish identity. In fact, the scholarly study of Judaism became one of the central achievements of German Jewry in the nineteenth century, admired by Jews elsewhere in Europe and in America.

Wissenschaft des Judentums was an attempt to bring Jewish studies under the aegis of a reigning ideal. Wilhelm von Humboldt, the founder of the University of Berlin, had argued that "the pure idea of *Wissenschaft*" was the essential element in every academic enterprise. For the individual it formed a sound character. It was not a means, but an end in itself. The moralism and rhetorical tone of eighteenth-century historiography thus gave way to a quest for objectivity, a *Verwissenschaftlichung*. Generalizations fell in favor of detailed description and—most important for the inclusion of the Jews—the concept of history broadened from a recounting of military and political events to embrace the evolution of culture and religion. The historical spirit everywhere displaced what the legal thinker Friedrich Karl von Savigny, one of the principal shapers of the new mentality, regarded as the shallow self-sufficiency of the preceding half century. The new historicism, which reached its apogee in Ranke, eschewed judgment by external criteria in favor of understanding each culture on its own terms.

Leopold Zunz became the chief Jewish exemplar of the Wissenschaft ideal applied in life and in writing. The origins of Zunz's extraordinary erudition in the sources of postbiblical Judaism lie in his early traditional Jewish education in the Jewish free school in Wolfenbüttel. His scholarly method—philology, in the broad sense of literary history—was the product of his studies at the University of Berlin, influenced mainly by its two great scholars of antiquity, the unromantic, empirically oriented student of Homer, Friedrich August Wolf, and the theoretician of philological method, August Boeckh. Unlike his friends in the Verein, Zunz did not study philosophy at the university; his scholarship was not aimed at deriving a spiritual essence of Judaism. Yet, unlike traditional scholars, he studied texts within a secular, not a sacred framework. His interest lay in mastering the enormous corpus of medieval Jewish creativity in order to place each work within its historical context, discerning continuities and influences. In 1822 Zunz became the editor of the first scholarly Jewish periodical, the *Zeitschrift für die Wissenschaft des Judenthums*, and was also its most important contributor.

Zunz's motivation for his task was complex. Most fundamentally, he believed that in an age when scholarly objectivity was an indispensable cultural shibboleth, and knowledge was expanding into the remotest areas, Jews could not be considered full participants in German culture unless they applied scientific method to their own tradition. Already in 1818 he had expressed desolation that "our field of scientific endeavor alone is languishing."[5] Approaching Jewish sources with the tools of modern scholarship would bring respect both to the scholars and to the objects of their work. It would produce a specifically Jewish contribution to the task of all scholarship: understanding the nature of humanity. Zunz also had a specifically religious motive. He hoped that historical study would make it possible to distinguish the permanent from the transitory in Jewish history and also, therefore, the divine from the merely human.

Both the Verein and its periodical were short-lived. The members did not succeed in formulating a new rationale for Jewish existence strong enough to counterbalance the growing discrimination against educated Jews especially evident in the Prussian decision of 1822 excluding them from public teaching positions. They also felt isolated from their fellow Jews who failed to share their vision or financially support their cause. They regarded their contemporaries contemptuously, either as ongoing adherents of rabbinism and hence mired in a culture wholly inappropriate to the times or as crass materialists who had no appreciation for any culture. Zunz complained bitterly that few Jews outside the Verein itself read its *Zeitschrift*, which ceased publication after three issues. Orthodox Jews could not accept its critical premises; nonorthodox Jews had little interest in detailed historical studies of premodern Judaism. Few could cope with its erudite unpopular style, intended not to advance popular education, like *Sulamith*, but to prove that Jews did not lag behind others in applying Wissenschaft to historical sources. Likewise Christian scholars to whom Zunz sent issues either responded only perfunctorily, misunderstood its intent, or expressed themselves negatively. The result was severe demoralization.

Yet Wissenschaft des Judentums itself survived the demise of the Verein. Although he was forced to carry on his scholarly work in spare time while earning his living as a journalist and Jewish schoolmaster, Zunz continued to bring to light and study systematically the immense and largely unknown corpus of postbiblical Jewish literature. Unlike the maskilim, he did not draw selectively upon the past to reinforce desired norms of conduct; he was interested in the totality of Jewish creativity, regardless of immediate relevance or capacity to edify. In the *Zeitschrift* he had written a long and influential article on Rashi, the medieval Ashkenazi exegete, whom he held up as a man intellectually limited by the age in which he lived. Nonetheless, Zunz's major scholarly project after the demise of the Verein indicated clearly that he had not abandoned the possibility that Jewish scholarship would exercise both a political and a religious influence on German Jewry. His *Die gottesdienstlichen Vorträge der Juden, historisch entwickelt* (The Sermons of the Jews, Historically Developed, 1832), the first significant book-length product of Wissenschaft des Judentums and a work of lasting scholarly value, focused on a topic then in dispute: whether the Jews possessed their own sermonic literature or whether, as the Prussian government held, the giving of sermons in the synagogue was an innovation and hence inadmissible. Zunz documented that the Jews had a well-established homiletic tradition and sought to justify its revival in modern form.

Zunz would not produce another major work as engaged with the present as *Die gottesdienstlichen Vorträge der Juden.* He continued to believe that gaining Christian respect for Jewish scholarship would, in turn, gain respect for the Jews and therefore advance the cause of Jewish emancipation. He wrote, "The equal status of the Jews in public ethos and in life will emerge from the equal status of the Wissenschaft des Judentums."[6] But the contemporary Jewish community ceased to be his frame of reference. He withdrew himself from the movement for religious reform and eventually rejected it; he was distressed that the new generation of rabbis was distorting the scholarly study of Judaism to make it fit the mold of theology. His goal now was to bring the study of Jewish literature into the orbit of the university. But in this he was repeatedly unsuccessful. Wissenschaft des Judentums did not become an organic element of the scholarly enterprise in Germany. It remained in a channel of its own. In non-Jewish eyes integration of the Jews into German society did not imply integrating their cultural heritage, not even its scholarly study done with the tools of German Wissenschaft.

Zunz was a historian of Jewish creativity, not of the Jews. He believed that their religion and culture were the only significant elements in the

15   Leopold Zunz, founder of Wissenschaft des Judentums,
oil by Moritz Oppenheim, around 1875

life of a people that for most of its historical existence lacked political sovereignty. As creators of culture, the Jews actively produced a unique history; their relations with the external world, however, were no different
from those of any other oppressed group. The Jews' outer history, Zunz
wrote, "is not their own, not the powerful, freely expressed deed, but
something alien, an imposed defense along with suffering"[7]

It was Isaac Marcus Jost, Zunz's boyhood friend, who became the first
Jew in modern times to concentrate on the external relationships and
write a comprehensive history of the Jews. Jost had studied in Göttingen,

the focal point of historical studies in Germany at the turn of the nineteenth century. There the historian and biblical scholar Johann Gottfried Eichhorn had encouraged him to undertake his ambitious project. From 1820 until 1828 Jost published nine volumes of his *Geschichte der Israeliten* (History of the Israelites). His sober and somewhat prosaic writing was scholarly but not historicist. He attempted to portray the Jewish past critically and objectively, but lacked empathy for certain of its manifestations, especially rabbinism and mysticism. Intended for non-Jews as well as Jews, and especially for government officials, Jost's history stressed the loyalty that Jews had displayed to rulers wherever they had lived. The material was divided in such a way that it became more a compilation of the separate histories of Jews in various lands than the history of a single people. It was only their religion that provided a bridge across space and time. Later Jost justified this approach, claiming that Jewish history "is not something that stands alone, but an aspect of the history of the most important peoples and states with which the Jews have come into contact; the former complements the latter and offers it an element that hitherto has remained unknown or unconsidered."[8] Like Zunz, Jost too saw his work as playing a role in the process of integrating unjustly excluded Jewish elements into the German and European consciousness. As Zunz desired to bring the cultural legacy of Jewish literature into the orbit of the European cultural patrimony, Jost argued that the history of the European nations remained incomplete without consideration of the role played by the Jews.

Other Jewish historians in Germany were less concerned with making a contribution to general historiography and more intent on revealing their unique inner history to the Jews themselves. As a historian, the ideologist of religious reform Abraham Geiger was a historicist. The Jews' persistence in their faith, he argued, "is a historical fact that stands all alone, which allows of no parallel, and which for that reason must be explained entirely out of itself."[9] The principal intellectual influence on the young Geiger was Herder, from whom he learned to understand history not as events but as the evolution of the human spirit. Like Herder, and like Zunz, Geiger was not interested in the external history of the Jews, which lacked any rational principle of development. Properly understood, Jewish history taught the possibility of religious survival and creativity in the absence of political institutions and despite oppression. Its unity lay in the Jews' adherence to the monotheistic idea and the separation of their faith from every political connection. Geiger thus made of Jewish history a "history of the synagogue." Although the Jews had once been a people, they had become a "community of faith," the historical vessel of monotheism. The spirit of Judaism was the religious spirit par excellence. Viewed in this manner, the thrust of Jewish history provided no impediment to full emancipation: the historical essence of the Jews was not in conflict with complete political and cultural integration. What had always set the Jews apart and would continue to do so was their religious faith. When Geiger founded his own periodical in 1835, the *Wissenschaftliche Zeitschrift für jüdische Theologie* (Scholarly Journal for Jewish Theology), it was, despite its title, not devoted to systematic studies but to Jewish history as Geiger understood it.

As the Jewish historian Heinrich Graetz was to note a generation later, the enterprise of scientific historical study in Germany, as it developed in the post-Aufklärung decades, was not driven by a dispassionate historical curiosity but by "an irresistible drive to self-examination."[10] The past was both burden and inspiration, but, even more, it was potentially revelatory of the Jewish collective self. The Verein, Zunz, Jost, and Geiger, like Peter Beer, all sought liberation from the past through knowledge of it. But they also sought to give a historical dimension to a modern Jewish identity, whose contours still remained unclear. Historical study, though distanced from its object by criticism, was nonetheless able to provide for some German Jews a sense of continuity with earlier generations when the bridge afforded by Halacha became inadequate. Just how Jewish history flowed into the present would continue to be a point of difference, but those who remained Jews agreed that without the internalized consciousness of an examined and structured Jewish past, Jewish identity would not be able to withstand the temptations of ongoing integration and the pressures of persistent political rejection.

2. Religious Ideology

As the internal purpose of critical historical study was to reshape the relationship of modern German Jews to their past, the intent of the religious ideologies that appeared among them was to attain a new understanding of the Jewish religion that rendered it viable for present and future. During the first half of the nineteenth century four distinct positions emerge—roughly corresponding to the spectrum of Orthodoxy, Mediation Theology, Liberalism, and Rationalism among German Protestants of the same period. Each is associated with a major thinker, who brought it to fullest expression. Although the four men had much in common, they differed sharply on certain fundamentals, providing impetus for the crystallization of four religious groupings, which—in addition to the declining old Orthodoxy—would continue to characterize German Jewry into the twentieth century.

Each of the four ideologists was a unique personality who enjoyed the intense loyalty of his supporters and defended his position vigorously against its detractors. Samson Raphael Hirsch (1808–1888), who was born in Hamburg, grew up in a traditional but enlightened family, which saw in Mendelssohn's life the best evidence that orthodox practice and European culture need not conflict. The traditionalist Isaac Bernays, who was the first community rabbi in Germany to have attended university, was the chief influence determining Hirsch to become a rabbi. Like his mentor, Hirsch received a university education in addition to his rabbinical studies. His very popular first work, *Igrot tsafun. Neunzehn Briefe über Judenthum* (Epistles of a Hidden One: Nineteen Letters Concerning Judaism, 1836), established a new trend in German Judaism. It substituted for the old Orthodoxy, with its unthinking attachment to every traditional element, a self-conscious and positive response to modernity from the position of halachic Judaism, presenting an alternative to the more radical responses offered by religious reformers. It was not necessary for traditional Judaism to succumb to modernity since there was no contradiction between them.

Unlike Mendelssohn, Hirsch did not compartmentalize the Jewish and general spheres but sought to integrate them in personality and activity. He coined the influential self-designation of the Jew as *Mensch-Jissroeïl*, signifying the possibility of embodying at once the universally human and the specifically Jewish without inner conflict. He conveyed the same idea in the Hebrew motto *Torah im derekh erets*, which expressed the goal of joining the law and teaching of Judaism with an active life in state and society. Hirsch's approach was sufficiently different from the older orthodoxy to arouse animosity during his years spent as rabbi in Moravia. But it was too uncompromising in its adherence to Halacha to allow him to remain within the German Jewish collective community. In 1851 he became rabbi of the newly formed Israelite Religious Society in Frankfurt am Main, which was able to embody his ideas fully and inspire the formation of similar separatist groups in other German cities. Because Hirsch's modern Orthodoxy, or neo-Orthodoxy as it was soon called, did not venerate the old ways merely because they had been passed down through

k. k. Mährisch & Schlesischer Landes Ober Rabiner.

16   Samson Raphael Hirsch as chief rabbi of Moravia and
Silesia in Nikolsburg around 1848

the generations but sought to justify the basic elements of traditional
Judaism with modern arguments, it was a serious rival to those ideologies
that, to varying degrees, were ready to relinquish some of those elements.

Among the other ideologists of a modern German Judaism, the closest to Hirsch was Zacharias Frankel (1801–1875). Like Hirsch, Frankel
retained a deep attachment to the traditional Jewish life. He spent his
early years in Prague, studied at the University of Pest in Hungary, and
eventually became the rabbi of Dresden. More than his rivals, Frankel
was a man of the golden mean. Conservative in outlook, he eschewed
both militant orthodoxy and radical reform. He hoped to find a middle

path that would preserve the unity of German Jewry. Like Hirsch, Frankel also stated his position in terms of an integration of elements. But whereas *Torah im derekh erets* combined Jewish tradition with contemporary life, Frankel's "positive-historical" Judaism pointed to differences within Judaism itself. Adopting a term then current in conservative Protestant theology, Frankel held that the core of the Jewish religion was "positive," that is, revealed, and therefore not subject to rational criticism or to change. However, Judaism also developed within history and hence its traditions, including even its postbiblical laws, had been and could still be subject to reinterpretation. Frankel devoted his scholarship largely to the historical explication of rabbinic law, demonstrating that the Halacha had been innovative and leading to the conclusion that its historical development could be renewed in the present. He generally preferred to speak of "further development" rather than "reform" so as to signify that his goal was simply to continue a process endemic to Jewish history. He claimed to favor religious improvements, not innovations. Like contemporary Protestant Mediation Theology, Frankel sought to mediate between the demands of tradition and religious reform, faith and historical criticism. After he was chosen to head the Jewish Theological Seminary in Breslau, the first modern rabbinical seminary in Germany, his conservative approach to the tradition gained widening influence through its graduates.

The two remaining figures were decidedly more radical. Neither Abraham Geiger (1810–1874) nor Samuel Holdheim (1806–1860) easily found a substitute for the traditionalism of their early years. Geiger long felt a deep rift within himself between the desire to preserve the continuity of Judaism, which he expressed as a rabbi through the sermonic use of Midrash, and the need for relentlessly pursuing the historical truth with all of its consequences, which he espoused as a critical scholar through Wissenschaft. Only after much inner struggle did Geiger reject the necessity of creating an organizational schism between tradition-bound and enlightened Jews. Ultimately he decided to pursue the reform of Judaism within the communities, even though that involved practical compromises. But he always strained to purify Judaism of those beliefs and practices that he thought could not be from God because they conflicted with human moral reason. It was Geiger who gave a coherent ideology to what had heretofore been practically oriented and not deeply motivated efforts at religious reform. At the heart of that ideology was the notion of religious progress in history. Not only had Judaism developed during the cen-

17   Rabbi Zacharias Frankel, advocate of moderate reform
of Judaism

turies, adapting to changing circumstances, but it had moved toward a
greater understanding of God and the world. Although this progress had
not been steady, it was abundantly evident and could serve as precedent for
contemporary reform. The Jewish spirit, not Jewish law, provided continuity from age to age. In Germany this freer but nonetheless historically oriented approach to Judaism, though in the early years often broadly called
Reform, later assumed the institutional designation of *Liberal*.

Whereas Geiger was willing to compromise, at least in practice, Holdheim, like Hirsch, eventually preferred to be the spiritual leader of those

Jews who fully shared his views. He had begun his life as a strictly Orthodox Jew in the province of Posen but moved step-by-step away from tradition, until he assumed a position on the radical extreme of the Reform movement. Of the leading German rabbis he was the least bound by historical precedent. Convinced that earlier stages in Jewish history could offer little help in shaping a Judaism for the present, Holdheim called for revolutionary change, a Judaism based not on Halacha but on the subjective religious needs of the modern Jew and grounded in the values of European culture. For the Judaism of law, which had been appropriate while the Jews possessed their own state, and to a limited extent also during their existence in the ghetto, Holdheim wanted to substitute a religion of prophetic morality, expressed in the autonomous individ-

18 Rabbi Abraham Geiger, the most significant thinker
and scholar of the Jewish Reform movement

ual's own decisions of daily life. Unlike Geiger, Holdheim demanded full consistency between belief and practice. In 1847 he became the rabbi of the Jewish Reform Association in Berlin, a circle of laypeople who shared his opinion that, in its expression of Judaism, the existing Jewish community was hopelessly out of tune with the zeitgeist. During the second half of the nineteenth century his rationalistic ideology, as represented by the community he served, became known in Germany specifically as *Reform Judaism*.

Despite the differences among these four men and the ideologies they represented, they had much in common that set all of them apart from the old Orthodoxy. Each had studied in a university, each was a rabbi of the new type, who educated and ministered to his community much in the manner of a Christian clergyman. Each dressed according to the fashion of the time; even Hirsch, during his early years, did not wear a full beard. All spoke and did most of their writing in German. On the pulpit they wore the robe and collar bands that were the mark of clergy generally. An important part of their rabbinical duties was the regular delivery of religiously and morally edifying sermons. The services in their synagogues were decorous, the music according to Western patterns. None of the four regarded these formal adaptations as violating the biblical prohibition against imitating the Gentiles. In appearance, manner, and function they had more in common with each other than with the rabbis of Eastern Europe. Together, they were the spiritual representatives of a new, coherent, and readily differentiable phenomenon: a specifically German Judaism.

Indeed, Eastern Europe symbolized for all of them a cultural backwater that evoked disdain. They had only contempt for the Polish melamdim and their traditional style of Jewish education. None had any fondness for the pietistic Hasidic movement, which dominated in the East. Despite some proclivity to Romanticism in Hirsch and Frankel, they were all fundamentally rationalists. They abandoned the Jewish mystical tradition, the Kabbalah, then still alive in Poland and among some of the old Orthodox in Germany, as irreconcilable with modern modes of thought. None of the four established a yeshiva. The concentrated study of talmudic texts unrelated to the needs of daily life was not an ideal even for Hirsch, who devoted his own writing especially to an explication of those religious books that were of most significance and usefulness to the average Jew: the Bible (above all, the Pentateuch and Psalms) and the prayerbook.

All four men were unambivalent proponents of emancipation and acculturation. They believed that as Jews they could be as German as the

Gentiles and they were eager to participate fully in political and cultural life. None believed that the Jews were a nation in the modern sense; it was rather religion that bound Jews together. Land and soil were never Israel's bond of unity, Hirsch insisted, but rather common obedience to the revealed laws of the Torah. Because the unity of the Jews was anchored in the ideal realm of religion rather than the earthly one of statehood, the eternality of Israel was guaranteed, even if Jews chose to accept fully the obligations of citizenship to a state not their own and to participate in a culture they had not created. As Frankel wrote in 1842, "The Jews' nationality is entirely spiritual, conditioned by faith: they are an entity only insofar as they preserve their faith. Thus the Jews constitute only a religious community, just like every other denomination that exists in the state."[11] Although Hirsch did not relinquish the religious hope of the final restoration of Israel to its land and certainly did not remove it from the prayerbook, he believed that the messianic return would occur only upon God's initiative at the end of days. Meanwhile, there was no reason German Jews should refuse to play an active role in the political life of states to which they felt bound by feelings of political loyalty no less intense than those of non-Jews; Jewish law and the obligations of citizenship did not conflict.

All four men recognized that Judaism was more difficult to preserve under conditions of emancipation. But, unlike the old Orthodox, they insisted that it was possible to meet the challenge by modernizing Judaism to varying degrees. They were also in agreement that, as desirable as emancipation might be, they would not pay a religious price for its complete achievement. Hirsch said explicitly he would forego emancipation if it entailed any infringement of Orthodox Judaism. And even Holdheim, who held that Jewish law must give way in every instance before the demands of the state, insisted that the Jewish religion as he defined it—the belief in one God and the prophetic morality—stood above the age and could not be sacrificed for any political purpose.

Similar to the wholehearted affirmation of emancipation among all but old Orthodox Jews was the positive relation to German culture. Neo-Orthodox Jews no less than Reform Jews read German literature and philosophy; they went to the theater and the concert hall. Hirsch did not believe that such activity violated Judaism. On the contrary, he himself frequently cited Lessing and Schiller; his writings revealed the influence of Kant and Hegel. All four ideologists presumed to find in German high culture moral values that reinforced those to be found in Jewish sources.

Jews in Eastern Europe and Asia differed from their coreligionists in Germany not only in such matters as style of worship but more crucially on account of their lack of secular culture.

All streams of German Judaism also shared a fundamental doctrine: the "mission of Israel." Just as non-Jewish German writers, initially in response to French domination, argued that Germany had a cultural mission among the nations, so the Jewish ideologists posited that the Jews had their own spiritual and moral mission within Germany. As early as the eighteenth century Moses Mendelssohn argued that the Jews were chosen by Providence to be a priestly people, whose task among the nations was to call attention to its unadulterated idea of God and high morality. Following Mendelssohn, Hirsch's writings from the very first repeatedly expressed this idea. One of the correspondents in his *Igrot tsafun* instructs the other: "Consider for a moment the image of such an Israel, living freely among the nations, striving for its ideal! Every son of Israel a respected, widely influential priestly exemplar of justice and love, disseminating not Judaism—which is prohibited—but pure humanity among the nations!"[12]

For the religious reformers the mission idea was even more decisive. They addressed Jews who had largely given up return to Zion even as a distant God-initiated event and for whom the Halacha was no longer a divinely ordained norm. If their readers and listeners were to remain Jewish other than out of habit or familial piety, and despite the pressures to convert to Christianity, then they required a doctrine that rationalized their persistence in the most grandiose terms. The mission of Israel idea served that purpose. It held that Europe had not yet absorbed all that the Jews had to offer. To remain a religious Jew was therefore not a selfish but a magnanimous act, not a withdrawal from the larger society but the expression of confidence that Judaism could raise that society's spiritual level.

The mission of Israel was the most extreme response to the alleged depravity of the Jewish religion argued by the enemies of emancipation; it was, in effect, the chosenness of Israel turned outward. No matter that in practical fact few Christians believed they still had anything to learn from the Jews; for the Jews themselves the mission of Israel was the most powerful doctrine of self-justification. Thus Jewish particularism ceased to be an end in itself, becoming instead the means toward a greater goal: the universal acknowledgment of the God of Israel and God's moral precepts for humanity. And thus the survival of the Jews became more, not less, significant in an age of emancipation.

Notwithstanding such commonalties, the four religious ideologies also displayed fundamental differences. These may be understood as focusing on three major issues: the source and nature of divine authority, the reflection of that authority in the sacred texts of Judaism, and the practical implications of the theoretical positions.

With regard to the source of divine authority, the positions of neo-Orthodoxy and radical Reform are the most precise. Hirsch fully retained the traditional conception that God verbally revealed the entire Written and Oral Law at Sinai: there is no human element in them at all; the revelation is entirely supernatural and unconditioned by history. Like Mendelssohn, Hirsch believed that no historical change could alter it; only God could do so in a similar revelatory act. The duty of the Jew was therefore simply to believe every revealed doctrine and to obey every revealed law. Neither did Hirsch, like some of his antagonists, distinguish between moral and ritual laws. All are equally and eternally the will of God.

Samuel Holdheim's position stands out most clearly from Hirsch's since it determines divine authority to lie entirely within the contemporary individual and not at all in an ancient supernatural act of revelation: "Conscience is that indubitable religious revelation to which Judaism attaches its teaching. . . . Reason not only has an important voice in matters of religion; it is the surest criterion for assessing everything that is taught in its name."[13] The autonomous individual, in turn, was guided by the highest values of the contemporary age. God, in the past and in the present, was merely the source of religious illumination. What set the ancient Israelites apart historically was that their leaders attained a higher degree of such spiritual illumination than did their neighbors, but the words they formulated were human and limited by their times. Present-day Jewry, Holdheim believed, was not bound by their formulations or practical conclusions; it was within its power, through fresh illumination, to rise above the religious level of its ancestors.

Like Holdheim, Geiger understood revelation as nonverbal illumination and rejected Hirsch's adherence to an unchanging, externally revealed law. He defined obedience to God as "obedience to the divine within us, to the God-given moral consciousness."[14] Geiger likewise held that revelation was continuous and progressive. However, he differed from Holdheim in two respects. First, he emphasized that the ethical monotheism reflected in the writings of the biblical prophets could not be fully understood as merely a step forward in a process of historical religious development. It appeared only when the prophetic religious genius suddenly attained a far higher level of religious consciousness because the spirit of God had dramatically revealed itself to the human spirit. Second, Geiger stressed that contemporary culture, which Holdheim made normative, was only a stage in the further development of the human spirit. He was therefore less negative about the religious value of earlier periods of Jewish history and more reluctant to give normative status to the present.

Interestingly, the conservative Frankel adopted a position similar to Holdheim's in that he too ascribed revelatory authority to the present. However, for Frankel such authority lay not in the zeitgeist, external to Judaism, but in the collective will of average religious Jews: "There is a revelation too in the common consciousness of a religious community which, as long as it remains that group's living common possession, deserves as much recognition as the unmediated divine one."[15] Therefore, in Frankel's view, no religious reformer had a right, for reasons of rationality, to alter norms the people themselves had not cast aside.

These differing conceptions of revelation implied differing attitudes to Judaism's sacred texts. Hirsch remained adamantly opposed to any attempt to humanize or historicize either Bible or Talmud. He rejected Wissenschaft des Judentums precisely because it potentially undermined their divine and superhistorical origins. Put bluntly: "Better to be a Jew without Wissenschaft than to have Wissenschaft without Judaism."[16] In his own writings he carried forward the traditional hermeneutic approach to the text, especially to the Pentateuch, by supplying symbolic interpretations intended to appeal to the moral and aesthetic consciousness of his modern readers. New human meanings could legitimately be added to divinely revealed sources.

Closest to Hirsch's position—and hence the object of his most severe polemics—was Frankel's positive-historical Judaism. The conservative school held, with Hirsch, that the Written Law was an accurate reflection of God's word and it shared an almost equal devotion to full religious observance. However, Frankel and his disciples distinguished between the Mosaic foundation and the later structure of rabbinic Judaism that was built upon it. The Talmud, they held, was a work mingling divine inspiration with human genius. Frankel's distinction between the status of Written and Oral Law had the consequence that he condemned biblical criticism but engaged actively in respectful, yet nonetheless historically critical studies of postbiblical Judaism. The practical implication was that rabbinic law, Halacha, having been created in history, could also develop continuously in history, subject only to the changing religious consciousness of the people.

Geiger and Holdheim were at one in their refusal to ascribe intrinsic divine authority to any text. Although the Bible possessed greater religious value, it was, no less than the Talmud, the work of humans, and contemporary humans had to discover what elements in the text were the true reflection of an eternally valid revelation. Therefore neither man placed any textual limits on the scope of Wissenschaft des Judentums. Geiger's approach to the rabbinic literature was, from the first, open and revolutionary. Under the influence of David Friedrich Strauss and the Tübingen school among Christian scholars, he adopted the method that Strauss had applied to his studies of the New Testament. Just as Strauss had shown that the Evangelists created a forced unity between the Old and New Testaments in order to make the former foretell the birth of Jesus contained in the latter, Geiger similarly argued that the rabbis of the Mishnah and the Gemara (the two historically consecutive portions of the Talmud) had purposely misunderstood the text of the Hebrew Bible in order to use its authority for their own legislation. Far from being a seamless web, the tradition in fact underwent historical change, thinly disguised by the Mishnah reading its views falsely into the Bible, and the Babylonian Gemara, in turn, projecting its opinions onto the Palestinian Mishnah. Geiger thus showed that religious evolution was present all along, even though it had purposefully been concealed. His historical criticism especially angered the conservatives—who themselves believed in historical study of rabbinic texts—because it seemed to imply that the Rabbis were deceitful. However, in humanizing and historicizing all sacred texts Geiger did not deprive them of their religious significance: they were all "documentary evidence of the spirit of Judaism" and, as such, links in a spiritual chain that continued to the present. Moreover, the ancient Rabbis, in going behind the letter to the spirit of biblical legislation, were an attractive model for contemporary Jews.

It is in this positive evaluation of the Rabbis as links in a spiritual chain of tradition and as models for reform that Geiger's liberal and evolutionary theology parts company with Holdheim's dialectical rationalism. Unlike Geiger, Holdheim saw little possibility of upholding the continuity of Jewish religious history; the contemporary age represented too radical a departure from the past. For Holdheim the texts were not links in a chain but documents that reflected a religious milieu radically different from the present. The Talmud, and certainly the Bible, possessed religious value, but only as sources from which present-day Jews might select those passages that still appealed to contemporary religious conscience and reason. Whereas Geiger's historical approach replaced the old continuity based on identity of content among the sources with a new continuity based on gradual religious development, Holdheim distinguished contemporary Reform Judaism sharply from rabbinic Judaism and objected severely when colleagues read modern views on such subjects as the religious status of women back into the Talmud.

The final significant point of comparison among the four religious ideologies lies in the practical implications of their theoretical positions. For Hirsch the verbal revelation of the entire corpus of Written and Oral Law contained in Torah and Talmud necessitated rejection of any religious reform that violated God's manifest, unchanging, and fully expressed will for all generations. Hence, despite its openness to European culture, neo-Orthodoxy drew the line clearly at Halacha, considering no law less important than another and requiring full obedience to every commandment. "*La Loi* and not *la foi*, law—and not faith—is the catchword of Judaism; obeying, not believing and hoping and praying, makes the Jew a Jew."[17] According to Hirsch, Judaism was a wholly "positive" and objective religion that left little room for collective or individual dissent. Only customs that had no basis in law might be abandoned or modernized.

If Hirsch's position allowed for the least change, Holdheim's allowed for the most. Unbound either by verbal revelation or by the restraints of historical linkage, Reform Judaism in Germany was free not only to abandon venerable customs like the head covering at prayer for men but even to move the biblically ordained observance of the Sabbath on the seventh day from Saturday to Sunday. Holdheim believed that the dietary laws and similar rituals reflected the primitive religious consciousness of an earlier age. Not only were they wholly dispensable, but, because they set the Jews apart, such laws delayed the messianic age when all religions would become one. Proper religious praxis, Holdheim believed, in agreement with Kant, consisted not of obedience to ceremonial laws but of freely chosen moral acts.

Frankel and Geiger occupy less clearly defined positions in the middle. Like Hirsch, Frankel held that law was essential to Judaism. Perhaps even more than Hirsch, he possessed a romantic veneration for tradition and strenuously opposed most substantive reforms. Of the major Jewish religious ideologists he was most similar to the Christian Pietists in Germany, like them stressing the importance of faith and sentiment. Yet part of that same romanticism was Frankel's confidence in the collective religious consciousness of the Jewish people, and that consciousness was subject to gradual historical change. Thus Frankel could be more flexible than Hirsch, even entertaining the possibility of dropping the second days of certain holidays from the Jewish calendar. His goal, "preservation through progress,"[18] depended upon creation of a leadership emotionally at one with the collectivity and therefore able to pluck out only what had already died within it while, above all, preventing rift within the community.

Geiger was less in sympathy with the Jewish masses. Though he ultimately chose not to abandon the general Jewish community, he believed that reform-minded rabbis, versed in the spiritual history of Judaism and standing on the "height of the age," needed to take the initiative in a disunited community: "The willpower of the collectivity is broken; the will of the individual must steel itself."[19] Geiger neither accepted ritual law as the word of God nor rejected it outright. Rather he distinguished between eternal moral laws and ritual ones, the latter being means to religious ends but not ends in themselves. Possessing only instrumental religious value, ritual laws could be abandoned or altered when they no longer served their purpose. In specific instances, Geiger favored far more radical reforms than Frankel. He supported use of the organ in worship and abandonment of prayers for the return to Zion. On one occasion he privately referred to circumcision as "a barbaric bloody act that fills the father with anxiety"[20] and envisioned its eventual abandonment. However, as "bearers of the spirit," the rituals were to be maintained as long as they did not become mere rote observances, as long as they "stimulate our religious and moral sensibility."[21]

These ideological positions all emerged in Germany during the decade between 1835 and 1845 against a backdrop of increasing factionalization and friction in the larger Jewish communities. Their influence was felt as laymen made divisive decisions about religious leadership and entered into controversies with one another.

3. Practice

During the second quarter of the nineteenth century the decline in traditional observance among German Jews, which had begun earlier, went forward with greater rapidity. Except in the smallest communities, where religious conformity could more easily be maintained by informal pressures, Jews increasingly differed in their degree of observance. As ever larger numbers of children attended non-Jewish schools, they underwent an early acculturation, which frequently limited the role that Judaism played in their adult lives. Those practices that conflicted with complete economic integration, such as strict observance of the Sabbath, or that set the Jews most sharply apart from non-Jews, like observance of the dietary laws, disappeared earliest. The celebration of Jewish holidays in the home possessed greater staying power, but there are also contemporary reports of Jewish houses adorned with Christmas trees. Although the Reform movement gave centrality to the synagogue and urged women, as well as men, to attend religious services, the sense of obligation to pray diminished. In the larger communities the houses of worship were rarely filled except on the High Holidays, even though their capacity was considerably smaller than the population of adults. For an increasing number of German Jews, their level of secularization had simply reduced the role of religion in their lives to a minimum, and the nature of what remained did not greatly concern them.

The Reform movement shied away from directly confronting the diminution of observance in the private sphere. Only one notable attempt was made to establish a more liberal Halacha in all its details. But that effort, by Michael Creizenach (1789–1842), a teacher at the Frankfurt Philanthropin, failed to make any impact. His *Shulḥan Arukh* (1833–1840), named after the sixteenth-century code of Jewish law, could not establish revised norms among Jews who had given up ritual practice almost entirely. Moreover, its grounding in the Talmud was not attractive at a time when rabbinic Judaism was in severe disrepute not only among Christians but among many Jews, who believed that the Talmud was the spiritual counterpart of the ghetto.

Those Jews who had attended a university were the more likely to be estranged from Judaism. Their advanced secular studies, their contact with educated non-Jews, and their exposure to philosophical systems inimical to Judaism left many of them feeling little in common with coreligionists who had not shared their experience. They considered themselves universalists, practiced few, if any, Jewish rituals, and wondered what, aside from the accident of birth, still made them Jews. What remained, some of them said, was only a sense of filial piety and the feeling that conversion was an affront to their integrity.

Within the communities observant and secularized Jews maintained social as well as religious distance. In Hamburg, for example, traditional families and those belonging to the temple avoided intermarriage with one another. There, too, on one occasion in 1841, a public banquet to raise funds for the local Jewish Free School served non-kosher meat, undoubtedly with the expectation that observant Jews would not attend. Even in the smaller communities factionalization became more common, especially where restrictive legislation still prevented the less traditional Jews from leaving for the freer atmosphere of the larger city. With widening religious differentiation philanthropy and social welfare work became the principal common ground. A Jewish critic of the community leadership in Berlin deplored its lack of attention to Jewish education but deemed its care of the poor "exemplary."[22] Jews who rarely attended synagogue not only paid their taxes to the community but also contributed to voluntary Jewish charities. Giving to the Jewish poor became a substitute for religious observance, relieving any possible sense of guilt about abandoning practices instilled by parents. Charity was also the performance of a moral commandment whose value was fully recognized by non-Jews.

Even as religious indifference and factionalization within German Jewry were increasing, however, an important new element emerged that gave it a sense of greater strength and solidarity—a vigorous Jewish press. The Jewish periodicals in Germany of the preceding period, such as the Hebrew *Ha-Me'asef* and the German *Sulamith*, were vehicles for Jewish enlightenment, contributed to and read, in the first instance, by the maskilim and, in the second, mostly by the new generation of Jewish educators. Neither was able to direct itself to a larger circle of readers. The *Allgemeine Zeitung des Judenthums*, which began to appear in 1837 in a large format modeled on the general press, was distinctly different from its predecessors. Instead of appearing monthly, it was published at first three times a week and then weekly. It called itself "an impartial organ for every Jewish concern." Unlike the scholarly periodicals that had been founded earlier by Zunz and Geiger, or that which Frankel was to establish shortly thereafter, its principal aim was not to further Jewish Wissenschaft but to create a lively awareness of contemporary Jewish history. Whereas it may otherwise have seemed that Judaism was in decay and dissolution, the AZJ created the sense of a new Jewish world that had emerged from the ghetto. Its editor was the inveterately optimistic Ludwig Philippson (1811–1889), a young preacher (later rabbi) in Magdeburg and a member of the moderate wing of the Reform movement. Although more liberal religiously than Frankel, he too was intent on preserving the unity of German Jewry and saw his newspaper as the most effective tool for achieving that end. A man of extraordinary energy, Philippson edited the AZJ for more than fifty years, and it continued after his death until 1922. In 1845 it reached 1,600 subscribers and was read by many more. It was the first widely disseminated Jewish newspaper.

The *Allgemeine Zeitung des Judenthums* focused its attention upon German Jewry, especially the struggle for complete emancipation in the various German states. It refuted the antisemites and praised the Christian and Jewish champions of equal rights. Regular news reports, some reprinted from the general press, others sent in by correspondents, informed readers about events of Jewish interest wherever Jews lived. They could take pride in reading of young Jews who had attained some notable achievement in the arts or sciences and share concern in cases of Jewish misfortune. The paper showed a persistent interest in the Jewish settlements in the Land of Israel and mounted fund drives to help get the

19   The rabbi and publicist Ludwig Philippson

new settlers established as artisans and farmers. When a ritual murder accusation was made against the Jews of Damascus in 1840, the AZJ urged a sense of solidarity with Jews far removed from the German cultural orbit. Thus it was able to appeal to readers for whom religion had ceased to be of great interest but who continued to be vitally concerned with Jewish rights in Germany and with the welfare of their coreligionists abroad. It also reached numerous Jewish readers in Eastern Europe who formed their image of German Judaism from its articles. Of course, Philippson devoted attention to "theology" as well as to "politics," and he was no more averse to taking a position on religious issues than on political ones. Practical reforms in various communities usually received favorable treatment. But contrary views also found room in his newspaper, as did advertisements for the works of Orthodox writers like Samson Raphael Hirsch. During the period of his editorship the AZJ did not become a party organ in the narrow sense. The stories and poetry that it contained (though not of the highest literary quality) also widened its appeal to women, who were thought to be the more interested in such matters. In short, despite its reformist orientation, the *Allgemeine Zeitung des Judenthums* was a centripetal force that gave German Jewry a sense of self-understanding and unity it had not earlier possessed.

Similar but less successful was *Der Orient*, which appeared from 1840 to 1852 and was edited by the orientalist and Leipzig University *Privatdozent* Julius Fürst (1805–1873). Like the AZJ, *Der Orient* claimed to be free of partisanship, though devoted to showing the progress of the Jewish spirit. But it wanted to be more serious and scholarly, the latter especially with its literary supplement, which contained articles of lasting significance. As its title indicated, it gave special attention to the Jews of the East, in keeping with its editor's own interests, and relatively less to the Jews of Germany. If *Der Orient* was too scholarly for some Jews, another new newspaper, with which Fürst was also associated, was designed to have broader and more popular appeal. First appearing in 1842 and called *Sabbath-Blatt*, it was sent out weekly so as to reach its subscribers in time for the Sabbath. Each four-page issue began with an interpretation of the weekly scriptural reading followed by articles and stories intended for popular education and entertainment. Reading the *Sabbath-Blatt*—or another of the Jewish newspapers that proliferated in these years—on the Sabbath became a way of marking that day with a Jewish act, whether or not one also attended synagogue.

Likewise reflecting the collective self-awareness of German Jewry was the publication of Jewish books in the German language. Some of them were printed sermons, others translations of classical Jewish philosophical works, popular histories and biographies, and abundant textbooks for children. Most important was the appearance of a series of new Jewish translations of the Hebrew Bible. Mendelssohn's German Pentateuch, printed in Hebrew characters, had been a device for teaching Jews the German language. It departed frequently from the literal text of the original in order to present more literary German formulations, freely leaving out some words and introducing others not in the text. The new translations had a different intent: they sought to render the Hebrew as literally as possible for readers who no longer had full access—or had no access at all—to the original, whose Bible was now the German Bible, and who required a Jewish text free of Christology. Joseph Johlson, a teacher at the Frankfurt Philanthropin, was the first to publish a Pentateuch translation of this kind in 1831. It was, he admitted, difficult to free himself of the Mendelssohnian renderings, which he had learned in his youth, but he was determined to produce a "precise and literal translation."[23]

In addition to numerous new German versions of various individual biblical books, the following years witness the appearance of four major Jewish translations into German of the entire Hebrew Bible: an inexpensive and widely circulated *Deutsche Volks- und Schul-Bibel für Israeliten* (German Folk and School Bible for Israelites) published with Hebrew text and commentary by the preacher of the Hamburg Temple, Gotthold Salomon (1837), a more scholarly and often reprinted translation edited by Zunz (1838), a multivolume text with commentary by the moderate Reformer Salomon Herxheimer (1841–1848), and a family Bible done almost single-handedly by Ludwig Philippson (1841–1849). Samson Raphael Hirsch's Pentateuch translation and commentary, which for religious reasons avoided biblical criticism, began to appear only in 1867, though an earlier Pentateuch under Orthodox auspices had already been published from 1847 to 1852. This extraordinary activity attests to the Bible's rapid displacement of the Talmud as the focal religious source for most German Jews. Its veneration united modernist and traditionalist Jew, as also Jew and Gentile.

By the end of the 1830s, however, much of German Jewish literary productivity had assumed a more partisan cast. Not only do the controversies of the following decade produce an outpouring of tracts and countertracts, but new periodicals appear that avow clear ideological positions. The very name of the monthly *Der Israelit des neunzehnten Jahrhunderts* (The

Israelite of the Nineteenth Century), which the radical Reform rabbi Mendel Hess began to publish in 1839, attests to its character as the organ of those Jews who sought to break sharply with the past. Its editor's purpose was to liberate Judaism from those elements that he regarded as bringing dishonor and standing in the way of religious progress.

In 1845 the opposite extreme was forcefully represented in the press for the first time with the appearance of *Der treue Zions-Wächter* (The Faithful Guardian of Zion), a weekly edited, with the support of Rabbi Jacob Ettlinger, by Samuel Enoch, who served as the director of a Jewish school in Altona. If Hess urged religious progress, Enoch argued resistance to it. Established in the wake of the first assembly of Reform rabbis, the posture of the new paper was explicitly defensive: the believers in the old ways had to oppose even the slightest changes lest they open the floodgates to radicalism; Judaism and religious progress, even the most measured, were antithetical. With the appearance of *Der treue Zions-Wächter* German Orthodoxy entered the public sphere as a religious party in Germany to confront the crystallizing parties favoring various degrees of religious reform. Through a Hebrew supplement the Orthodox were further able to disseminate halachic discourses, answers to questions on ritual matters, and religious poetry. In the fight against an increasingly active Reform movement, Orthodoxy of the old type emerged from passivity and became a more clearly defined form of Jewish self-understanding.

Division within the communities manifested itself also in the criteria set for religious leadership. Should the rabbi of a community be, above all, pious and able to swim in the "sea of the Talmud" or was it more important that he be a modern scholar and man of his age? Often Jewish communities demanded that rabbinical candidates somehow fit both descriptions. When the lay leaders in Krefeld sought a new rabbi in 1844, they were looking for a "competent talmudist" who could justify moderate religious improvements by reference to rabbinic law. But "no less must he be versed in modern scholarship as well as fully able to manage our internal affairs vigorously and represent us worthily to the outside world.[24] Their rabbi was also expected to possess an imposing appearance and the talents of a popular preacher.

By the 1840s there were indeed men in Germany who combined knowledge of classical Jewish sources with a university education. Gradually they displaced the rabbis of the old type, who lacked formal secular study. Some German states either insisted upon or encouraged the appointment only of rabbis who had attended a university. In Bohemia philosophical study had been a requirement since 1797, though it had proven mostly unenforceable for lack of suitable candidates. In Prussia, where rabbis enjoyed no official recognition, the acquisition of the doctorate from a German university served as a substitute for the state certification that was granted only to Christian clergy.

The early religious reformers had found few rabbis who supported their cause and at first believed that the rabbinate was an institution doomed to irrelevance. The lay "preacher," through his sermons, became the religious authority for those attending the modernized services in Berlin and at the Hamburg Temple. In the succeeding decades, however, young men with a talmudic education, gained in childhood, began to study at universities with the intention of becoming "theologians." They were prepared to take on both the new functions of preacher and pastor and the remaining specifically rabbinical duties of rendering decisions in matters of ritual and personal status, such as divorce. Thus, by the 1830s, the rabbinate was no longer an institution associated exclusively with old Orthodoxy and with resistance to all change. It had entered the process of modernization. The university-educated rabbis, ranging in viewpoint from radical Reformers to neo-Orthodox, regained the respect of modernizing Jews for an institution some of them had earlier wanted to inter.

This university-trained rabbinate, though still a minority among the Orthodox at mid-century, became a distinguishing characteristic of German Jewry. The title of doctor before his name gained increasing currency among German rabbis even as it remained rare or nonexistent elsewhere in Europe. Neither to the east, in Russia and Poland, nor to the west, in France, did an equivalently educated rabbinate emerge, mainly because the German example of a Christian clergy with a higher secular education was lacking. By the late 1840s several dozen rabbis and Jewish preachers possessed the doctorate. Others had studied at universities without achieving the degree.

Preponderantly, secularly educated rabbis were advocates of religious reform, which to varying degrees was then spreading even to smaller towns in Germany. Most German states, especially in the southwest, favored the appointment of rabbis bent on making reforms and supported their efforts. However, Prussia, during the 1830s, continued to look askance upon men who favored religious innovations, even those as uncontroversial among most Jews themselves as the delivery of a German sermon. In Bavaria policy shifted rapidly with the coming to power of an ultramontane government in 1838. It now limited the appointment of new rabbis only to Orthodox men, "not to candidates who subscribe to a pernicious neology," and prohibited the attendance of Bavarian rabbis at the reform-minded rabbinical assemblies of the 1840s. Those rabbis favorable to religious reform left Bavaria for communities elsewhere.

In some communities, Brunswick for example, the transition from a premodern to a modern rabbi went smoothly and without controversy, in others it brought into the open divisions that had been quietly developing. At the end of the 1830s the Jewish community of Breslau became the arena for a bitter and protracted dispute between the old rabbinate and the new that revealed both the extent of religious change German Jewry had already undergone and its direction for the future.

In April of 1838 the lay leadership of the Breslau Jewish community, with its more than 5,000 Jews, advertised on the front page of the *Allgemeine Zeitung des Judenthums* for an assistant rabbi who possessed all the requisite qualifications of a modernist. The advertisement was evidence of the coming to power of a lay leadership in the community that favored reforms as well as a presumed new attitude on the part of the Prussian government that would allow them. The leading candidate applying for the position was Abraham Geiger, whose writings had already marked him as the most learned and forceful spokesman for religious change. Activist as much as scholar, he yearned for the opportunity to expound his ideas within a major Jewish community. The chief rabbi of Breslau at the time was Solomon Tiktin (1791–1843), a typical representative of the earlier style of rabbinate and a sworn opponent of religious reform. Together with his supporters in the community, he strenuously opposed Geiger's election, and when he was chosen by a vast majority of the electors, the Orthodox attempted, without effect, to discredit him before the Prussian government. Even the compromise effort to allow Geiger to assume the title of preacher and not rabbi failed when Geiger refused to accept it. For the first time in Germany an avowed Reformer assumed a rabbinical position in one of the largest Jewish communities in Germany.

The Breslau controversy, which was not finally resolved for four years, focused the attention of German Jewry upon the progress of acculturation and its effect on the choice of religious leadership. Tiktin became symbolic of the old order that was passing, Geiger of the new. The younger rabbi's sermons filled the largest community synagogue each Sabbath, which in recent years had happened only on holidays, while Tiktin's authority contracted to an ever smaller circle. It became apparent that two such different rabbis could not serve together within a single religious framework.

The solution finally reached in Breslau was to allow each faction to be served exclusively by its own rabbi and worship commission while the community remained united for matters of general administration and social welfare. In succeeding years the Breslau model was copied in Berlin and in other larger communities. It gave evidence that neither Orthodoxy nor Reform could expect to impose itself on an entire community of any size. In a permanently pluralistic environment each would have to be satisfied to serve its own adherents and conduct its own ritual.

The events in Breslau were significant in another respect as well. In justifying Geiger's election to the Prussian authorities, the lay leadership had sought opinions from those German rabbis who were presumed to be affirmative of the legitimacy of Geiger's religious orientation. The seventeen respondents, mostly younger men with a doctorate and all serving German communities, agreed that Judaism had indeed developed in history, as Geiger argued, and that therefore the contemplation of further progress was entirely legitimate. Moreover, it was not a religious violation for a rabbi to apply modern historical scholarship to the beliefs and practices of Judaism; free inquiry did not conflict with the rabbinical office. The election of Geiger and the consensus among the respondents, despite some points of difference, demonstrated the extent of influence that had been gained by the Reform ideology.

In Hamburg, too, the Reform faction, now more clearly identified as the leading edge of an increasingly self-conscious movement, pressed forward. Although its members still had to pay full dues to the general community as well as into its own treasury, the Hamburg Temple Association had grown in size and local influence. In 1841 it sought permission to construct a new building that would have room for 800 worshippers instead of the current 250, with the intent of expanding its membership to less affluent members of the community. That aroused the virulent opposition of the community rabbi, Isaac Bernays, for it meant that this new structure would lend greater scope and fresh visibility to a faction that he believed only legitimized religious indifferentism. But, as in Breslau, the climate within the Jewish community and outside of it was now more broadly favorable to religious reform than had earlier been the case. Bernays was unable to persuade the Hamburg Senate to prevent construction of the new temple and had to confine himself to warning faithful Jews against reading their prayers from its prayerbook.

However, in the meantime, the Reform movement had developed its own divisions, which now became evident. As religious radicalism gained ground in Christian circles, its counterpart appeared among German Jews. In the more liberal atmosphere of the 1840s dissident factions emerged at the edge of all three faith communities. The Protestant Friends (later, Friends of Light), formed in 1841, adopted a set of principles declaring it their right to subject all the elements of their faith to the scrutiny of reason. Three years later liberal Catholics established the German-Catholic movement, which turned against the Roman hierarchy, attempted to revert to the New Testament foundations of Christianity, and favored the use of German rather than Latin in the Mass. This ferment had a profound impact upon a thin layer of Jewish intellectuals then coming to maturity. Along with internal Jewish motives, it drew them together to organize their own religious societies in Frankfurt and Berlin.

The men who joined together as the Jewish Friends of Reform in Frankfurt in the fall of 1842 were, as far as can be determined, nearly all graduates of German universities recently embarked upon professional careers. Some were the sons of affluent and prominent Frankfurt Jewish families. They were all fully Germanized in culture and far removed from traditional Jewish belief and practice. As Jews, they suffered professional and personal discrimination, the more unfairly, they believed, as their Jewishness was so peripheral to their lives. Yet, mostly for family and social reasons, they remained attached to fellow Jews. What brought them together was not so much a desire to reaffirm their Jewish identity as to correct the mistaken impression in the non-Jewish world that they were not different from all other Jews. Their program repudiated rabbinic law and the belief in a Messiah who would return the Jews to their land. In noting that even the biblical faith was capable of "unlimited development," they removed every fixed element from Judaism, dissolving it entirely in the stream of history. The group was distinctly anticlerical, paralleling trends in Christianity. They complained of the rabbis, who were dragging their feet, compromising their consciences for the sake of preserving unity and historical continuity. Although its membership never exceeded forty-five, the group's ideas reverberated through the Jewish press. Not surprisingly, they met almost unanimous opposition, from Reform rabbis as well as from traditionalists.

In 1843 a major controversy erupted within the Frankfurt community over whether an uncircumcised male could be admitted to the Jewish community. Some fathers preferred to baptize their sons rather than subject them to the operation, others simply omitted it. The Friends of Reform favored the substitution of an initiation ceremony, equivalent for male and female infants, in place of circumcision, which they opposed not only for medical reasons but also because it set the Jewish male physically apart from the non-Jew. However, on this issue as well, the Frankfurt radicals found themselves with little support outside their own narrow ranks. Reform as well as Orthodox rabbis reaffirmed the legal and symbolic centrality of the rite in Judaism.

In Berlin, as in Frankfurt, the number of university-educated Jews had grown considerably. By 1844 it was estimated that more than seventy possessed a doctorate. Dissatisfied with the slow pace of Jewish religious reform in a city where few of them had family roots, a large portion of this group decided to band together independently and set forth their own program. The intellectual impetus for their Association for Reform in Judaism, established in 1845, came from Sigismund Stern (1812–1867), a teacher in a Berlin school for Jewish boys who had been greatly influenced by Hegelian philosophy. It was his belief that a reformed Judaism could enter the history of Europe, not separately, but as an active and integrated spiritual component, even as Jews became active and full participants in the political life of the Prussian state. As its opponents repeatedly pointed out, the broader impetus for the formation of the group was the German-Catholic movement, for which it represented a Jewish counterpart, a "German-Jewish church." Like the German-Catholics, the association believed that religious progress should be advanced through democratic synods and sought—though unsuccessfully—to create such a synod for all of German Jewry.

Like the Frankfurt Friends of Reform, the Berlin group repudiated ritual laws, but its leading members were less ambivalent about preserving Judaism. They spoke of "fragmentation," of the inner conflict produced by a transformed religious consciousness at odds with the inherited beliefs and prescribed rituals of rabbinic Judaism. "The petrified teaching and our lives have forever parted company."[25] They wanted an intellectually consistent and emotionally appealing religion that they could pass on to their children, who lacked the nostalgic memories of their own youth. With little concern for established practice, they proceeded to compile a prayerbook, guided mainly by what they believed to be their own religious needs. They held their first religious services, which attracted some six hundred worshipers, for the Jewish New Year in 1845. Not unexpectedly, these services were unprecedented in their departure from tradition. Most of the men did not cover their heads; women sat, separated from them, but on the same floor. Although the Torah was read in Hebrew, nearly all of the

20   Executive board of the Reform Congregation in
Berlin, 1855

prayers in the much abbreviated service were said in German paraphrases
of the originals, and an organ accompanied the choir, composed of both
men and women. The traditional sounding of the ram's horn, considered a
disruptive ritual laden with mystical associations, was not heard.

Although similar stirrings occurred for a time in Breslau, Königsberg,
and a few other cities, the Reform association did not achieve its larger
goals of initiating a countrywide movement for radical religious reform.
It did, however, persevere in Berlin as the "Reform congregation" of the
city and was able to persuade Samuel Holdheim to become its rabbi. The
weekly services, soon held exclusively on Sundays, and its independent
religious school served the needs of a modest number of families, and it
continued to exist into the Nazi period. Far more radical than the Hamburg Temple, it remained unique in German Jewry, most closely paralleled by the "Classical" Reform Judaism that developed a generation later
in the United States.

The emergence of a radical laity in Germany occurred at a time when
the Reform rabbinate was coming together to set forth its own more
moderate program. Upon the initiative of Ludwig Philippson, three rabbinical assemblies were held: in Brunswick (1844), Frankfurt am Main
(1845), and Breslau (1846). They were prompted by the example of similar conferences of Christian theologians and other professional groups,

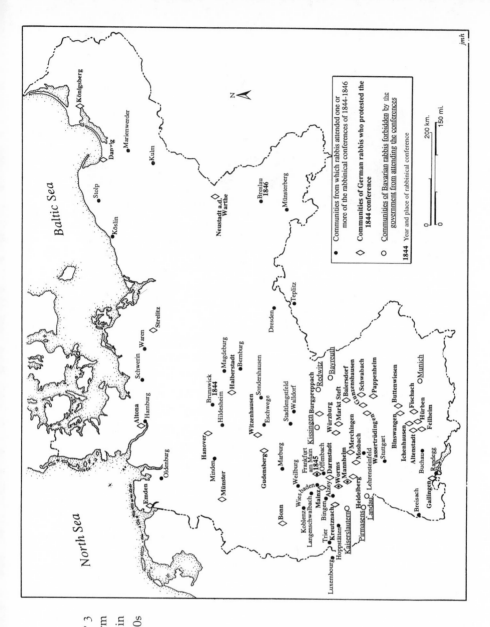

MAP 3

Religious Reform
and Its Opponents in
the 1840s

Legend:

- Communities from which rabbis attended one or
  more of the rabbinical conferences of 1844-1846

◇ Communities of German rabbis who protested the
  1844 conference

○ Communities of Bavarian rabbis forbidden by the
  government from attending the conferences

1844 Year and place of rabbinical conference

200 km.

150 mi.

North Sea

Baltic Sea

Königsberg
Dan'zig
Marienwerder
Kulm
Stolp
Köslin
Mariemberg
Breslau 1846
Münsterberg
Neustadt a.d. Warthe
Teplitz
Dresden
Strelitz
Waren
Schwerin
Hamburg
Altona
Oldenburg
Emden
Magdeburg
Bernburg
Halberstadt
Brunswick 1844
Hildesheim
Witzenhausen
Sondershausen
Eschwege
Hanover
Minden
Münster
Gudensberg
Marburg
Weilburg
Bonn
Koblenz
Langenschwalbach
Wiesbaden
Trier
Bingen
Kreutznach
Mainz
Alzey
Worms
Hoppstädten
Kaiserslautern
Luxembourg
Pirmasens
Landau
Lehrensteinfeld
Heidelberg
Mannheim
Merchingen
Mosbach
Wassertrüdingen
Breisach
Gailingen
Randegg
Buchau
Altenstadt
Ichenhausen
Binswangen
Fischbach
Hürben
Fellheim
Buttenwiesen
Stuttgart
Schwabach
Pappenheim
Gunzenhausen
Baiersdorf
Markt Steft
Würzburg
Redwitz
Bayreuth
Munich
Frankfurt am Main 1845
Offenbach
Darmstadt
Kissingen
Burgpreppach
Stadtlengsfeld
Walldorf

which were becoming more common at that time, by the desire to assert rabbinical authority over the laity, but mostly by a common wish to give status and sanction to an integrated program of religious reform.

The forty-two men who attended one or more of the assemblies were almost all representatives of the new rabbinate that had emerged in the preceding decade. They came from large and small communities: from Breslau, Frankfurt, and Hamburg, but also from Alzey in Hesse-Darmstadt, Randegg in Baden, and Weilburg in Nassau. The majority possessed a doctorate; their median age was about thirty-six. In religious views they ranged from radicals like Holdheim, through a more restrained faction that included Geiger and Leopold Stein, to distinct moderates like Frankel, who attended the second of the conferences. The deliberations were conducted according to parliamentary procedure and the discussions officially recorded, lending the assemblies the character of an official body.

On some matters, such as seeking abolition of the demeaning oath that Jews were still forced to swear when giving testimony in certain German states and the compatibility of Judaism with the obligations of citizenship, unity reigned among the participants. On other matters basic differences appeared. Two such issues deserve special attention. The one was the question of using Hebrew in the service, which was discussed at great length during the Frankfurt conference. The rabbis were agreed, on the one hand, that there was no halachic objection to prayers being said in any language and, on the other, that Hebrew should not be immediately abandoned. But they differed on whether it should be indefinitely preserved as an integral element of Jewish worship. After a narrow majority decided that its preservation was only subjectively and perhaps not permanently necessary, Frankel left the assembly and thereafter separated himself from his less conservative colleagues. His more organic and historical view of Judaism was incompatible with the notion of Hebrew as only the vehicle for a content that could be conveyed in whatever tongue the worshiper felt most at home.

The second issue, the Sabbath, stood at the center of the deliberations in Breslau. Here it was the radical Holdheim who found himself in almost complete isolation. He argued that the Sabbath could properly be sanctified only on a day when it was possible for Jews to rest. Since their occupations required many Jews to work on Saturday, there was no choice but to take the radical step of observing the Jewish Sabbath on Sunday. However, if most of his colleagues could conceive of prayer with a minimum of Hebrew, they could not imagine a Jewish religious day of rest removed from its traditional position on the Jewish calendar. As a consequence, Holdheim did not even ask for a vote. Like Frankel, he was forced to find support for his position outside the circle of his assembled rabbinical colleagues.

In their other discussions the assemblies addressed both ideological and practical issues. They reaffirmed the centrality of the messianic idea in Judaism, but as a strictly universal conception, dissociated from return to the Land of Israel, they spoke in favor of the Jews' religious mission among the nations, and they allowed Jews in government service to work on the Sabbath. In a series of votes on liturgical issues they lent support to practical reforms—such as the introduction of an organ and the alteration of prayers for the restoration of the sacrificial cult—that were not yet instituted in most communities. Although the matter did not come to a vote, for "lack of time," the third assembly also heard a committee report that argued for the religious equality of Jewish women as worshipers in the synagogue, making prayer obligatory for them no less than for men and counting them in the minyan, the prayer quorum of ten.

The effect of the three assemblies was mixed. On the one hand, they gave clear evidence of a new rabbinate favorable to some degree of religious reform, which could conduct its affairs earnestly and with dignity before the public. They also succeeded in raising religious issues to renewed prominence within German Jewry. In the decades following the assemblies many of their proposals were in fact instituted piecemeal in various communities. However, they failed to establish a permanent institution, they distanced the left and right wings, and—obviously without intent—they stirred new life among the Orthodox. The latter circulated a protest, eventually signed by 116 mostly German and Hungarian rabbis, giving indication of the continuing strength of the traditional leadership. Samson Raphael Hirsch declared that by their words and actions the assembled rabbis had shown that they no longer considered themselves Jews. The chief rabbi of Prague, Solomon Judah Rapoport (1790–1867), who had earlier proven himself a master of modern historical scholarship, wrote that the institution lacked legitimacy since, according to Jewish law, no contemporary rabbis could contradict decisions made by earlier— and hence more authoritative—rabbinical bodies. Not only did *Der treue Zions-Wächter* now marshal the Orthodox forces against Reform, but in various communities the Orthodox showed new initiative by establishing some forty reading circles for the study of rabbinic texts and other traditional literature. The assemblies might have had a more profound effect and continued beyond 1846, however, were it not that religious interest in Germany among Jews and Gentiles gave way rapidly to absorption with political events. And the years of reaction, which followed the abortive revolution of 1848, were not conducive to united activity on behalf of religious liberalism.

By the end of the 1840s, then, German Jews were permanently divided with regard to their spiritual and religious self-understanding. They had sought to understand their history; they had set forth and debated a variety of ideological positions along with their practical ramifications. The fundamental points of agreement and those on which there were unbridgeable differences had been determined. Clearly distinguishable as a whole from Jews elsewhere, German Jewry possessed its own religious spectrum that reflected its composite character.

5 | Judaism and Christianity

As long as Jews and Christians in Germany lived entirely within their own milieus, each studying their own literature, speaking their own language, and sharing their own particular hopes, the Jewish and Christian religions were integral elements within encompassing spheres that included not only religion but the full range of cultural and intellectual life. However, among Christians the process of secularization in German thought, beginning in the seventeenth century, gradually removed culture from the sphere of religion, while among Jews the process of acculturation, beginning a century later, progressively narrowed explicit affirmations of Jewish distinction to religion alone. As Jews increasingly desired to become Germans, and as being German—at least in enlightened circles—became possible without being Christian, Jews and Christians alike came to believe that in the future Jews would share in the common culture and differ from Christians in their religion alone. The Jewish faith thus took on a new centrality as the only remaining explicitly Jewish identity. If acculturating Jews ceased to be committed to Judaism as a religion, then no accepted justification remained to keep them apart.

As Jews increasingly identified with their cultural milieu, it became especially important for them that the most prominent German thinkers should value Judaism positively with regard both to its role in history and its viability in the modern world. Yet in nineteenth-century Germany that did not occur. In various ways, but with remarkable consistency, modern Christian thinkers and scholars in Germany—like their medieval forebears and like their counterparts elsewhere in Europe—deprecated historical Judaism and declared that its contemporary manifestations had no significant future. For their part, German Jews responded to this religious environment in various ways. A small number, who accepted the superiority of Christianity, became Christians, including a few for whom the new faith became central to their life's work. Jewish religious reformers, for a time, looked to Christianity for guidance in their work, but then became more critical. Among the intellectual elite there emerged a polemical stance toward Christianity that found expression in religious philosophy, historical writing, and practical efforts to deter apostasy. Endeavors to bring Jews and Christians together as equals encountered severe opposition. Successes were few and of limited consequence.

1. Christianity Against Judaism

During the entire course of modern German-Jewish history the friendship between Gotthold Ephraim Lessing and Moses Mendelssohn served as a paradigm for the ideal relationship between Christian and Jew. Yet, from the first, Lessing's regard for Mendelssohn had been based on human qualities which, to his pleasant surprise, he found could exist even among Jews. Lessing, the most tolerant of the German enlighteners, did not attribute Mendelssohn's virtues to his religious faith. Like the medievals before him, he held that Christianity had superseded Judaism. It was, he believed, a more advanced stage than its predecessor in the religious education of humanity. In various forms the greatest German thinkers and scholars who followed Lessing expounded similar ideas, forcing Jewish writers of the nineteenth century to assume a polemical stance vis-à-vis Christianity.

Johann Gottfried Herder's understanding of Judaism resembled that of Lessing but was more extreme both positively and negatively. Like Lessing, he recognized that the ancient Hebrews played a significant role in the religious and moral progress of the human race. It was the law of Moses that enabled a horde of nomads to become a cultivated nation; the religious poetry contained in the Hebrew Bible, to which Herder devoted much sympathetic attention, was to his mind an unparalleled achievement. However, not only did Christianity represent a higher form of religion, Pharisaic Judaism marked a distinct religious decline. The Jewish people, Herder believed, failed to live up to its promise: "In short, it is a people that was corrupted in the process of its education because it never attained the maturity of a political culture on its own soil and therefore also not a true feeling of honor and freedom." Unable to establish a durable state of its own, the one-time people of God became a "parasitic plant upon the trunks of other nations."[1] The exile of the Jews was the consequence of their own spiritual failure. Their history, once sacred, became entirely secular.

Belief in the spiritual decay of the Jewish people did not necessarily entail opposition to Jewish emancipation. Herder was a vigorous opponent of laws that discriminated against Jews, as was Wilhelm von Humboldt. But Humboldt, too, regarded Judaism as only the remnant of an ancient yet long moribund faith that modern Jews would soon leave behind. He became the champion of Jewish equality in the expectation that emancipation would assure its demise. His assumption was that only exclusion had made the Jews cling to empty ceremonies that set them apart. Given political and social integration, religious separation would be unable to persist. As a man of the Enlightenment, Humboldt did not expect Jews to accept Christian dogma, but he did expect them to adopt Christianity as the religion most reconcilable with humanist culture.

Like Humboldt, Immanuel Kant associated Judaism with external acts devoid of true religious content. He readily adopted the definition of Judaism, first propagated by Paul in the New Testament and later echoed by Spinoza and Mendelssohn, that made Judaism distinctive as a religion of statutory laws. But Kant went further in completely denying that the law could have religious value. In his eyes Judaism was not a proper religion at all since it demanded obedience rather than independent moral judgment. Moreover, as a universalist, Kant was appreciative of historical religions only insofar as they served as vehicles for a universal rational faith. Judaism, with the particularism of its ceremonies, was inherently incapable of rising to the level of the universal religion. Christianity, on the other hand, did have that capacity. New seeds of the true religious faith, beginning to sprout among Christians, would make possible the development of a church that visibly represented the invisible kingdom of God on earth. But Judaism was inherently incapable of sharing in that future church. It had come into existence as the constitution of a political state, which it managed to outlive only through political faith in its messianic reestablishment. The God of the Jews was an autocrat, not the source of morality; their narrow belief that they were the chosen people necessarily evoked enmity. Even more sharply than Lessing or Herder, Kant differentiated Christianity from Judaism: "We can begin the general history of religion, insofar as it is to be systematic, only with the origins of Christianity which, in fully abandoning the Judaism from which it emerged, was founded upon an entirely new principle and brought about a complete revolution in doctrine."[2] Kant did believe that, like enlightened Catholics and Protestants, enlightened Jews could be regarded as "brothers in faith," but only if they would cast off "the garment of the old religious practice, which has lost its purpose and serves rather to inhibit all true religious sentiment."[3] If Jews would accept a purely moral religion, like the religion of Jesus, they could be part of the universal church, but, in terms of religion, they would then no longer be Jews.

In associating his radical religious views as closely as possible with Christianity, Kant had to stress its rational and universal elements, and he could do so the more readily by contrasting them with Judaism. However, by the end of the eighteenth century, Christianity in Germany was beginning to undergo a romantic revival, which returned it to its own historical traditions and declared the purely moral religion of Kant religiously inadequate. Friedrich Schleiermacher was the foremost representative of this trend. Unlike Lessing (and later Hegel), Schleiermacher did not envisage a single continuous history of religion that led from Judaism to Christianity to a universal philosophical religion with Christian symbolism. It was entirely wrong to view Christianity as "a modification or a renewal and continuation of Judaism."[4] In his view the two religions did not share the same "genus"; each had its own revelation and its own history. Nor were they on the same religious level: Christianity represented a higher form of monotheism than either Judaism or Islam. Schleiermacher believed that Judaism was "almost at the point of extinction" and he encouraged Jewish friends, like Henriette Herz, to convert. Such conversion, however, could not mean for Schleiermacher, as for Humboldt or Kant, the mere acceptance of Christianity as the religious element in European culture or adoption of the religion of Jesus. It meant, according to ancient belief, to become a "new person." Mendelssohn had shared the common ground of natural religion with his Christian friends. Schleiermacher removed that ground between Jews and Christians by restoring the difference in essence between the two religions, erecting anew barriers the Jewish enlighteners had consigned to the past.

Hegel differed in not sharing Schleiermacher's desire to separate Christianity from the more encompassing history of religion. The tendency of his thought went in the opposite direction. Christianity, and with it Judaism, became once again stages in the development of religion, as they were for Lessing and Herder, except that now religion was encompassed within the larger category of Spirit. In his early writings Hegel displayed a marked animus toward ancient Israel, which he characterized as passive and morally ugly. Following Kant, he declared that the spirit of Judaism failed to achieve freedom: "Spirit had nothing left but the stiff-necked pride in this obedience of slaves to laws not of their own making."[5] In his mature thought, however, Hegel integrated ancient Judaism into the dialectical process of spiritual development, ascribing to it a positive and necessary role. It was a "spiritual thrust" opposed to paganism, which for the first time clearly separated spirit from nature. That, in turn, made possible both morality and history. But whereas Judaism fully recognized God's "sublimity," it failed to acknowledge the divine presence within the human being and hence remained one-sided and subservient to an external God. Only the Christian religion, with its doctrine of the incarnation, was able to comprehend God as pure spirit. It satisfied all spiritual aspirations and was therefore the "absolute religion." Yet, unlike most of his contemporaries, Hegel did recognize the continuing influence of Judaism, since spirit always retained within it those gradations it seemed to have left behind. For Hegel, then, the contribution of Judaism to spiritual development was positive and it was retained within the World Spirit, but it had long been fully absorbed. The survival of Judaism as a separate religion into the present was simply anachronistic.

Like Hegel, radical Left Hegelians posited an essence of Judaism that did not change, and therefore they denied that Judaism itself could have a history. They differed from their master in that they emptied that essence of any moral value. Ludwig Feuerbach (like Karl Marx after him) declared both ancient and modern Judaism "the religion of petty egoism."[6] Bruno Bauer called the distinguishing characteristic of Judaism "exclusivity" and thereby explained the Jews' ongoing conceit and arrogance.

Hegel's conception of Judaism also directly influenced scholars who dealt in greater detail with its history. Similarly to Hegel, the historian Heinrich Leo, in lectures that he gave four times at the University of Berlin during the 1820s, declared "abstract monotheism" to be the chief characteristic of the Jewish religion. However Leo, whose dislike of Jews was undisguised, went beyond Hegel in determining that their religious faith was closely linked to their qualities of character, namely, their "truly corrosive and disintegrative intellect," which still manifested itself in their contemporary business activities. Even more extreme were the views of F. W. Ghillany, professor and city librarian in Nuremberg. In a book of nearly eight hundred pages, *Die Menschenopfer der alten He-bräer* (The Human Sacrifices of the Ancient Hebrews), he lent credibility to the blood accusation made against the Jews of Damascus in 1840 by arguing that ritual murder was simply a remnant of the human sacrifices that Ghillany believed had been practiced regularly in ancient Israel. The customs associated with circumcision were likewise a survival of the same ancient rite in which Israelites ate the flesh and drank the blood of their sacrificial victims.

If German Jews could discount Leo's and Ghillany's denigration of their heritage as the ramblings of their enemies, they could less easily dispose of the more benign Hegelian view that the Jewish contribution to Western culture had long ago been fully absorbed. When the volume of the Ersch and Gruber *Allgemeine Encyklopädie der Wissenschaften und Künste* (General Encyclopedia of the Sciences and Arts) that was devoted to Jews, Judaism, and Jewish literature appeared in 1850, the article on Judaism concluded that contemporary Jews were caught in a sad dilemma: to cling to letters robbed of spirit or to accept the prospect of a certain dissolution of their religion. The author, the noted Protestant Bible scholar Eduard Reuss, did offer a consolation in noting that Judaism "has in fact entirely fulfilled its vocation for humanity and bestowed upon it a benefaction that appears the greater since it cannot be lost in the future."[7] Reading Reuss's essay, Jews could take pride in their historical achievement, but they were left with no religious reason for continuing to live as Jews.

Regardless of whether they believed Christianity to be radically different from Judaism or to be dialectically related to it, Christian thinkers in Germany invariably held that Judaism possessed no creative potential in the present and future. The noted Göttingen biblical scholar Heinrich Ewald, for all of his appreciation of the Hebrew genius, repeated the old dogma that with the sprouting of Christianity the Jewish trunk on which it had grown "withered forever."[8] Commonly, Christian writers called Judaism an "antiquated religion" and denied that it was capable of modernization. Therefore they regarded religious reform among Jews as nothing more than the gradual abandonment of Judaism. Those who favored it, like the enlightened Berlin educator and orientalist J. J. Bellermann, thought that reform would lead toward acceptance of Christianity; those who were ambivalent about it, like the Prussian government councilor Karl Streckfuss, believed that it approached a dangerous Deism or sectarianism. But none legitimated it as a genuine revival within Judaism itself.

Orthodox Judaism, they held, was authentic, but it was incapable of development; Liberal Judaism was no longer Judaism. Only Christianity, and
especially Protestantism, was capable of religious progress. Judaism would
always have its place in history, Streckfuss believed, but it was prideful of
Jews to insist that it continue to be an influence not only in their own lives
but in the religious life of Europe.

In the debate over Jewish emancipation, the Christian judgment of the
Jewish religion played a large role. The Heidelberg rationalist theologian
H. E. G. Paulus believed that as long as Jews did not abandon the talmud-
ism and "good-for-nothing ritual practice" that was propagated by traditional rabbis and underlay their ethnic separation, they could hope only
to be subjects but not citizens. Similarly, Streckfuss held the Jews incapable of emancipation as long as they observed their ritual laws. Were not
those Jews most likely to engage in questionable business practices to be
found among the most observant? Yet, at the same time, Christians mistrusted all Jews who had ceased to be Orthodox. If they were not loyal to
their own faith, could they be expected to be loyal to the state?

Christian writers, like Streckfuss and the Stuttgart orientalist August
Gfrörer, who both claimed to be friendly to the Jews, were convinced that
only oppression had kept Judaism alive and that it could not maintain
itself in a more hospitable environment. The decay of Judaism would necessarily parallel the gradual emancipation of the Jews. Yet only when its
ruin was complete and Judaism had ceased to exist could Jews be fully
absorbed into the state. Streckfuss and others of similar views were not
willing to allow that Jews remain religiously distinct after complete
emancipation. Jews could not simultaneously demand political unification
and still insist, as well, on religious separation. The same views were
expressed vigorously in Protestant popular writings, which invariably
made conversion to Christianity a prerequisite for complete equality.

In their desire to bring Judaism closer to Christianity, Streckfuss, as
well as the Bavarian government official and theologian J. B. Graser, did
argue that the Jews be allowed to establish professorships for Jewish theology at German universities. But their views in this regard were exceptional. For the most part, individuals and governments took a dim view
of allowing Judaism to be represented in higher institutions of learning.
The efforts of Ludwig Philippson and Abraham Geiger to gain permission for a Jewish theological faculty and the repeated petitions by Leopold
Zunz to the Prussian government for a professorship of Jewish studies at
the University of Berlin were without success. Even during the liberal

tide of the year 1848 Zunz's request was refused. The university informed him that because such a position would strengthen Judaism in its particularity it would mean giving a "special privilege to the Jews, a misuse of the university."[9]

University instruction in the Hebrew Bible and postbiblical Judaism was thus left in the hands of Christian scholars, of whom the most prominent by the middle of the nineteenth century was Franz Delitzsch. In addition to his widely acknowledged expertise as a leading biblical exegete, Delitzsch possessed a knowledge of Talmud and Midrash unparalleled by any other German Christian of his day. He worked in close conjunction with Jewish scholars, who greatly admired his work and valued him as a friend. Delitzsch published important works on Hebrew poetry and contributed numerous scholarly articles on postbiblical Hebrew literature to Julius Fürst's *Der Orient*. Toward the end of his long life, he vigorously defended Judaism against the accusations of antisemites and thereby gained the immense gratitude of the Jewish community. Yet Delitzsch's interest in the Jewish religion, as he readily admitted, had an ulterior motive from the very first: he hoped that his knowledge of Judaism would enable him to win Jewish souls for Christianity. Early in his career he had dissociated himself from all efforts to hinder or delay Jewish emancipation; like the young Luther, he believed that Christians' loveless treatment of the Jews was a blot upon their faith. But already in 1838 he put the Jews on notice: "I have begun to learn your languages and scrutinize your literatures for no other purpose and from no other motive than to preach to you the gospel of the crucified Christ."[10] At various times he played an active role in missionary societies in Saxony and Bavaria and later published the missionary periodical *Saat auf Hoffnung* (Hopeful Sowing). Letters that he wrote to Jews bore a red seal with the inscription in Hebrew: "See, your Redeemer has come!"[11] Delitzsch was especially proud of his translation of the New Testament into Hebrew, which he had undertaken for the benefit of Eastern European Jews. And, indeed, he was successful in leading some Jews to baptism.

Christian missionary activity among Jews in Germany, never entirely absent, had gained fresh impetus during the religious revival that followed the defeat of Napoleon. In 1818 the London Society for Promoting Christianity Among the Jews published a new edition of the Boston historian Hannah Adams's history of the Jews. The following year it began to appear in a German translation, becoming the first history of the Jews in the German language to extend down to the present. The society's edition made even more explicit Adams's own missionary intent. It concluded by calling upon its readers to support the missionary enterprise and "to pray often and fervently for the promised conversion of the Jews."[12] In 1822 the London Society became more active in Germany by establishing a branch in Berlin with the express approval of the Prussian monarch. Its first president was the war minister von Witzleben, who was followed in office by other Prussian generals. Among its founders and officers was August Tholuck, the Pietist theologian who, for a time, taught at the Berlin University. Tholuck delivered lectures at the university on rabbinic and oriental literature. He also held weekly discussions on missionary activities with Christian students and persuaded a few of his Jewish students to convert. Missionary societies were founded, as well, in other German cities during the third decade of the century, mostly under the influence of the London Society. Some lasted only a short time; others continued for decades.

It was not unusual for prominent personalities—in government, in the church, and in the universities—to lend their support to these societies. The Prussian monarchs provided the Berlin society with an annual personal contribution as well as free postage. Frederick William III himself, for a time, served as godfather at Jewish baptisms and gave the new converts a royal gift. When Tholuck left for Halle in 1825, his place in the society was taken by Ernst Wilhelm Hengstenberg, the most prominent theologian of the new Protestant Orthodoxy and editor of the influential *Evangelische Kirchenzeitung,* where reports appeared on the society's work. Beginning in 1827 regular Sunday sermons intended for prospective converts were given in one of the churches in Berlin.

For their part, Jews did not engage in missionary activities on behalf of Judaism. Not only did they argue that their religion was not a missionary faith, but it is almost certain that they would not have been granted permission for such activity by any German state. Until 1848 Prussian policy wavered between outright prohibition of conversion to Judaism and depriving converts of their political rights. In this period only a handful of Christians converted to Judaism, mostly in cases of prospective marriage.

The mission to the Jews in Germany was only modestly successful. Liberals opposed it; most Christians showed little interest. A large proportion of converts chose baptism strictly for mercenary reasons and some later returned to Judaism. Their questionable motives created a dilemma for Christians: whether to admit that Jews could be fully German without conversion or to encourage their baptism, even for the wrong reasons, in the hope that they—or at least their children—would fully accept their new faith. The number of converts attributable directly to missionary activity remained small—little more than a dozen per year—largely from the proletariat or the intelligentsia, few coming from the middle class. Most Jews who had determined to convert chose to do so in as inconspicuous a manner as possible and not under the auspices of the missionary societies. Some, who might have been candidates for conversion because they had ceased to believe fully in Judaism, turned to a religiously reformed Judaism as an alternative to conversion. Indeed, the missionaries vigorously attacked the Reform movement both because it provided its own alternative to Jewish Orthodoxy and because Liberal Jews, even if they converted, were less likely to accept the Christian Orthodoxy they propagated. However, the Berlin Society for Promoting Christianity Among the Jews could soon claim that it had achieved some success not only with poor Jews looking for financial reward but also with Jewish physicians, painters, musicians, jurists, and mathematicians. Some of their converts, in turn, became missionaries themselves. The presence of the missionary societies in Germany and their support by prominent personalities once again communicated to the Jews that Christians still regarded Judaism as a lesser religion than Christianity, a view that, as we have seen, was reinforced on the highest intellectual levels by philosophers, theologians, and historians. Although the vast majority of German Jews resisted the pressure to convert, for those no longer secure in their own faith the temptation was very great.

2. Jews as Christians

It is not possible to generalize about those German Jews who chose to leave Judaism for Christianity. They came from different strata of the Jewish population, though mostly from the cities. Some grew up in Orthodox homes, others in enlightened ones. Their motivations differed greatly, ranging from sheer cynicism to genuine conviction. After conversion some retained close ties with fellow Jews, others tried to make a clean break with the Jewish environment in which they were raised. A few became prominent as leading representatives of their new faith. It is estimated that in Prussia alone about five thousand Jews converted to Christianity between 1800 and 1848, a large majority of them in Berlin.

By mid-century the rate had begun to decline as hopes for complete acceptance brightened.

The discrimination that Jews continued to suffer in Germany was without doubt the principal factor motivating most of the conversions. The Jews' efforts at acculturation had made them feel German. But such efforts did not persuade non-Jews that they were now qualified not merely to participate in German society but to join the ranks of its political and intellectual elite. Jews who desired state offices or teaching positions had no choice but to convert to Christianity. Similarly, if they wished to influence German culture through their writings or to enter the formal and informal social circles of all but the most enlightened Christians conversion was the prerequisite. It was not unusual for parents to baptize their children so that they might enjoy the benefits of joining the majority, while themselves remaining Jewish or converting only at a later time. Some Jews rationalized their conversions in the language of philosophy or religion in order to provide themselves and their acquaintances with a lofty justification for an act of clear self-interest. But for others, even where personal advantage played some role in their conversion, genuine ideal considerations seem also to have been present.

In the spirit of the Enlightenment Moses Mendelssohn had argued that Judaism was an entirely rational religion with no supernatural dogmas that set it apart. It was distinguished only by its ritual laws. In the following generations some Jews who had given up observance of the law came to believe they were thereby also abandoning Judaism. Along with Christian writers on Judaism, they viewed their community as a decaying remnant that had lost its vitality. Kant's conception of a universal moral religion, which they could believe represented a future beyond both Judaism and dogmatic Christianity, was especially attractive. Some accepted Humboldt's contention that Christianity was inextricable from European civilization and that, therefore, in order to become fully European, the Jews would have to accept the Christian heritage as their own. To adopt Christianity as an integral element of a culture they had already acquired created less of a rupture in their lives than had conversion to Christianity in earlier times. The Catholic theologian Ignaz Döllinger believed that as Jews became German in thought and manner they necessarily also began to think and act as Christians.

The motivation for such a conversion was poignantly expressed in a famous letter that Abraham Mendelssohn, Moses Mendelssohn's second son and the father of the composer Felix, wrote in 1820 to his daughter

Fanny upon her confirmation in the Lutheran church. Abraham confessed that he had doubts about human immortality and even about God's existence. But he did sense the "inclination to all that was good, true, and just," to be found in all human beings, and following that inclination was his religion. The historical form of that moral faith was inessential to it and hence subject to change: "Several thousand years ago the Jewish form reigned, then came the pagan, now it is the Christian."[13] He and his wife had raised their daughter as a Christian because it was "the form of belief shared by most cultured people." For Abraham (who himself became a Christian shortly thereafter), and no doubt for many others like him, conversion was not the adoption of a new faith but only the exchange of older, outdated vessels for those employed by the dominant majority to contain the same moral and cultural values.

Although some Jewish parents baptized their children, others were deeply grieved when their offspring took a step that they could not condone. Children therefore sometimes waited until their father and mother had died before formally entering the church. Joseph Arnstein, a son of the prominent Jewish court factor family of Vienna, pleaded with his parents to accept his step and give him their blessing, but apparently in vain. Simon Veit, for a time the husband of Moses Mendelssohn's daughter, Dorothea, was more accepting of his two sons' conversion. In this instance the plea for tolerance came from the side of the parent. To his son Philipp he wrote:

> So, my dear son, as long as we differ only in religion but are at one in our moral principles, no separation will ever occur between us. Only do not believe, when you have gone over to another religion, that the millions of people who have different religious principles are poor sinners and hated by God or that they can have no share in eternal salvation.[14]

Conversion to Christianity was especially common among Jewish women who were attracted to the Romantic movement. Unlike the Jewish rationalists, they could not accept the universal moral faith of Kant as an adequate expression of their religious needs. Three of the most prominent among the Jewish women who hosted salons at the end of the eighteenth century all converted to Christianity out of religious conviction. Dorothea Mendelssohn at first became a Protestant, confessing to Schleiermacher that she believed Protestantism to be the religion of Jesus, the religion of culture, and thoroughly unlike Judaism, which she had come to abhor.

Later, along with her husband Friedrich Schlegel and other members of
the Romantic movement, she became a Catholic, fervent in her piety and
eager to win converts among her friends. The daughter of the *Aufklärung*
Jewish philosopher who had argued that salvation was possible for the
righteous of any faith community came to believe that there was no salvation outside the Catholic church. She pitied her relatives who had
remained Jewish and hence necessarily lacked true religious feeling.

Dorothea's friend, the much admired Henriette Herz, became the soul-
mate of Friedrich Schleiermacher. He was a regular guest in her house,
discussed his work with her, and won her over to his highly personal form
of Christianity long before she actually converted, upon the death of her
mother. For Henriette Herz Christianity alone offered what she required:
a "religion of the heart." Similarly, the most talented of the Jewish salon
hostesses, Rahel Varnhagen, eventually became a serious Christian. To be
sure, Rahel remained highly aware of her Jewish origins. Being a Jew, she
noted, meant to suffer. It meant the necessity of repeatedly trying to
legitimate oneself in a society that remained suspicious of outsiders. But
although as a romantic she believed that without such suffering there
could be no profound insight, the burden of Jewishness in time weighed
more heavily upon her than she could bear. As a religion Judaism had no
attraction whatever for Rahel. In its traditional form it seemed immature,
a faith of *Kindermenschen,* in its modern variation a barren rationalism
that could not speak to the individual soul. Long before her conversion
Rahel celebrated the Christian holidays and already considered herself
spiritually a Christian. After she became a Protestant she read deeply in
Christian religious literature and was especially drawn to the seven-
teenth-century mystic Angelus Silesius. Shortly before her death, Rahel
confessed to her husband, Varnhagen von Ense, that she had wept over
the passion of Jesus and the sufferings of his mother Mary. Her religious
identification as a Christian was complete.

None of these women turned to Christianity insincerely for the sake
of practical advantage, nor did they believe that their religion of origin
and religion of choice were fundamentally alike. In a highly personal,
even mystical Christianity they found the satisfying emotional elements
they believed were necessarily absent both in Judaism and in the religion
of the Enlightenment. Neither the traditional Judaism of law nor the rationalism of its early modernizers could attract them. Living as Christians, in their case, was not simply a concomitant of acculturation; it was
a necessity of their own religious experience.

21   The Berlin salonière Rahel Varnhagen

In the generation following the Jewish salons, similarly sincere Christians appear among prominent male converts, and a few of them even play significant, specifically Christian roles in church and society. Though Christians, these men continue to have a personal or ideological relationship to their community of origin that expresses itself sometimes on behalf of their one-time coreligionists, sometimes in opposition to their interests. One of the most prominent was Johann Emanuel Veith (1787–1876), who adopted clerical status and achieved fame as the preacher at St. Stephan's Cathedral in Vienna. Even as a Christian Veith apparently felt a moral obligation to his community of origin for, as Austrian Jews long remembered, at the time of the blood libel fomented against the Jews of Damascus he swore upon the pulpit, crucifix in hand, that the charge was patently false. Veith's brother not only remained

Jewish but was the secretary of the Vienna Jewish community. The case of Paulus (Selig) Cassel (1821–1892) is similar. Cassel too became a Christian preacher, though of the Evangelical Church. Like Veith—and like Delitzsch—he defended the Jews against their enemies, in his case, toward the end of his life, against the accusations of Heinrich von Treitschke and Adolf Stöcker. Cassel was highly knowledgeable in Judaism and wrote important works on Jewish history both before and after his conversion in 1855. He too had a brother (who broke off relations with him after his conversion), David Cassel (1818–1893), himself one of the most productive Judaica scholars of the nineteenth century.

A third convert from Judaism attained yet greater influence as a member of the Christian clergy. August Neander (1789–1850) had come under the direct influence of Schleiermacher, whose Romantic Christianity of religious experience became determinative for his own personal faith. With the assistance of his mentor, Neander became professor at the University of Berlin where he gained a reputation as the foremost church historian of his day. Like Veith, Neander too defended the Jews against the ritual murder accusation of 1840, but he also opposed allowing them to teach at the university when that subject was raised seven years later. As a Christian, he was—in keeping with his name—a "new man" who had left the religion of law for the religion of love. Like Schleiermacher, he held that Judaism and Christianity were irreconcilably opposed.

Among the Jewish converts who became serious Christians in Germany during the early nineteenth century, one stands out for his political significance. Friedrich Julius Stahl (1802–1861) was born Julius Jolson to an Orthodox Jewish family living near Würzburg. In 1819, at the age of seventeen, he converted to Lutheranism, the minority form of Christianity in Bavaria. A few years later the entire family followed his example. As a political thinker Stahl propounded the idea of the "Christian state," which served as a major theoretical bulwark against the increasingly impatient forces for democratization in Germany. After he succeeded the likewise converted Eduard Gans in his position as professor of law at the University of Berlin in 1840, Stahl achieved extraordinary influence as the champion of divinely sanctioned personal Absolutism in Prussia. His lectures in the largest auditorium of the university were attended by the elite of Prussian officialdom. In the years of political reaction after 1848, he was the acknowledged theoretician of the Conservative party. He sat in the Prussian Upper House and for more than a decade served as president of the German Evangelical Church Congress.

22 Friedrich Julius Stahl, advocate of the idea of the
Christian state in Prussia

That a baptized Jew could play so central a role in conservative thought
and institutions attests to the degree to which all strata in German society still regarded conversion as sufficient for the complete legitimation of
born Jews.

Stahl's Christian state necessarily excluded Jewish participation. In
order to maintain its specific religious character, it could tolerate neither
Jews nor Deistic sectarians in positions of leadership. Belief in the reve-

lation of the New Testament, Stahl held, was prerequisite to the exercise of political rights—though not of civil rights, which could be given equally to all inhabitants. Yet, despite his Christian fervor, Stahl did not denigrate the traditional Judaism of his own origins. He believed that, unlike its Reform variant, which had no solid principles, the original Judaism was a "genuine" though rapidly disappearing faith. If Stahl did not urge the prohibition of religious reform among Jews, it was only because he believed that any modernized Judaism could not long maintain itself and that its adherents would soon become Christians. It was the obligation of state and society to encourage that process. "Christendom must acknowledge the conversion of Jews and pagans as a high demand placed upon it by God," he wrote in 1847.[15] Thus Jews who remained loyal to Judaism of course saw Stahl as their enemy, a Christian whose political theory, in principle, excluded their hopes of gaining full equality. For Stahl the political status of the Jews was not a question of alleged Jewish faults or lack of sufficient acculturation. The nature of the state itself required exclusion of even the most assimilated Jews from its positions of authority. More Christian than most Christians, Stahl defended an ideology that withheld full emancipation from any Jew who did not follow his own example.

3. Judaism Against Christianity

The acculturation that German Jews sought to attain forced them to confront a difficult dilemma. On the one hand, they had read the important philosophical writers and were influenced by their views. Indeed, acculturation required entering the world of the great thinkers that dominated German intellectual life in the late eighteenth and early nineteenth centuries. To varying degrees Jewish intellectuals and religious leaders, both Reformers and Orthodox, became Kantians, Hegelians, or Schellingians. They also read Christian theology and gained a closer understanding of Christian religious practice. It was not possible, they recognized, for Judaism to survive in modernity if it remained oblivious to its intellectual and religious milieu. But, on the other hand, as we have seen, the great German philosophers and theologians as well as the historical writers on Judaism invariably placed the Jewish religion on a lower level than Christianity. They reiterated the traditional Christian view of supersession, simply clothing it in new philosophical or scholarly garb. It thus seemed that if acculturation meant adoption of the prevailing views concerning their own religion, and if religion had become the principal point of distinction between Jews and non-Jews, then the necessary conclusion could only be conversion to the superior faith. Likewise, in matters of religious praxis, if Christianity possessed a monopoly on forms appropriate to modern religious symbolism, then the synagogue would have to imitate the church more and more until it completely lost its distinctive character.

Thus German Jews responded to their intellectual and religious environment with great ambivalence. They wanted to live fully within the German cultural milieu, but that milieu continued to be imbued with Christian ideas and Christian symbols. This was the more true in the period following 1815, when historical Christianity enjoyed a revival in Germany and succeeded in dispelling the universalizing rationalism of the Aufklärung. In order both to become Germans and to remain Jews it was therefore necessary not only to adopt German culture but also to depart from it sharply where it touched upon the historical and contemporary role of the Jewish religion. Thus we find that the most important Jewish theologians in the first half of the nineteenth century invariably take issue with the major Christian thinkers on their conception of Judaism. Although they are clearly influenced by the concepts and terminology of contemporary German thought, the motivation and thrust of their work is a sharp polemical reassertion of Judaism against Christianity.

Three systematic Jewish thinkers in Germany produced important theological works during the years between 1835 and 1842. One of them was a physician, Salomon Ludwig Steinheim (1789–1866); two were Liberal rabbis, Salomon Formstecher (1808–1889) and Samuel Hirsch (1815–1889). Their abstruse and difficult major writings were not read by large numbers, but they did have a broader impact when they presented their ideas more briefly in popular works, sermons, and articles in Jewish newspapers. The writings of all three men attest to the need they felt to bring Judaism into contact with German philosophy and at the same time to detach it from the place that German philosophy and Christian theology had assigned it.

Of Steinheim, who grew up and spent most of his adult life in Altona, we know that he had himself once considered conversion, and it may be that, in personal terms, his theology was a grand effort to erect a theoretical barrier against such defection. Steinheim realized that Mendelssohn's interpretation of Judaism as distinctively law—which was also the Christian view—encouraged conversion on the part of those who no longer believed that law to be divine. His own conception of Judaism abandoned the legal distinction in favor of a doctrinal one: what formed Judaism was a revelation that did not consist of ritual commandments but of the self-revelation of a transcendent God who created the universe and granted human beings free will. This truth, which speculative reason could not have attained on its own, set Judaism once and for all sharply apart from its pagan surroundings and became its unchanging essence. Although the Jewish people's understanding of its faith progressed during the course of history, the revelation itself was perfect and complete from the first. Steinheim's severe limitation of the role of reason in religion—likewise a departure from Mendelssohn's view—discouraged apostasy since it removed the bridge whereby Jews could and did travel from Judaism to Christianity. Like Schleiermacher, Steinheim held that the two religions were different in principle and that they did not share a common religion of humanity.

In setting the revelation contained in the Hebrew Bible above history, Steinheim undermined the conception common to most Christian thinkers since Lessing that, both in content and form, ancient Judaism was simply an early historical manifestation in a larger history of the human spirit and that its preservation by the Jews was a mark of their religious backwardness. The revelation, according to Steinheim, is true for all time, for all who will accept it, and it is entirely independent of the cultural level of those to whom it was first revealed. Ancient Israel was not the source of its God concept; it was only its "trustee" or "bearer." In a sense Steinheim turned Kant upside down: Judaism remained the religion of moral freedom; Christian doctrines, which incorporated pagan elements, had compromised it. To remain a Jew was to accept Steinheim's own confidence that "sooner or later revelation, in its pure and unadulterated original form, will complete its victory over paganism, however much the latter may stiffen and resist."[16]

Like Steinheim, Salomon Formstecher also wrote a defense of Judaism intended to refute the claims of Christianity against it. Invariably, he noted, Christian philosophical and theological systems reflected their authors' emotional attachment to Christianity and their prejudice against Jews and Judaism. In response, Jews themselves needed to formulate a religious system that did full justice to their own religion, one that showed the Jew "that his religion had not yet died of old age and needed to be buried, but that it still possessed great vital energy."[17] Against

Christian writers Formstecher therefore set out to show that Judaism, without departing from its own essence, contained what non-Jews denied it: the capacity for progress toward the universal religion of civilized humanity. For some of his conceptions he was indebted to Schelling or Fichte, for example his differentiation between the religions of nature and spirit. But he departed sharply from all Christian writers in asserting that Judaism was the spirit's only pure and complete religious expression. Like Steinheim, Formstecher understood Christianity as an amalgam of paganism and Judaism, although he valued Protestantism as a protest of the Jewish element within Christianity against its pagan components and gave greater emphasis to its positive role—and that of Islam—as agents of Judaism in bringing the religion of spirit to the pagan world. Once that mission was complete, however, Christianity would cease to exist. Judaism, shorn of the few particular elements that for the present were still necessary to preserve it, would emerge in fully universal form as the absolute religion, adopted by all humanity.

The origins of Samuel Hirsch's theological work, by his own testimony, lay in a deeply felt injury: despite the German Jews' effort to acquire the culture of their age, despite the successful completion of their "years of apprenticeship," both church and state had extended no more than tolerance to their religion. Because they denied its religious value, they refused to grant it equal status with Christianity. Like Steinheim and Formstecher—except this time more in relation to Hegel and with a more radical theology—Hirsch therefore set forth his justification for Judaism's religious value and continuing universal relevance. From Hegel he adopted the idea that human history is the history of the idea of freedom. But Hirsch removes that idea from Hegel's dialectical scheme. Hegelian philosophy, with its notion borrowed from Christianity that virtue can emerge only in necessary opposition to sin, contradicts the freedom of individual human beings. It is therefore not biblical, but "nothing more and nothing less than the most sublimated paganism."[18] True freedom, which began with Abraham, must mean that humans neither necessarily sin nor are ever free from its temptations.

By arguing that the idea of freedom, which for Hegel was the thrust of human history, has its origins in Judaism, while its most significant negation, original sin, is characteristic of Christianity, Hirsch makes the case that, far from being an anachronism, Judaism is nothing less than the religious foundation of the modern age. From his point of view Hirsch is therefore not hyperbolic when he concludes: "But Judaism can never per-ish because its destruction would mean the destruction of the world."[19] In effect, Hirsch does to Hegel what Steinheim had done to Kant: he reverses his mentor's view of the relative moral and religious status of Judaism and Christianity. According to Hirsch, Judaism is not a stage in the dialectical process; it is its consummation.

Steinheim, Formstecher, and Hirsch all spoke the language of contemporary German philosophy. Their works are unintelligible apart from it. They freely incorporated elements from the leading thinkers and their systems are clearly indebted to them. But their purpose was not to write a Jewish version of Kant's or Hegel's religious philosophy. They wrote to persuade Jews and non-Jews that Judaism was not as German philosophy and Christian theology had defined it. Theirs was a polemical response, as in the disputations of the Middle Ages, but based on contemporary thought rather than Scripture. In each instance they argued that neither modern philosophy nor modern Christianity had successfully freed itself of pagan elements, that Judaism was the religion that possessed purer ethical doctrines. They drew Christianity closer to Judaism by stressing the Jewish faith of Jesus, but they also saw it as religious decline rather than advance. They portrayed Judaism as a religion that had not been superseded by its daughter faith. On the contrary, it had remained pristine while Christianity had been forced to make compromises. Judaism not only stood at the beginning of Western religious development, it would play a role—or even the principal role—in its future. Needless to say, Christians did not accept the implications of these systems, which in respect to Judaism utterly contradicted their own views. They could argue plausibly that the Jewish theologians had tailored their understanding of historical Judaism to make it seem more ideally suited to the modern age than it was in fact. But even if they did not convince non-Jews, Steinheim, Formstecher, and Hirsch did give philosophically educated Jews grounds for believing that Judaism could be reconciled with a freely chosen morality and with spiritual progress.

The felt need to reassert Judaism against Christianity, which prompted the Jewish systematic thinkers, played a large role also in the scholarship and Reform ideological writings of Abraham Geiger. In his youth Geiger envied Christianity because some of its scholars were willing to apply critical research to its sources—Wilhelm Vatke, for example, to the Old Testament, David Friedrich Strauss to the New. Moreover, it was actively reforming itself, discarding outmoded ideas and preserving its genuine treasures. Christianity would therefore have a role in the culture of the new Europe, while Judaism, as long as it remained unchanged, was destined to disappear. In 1836 he wrote in a personal letter: "Dear friend, look at the high standing of Christian theology in all of its systems, how it always keeps up with modern scholarship, whereas Jewish theology just keeps on precociously crawling around."[20] The Protestant Reformation, Geiger believed, was of great importance to Jews because it made them feel most deeply the need for their own reform of Judaism. In his *Wissenschaftliche Zeitschrift für jüdische Theologie*, itself modeled on Christian periodicals, Geiger regularly reviewed Christian theological and historical literature. He was persuaded that rabbis required familiarity with Christian theology since its impact would sooner or later extend to Judaism as well. During the 1830s and 1840s Geiger looked to the historians of the Tübingen school as a model of critical *Wissenschaft*.

Increasingly, however, Geiger became a severe critic of Christianity. He had always opposed the superficial imitation of Christian practices, which he called "Christeln," and insisted that Judaism must maintain its "religious independence." Also, as he read Christian writers on Judaism, he polemicized against what he regarded as their distortion of Judaism and the conclusions that they drew from it against Jewish emancipation. After mid-century Geiger became ever more convinced that contemporary Christianity had reverted to struggling against the secular world. No longer a force favoring progress, it had become a pillar of reaction, turning its back on Wissenschaft and culture. Catholicism had separated itself from the development of the human spirit and it was likewise doubtful whether Protestantism could be resuscitated. "The church is sinking ever deeper into the Middle Ages; it has lost all connection to the living spiritual forces of the present."[21] Christianity, he believed, had now become a model for Jewish Orthodoxy, no longer for Reform. The radical thinkers among Christians had left their religious origins behind.

Yet Christianity continued to attract Jews. Even though the rate of conversions had declined, some Jews were still drawn to it as a faith they believed more adequate to modern life. Geiger's response was to portray for prospective converts the full range of Christian dogma. Christianity, as represented by the thinking of Hengstenberg and Stahl, he wrote in a popular pamphlet, demanded acceptance of the incarnation and the trinity. Of course, there were Christian clergy who would make conversion easy, but they misrepresented their faith. Geiger began to argue more strongly that only Judaism, with its strict ethical monotheism, could be the religious foundation of modern culture. The reactionary course of

Christianity in the nineteenth century, he believed, had shown its incapacity to fill that role.

Possibly because the Reform movement had weakened barriers of specific belief and practice between Judaism and Christianity, the rabbis associated with it were constrained to stress the larger differences in worldview. Orthodox Jews, less threatened by Christianity, rarely engaged in extended polemics. From their point of view the larger the role played by Christianity in German society, the more favorable was the atmosphere for Orthodox Judaism. The real threat to Jewish traditionalists (as to their Christian counterparts) came from secularism. Nonetheless, Orthodox Jews did oppose the missionary societies and—as had Mendelssohn—frequently noted that, in contrast to Christianity, Judaism was not a proselytizing religion. Also, like the systematic thinkers, Samson Raphael Hirsch ascribed to Christianity no more than an intermediate role in religious history, played out between its Jewish origins and the messianic acknowledgment of Judaism alone as the world religion.

For Reform Jews, in particular, the relationship to Christianity touched upon religious practice as well as principles of faith. The early Reformers eliminated or altered prayers that referred in a deprecating fashion to non-Jews. As we have seen earlier, they adopted a wide variety of Christian forms deemed appropriate for all modern religion, including Judaism. Synagogue structures were modeled on churches, sermons followed the pattern of Christian homiletics, Jewish children were confirmed, and in some places organs accompanied the worship. However, beginning in the 1830s a strong counter current makes its appearance. A Berlin Reformer complains, "Yes indeed! That's the problem with our Jewish situation, that we measure it by a Christian measuring stick."[22] The rise of greater historical awareness prompted by Wissenschaft des Judentums now leads to the abolition of some recently adopted Christian forms or to lending them a more Jewish character. Israel Jacobson had wanted to make his temple in Seesen as much like a church as possible with the exception only of specifically Christian symbolism. A generation later Jewish community boards were looking for appropriate Jewish models that would awaken Jewish historical memories: the Temple of Solomon, the Moorish style of medieval Spain, or the pre-Gothic architecture common to early synagogues and churches. Similarly, the first regular Jewish sermons in the vernacular closely resembled those delivered in the more enlightened churches. They too stressed the universal truths of natural religion and the inner happiness to be gained by moral conduct. But once Christian homiletics, under the influence of Schleier-macher, began to assume a more Christological character, Jewish preach-ers likewise resorted to more specifically Jewish themes. Increasingly, they cited texts not only from the Hebrew Bible, common to Jews and Christians, but also from the Rabbinic literature. Zunz's work had revealed an indigenous Jewish homiletical tradition on which they could build. By the 1830s Jewish confirmation ceremonies were also taking on a less Christian character, stressing knowledge rather than the confession of faith. Catechisms become less universalistic and more specific, until one published in 1859 is entitled *Katechismus der Unterscheidungs-lehren des Juden- und Christenthums* (Catechism of Teachings Differen-tiating Judaism from Christianity). Least capable of Judaization was the organ. Until the nineteenth century it was precedented only by the use of a musical instrument in the synagogue of Prague and it was so closely associated with the church that Orthodox and some Conservative Jews continued to reject its use as Christian. Yet even in this instance Abraham Geiger tried to make the argument that the modern organ was prece-dented by a similar musical instrument played by Levites in the ancient temple in Jerusalem. Thus, in specific matters of practice, as in grand the-ological systems, even Liberal German Jews—or at least their spiritual leaders—were defining Jewish religious identity less as in convergence with Christianity than as historically and essentially different.

4. Between Jews and Christians

The Christian deprecation of Judaism and the Jewish response of self-assertion against Christianity sustained separation between Christians and Jews. With few exceptions, Christians excluded Jews from the formal and informal groupings in which they came together for professional and social purposes. For their part, Jews felt more comfortable among their own, where they did not need to worry about unintentionally giving offense to a non-Jew or, if they were observant, being tempted to violate the Sabbath and dietary laws. As a result of the hesitancies on both sides, ongoing social contact between Jews and Christians was not common. Rare too were more formal frameworks in which Jews and Christians could come together as equals.

In the villages and small towns where most German Jews still lived, and where Christians and Jews alike remained pious and observant, reli-gious barriers separated the two groups into clearly differentiated societies. Sermons delivered in churches and religious instruction in Christian schools kept alive a tension just beneath the surface of day-to-day relations. Jews still had to worry, as in medieval times, that some incident might unleash an outbreak of religious anger. Nonetheless, in the countryside contact between Jews and Christians was generally more extensive than in the cities, where Jewish communities were larger and socially more self-sufficient. Jewish and Christian families, which had lived together in the same village for many generations, could hardly be strangers to one another. In times of need neighbors assisted one another regardless of religion, and occasional friendships were formed despite religious obstacles. There was a bond also in a common piety—as against the more secularized worldview of city folk—even though that piety was expressed in different traditions.

Religious distinctions were least significant among those Jews and Christians who were furthest removed from their respective religious communities. Jewish beggars, traveling musicians, and vagabonds, lacking roots in any one place and little concerned about respectability, frequently established close relations with non-Jews of their class. At the other end of the economic spectrum, wealthy Jews sought social contact with the most influential Gentiles. At the time of the Congress of Vienna Fanny von Arnstein hosted the most prominent delegates in her palatial home. In Hamburg members of leading Christian families regularly visited the home of the wealthy and public-spirited banker Solomon Heine. However, it was less common for even the most affluent or eminent Jews to be invited, in turn, to the homes of Christians. To attend a soiree in a Jewish house was, after all, merely a foray; to have brought Jews into a Christian house would have been an acknowledgment that they were acceptable in one's own social sphere.

During the last decades of the eighteenth century and the first years of the nineteenth, extensive social contact between Jews and non-Jews took place in the salons hosted by Jewish women in Berlin. The Christians who attended were mostly younger men, some of them nobles or writers, who were looking for a more interesting and open social milieu than that offered by the highly structured and culturally uninteresting social life of the court. During lively discussions of the most recent works of German literature it was possible to forget who was a Jew and who a Christian. Nonetheless, although the salons offered a common meeting place, the gatherings represented requests for social and cultural acknowledgment that were issued by Jews to Christians; they did not create a sociability in which Jews and Christians participated as equals.

There were, of course, in addition to a wide variety of incidental casual contacts, individual instances of genuine friendship between Christians and Jews. David Friedländer, Mendelssohn's disciple, enjoyed lasting warm relationships with a number of prominent Christians. The scientist Alexander Humboldt, one of the least prejudiced outstanding Christians and among the most friendly to Jews, on one occasion confided to the older Friedländer his scientific plans and aspirations because, as he wrote, "It is so important for me to be understood by a friend such as yourself."[23] Encounters in the Jewish salons resulted in some ongoing, though often ambivalent relationships. Later Gabriel Riesser would enjoy the close friendship of many non-Jews. But it seems that even in the most liberal Christian circles during the years before 1848 relationships with Jews that had no instrumental purpose were the exception to the rule.

In formal societies organized by Christians religious barriers against Jews were common. The success of Jews in gaining admission to societies devoted to a particular purpose varied depending on the nature of the association. Those with medieval roots and Christian traditions were the most likely to exclude Jews. Newer societies, especially those based on a common profession or serving a charitable purpose, were more accommodating. In 1833, for example, a Jewish practicing physician was among the founders of the Munich Medical Association and, in 1850, of the Bavarian Medical Widows' and Orphans' Pension Society. Socially oriented associations were more exclusive. In Frankfurt, for example, Jews were not admitted to the leading literary societies or to the Frankfurter Club. The situation was similar in Hamburg. In fact, just as Jews were beginning to seek social integration in greater numbers, Christians raised higher the formal barriers against them.

The Jewish experience with Freemasonry in Germany is the best example of the difficulty Jews experienced in penetrating a formal organizational structure where Jews and Christians would share a common social milieu. Since the ideals of Freemasonry, as formulated in the eighteenth century, reflected the humanism and universalism of the Enlightenment, the Masonic lodges seemed to provide a setting in which those ideals that the Haskalah had adopted as its own and that were repeatedly stressed by the Reform movement could be venerated in common by Jew and Gentile. For Jews alienated from their own tradition, the quasi-religious character of Freemasonry, based on a universal Deism, also offered a channel of religious expression that could supplement or replace Jewish worship and practice. Here then, in theory, Jews and Christians could establish the deepest moral and social bonds while each segment remained associated with its particular religious community. However, unlike their counterparts in England, France, and Holland, the Freemasons in Germany, with occasional exceptions, continued to begrudge the Jews admission to their lodges during the first half of the nineteenth century. In Prussia the barrier remained intact until shortly before it was raised even higher with the rise of racial antisemitism in the last decades of the century.

In Frankfurt am Main both the existing lodges closed their doors to even the most acculturated Jews of the city, prompting eleven of them (together with a single Christian) to form their own lodge in 1807. But, to the members' distress, they were able to gain recognition only outside Germany. Non-Jews who joined the Lodge of the Breaking Dawn were not from the established Frankfurt families; the Jewish members, by contrast, represented a youthful economic and cultural elite. Prominent among them were the elected officials of the Jewish community and the intelligentsia associated with the Philanthropin. Clearly there was a social imbalance between the Jewish members and the few unprejudiced non-Jews who had chosen to join them and who were honored with the lodge's positions of leadership. In the 1820s the number of Christian members declined until it was merely symbolic, and the Frankfurt lodge became, in effect, a Jewish social circle that was incompletely absorbed into the Masonic structure. The historian Isaac Marcus Jost, himself an active member, mentioned only its specifically Jewish purposes: to further the Jews' "respectability in the outside world and their strength of character within."[24] The "Masonic Lodge of the Israelites in Frankfurt," as Jost called it, may have been dedicated to universal ideals, but the social context for expressing them had remained almost exclusively Jewish.

Contact between Jewish and Christian scholars of the Near Eastern literary heritage was rare. The former worked mostly as rabbis and did their research whenever they found the time; the sphere of the latter was the university. Unusual was the participation of half a dozen Jews among the forty-nine scholars who attended the first gathering of German and foreign orientalists held in Dresden in 1844. Abraham Geiger, Zacharias Frankel, and the young bibliographer Moritz Steinschneider gave lectures at the meeting. Geiger used the occasion to scold the Christians present about their neglect of rabbinic literature, which, he argued, was essential for biblical studies. Frankel demonstrated that fragmentary Aramaic translations of the Bible were earlier and therefore more important for understanding the Bible than the Greek Septuagint, which was far better known among Christian scholars. And Steinschneider made a plea for the philological value of postbiblical Hebrew literature. All three lecturers urged the Christian orientalists to look more closely at the specifically Jewish traditions. In succeeding years Jewish scholars were welcomed as contributors to the prestigious *Zeitschrift der Deutschen Morgenländischen Gesellschaft.* However, the orientalists at the meeting in 1844 elected no Jews to be their officers. Nor was a Jewish scholar of the stature of Abraham Geiger, though admired by colleagues like David Friedrich Strauss and August Gfrörer, selected for membership in any German academy.

Only for a very short time did a common religious forum come into existence that included Jews alongside Catholics and Protestants. In 1837 a distinguished Catholic convert from Protestantism, Julius Vinzenz Hoeninghaus, began to publish in Frankfurt am Main his twice-weekly *Unparteiische Universal-Kirchenzeitung,* specifically intended for all three religious groups. To edit the Jewish division he recruited Michael Hess, a senior teacher at the Philanthropin, and his colleague, the historian Isaac Marcus Jost. In the first issue the two Jewish editors wrote with apparent enthusiasm:

> Here we are not one-sided advocates of particular views or proponents of particular directions. Rather, as we honorably recognize the various religious parties of our Christian brothers, we are ourselves recognized with equal honor and we join together in the common task. Just as we fulfill our duties alongside each other in the state, so we shall gladly devote our energies in the same measure to disciplined scholarship.[25]

Soon more than two dozen rabbis and Jewish educators, ranging from religious conservatives to radicals, were listed along with Christian professors, court preachers, high church officials, and common clergy as coworkers on the journal. Some articles in the Jewish section were aimed at informing Christians about historical and contemporary Judaism, others were devoted to internal polemics over religious reform. Jewish news items

appeared next to Christian ones; Jewish books were reviewed in a section
on current theological literature. However, as the journal gained a larger
readership, it aroused severe opposition, especially in Protestant circles,
where its editor was accused of Jesuit tendencies. When its distribution was
prohibited in Prussia, the *Kirchenzeitung* was unable to carry on and
ceased to exist at the end of one year. Hoeninghaus announced a new journal strictly for Catholics, while Jews turned to their own separate newspaper, the *Allgemeine Zeitung des Judenthums*, likewise founded in 1837.

  Not until the middle years of the following decade, with the resurgence
of religious liberalism and the appearance of radicalism among both
Christians and Jews, does the spirit in the non-Orthodox camps on each
side shift away from polemic and toward a new search for common
ground. In 1844 Ludwig Philippson launched a short-lived devotional
periodical intended to cross religious boundaries, which he called *Reli-
giöse Wochenschrift für gottgläubige Gemüther aller Confessionen* (Religious Weekly for Believing Spirits of all Denominations). That same
year Joseph Levin Saalschütz (1801–1863), preacher of the Jewish community in Königsberg, argues that Judaism and Christianity are at one
with regard to all basic elements of morality and religion, differing only
on dogmas that likewise not all Christians accept.[26] A truly Christian
state would therefore be no different from a Jewish one. Each would rest
on the same foundation. Although Saalschütz's point is political, he reverses the thrust of discourse from the stress on Jewish differentiation,
which characterized the systematic Jewish thinkers, toward the reconciliation and minimization of differences that had been typical of the Haskalah generation. Similar was the view of Sigismund Stern, the ideologue of
the Berlin Reform Association, that a modernized Judaism is sufficiently
like Christianity to be recognized as a state religion alongside it.

  From the Christian side religious radicalism was now seeking to reconcile Protestantism and Catholicism on the basis of German nationalism and a simplified common Christian faith. The suspended Catholic
priest Johannes Ronge hoped that his rationalistic "German Catholicism" would unite radical Protestants as well as Catholics in a single national church. As we have seen in the previous chapter, this was also the
period when unprecedented religious radicalism appeared among the
Jewish laity in major communities, especially Frankfurt and Berlin.
Thus, in 1846, Carl Scholl, a German-Catholic clergyman in Mannheim,
could welcome the reform of Jewish theology "which, in accordance with

its spirit, aims at the same goal as the German-Catholics" and raise the possibility of uniting Catholicism and Protestantism with a reforming Judaism. However, the basis of the proposed unification would nonetheless be Christian, with Jews expected to acknowledge Christ as the "founder of the new world of the spirit."[27] For their part, Jewish radicals were stimulated by the analogous trends in Christianity. They maintained relations with the Christian radicals and a few joined the German-Catholics or the later Free Religious Communities. However, most Jews were unsympathetic to the German-Catholics and Protestant Friends of Light. Recognizing that a Christianity that abandons dogma and stresses freedom and brotherly love must exercise "a significant attraction" for many Jews, the moderate reformer Ludwig Philippson condemned the radicals both for their humanistic theology, which substituted individual consciousness for revelation, and for the notion—present in their circles no less than among the traditionalists—that Christianity had passed beyond Judaism.

The most intimate relations between Jews and Christians were, of course, through marriage. However, unlike in France where civil marriage was obligatory, in Germany during the first half of the century such unions were nearly always religious and required conversion of the Jewish partner. In the rare instances in which mixed marriages did occur before 1848, the ceremony took place in a church and the parents were required to raise their children as Christians. Thus when the first rabbinical conference, held in Brunswick in 1844, proclaimed that "the marriage of a Jewish man with a Christian woman, marriage between adherents of monotheistic religions in general, is not prohibited provided that the laws of the state allow the parents to raise the children from such a marriage also in the Jewish faith,"[28] it was without practical consequence since no German state at the time gave such permission. Gabriel Riesser did advocate the legalization of mixed marriages as early as 1833, but only because he believed that it would diminish the pressure for insincere conversions. After 1848 mixed marriages without conversion gradually gained wider legality and a few of the most radical rabbis agreed to conduct ceremonies for mixed couples. For one such occasion Samuel Holdheim devised a nondenominational set of vows, which referred only to the universal God "whom I recognize in my heart."[29] Such instances, however, were few. Interreligious marriages of any sort between Jews and Christians were still far from common.

23   The funeral of soldiers killed in the Revolution of March 1848
Preacher Isaac Noah Mannheimer and Cantor Salomon Sulzer are at the
center of the picture.

Finally, during the revolutionary year of 1848, as Jews fought together
with Christians on the barricades, they also came together briefly to
mourn their dead. In Vienna the Jewish preacher Isaac Noah Mannheimer
and the cantor Salomon Sulzer joined Catholic and Protestant clergy at a
common grave site to eulogize the fallen of the March Days. It was an unusual—and often recalled—instance of mutual religious recognition.

6 | Becoming German, Remaining Jewish

1. The Problematic Acquisition of German Culture

In the eighteenth century the number of Jews in Germany who could claim the possession of German or European culture was minute. Living in social separation, educated in Jewish schools, speaking their own Western Yiddish (Judeo-German) language, the vast majority regarded themselves, and were regarded by others, as not only religiously but also culturally distinct. The religious barrier between Jew and Christian was likewise a cultural barrier between Jew and German. Moses Mendelssohn became so celebrated a phenomenon because his life represented prominently for the first time a separation of culture and religion. He had succeeded in becoming culturally German while remaining religiously a Jew. His extraordinary contribution to German letters, combined with an active role in the Jewish community of Berlin, proved that a Jew could indeed live productively in both worlds. It is not surprising that Mendelssohn served as a model of acculturation for German Jews throughout the nineteenth century, especially for the Orthodox, who could stress repeatedly that acculturation did not necessarily entail any compromise of fundamental Jewish belief or practice.

Mendelssohn had adopted the culture of the German Enlightenment. Its ideals were the application of reason in society, state, and religion along with the display of moral virtue in individual life. Its universalism had in principle necessitated embracing even Jews. So powerful was the attraction of the *Aufklärung* for German Jews on account of its hopeful vision of a united humanity that, intent upon gaining social and political equality, they continued to appeal to its ideals well into the nineteenth century. However, only the earliest and numerically most limited stage of Jewish acculturation in Germany took place under its aegis. By the last decades of the eighteenth century the intellectual and moral ideal was no longer the liberation of the mind from superstition and prejudice but the attainment of *Bildung*. Whereas the Enlightenment had related virtue particularly to reason, this new ideal focused more broadly upon individual character, including the cultivation of an aesthetic as well as a moral sensibility. It called for the unfolding of multiple talents and qualities within the personality. The individual who was truly *gebildet* would manifest the achievement in every aspect of life. The ideal of Bildung gradually shaped a new social entity in Germany, the *Bildungsbürgertum*, a class that owed its standing not to privilege but to cultural and moral attainment.

The process of Jewish integration involved a twofold adaptation. Even as Jews, accumulating various degrees of wealth, assimilated to the economic class of the bourgeoisie, culturally they sought to rise to the status of the Gebildeten. Both were entities only then coming into existence and hence apparently open to individuals whose roots lay outside the earlier social order. To be considered cultivated required not only the demonstration of personal morality and intellectual capacity but also the ability to appreciate literature, art, and music and the possession of social grace. Perhaps, above all, it required being fully at home in the German language. Bildung had little to do with family or social status; its realization depended upon individual effort and talent. It was this status that growing numbers of German Jews sought to achieve during the first half of the nineteenth century, in part because it was often made requisite for the attainment of political and social equality but in part also because of its intrinsic attraction. For those Jews who no longer found personal meaning in the Jewish religion, the attainment of culture became a spiritual quest. For them, as for some Christians, Bildung served as a secular religion whose significance was ultimate. But even observant Jews ceased to regard acculturation as a danger to Judaism. Whereas eighteenth-century rabbis had viewed Mendelssohn's translation of the Pentateuch into German with grave suspicion, Samson Raphael Hirsch was not alone among the spiritual leaders of Orthodox Judaism two generations later in praising "our beautiful German tongue" and in recommending the classical German writers. In fact, Orthodoxy, on account of its greater religious separation, tended to stress the more fervently that in the cultural realm traditionalists could be as German as modernists.

If the Aufklärung had directed Mendelssohn and some of his disciples especially to the pursuit of philosophy, the regnant ideal of Bildung at the beginning of the nineteenth century drew Jews to literature and the performing arts first, and most broadly, as consumers of culture, then more narrowly as its producers. As Jews gained the capacity to read German, first in Hebrew letters and later in Gothic ones, the libraries in their homes made room for non-Jewish books alongside of, and eventually in place of, Hebrew and Western Yiddish ones. Jewish women, like their Gentile counterparts, were especially drawn to belles lettres, while their husbands tended to prefer philosophical writings and periodical literature. By the first decades of the nineteenth century German reading had become a passion among urban Jews. When possible, they joined lending libraries and reading societies established by non-Jews; when they were excluded, they formed their own. In Frankfurt am Main, where they were not admitted to Gentile societies, they created no less than four of their own—one with as many as one hundred members—between 1801 and 1804. Here they could gather in the society's own rooms to read books and current newspapers. Having gained wealth, they now sought culture. A local newspaper reported: "The Jews in Frankfurt, who . . . have become very elegant but haven't as yet really changed their inner selves, now want to attend to cultivating the latter as well."[1] As Jews became avid readers of German books, a growing number entered actively also into their sale and publication.

Which German writers did the Jews venerate most during the early decades of the nineteenth century? Their preferences were not determined exclusively nor perhaps even primarily by literary criteria. For the average Jew, content was more important than form. Invariably and not surprisingly, they held Lessing in the highest regard and continued to purchase his writings long after he had been overshadowed by later writers. For Jews, *Nathan the Wise* was more than a play; it was the symbol of their hoped for acceptance within German society as equals. Hence its reading was obligatory. Ludwig Börne may have been scoffing, but he was probably only exaggerating slightly when he wrote of *Nathan* in 1807 that it was a book "every Jew who lays claim to Bildung reads a few dozen times and praises to the skies as the most beautiful work of art even if he doesn't understand one word of it and it bores him to tears."[2] In the course of the nineteenth century the devotion to Lessing grew even stronger, especially when his vision seemed imperiled by political reaction.

Unlike Lessing, Friedrich Schiller did not befriend Jews nor did they seek him out. His contact with Jews in Weimar was most limited, and he was not a public advocate of their cultural or political emancipation. He did think highly of *Nathan the Wise*, but few Jews appear in his own writings and none of them are either significant or depicted as especially virtuous. During his lifetime even Jews with a secular education paid Schiller relatively little attention. However, in the course of the nineteenth century, his popularity increased sharply. If Lessing represented for German Jews the writer who first attested to their moral virtue, Friedrich Schiller evoked their admiration for his presentation of a broad humanitarian vision in which they wanted to share. Schiller's enthusiasm for freedom and human dignity, his idealism and high-minded morality, seemed easily reconcilable with traditional Jewish values. In 1842 Gabriel Riesser could claim that it was always easier to find ten enthusiastic admirers of Schiller among his coreligionists than one who was a devotee of Goethe. Schiller became the favorite writer of Jewish educators and teachers. "Jewish young people got their education from Schiller. From him they learned how to read, to think, and to feel."[3]

Although, unlike Schiller, Goethe had considerable personal contact with individual Jews, some of whom made the pilgrimage to him in Weimar, he was the last of the three classical German writers to gain broad acclaim among Jews. In part that may have been due to Goethe's well-known disparaging remarks about the Jewish ghetto of Frankfurt, which he visited on various occasions as a young man, and his opposition to Jewish political emancipation; Berthold Auerbach thought him an enemy of the Jews. But more basically it was due to the nature of Goethe's writings, which were less in tune with Jewish ideals and aspirations than those of Lessing and Schiller. Religious Jews could not identify with the pursuit of sensuality in *Werther* and in *Faust*, while politically oriented Jews resented Goethe's elitism and his opposition to the democratic trends on which they pinned their hopes. Goethe, too, was not a popular writer like Schiller, his writings less easily comprehensible by average Jews and less appropriate for the Jewish school. Only late in the century did Goethe gain a larger following among Jews, who then played a disproportionate role in Goethe studies. And yet if Jews collectively were late to appropriate Goethe, individual Jews were among his first admirers. In the salons of Henriette Herz, Dorothea Mendelssohn, and especially the celebrated Rahel Varnhagen, Goethe's writings served frequently as the topic of conversation. Whereas Rahel had little regard for Schiller, her veneration for Goethe as the profounder poet became a religious cult to which she eagerly sought converts—among them the young Heinrich Heine. These Jewish women, less bound by Jewish religious and political considerations, less influenced by conventional taste, and more sensitive to Goethe's genius than most contemporary Christians, played no small role in spreading Goethe's fame.

Whatever their German cultural importance, however, the Berlin salons were a peripheral phenomenon in the Jews' quest for Bildung. They involved only a small number, mostly at the edge of Jewishness or moving beyond it into Christianity. More broadly significant for the Jews' acculturation is their increasing participation in public performances. In the last decades of the eighteenth century theaters moved from the courts of the nobility to the bourgeois space of the city. With remarkable rapidity Jews thereupon joined Christians in the audiences, thus publicly displaying their claim to shared artistic interest. The number of Jews attending performances in the centers of early Jewish acculturation—Berlin, Königsberg, Breslau, and Vienna—astonished contemporary observers. Even in Fürth, a center of Jewish Orthodoxy, at least fourteen of twenty-one founders of a theater in 1816 were Jews. When a benefit performance was held three years later, Jews occupied more than one third of the seats, and one traditional Jew absented himself when the mayor called a meeting of the theater's stockholders on the Sabbath. Similar was the Jewish enthusiasm for musical performances, although Jews could be excluded from attendance when these were held in more informal settings. In Frankfurt, where Jews were not sold tickets to amateur concerts organized by a Christian group of music fanciers, they formed their own society, presenting concerts attended (without charge) by Jews and Christians alike.

During the eighteenth century, when the number of Jews determined to acquire German culture was exceedingly small, when the Aufklärung was proclaiming the possibility of finding talent and virtue among representatives of every people, and when Moses Mendelssohn provided an example of the most successful acculturation, the enlightened German public could find merit in Lessing's idealized portrayal of the Jew Nathan. A generation later, when the universalistic Enlightenment had given way to a more narrow and nationalistic Romanticism, it seemed strange to count Jews among true Germans. Yet as they rose in the economic order and made claims to full political equality, Jews often based their argument for emancipation upon their attainment—or potential attainment—of German Bildung.

In fact, however, despite their best efforts, most German Jews were not able to achieve full acculturation with ease. As long as they were born into families that spoke Yiddish and educated in traditional Jewish schools, German culture was not a formative influence in their lives. They only made the decision to acquire it as adults. As a result, their acculturation was often hasty, incomplete, and superficial. Giving up religious observance, pursuing secular pleasures, and adopting the most recent fashions in dress were easier steps than cultural achievement. During the first decades of the nineteenth century those with pretensions to enlightenment or Bildung, but in fact lacking both, had become a sufficiently common phenomenon to attract general attention. Jewish and Christian writers spoke of them as miseducated (*verbildet*) or as possessing only a pseudoenlightenment (*Afteraufklärung*). Critics focused especially on the mannerisms that partially acculturated Jews displayed in conversation, which, despite their best efforts, they could not easily expunge. These mannerisms were called *Mauscheln* (from the name Moses as pronounced in Hebrew or Yiddish among German Jews) or *Jüdeln* and included the persistence of errors in syntax and pronunciation, characteristic intonations, occasional Yiddish words, and hand gestures. Mauscheln was especially characteristic of Jews recently arrived in the city from the countryside and seeking to adapt themselves quickly to their new environment.

An unprecedented Jewish figure now appears on the German stage, neither a villain like Shylock nor a hero like Nathan, but the incompletely acculturated Jew, who is worthy neither of hatred nor admiration but only of contempt. The most prominent, though by no means unique, examples occur in the anti-Jewish play *Unser Verkehr* (Our Crowd). This one-act farce by the physician Karl Borromäus Sessa was first performed in Breslau in 1813 with little success. However, once it was produced two years later in Berlin—over local Jewish objections that only gave it more attention—it gained extraordinary notoriety. Well-attended performances took place in various German cities and illustrated editions of the work enjoyed ongoing popularity. The main theme of *Unser Verkehr* is generational change and continuity. The older generation of German Jews is represented by Abraham, a small-town dealer in secondhand goods who speaks the Yiddish jargon, is contemptuous of non-Jews, and worries only about increasing his wealth. Abraham's best advice to his son, Jacob, is to

24 Front cover of the antisemitic farce *Unser Verkehr*
(Our Crowd)

become rich. Unlike his father, however, Jacob has cultural pretensions and believes that he can change his character at will: "I'm gonna throw away the Jew; after all, I'm enlightened—ain't nothing Jewish about me!"[4] He claims he can dance, speak French, recite poetry; he has begun to learn aesthetics and can write theater reviews. Such a "genius" can easily become a *bel esprit*. In the big city Jacob encounters other Jews who are further advanced upon the path of acculturation but just as ridiculous. The highly affected Lydie (alias Liebche), a parody of the Jewish salonières, is unable to expunge her former self, which keeps on showing through her new persona. Isodorus Morgenländer, who has studied at no less than sixteen universities and whose speech is free of Mauscheln, talks only pretentious nonsense. He has learned the language of literature but not the appropriate speech of conversation. A self-hating Jew, he tries to dissociate himself from fellow Jews, but his values remain the same as theirs. Jacob's attempt to purchase respectability with money and with the false veneer of Bildung fails totally and he appears in the final scene pathetically reduced to the peddling that supports his father. The message of the play is obvious: Jews cannot acculturate; they can only degrade German culture. The younger generation may make abortive efforts to attain Bildung, but the results are necessarily grotesque and laughable. The Jewish character expresses itself in deceitful exploitation of the non-Jew (as well as of the Jew) and that character is unchangeable. Jewish acculturation cannot help but be superficial and inauthentic, a cloak that scarcely hides the incorrigible "eternal Jew" who lurks beneath it.

The social and political implications of the play were doubtless clear to its readers and audiences, and it is not surprising that the Jews were shocked by it. Börne noted that *Unser Verkehr* was not making fun of a few humorous attributes—which other distinguishable groups in German society possessed as well—but of allegedly invariable and permanent qualities of character. A Jewish physician in Fürth, Simon Höchheimer, wrote a counterplay whose main character, Nathan Weismann (!), is a truly enlightened and fully bourgeois contemporary merchant and manufacturer. But Höchheimer's verbose apologetics, which attempted to distinguish exemplary high-minded and cultured Jews from those who indeed possessed the caricatured defects, lacked all literary merit and effect. The figure of Nathan could not be revived at a time when Jews in larger numbers, and still to varying degrees culturally unassimilated, were actively seeking social and political acceptance in an atmosphere unfavorable to their aspirations.

Christian playwrights continued to create Jewish figures on the German stage who serve preponderantly as the butt of ridicule. Seldom are they villainous or dangerous, even more rarely virtuous. The Jews' change in economic status is marked by the more frequent appearance of bourgeois occupations, but their qualities of character remain the same. They serve as targets of resentment at the ongoing Jewish penetration into the inner sanctum of German society and culture, which is most easily assuaged by making them appear ludicrous. Exceptional is Karl Gutzkow's popular historical tragedy *Uriel Acosta* (1846). Based on the life of a Jewish heretic in Amsterdam in the seventeenth century, this *Judenstück* (Jew-piece), as it was widely known, is, like Lessing's *Nathan the Wise*, essentially a plea for tolerance. However, although it portrays admirable as well as despicable Jews, it does not root tolerance in Judaism. Within the Amsterdam community, it makes clear, there was no place for independent minds like Acosta—or, for that matter, Spinoza, who appears briefly in the play. Tolerance, Gutzkow is saying, represents a virtue that some Jews can achieve, but it is not clear they can do so without ceasing to be Jews.

Non-Jewish playwrights could muster little poetic sympathy for what in the first half of the nineteenth century was the principal concern of most Jews: their achievement of political equality. With Jews rapidly climbing the economic ladder, their lack of rights did not seem a subject worthy of serious drama. Nor could Jews themselves present it believably in artistic form, at least not directly. The one play that touched upon the subject did so only in veiled form.

In 1823 Michael Beer (1800–1833) became the first Jew to have a play produced on the German stage. His popular one-act tragedy *Der Paria* (The Pariah), written in occasionally rhyming verse and initially presented at the Royal Theater in Berlin, tells a moving story of gross injustice. The setting is faraway India, where Gadhi, his wife Maja, and their son live the miserable lives of untouchables. Yet, though he stands at the bottom of the social ladder, Gadhi is morally far above the highest caste. His actions, which eventually necessitate suicide together with his wife, are clearly more noble than those of the raja who seeks to take away his wife. By choosing the distant Indian setting, Beer made the message of the play universal—and that, without doubt, not only contributed to its effect but also made it persuasive to his audiences. Eckermann, Goethe's close friend, noted that Beer's pariah "can reasonably serve as a symbol for the degraded, downtrodden, and despised among all peoples."[5] Yet contemporaries also saw in Gadhi a reflection of the Jews' complaint as the victims of injustice. Although only by gross exaggeration was the lot of German Jews as grievous as Gadhi's, certain lines of the play too obviously reflect Jewish sentiments to have been written without them in mind. At one point Gadhi pleads:

> Might I but be a person among persons!—oh alas! . . .
> Give me like status with you and see if I am not like you!
> I have a fatherland; I will defend it.[6]

This is clearly the language of German Jewry's quest for political emancipation. But it had to be contained in a few lines, for, as Berthold Auerbach noted, were Beer to have presented a Jew as tragic hero upon the stage in 1823, the character would have been unpersuasive to audiences accustomed to seeing Jews only in the context of farce. An unfamiliar pariah could arouse sympathy; Jews could evoke only disdain.

Just two years earlier Heinrich Heine (1797–1856) had likewise written a play in which the Jewish plight appeared only in disguise. The hero of his *Almansor* is a Muslim pressured to forsake his heritage and to live fully as a Christian in sixteenth-century Spain. Heine, too, in this instance thought it more prudent and persuasive to transpose the contemporary (and personal) Jewish *misère* to another religious group living in another country and another age.

2. "The Jew That Can Never Be Washed Off": Heinrich Heine

Heine's place in German and in Jewish history has been the subject of ongoing dispute. Non-Jews at various times regarded him as not fully German on account of alleged Jewish characteristics; some Jews, especially in the early years, rejected Heine not only on account of his apostasy but also because they believed the character of his work un-Jewish. Yet for the entire nineteenth century, and until Franz Kafka, Heine's writings represent the most important contribution to German literary culture made by anyone who was born a Jew. "Whoever deals with modern German history," wrote the historian Golo Mann of Heine, "must attempt to describe his character and thought as best he can."[7] Moreover, Jewishness remained a recurrent theme in Heine's life and an important stimulus to his creativity as a writer; he cannot be adequately understood without giving it ample attention. Nor can one ignore his striking images of medieval and contemporary Jews. Finally, since Heine was an ongoing issue among

Jews who did not convert, their evaluation of his personality and writings serves as a touchstone for understanding Jewish cultural attitudes. Our concern with him cannot include the totality of his literary contribution; we shall neglect those portions of his work that do not bear on Jewish matters. It is Heine's Jewish identity, which persisted after his conversion and reemerged more strongly in the last years of his life, that requires close attention.

Heine cannot be "claimed" for Judaism any more than he can be classified by ideological or literary categories. He was consistent only in being ambivalent, in his refusal to be pigeonholed, and in insisting upon his artistic freedom. What he had to say about Christianity, about Judaism, about democracy, and about Germany is notoriously inconsistent, sometimes the product of changing moods, of recent experiences, or of the identity of his correspondent or partner in conversation. Like Goethe, whom he admired greatly, Heine's only unswerving loyalty was to his poetic task. Jewish themes and characters are abundant in his writings, though we must not suppose that they dominate in his work. At various stages in his life Heine chose to dwell on them. Whether his contribution as a whole is determined by his Jewish origins and ongoing Jewish identity is a difficult, perhaps unanswerable question. Certainly, Heine drew on multiple literary traditions and is better categorized as a German than as a Jewish writer. Yet it can be argued that the "Jew that can never be washed off" (*der nie abzuwaschende Jude*), an expression he used in a letter of 1823—two years before his conversion—kept him always at a distance from what he surveyed, sharpened his vision, and thus contributed significantly to his artistic achievement.

Heine's immediate family was already a step removed from medieval Judaism. Young Harry grew up in French-controlled Düsseldorf, not in a ghetto. He learned proper German at an early age and received at best a perfunctory Jewish education. As an adult he remembered only a few Hebrew words. Of Jewish celebrations only the festival of Passover seems to have made a lasting impression. Initially, he tried to ignore his origins. As a student in Bonn and Göttingen Heine associated mostly with non-Jews. It was only when he came to study in Berlin in 1821 at the age of twenty-three that he became acquainted with a group of Jewish university students that made him reflect on his own identity. Heine joined the Verein für Cultur und Wissenschaft der Juden (see chapter 4), where he came to know, among others, its president, Eduard Gans, and the editor of its *Zeitschrift*, Leopold Zunz. Within the membership of the *Verein*,

Heine found, for the first time, men of his own generation and no less acculturated than he, who, in the wake of renewed Jew-hatred, were struggling to reformulate Judaism in terms of the regnant Hegelianism, to which Heine was also drawn, and to anchor their Jewish consciousness in serious historical study. The uncertainty and daring of their enterprise lent it a dramatic appeal lacking in the contemporary efforts at religious modernization. Heine even promised to write an article for the association's journal on the "great anguish of the Jews (as Börne calls it)." The group and some of its individual members made a permanent impression on Heine. His active participation in the Verein, though lasting only a few months from the fall of 1822 until he left Berlin the following year, was Heine's only positive relationship with an association of Jews.

The Jews of the Verein were clearly different from the other varieties about whom Heine was writing in his student years. In 1822, on a trip to Posen, he had encountered Polish Jews who aroused both his disgust at their appearance and his sympathy on account of their poverty. He also admired their wholeness of character, which German Jews, torn between Jewish origin and attractions foreign to it, no longer possessed. Thus Heine continued to display a wistful envy of traditional Jews. They alone, he believed, had remained authentically Jewish; their consistent and rigorous rabbinic Judaism was the only genuine article. Yet for himself he had neither the inner strength nor inclination to live the life of a traditional Jew. He described himself as "the born enemy of all positive religions."[8] In venerating a Judaism so far removed from his own, it was easier to justify his own distance from any of its forms.

Heine had only contempt for efforts to modernize Jewish religious practice. Reformers like David Friedländer provoked his scorn. Judaism, he was certain, could not be brought up-to-date by superimposing a few externals drawn largely from Christianity. "Band-Aids" would not cure it. Nor did Heine have high regard for Jews who remained nominally Jewish but who had, in fact, substituted bourgeois values for religious ones. Because the Verein fitted into none of these categories and because he possessed genuine respect for its ideals, Heine had the severest difficulty in justifying to those members he valued most his abandonment of their cause for a selfish end.

In an atmosphere increasingly unfriendly to Jews, marked by the Prussian law of 1822 that definitively excluded Jews from academic teaching positions and in Heine's own life by Christian acquaintances turning against him as a Jew, he began to think seriously of conversion. Almost

two years before taking the step he was already rationalizing the possibility to Moses Moser, his closest friend from the Verein, as opening the
way for a greater devotion to the cause of advocating rights for unfortu-
nate fellow Jews. But he still held such an act, if taken for the sake of practical advantage, to be beneath his dignity. In his resistance he wrote privately of "a profound antipathy for Christianity" and immersed himself
in Jewish studies. Yet, in the end, he took the fateful step. On June 28,
1825, at the age of twenty-seven, he was baptized Christian Johann
Heinrich Heine. Officially, he thereby ceased to be a Jew, but neither
Heine himself nor the public he addressed believed that it had seriously
changed him.

The inner struggle over the conversion continued after it had taken
place, except that guilt and self-reproach now replaced self-searching
and rationalization. The conversion of Eduard Gans a few months after
his own enabled Heine to project onto Gans what he really felt about
himself: "I think of him a lot since I don't want to think about myself."[9]
In a poem written at the time, but not published until later, he castigated
his former friend:

So you crawled to the Cross,
To the Cross that you despised,
That just a few weeks ago
You thought of trampling into dust!

As the president of the Verein Gans had been the captain of a worthy
vessel; his rush to abandon it was a shameful act. Similarly, it was inex-
cusable, Heine wrote much later, for Felix Mendelssohn, as the grandson
of the famous Jewish philosopher and a man of independent wealth, to
have composed pious music for the church. Of his own conversion Heine
wrote that he regretted it very much and that he was now detested by
Christians and Jews alike. On one occasion, a few months after his baptism,
he attended the Reform temple in Hamburg, taking perverse delight when
the preacher, Gotthold Salomon, castigated opportunistic conversions.

During the period in which he was contemplating conversion and for
a short time thereafter Heine occupied himself with Jewish themes.
"Donna Clara," written in 1823 and reflecting an experience in his own
life, is the first Heine poem in which a Jewish character appears. As in
Almansor, the setting is medieval Spain, except that here the mysterious
handsome knight and lover of the alcaide's Jew-despising daughter sur-
prises the reader in the last verse when he reveals his hidden identity:

I, Señora, your beloved
am the son of the much admired
Great and learned Rabbi
Israel of Saragossa.

Unlike Lessing's early play *Die Juden*, in which a similarly noble character reveals himself as a Jew, there follow upon this concluding verse no
high-minded statements about mutual tolerance. The consequences of the
revelation, by a Jew whose father Heine deliberately called "Israel," are
left unspoken.

During these same years Heine was also working on the story that
would, more than any other of his works, establish his name within the
literary canon of German Jewry. Writing *Der Rabbi von Bacherach* (The
Rabbi of Bacherach) was not just an endeavor to produce a first novel in
the style of Sir Walter Scott; it was an exploration of his self as a Jew. He
claimed that the project was motivated only by love, not by the quest for
fame, since it could only arouse enmity among non-Jewish readers. To
prepare for writing the tale he read Jewish history seriously for the first
time and sought information about Jewish traditions from his friends.
"The spirit of Jewish history reveals itself to me more and more," he
wrote to Moser at the time.[10] Begun while he was still a Jew as a futile
attempt to anchor himself within Judaism, it was continued after his baptism as evidence that he had not entirely given up his obligations as a Jew
after all. Only when it proved impossible to continue the task, perhaps
more for literary reasons than for Jewish ones, did Heine drop the project.
Thereafter, non-Jewish concerns and interests increasingly drove out
Jewish ones.

Heine's medieval story begins idyllically at the table of Rabbi Abraham
and his wife, "the beautiful Sarah." Together with friends they are celebrating the festive Passover meal recalling the redemption from Egypt.
The tranquillity of the scene is destroyed when two strangers posing as
Jews drop the corpse of a dead Christian child beneath the rabbi's table. In
desperation, he flees with his wife at the first opportunity. Leaving the
ancient Rhineland town and its small Jewish community behind, Abraham
and Sarah journey up the Rhine in the dark of night. Here the first chapter—all we can be certain was completed at the time—ends abruptly. What
is remarkable in this chapter is the great empathy Heine displays for the
lot of medieval Jews, victimized by the dread ritual murder libel. Missing
almost completely is the ambivalence and ironic wit that he would display

so often thereafter when he dealt with Jewish subjects. If Heine could not identify fully with most Jews—and certainly not with the rabbis—of his day, he could project himself sympathetically into the small-town medieval milieu, where Jewish life, as pictured in that first chapter, was physically endangered but also strong and whole.

In succeeding years Heine had few sustained contacts with unbaptized Jews except for members of his family. There is no evidence that he paid

25   Heinrich Heine, oil by Julius Giere, 1838

any attention to the theological and practical conflicts that split German Jewry into factions during the 1840s. Although he was otherwise well informed about events in Germany, the leading Jewish religious figures of the period go unmentioned in his published writings and extant correspondence. On the other hand, the Christianity that had been so abhorrent to him earlier now occasionally receives more favorable treatment, at least in the Protestant form in which he had adopted it, and it becomes his base for attacking the Jesuits. Heine admires Jesus as a social reformer, though he repeatedly stresses that the founder of Christianity was a Jew. But, more essentially, Heine's trajectory away from Judaism is determined by his adoption of a sensualist philosophy and way of life that he defined as Hellene or pagan, which he realized set him apart from Judaism whether ancient or modern. For Heine, in contrast both to traditional Judaism and to its modern interpreters, the aesthetic ideal stood above the ethical. Jews and Christians—he branded both "Nazarenes"—had turned away from beauty to an excessive concentration on spirit. For a time he was drawn to the utopian socialism of Saint-Simon, though he always eschewed economic determinism and could not identify with the masses. He remained deeply fearful of political and social revolution. It was as an outsider to every narrow religious and political category that Heine wished to be known.

Having developed sufficient distance from his earlier personal Jewish struggles, Heine was now easily able to look upon Jews and Judaism with the same wit and irony that he applied to other subjects. In the years after his conversion, he continued to include real and imagined Jews in his prose and poetry, holding up a mirror that reflected much of the reality of Jewish life. Three most memorable figures occur in Heine's *Die Bäder von Lucca* (The Baths of Lucca, 1829). The Marchese Cristoforo di Gumpelino is a wealthy Jewish parvenu become a pious Catholic, whose absurd cultural pretensions, characteristic of certain German-Jewish apostates, render him utterly ridiculous. His servant Hirsch has changed his name to Hyacinth but he has remained—also in caricature—a modern Jew of the Reform persuasion. For him the old-time Jewish religion is no religion at all, but only a misfortune. Like the aristocratic pretender Gumpelino, the utterly bourgeois figure of Hyacinth, intent on acquiring culture through his association with Gumpelino, is modeled on a Hamburg Jew of the author's acquaintance. Heine ceases to be devastatingly satirical only when Hyacinth describes a third and very different Jew. Moses Lump, a dirty Hamburg peddler, has remained untouched by the desire to be anything other than he is. "He doesn't have to sweat away at acquiring Bildung." He has no intention of changing his religion or even his name. All week long he struggles for his meager living, but on the Sabbath, amidst family and Jewish food, he is happier than any Rothschild. Moses Lump is the only contemporary Jew that Heine can portray with sympathy: one who has not been seduced by the desire to take on a new identity and thereby to sacrifice something of himself.

Heine's mostly dormant Jewish consciousness during the 1830s was awakened by the Damascus blood murder libel in 1840. In articles that he wrote at the time, Heine for once involved himself explicitly as a partisan of the Jews, though he also recognized the broader political and moral implications of the affair. Unlike Rahel Varnhagen, who had felt no sympathy as a Jew for fellow Jews during the "Hep Hep" riots of 1819, Heine now openly expressed his solidarity with them. He criticized French Jews for being so assimilated that they lacked enthusiasm for aiding their brethren in Damascus. And he expressed unstinting praise—exceptionally in the instance of a modern Jew—for the lawyer Adolphe Crémieux, because he was willing to undertake the rescue of his coreligionists while other Frenchmen, Gentile and Jewish, hesitated to act. The revived blood libel also returned Heine's thoughts to his unfinished *Rabbi von Bacherach*. He now added to it and published a fragment consisting of two chapters and part of a third. But as Heine has changed in his relation to Judaism, so too has the tone of his story following the end of chapter 1. When Abraham and Sarah enter the ghetto of medieval Frankfurt am Main, leaving behind the romantic atmosphere of their rural town, they encounter Jews who are more caricature than real. Like Gumpelino and Hyacinth, the new characters are held at a distance. Heine is unwilling or unable to portray them in any depth.

Heine returned to his Jewish roots more wholeheartedly only about a decade later, after the nerve disease from which he had long suffered became so acute that it confined him to his room. During nearly eight painful years spent in his "mattress-grave," he turned to belief in a personal God and to reestablishing an inner relationship to Judaism. Chastened by his paralysis and pain, he wrote, "No longer am I the zestful, rather corpulent Hellene who used to smile condescendingly at gloomy Nazarenes. Now I am just a deathly ill Jew, an emaciated picture of misery, an unhappy human being!"[11] Heine did not become a religious dogmatist nor did he begin to observe Jewish customs, and he decidedly did not lose his characteristic wit. But he did undergo what he called a "reawakening of religious feeling" and he turned for inspiration to the Bible—especially to the Old Testament. He identified himself with the figure of Moses, not as the humble servant of God but as a leader dedicated to social justice and as a creative artist who fashioned Israel as a people of God and an exemplar to the nations. When pious Christians wondered whether, like Paul, he had had a decisive religious experience, he wrote that he associated Damascus with blood libel, not religious conversion, and that his own illumination had come from the Bible of the Jews.

It was during these last years that Heine published three long poems on Jewish themes that make up the third book of his *Romanzero*, called, after Byron, "Hebrew Melodies." In the first of them, "Princess Sabbath," Heine elaborates and garbs in exotic myth a motif already present in the plainer description of Moses Lump: the impoverished, bedraggled weekday Jew, transformed—here from a dog into a prince—by the magical spirit of the Sabbath. For a day the Jew is free to celebrate with song and Sabbath food, but his joy ends with the conclusion of the Sabbath when the protective magic circle breaks and he becomes a dog once more. The second and longest poem, "Jehuda ben Halevy," is based on the life of the most famous of the medieval Hebrew poets, Judah Halevi, whose yearning for Jerusalem remained tragically unfulfilled. Its structure is complex and it contains both humorous relief and contemporary allusions. But like "Princess Sabbath," it is essentially serious. The older Heine could identify to a high degree both with the spiritual exaltation of the simple religious Jew and—more personally—with Judaism's greatest poet. Nonetheless, he continued to scorn religious fanaticism in whatever camp it might appear. The third poem, "Disputation," which pits a Jewish polemicist against a Christian one in medieval Toledo, is filled with contempt for the clerics of both faiths. Heine concludes it with the often cited verse:

> Who is right I do not know—
> Yet to me it seems quite clear
> That the rabbi and the monk,
> Both of them do stink.

The ending is telling because it strikes the reader so sharply that Heine, as a Jew, did not change so much after all, certainly not enough to give up the critical distance that, as an artist, he required from every dogma. Sometimes in his writings Heine admired Jews, more often he satirized them, frequently and out of personal experience he sympathized with their plight. But he always avoided both sentimentality and complete identification. "Disputation," with its funny irreverent note at the end, was a necessity for Heine—not only as an independent religious spirit but also as a poet.

A German who lived outside of Germany, Heine was a Jew who lived outside of Judaism. For him, the two peoples to which he belonged, in each case only problematically, were closely related. "How striking," he wrote, "is the deep feeling of affinity that reigns between the two moral peoples, the Jews and the Teutons."[12] Heine did not give up his own relationship to either one. He could not, because each identity—whether he willed it or not—continued to dwell within his own. From the German side Heine was attacked as un-German, and his writings did not easily enter the canon of German literature. He disturbed the German conscience; his works were banned as politically and morally dangerous. From the Jewish perspective it is ironic that the most important German cultural figure produced by the Jews in the nineteenth century was an apostate, who might have remained at least nominally Jewish if, as he once wrote, the laws had permitted the theft of silver spoons. Yet, even then, Heine would have been neither a traditionalist nor a modernist Jew, but set apart within a self-defined territory of his own: "as Heine will and must always be Heine."[13]

It is not surprising that the reception of Heine's work among German Jews was initially unfavorable. To the Jews of his own time Heine was mostly an embarrassment. Critique and dissociation only gradually gave way to admiration and appropriation. Gabriel Riesser, who possessed a personal animus against Heine, believed the poet to be a non-Jew, not only because he had converted but because "as a writer he never with so much as a single word represented or expressed Jewish convictions."[14] Although Heine did indeed possess exceptional wit, that was not a Jewish quality. It was the task of the Jewish writer, to Riesser's mind, to argue soberly for Jewish rights, not to poke fun at everyone.

Ludwig Philippson, the rabbi and editor, shared Riesser's sentiments when he first wrote on Heine in 1841. He did admit enjoying the "amusing figures" of Gumpelino and Hyacinth. Such individuals, he noted, were quite common in the 1820s. But he did not like the later parts of the *Rabbi von Bacherach*. Philippson, who wrote fiction himself, believed that stories set in the Jewish past should treat customs reverently if they were still viable or allow them to be forgotten if they were not. But they should not be transformed into "playthings for your feeble trickeries." Nor did he appreciate Heine's irreverence, and he was later very angered by

"Disputation." Like Riesser, Philippson was too involved with Jewish concerns in the present to look benignly upon writings that lacked such
engagement. Both men possessed ideological and moral commitments
that made Heine's frivolities appear dangerous and un-Jewish.

However, once the positive sentiments about the Bible and about his
own identity as a Jew, which Heine expressed late in his life, became generally known, and as his fame grew in Germany, the attitude to Heine
among German Jews began to change. Increasingly, they saw him as a
wayward son who had never finally abandoned his people; they bought
his books and placed them beside the other German classics. This shift is
nowhere as striking as in the last volume of Heinrich Graetz's *Geschichte der Juden* (History of the Jews), published in 1870. In this standard work the Jewish historian clearly claimed Heine (and Ludwig
Börne) for the Jewish people. "Having shot up out of Jewish soil and only
watered by European culture," they both possessed wit, a thirst for social
justice, and an insistence on telling the truth that Graetz defined as
"archetypically Jewish." Heine and Börne appear here as heroic figures,
who pierced the armor of German prejudice. They were "angels of vengeance who brought the Germans more blessing than did their guardian
angels." Though they were both apostates, Jewish blood flowed in their
veins; there was a "Jewish-talmudic electricity" in their lightning bolts.
If they left Judaism, it was only to launch a more effective attack on the
enemy camp from within. Despite all claims to the contrary, they had
proven Jews did possess aesthetic sensibility. Of the two men, however,
Graetz preferred Heine, whom he regarded as the deeper Jew. Later Jewish writers, both Zionist and anti-Zionist, would share Graetz's appreciation, though they used different—and contradictory—arguments of
their own. Thus Heine, with an irony he would no doubt have appreci-
ated, eventually became among nearly all German Jews a member of
their people whose conversion they regretted but whom they viewed in
a light that exposed little but the honor he had brought both to them and
to Germany.

3. Other Literary Figures

Though now nearly forgotten except among literary historians, during
his lifetime Berthold Auerbach (1812–1882) was among the most popular German writers both in Germany and abroad. He received numerous
honors for his work; he associated freely with members of the nobility

and with leading writers and intellectuals. His fame then rivaled Heine's and even today critics rank his writings directly after Heine's among contributions of nineteenth-century Jews to German belles lettres. Yet Auerbach and Heine were as different as night and day. As far as we know, Auerbach never even considered baptism. He remained an unhesitatingly identifying Jew, who cherished ongoing relationships with German Jewry's religious and political leadership, with Geiger, and with Riesser. His writings were not criticized as "Jewish" by non-Jews and they were universally admired by Jews. Auerbach was not a revolutionary in any sense. To his friend, the Jewish philosopher Moritz Lazarus, he wrote that "at peace with the world is the way I feel most comfortable in life."[15] His values were typically bourgeois. Like most other Jews, he favored moderate political change and like them he was an optimist about the possibility of achieving full emancipation. He trusted the Germans and was an ardent German patriot; in his view Israel had ceased to be a nation. When he

26 The writer Berthold Auerbach

gained fame as writer, his fellow Jews had no difficulty in claiming him as one of their own.

Auerbach began his life as a village Jew. He was born in the Black Forest village of Nordstetten in Württemberg to a family that boasted ten generations of rabbis on his father's side. Auerbach himself studied to become a rabbi and as late as 1840 was a candidate for the position of preacher in the Hamburg Temple. Preaching, he once admitted, always remained a part of his character. But he did not become a rabbi. He ceased to be traditionally observant and his Judaism became more a matter of loyal identification as a Jew than of active participation in the community and its institutions. "We are Jews on account of history and birth," he wrote.[16] In later life Auerbach visited the synagogue only occasionally, less for religious reasons than to "document" his Jewishness. When he attended services at the Berlin Reform synagogue with his children in 1862, he did so because "I have a need to demonstrate my sense of belonging to the collectivity and the children, who have to suffer in school and on the street because of their being Jews, should obtain a certain depth of feeling for their religious community."[17] Hearing the old liturgical melodies of his youth could still move him religiously, but he had become estranged from the theology of their texts and from the observance of Jewish law.

Among Auerbach's earliest writings were two long novels dealing with Jewish themes. In his *Spinoza* (1837) he provided a sympathetic portrait of the Sephardi Jew whose legacy was a universal one, whose pantheism he found personally attractive, and whose name, *Baruch*, he shared. In *Dichter und Kaufmann* (Poet and Merchant, 1840) he turned to Ashkenazi Jewry in the age of Mendelssohn, depicting through the unhappy career of the poet Ephraim Kuh the tensions and uncertainties that were released in the process of emergence from the ghetto. Auerbach admired Mendelssohn as he did Spinoza. To his mind they were the "two greatest Jews." Both novels, it has been argued, were Auerbach's attempt to explore his own identity as a Jew and as a writer. They were the first installments of a plan that Auerbach laid out in the introduction to *Spinoza* and still mentioned late in his life: to continue writing on Jewish themes through an ongoing series of novels on the Jewish ghetto.

Although *Spinoza* enjoyed numerous reprintings, his early novels—judged by nineteenth-century critics to be flawed as literature—did not establish Auerbach's fame as a writer. However, his *Schwarzwälder Dorfgeschichten* (Village Stories from the Black Forest), which began to appear in 1843, rapidly gained both critical and popular acclaim. Here Auerbach left the Jewish milieu behind and tried, as a Jew, to convey to non-Jews the character of their own rural life. The stories were attractive in their simplicity; they required little intellectual effort from their readers. As Auerbach idealized and sentimentalized it, the village—despite personal conflicts—was a haven from the stressful changes brought about by modernization. City folk were charmed by tales of a simpler, spiritually healthier life. Because Auerbach's own childhood had been spent in a Swabian village, he was able to craft persuasive portraits of Christian peasants, complete with local dialect and customs. The relatively few Jewish characters that occur in his tales are not caricatured or stereotyped. In Auerbach's village stories Jews and Christians live side by side with mutual respect, neither giving up their own religious identity. If these were in part actual memories of Auerbach's youth, they were certainly idealized to fit his ideological purpose. As Abraham Geiger noted, showing Jews peacefully and amicably integrated among Gentiles in works of literature could be more effective politically than explicit arguments for their emancipation. Heinrich Heine depicted mostly city Jews, who were often corrupted by the quest for wealth, social prestige, and the hasty, superficial acquisition of culture. The Jews in Auerbach's early tales remain uncorrupted, anchored not only in Judaism but in the village, where local German traditions prevail. Unlike Ludwig Börne, who took pride in being a German without local loyalties, Auerbach desired to be known as a Swabian and rejoiced when his fellow Swabians finally began to recognize him as a Jew who was their representative as well. He wanted to be something more than a political German, to have a folksy, common touch, and that required a local identity, not just a national one.

Like Riesser, Auerbach was a moralist and hence a severe critic of Heine's early writings. In 1836, when his literary activity was still contained within a Jewish orbit, Auerbach wrote a tract entitled *Das Judenthum und die neueste Literatur* (Judaism and the Most Recent Literature), which paralleled the contemporary assault on the liberal writers known as the "Young Germany" for their insolence and immorality. At this point in his life Auerbach identified himself strongly with the second generation of the Reform movement and especially with the ideas of Abraham Geiger that had just begun to appear in Geiger's scholarly periodical. For him, as for Geiger and the Jewish theological writers who wrote a decade later, Judaism was a religion that had developed and progressed in history from the Bible to the Pharisees and down to the present. From the beginning it had subordinated the world of the senses to that of the spirit, individual desires to religious principles. In Auerbach's eyes, therefore, Heine was fundamentally a non-Jew. His paganism cut this "modern Prometheus" off from both Germanism and Judaism, two identities that for Auerbach possessed a common moral foundation. For his part, Heine scorned Auerbach's village tales as "miserable, sentimental and religiously and morally insipid,"[18] while Auerbach, learning of Heine's view, wrote to his cousin: "For me Heine, to whom everything is good for a joke, is deeply repugnant and I, being who I am, must also be repugnant to him."[19] Like other German Jews, Auerbach later revised his evaluation of Heine, but moralism remained characteristic of the man and his work.

Heine was exceptional in his derision of Auerbach's writing. Nearly all German Jews celebrated Auerbach as living proof that a proud and loyal Jew could both win acclaim among non-Jews and write so persuasively about them in a traditional German setting. Moreover, his writings, unlike those of Börne and Heine, rarely provoked the condemnation of antisemites. His moderate political views and his charming rural stories were evidence that literary Jews could uphold rather than undermine German values. In the most widely circulated Jewish newspaper, the *Allgemeine Zeitung des Judenthums*, Auerbach's work received repeated favorable attention. Unlike Heine, Auerbach was not a critic of Jews and of Germans, but an affirmer of the inherited values in both their traditions. Ludwig Philippson liked the *Schwarzwälder Dorfgeschichten* better each time he read them.

Although as a young man he had noted that even liberal Christians could not easily refrain from denigrating Jews, Auerbach's faith that Germany would overcome its prejudices grew along with his own fame and social acceptance. When on one occasion, enchanted by Grimm's fairy tales, he came upon an antisemitic story, he wrote to his cousin that it was like having wounds ripped open. Auerbach lived long enough not only to witness the complete emancipation of German Jewry but also the beginnings of the new antisemitism. He finally bitterly complained that he had lived and worked in vain. Representative of his fellow Jews in their hopes, Auerbach also articulated their disappointment.

Like Auerbach, Moritz Gottlieb Saphir (1795–1858) was in his day one of the most popular writers in the German language, and his fame, too, did not last. But in other respects he was more like Heine and Börne: he converted to Christianity, he was a skilled wordsmith, and his enemies derided him as a Jew. Contemporaries and later writers, as well, treated this consummate satirist with scorn as a man without convictions who would sell his soul to the devil for personal advantage. Yet there was more than one side to Saphir, and his Jewish origins did not cease to be relevant after his baptism.

Saphir's childhood took place in a closed Jewish milieu. He was born in Lovas-Berény, a small town in Hungary, and spent the first years of his life acquiring a traditional Jewish education. His astonishing talmudic erudition, gained at the yeshiva in Prague, was sufficient to render him fit

27   The satirist Moritz Gottlieb Saphir, lithograph
by Kriehuben

for the rabbinate. Not until he was seventeen did he learn German and thereafter other languages as well. For a time he remained involved in Jewish affairs. At the request of the Jewish community in Pest, he composed a German prayer for a visit of the imperial couple to the synagogue and in a popular farce, which he wrote in Yiddish in 1820, he poked fun at the self-importance of a Jewish community autocrat. But he also published secular poetry and began drifting away from organized Jewry.

For the first thirty-seven years of his life—longer than Börne and Heine, with whom he liked to compare himself and with whom he was sometimes grouped by others—Saphir remained a Jew. His conversion, like theirs, was entirely opportunistic. Three months after it took place he was able to obtain a management position at the court theater in Munich. It is unlikely, however, that Saphir believed his Jewish origins would be forgotten—and he did not seek to hide them. To be sure, in his memoirs he referred to his Jewishness as a "congenital defect," but by this expression he meant only that anyone bearing the defect was at a severe disadvantage. Half humorously, he divided Judaism into three basic elements: Talmud, Jewish cooking, and martyrdom. The first of these, to which—unfortunately in his view—he had devoted his youth, he defined as a "a combination of the highest intelligence with the deepest obscurity." Once he was seduced by secular culture, he gladly left Talmud study permanently behind. Jewish cooking, however, remained for him, as for Heine, the most pleasant of Jewish memories. Really to appreciate Jewish dishes, he wrote with self-directed irony, you needed to be a *meshumet* (an apostate). Like Heine, too, Saphir preferred the sturdy, unbending traditional Jew to the newer variety that swayed back and forth in the breezes of modernity.

Most remarkable for a man of so few firm principles, Saphir consistently revealed deep sympathy with Jewish suffering and deprivation. In a brutal tale devoid of all humor he describes the extreme cruelty suffered by Jews in czarist Russia. On another occasion, writing in the year of his conversion, he composes a fictitious, macabre, and bitterly ironic letter to a Jewish woman whose twelve-year-old son has just died. Had she been able to raise him as a Jew, Christians would have said: "A Jew may not be a Jew!" And if as a Christian: "A Jew may not be a Christian!" Well aware of the Jewish situation in Bavaria, he adds that had her son wanted to marry as a Jew, he would have been forced to wait for another Jew to die before he could obtain a quota number: "Only the funeral torch of your coreligionist could have served him as his wedding torch!"[20] Unlike

Heine, Saphir did not late in life again call himself a Jew. But it is remarkable that his testament begins with words clearly reminiscent of a verse from Psalms said by observant Jews before retiring to rest at night: "My soul, O Lord, I lay in Thy hand."

In non-Jewish German eyes Saphir became a typical example of the Jewish writers' relationship to German language and culture. They were seen as virtuosos of linguistic manipulation; they could cite literary texts with amazing facility. But although they could be clever, comical, and entertaining, their writing was superficial, evanescent in its involvement with the fashions and scandals of the hour. Clever form mattered more than content. The German language itself was the rootless Jew's milieu, carried about in his wanderings from place to place. Saphir was a more extreme example than Börne or Heine, since in his case it could be argued that cleverness was an end in itself; it served no political or social cause. But Saphir himself saw the resort to wit as a specifically Jewish response to the rebuffs Jews were forced to suffer. It was, he noted, their only effective weapon and way of gaining recognition.

> Words and laments are easy enough to stifle, but even someone who has been gagged can laugh—laugh frightfully, laugh hideously. The Jews have chosen wit because in its service they can, in time, get to the rank of officer before some army order judges them by their certificate of conversion and not by their meritorious service.[21]

From Saphir a straight line extends to other masters of what became known as *Judenwitz* (Jewish wit). The founders and first major contributors to *Kladderadatsch*, the long-lived and popular illustrated political humor sheet, which appeared in Berlin beginning in 1848, were all of Jewish origin. And Jews continued to be among the major German satirists. But that was a mixed blessing. Immensely attractive in its liberation from conventional pieties, satire in an authoritarian society was also capable of arousing guilt in those that enjoyed it, a guilt that in some instances required condemning or at least denigrating such cleverness as alien.

That Judenwitz was not a necessary characteristic of Jewish writers, however, is well illustrated by Saphir's Hungarian countryman, Karl Beck (1817–1879), who used poetry less to entertain his readers than as a way of expressing social conscience. Beck made a name for himself mainly with a powerful volume entitled *Lieder vom armen Mann* (Songs of the Poor Man, 1846), which gave early and eloquent voice to the grief and anger of the proletariat. Jews appear in the volume initially in the guise of an unnamed Rothschild, representative of the entire family, whose wealth has gained him emancipation even as he has neglected to help other Jews achieve it. The poet asks rhetorically: "Have you liberated your own people, / That eternally suffers and hopes?" Symbol of a new capitalism more powerful than the nobility, the Rothschilds have become rich at the expense of the masses while giving neither them nor the Jews very much in return. The volume also contains a sympathetic poem entitled "Der Trödeljude" (The Jewish Hawker), which portrays the hopeless plight of a poor Jew, driven to despair because his son will be caught in the same entangling web of poverty and discrimination and will therefore have no choice but to become a Trödeljude like his father. Beck's identification with impoverished Jews was not, however, complete. Already in an earlier series of poems that he called "Das junge Palästina" ("Young Palestine"), adopting the critic Wolfgang Menzel's negatively intended description of the literary circle Young Germany, he had portrayed himself as fettered in the dungeon of his Jewish birth and fate. By the time he published *Die Lieder vom armen Mann*, and despite his atheism, he had escaped the Jewish web himself by converting to Protestantism three years earlier. Nor did Beck remain constant in his social vision, losing much of his fervor for democracy and social justice during the revolution of 1848 and becoming, like Saphir before him, a Habsburg loyalist.

At the same time that the most prominent Jewish writers were turning to the larger society for most of their subject matter, lesser-known men were looking back to the traditional Jewish milieu. Although Auerbach abandoned his early intent to write stories about the ghetto, the project was soon taken up by other Jewish writers, initially in the Habsburg Empire and then elsewhere as well. Leopold Kompert (1822–1886), the first important writer of Jewish ghetto stories, was one of a group of Bohemian Jewish intellectuals of similar age whose careers began at a time of Czech self-assertion and who soon found themselves internally divided among three cultural identities. They were the first generation of Bohemian Jews to grow up with formal advanced secular education. Mostly born in small towns or villages, they gravitated to larger cities to attend a gymnasium. Later they became students at the university in Prague and formed a literary circle called Young Bohemia, nearly all of whose most active members were Jewish. Drawn to the Czech cause, some began to write in the Czech language, but, following anti-Jewish riots in Bohemia in 1844 and rejection of their offer to participate in the development of a culture in the Czech language, they suffered severe disillusion. The hoped for Czech-Jewish rapprochement did not come about. Thereafter, they turned exclusively to German literature. Some remained actively loyal to Judaism, others only in name or not at all. One of their number, Siegfried Kapper (1821–1879), rebuffed by Czech intellectuals, turned to writing German novels on Jewish themes, while another, Moritz Hartmann (1821–1872), became active in radical politics and journalism.

Within this circle Kompert was unusual in that his literary fame rests almost entirely on the fiction he wrote about the Bohemian Jewish milieu from which he had himself emerged. He first gained larger public attention with a volume entitled *Aus dem Ghetto* (From the Ghetto, 1848), which was soon followed by a sequel, *Böhmische Juden* (Bohemian Jews, 1850). The two books together, he hoped, would "make it possible to have some idea of the poetry and the significance of a national life that has perhaps reached the point where both will be lost."[22] Kompert did indeed portray a Jewish life that still contained within it much poetic beauty. His descriptions of daily routine in the "Jewish street" possess much the same charm as Auerbach's portrayals of Swabian villages. Unlike the later writer on the Ruthenian ghetto, Karl Emil Franzos (1848–1904), Kompert did not deride Jewish superstitions or stress the ghetto's physical ugliness. But not all his stories are idylls of a traditional society that retains full confidence in itself. Some of them convey a Jewry that must endure not only the hardships and dangers endemic to Jewish life at all times but also new forces that are subtly yet surely bringing about its destruction.

An early Kompert story, generally judged to be one of his best, well conveys the problems faced in the initial stages of Bohemian Jewry's inner breakdown and its difficulties in coping with them. In "Die Kinder des Randar ("The Children of the Leaseholder"), Reb Schmuel, the lessee of an estate and tavern keeper who lives about half an hour away from the Münchengrätz ghetto, enjoys wealth and generally good relations with the local peasants, though anti-Jewish feeling lies just beneath the surface, ready to break out when there is a special cause for resentment. New difficulties become apparent in the younger generation. His son Moschele, who as a small child was attracted to the romantic idea of traveling to Jerusalem, becomes Moritz, who seeks a secular education only to find that as a Jew attempting to enter the Christian world he is treated unfairly. For a time he tries to identify with the hard-working impoverished peasants, but they are unwilling to be concerned about the welfare of Jews. The moral narrowness of the ghetto Jews offends him, though in this case too he sympathizes with their economic plight, which seems the harder to bear since Jews, unlike Bohemian peasants, do not resort to drink. Honza, his friend from the village, represents another exclusive world, that of Czech language and culture. This world too Moritz attempts to enter without success; as a Jew he cannot be fully a Hussite. In the end he becomes a physician in the ghetto. But his identity problem remains unresolved. He still does not know who he is. His sister Hannele follows another path out of the Jewish milieu that leads her almost to the point of baptism before she is rescued by her brother. The story well reflects the dilemmas of Kompert's circle in Bohemia, growing up amidst ghetto and peasant village, the old Judaism and a prejudiced Christianity, the Jewish, Czech, and German cultures.

Kompert's stories were persuasive because they conveyed an authentic image of traditional Jewish life. They were not apologetic. Among the frequent Hebrew and Judeo-German expressions used by his characters were even some potentially offensive to Gentiles: *Gallches* (shaved ones, meaning the priesthood), *Thumme* (impurity, meaning a church). Since he wanted Christians as well as Jews to read his stories, Kompert provided footnotes for unfamiliar customs and translations for foreign words. However, most of Kompert's readers were Jews. Philippson called the early stories "a gem of our literature," but suggested the author would have to be satisfied with the small circle that would be able to understand them.[23] Christians read Auerbach, who wrote about their own village life, but relatively few, it seems, were interested in either the inner life of the ghetto or the problems faced by Jews who sought to escape it. Kompert did hope that eventually Jews and Christians would learn to live together. Some of his later fiction pictured Jews as farmers and artisans, though here too their situation was fraught with problems. Toward the end of his life Kompert even considered civil marriages between Jews and Christians as a possible solution to the Jewish question. But he remained a lifelong opponent of conversion, served as a member of the governing board of the Vienna Jewish community, and devoted himself, in particular, to Jewish education. Two other Bohemian Jewish writers likewise played an active role in organized Jewish life: the poet and journalist Ludwig August Frankl (1810–1894) and the strictly observant Salomon Kohn (1825–1904), whose *Gabriel* (1854), a suspenseful historical novel on the subject of adultery and vengeance encompassing both the Prague ghetto and the Thirty Years War, enjoyed mounting success and was frequently translated.

Although ghetto stories, printed in Jewish newspapers and collected in books, became the leading genre of German-Jewish literature devoted to Jewish subjects through most of the second half of the nineteenth century, and spread to French, English, and American Jewry as well, they were not its only form. Jews also wrote plays, sometimes set in biblical times, sometimes in German surroundings. One of the most popular such plays was *Deborah*, a popular drama in four acts written by Salomon Hermann Mosenthal (1821–1877), a playwright born in Kassel who had settled in Vienna. *Deborah* was first performed at the Hamburg Municipal Theater in January 1849. Like some of Kompert's stories, its theme is the relationship between Jews and Christians. But as yet no Jews have been permitted to live in the Styrian village of the year 1780 in which the play is set. Its Christian population is prejudiced against them to varying degrees. The Jews who enter the region, among them the beautiful Deborah, are outsiders, forced to wander about furtively in the countryside. Despised by Christians, they are biblically vengeful, their forced response to the treatment they suffer. But the plot, which ends in reconciliation, presents an optimistic message: if Christians will be loving toward Jews, as their Christian faith demands, that, in turn, will bring out the best qualities among the Jews; although some mistrust will remain, living peacefully side-by-side is possible for the next generation. To a greater extent than the more profound Kompert, Mosenthal reflected the political optimism of German Jews, which had begun at the time of the play's setting, during the reign of Joseph II, and reached one of its peaks in 1848. Mixed audiences of Christians and Jews were enchanted by the play. It was frequently performed, translated into thirteen languages, and still reprinted as late as 1890. More thoughtful Jews, however, were appalled because the Jews and Judaism Mosenthal portrayed required moral salvation at Christian hands. One Jewish critic was outraged: "How far we have come from 'Nathan the Wise' to 'Deborah'!"[24] he exclaimed angrily. Mosenthal's play, he believed, appealed only to that Jew who was willing "to trample on his religion in order to get himself accepted by Christian society." In succeeding years Mosenthal complained of disadvantages he suffered as a Jew, but these did not prevent him from becoming a central figure in Viennese cultural life, gaining a reputation as a talented librettist and receiving a patent of nobility.

Although the creation of stories, plays, and poetry on traditional Jewish life was especially evident in the Habsburg Empire, Jewish writers elsewhere produced an abundant literature on the subject as well. One of the most skilled writers of ghetto tales outside Austria was Aron Bernstein (1812–1884), who was also a liberal political journalist, a popular writer on scientific subjects, and a principal founder of the Reformgemeinde in Berlin. During the 1850s Bernstein published two novellas, *Vögele der Maggid* and *Mendel Gibbor*, that both depicted traditional Jewish life in the small town of Fordon, in Posen, where he had been a Talmud student. Surprisingly, considering Bernstein's ideological attachment to the most radical wing of Jewish religious reform in Germany, these novellas—much more than Kompert's stories—present a romanticized and sentimentalized portrayal of unacculturated traditional Jews. His characters are depicted as loving and mutually supportive, genuine believers in God, and admirably devoted to Jewish customs and practices, which lend sanctity to their lives. Even the few Gentiles among them are mostly kindly folk, who have assimilated to their Jewish environment. Unlike some of Kompert's characters, Bernstein's Jews are not torn between the values of the ghetto and those of the outside world. They live contentedly among their own, speaking Yiddish with one another, abiding by Jewish law. Even the two yeshiva students in *Vögele*, who go to Berlin for secular study, return to settle as adults in the traditional Jewish society where they grew up. In contrast to many other examples of the genre, Bernstein's premodern Jews are not at all benighted souls who require enlightenment. On the contrary, they have much to teach the outside world about nobility of character and human dignity. Not surprisingly, critics accused Bernstein of wearing rose-colored glasses. They were also astonished that a religious radical should have written so movingly and uncritically about a form of Jewish life he had so completely rejected for himself. Yet perhaps Bernstein's novellas enjoyed such lasting success because, increasingly, German Jews were no longer engaged with the identity problems created by emergence from the ghetto, as Kompert conveyed them. The traditional self-contained Jewish society appealed to fully acculturated German Jews mostly as an object of nostalgia. It possessed an integrity that they could admire but that was no longer linked to their own personal lives. Bernstein's novellas were reprinted for decades and published anew during the 1930s.

Another form of specifically Jewish literary activity did not enjoy the same widespread and ongoing popularity. This was the writing of stories and novels intended to provide moral and religious instruction and shore up Jewish consciousness. Such literature, aimed at the emotions of average German Jews, was similar in its internal Jewish purpose to the writings of Jewish theologians, who addressed the intellect of the Jewish elite. Ludwig Philippson was the leading practitioner of this genre, which introduced heroic figures as models for contemporary Jews. But neither his writing nor that of other rabbis who used literature for a popular pedagogical purpose achieved lasting significance. One might thus conclude that Heinrich Heine and Ludwig Philippson represent the two poles of German Jewish literature in this period—in the one case, the highest literary achievement together with baptism and Jewish ambivalence; in the other, a mediocre fiction harnessed to unquestioned and complete Jewish commitment.

4. Political Writers

Aside from Friedrich Julius Stahl, whom we have discussed earlier, five important political writers emerge from German Jewry during the first half of the nineteenth century. Although all were marked by their enemies as Jews, they differed greatly with regard to their Jewishness: from enthusiastic affirmation to abandonment and self-hate. Gabriel Riesser and Johann Jacoby, who both remained Jews, first argued for equality for Jews and then expanded their political activity to the larger struggle for liberty and German unity. Ludwig Börne, after first writing on behalf of the Jews, early abandoned their cause for the sake of the universal one. Ferdinand Lassalle, although remaining a Jew, never associated himself publicly with the Jewish struggle for equality. Finally, Karl Marx, historically the most important of the five, has a place in Jewish history only at its very edge, as an extreme example of Jewish repudiation.

Among German Jews in the middle decades of the nineteenth century Gabriel Riesser (1806–1863) enjoyed unparalleled prestige. Whereas rabbis and theologians represented only a segment of the divided religious community, Riesser stood for a goal shared by all but the most traditional Jews: the attainment of full civil and political equality. Against the prevalent view he consistently argued that such equality was due the Jews immediately and without any condition other than that they be willing to take on the same obligations as their non-Jewish fellow citizens. Striving to obtain the rights unjustly denied them, Riesser believed, drew German Jews together as a "moral community."[25]

Riesser was born in Hamburg, the grandson of the militantly anti-modernist Rabbi Raphael Kohen and the son of Lazarus Riesser, who had tried to mediate between the traditionalists in Hamburg and the founders of the Reform temple. Riesser himself later joined the temple and served on its directorate. His personal religious views were close to those of the Frankfurt Friends of Reform, but he opposed their policy of pub-

28   Gabriel Riesser, champion of Jewish emancipation

licly repudiating particular elements of Jewish tradition they themselves rejected. Such self-criticism, Riesser felt, would lend support to the argument that Judaism was unlike Christianity in that it required fundamental religious reform before Jews could make a claim to equality. He did not want to give the impression—nor did he believe—that Judaism was an inferior religion. He consistently opposed the possibility that some Jews—an "enlightened aristocracy" that had abandoned alleged prejudices—might be granted rights while others, who clung to orthodox belief and practice, would be denied them. Riesser was invariably an opponent of state-enforced religious coercion, whether in support of Jewish orthodoxy, as in Prussia, or on behalf of religious reform, as in Saxe-Weimar. Although he defined Jewish identity in strictly religious terms and closely related his political ideals to religious ones, Riesser preferred to set religious issues aside until the political question had been resolved and could no longer play a role in the discussion. In any case, what mattered to him ultimately as a Jew were not the specifically Jewish questions of enlightenment and reform but the attainment of universal justice and freedom. To Riesser's mind that political aim was also the highest Jewish religious goal. As he put it most strongly to his fellow Jews, "Faith in the power and ultimate victory of the just and the good is *our* messianic belief: let us hold fast to it!"[26]

Riesser considered himself a representative of those secularly educated young Jews who were unwilling to pay what he called the "entry toll of the lie." They had grown up in enlightened homes; they were not fleeing from a narrow orthodoxy. Unlike the previous generation, their acculturation was complete. They were indistinguishable except by religion and felt no less German than non-Jews. Having gained spiritual equality, they were still denied its political counterpart. Their unresolved frustration had bred anger. Then the European political ferment of 1830 and fresh consideration of Jewish status in various German states, following more than a decade of Jewish political reversals, aroused new hopes for full civil equality.

When Riesser himself had obtained a doctorate in law from the University of Heidelberg summa cum laude in 1826, he was, as a Jew, denied a university position and, a few years later, likewise refused the right to practice law in Hamburg without undergoing "an innocent ceremony." Like hundreds of other Jewish intellectuals of his generation, he was forced to choose between a suitable profession and remaining Jewish. Riesser made his personal choice with a vengeance: he decided to devote

his life and legal talents to advocating the removal of such obstacles as had
thwarted his own career. Beginning in 1830, at the age of twenty-four,
Riesser wrote extensively on behalf of Jewish emancipation. Though af-
firming a sense of international Jewish solidarity, Riesser here emphasized that the German Jews no longer regarded themselves as a nation,
that their only home was Germany. What was eternal in Judaism was its
religious idea; Jewish nationhood was never essential to being a Jew. His
most novel appeal was as a German to Germans in terms of values that
the Jews too had come to share:

> The mighty tones of the *German* language, the songs of *German*
> poets, have kindled and nurtured the holy fire of freedom in our
> breasts. . . . We *want* to belong to the *German* fatherland; in all
> places we *will* belong to it. It can and may ask anything of us that it
> is entitled to ask of its citizens; willingly will we sacrifice everything
> for it—except faith and loyalty, truth and honor; for *Germany's*
> heroes and *Germany's* wise men have not taught us that through
> *such* sacrifices one becomes a *German*![27]

To pursue the cause of Jewish emancipation, Riesser founded a periodical, which he pointedly called *Der Jude* (The Jew, not The Israelite) and in
which he discussed in detail the deliberations then occurring on Jewish
rights in German legislatures. He also authored petitions on behalf of the
Jews in Baden and Hamburg.

For German Jews, including the modern Orthodox who were willing to
overlook his religious views, Riesser became the acknowledged political
champion. His effect on them was profound. Riesser gave German Jews a
sense of solidarity focused upon their shared political hope. They admired
his youthful idealism and indignation, his decision to sacrifice career
rather than conscience. He instilled Jewish pride, uniting a divided and
discouraged Jewry around the cause of emancipation. Geiger noted that,
thanks to Riesser, "civil equality became the rallying cry that called all
Jews to the colors."[28]

In various respects Riesser was a living refutation of the Jewish
stereotype. He was serious to a fault. He scrupulously avoided satirical
remarks, employing instead a more acceptably sober, legally informed
argumentation. Riesser's self-admittedly prosaic style could not persuasively be branded "Jewish." "The earnest, unyielding striving that is
aware of its higher purpose is only very seldom witty," he once wrote.[29]
Riesser submerged his own ego in the larger cause, he was clearly not a

cosmopolitan but an ardent German patriot, and he took care not to make frivolous comments about Christianity. Politically, he was a moderate who favored constitutional monarchy over the immediate institution of a republic, gradual political change growing out of the past, not revolution. Hence he was less vulnerable than the Jewish radicals. Unlike Heine and Börne, Riesser was neither politically nor religiously an embarrassment. Moreover, his unquestioned qualities of character made it impossible for his opponents to attack him personally. There is some truth to the statement made at Riesser's funeral that "in Riesser justice became a quality of character."[30]

Despite his close association with the Jewish cause, Riesser was able to gain extraordinary prominence in the German political arena in 1848. (See chapter 8.) Like Auerbach, Riesser was a Jew whose being Jewish—because so closely associated with German patriotism and political moderation—did not detract appreciably from his acceptability to Gentiles. Later Riesser became the first Jew to obtain a judgeship in Germany, when he was appointed to the Hamburg Superior Court in 1860.

The extent of Riesser's direct influence on Jewish emancipation is difficult to estimate. His writings, read by German statesmen and intellectuals, forced them to take a stand. He made the Jewish question an integral part of the discussion about Germany's future. But it was, without doubt, the steadily increasing influence of the liberal German bourgeoisie that played a much larger role in advancing Jewish emancipation than did Riesser's pamphlets. His greatest importance lies in the effect of his person and his writings on the Jewish community. On behalf of German Jewry he elaborated for the first time an ideology of insistence upon the right to define and retain one's Jewishness without thereby suffering any civil or political disability. That ideology remained the broadest common denominator among German Jews.

Riesser's experience as a Jew and his response to it are closely paralleled in the early adult years of another member of his generation, the Königsberg physician Johann Jacoby (1805–1877). Like Riesser, Jacoby grew up feeling himself a German but treated as an outsider. As a member of the still small circle of Jews who studied together with Christians at German universities, he had come into closer contact with non-Jews and felt—more keenly than did the Jewish merchant—the pervasive political and social discrimination. Referring to himself as a "comrade in faith and suffering," he wrote to Riesser of the need to raise the indignation of all Jews at the humiliation that many of them were far too ready to tolerate. In Gentile company, he noted in another early letter, it was never possible for him to forget his Jewishness, to avoid sudden feelings of apprehension, or to establish natural, unself-conscious relationships. Denied the *love* of Christians, young Jews tried to gain their *respect* instead. That led to remarkable intellectual development but also to undesirable qualities, like egotism and arrogance, which only raised higher the barrier of social exclusion. The only solution to this sad situation, Jacoby believed, was the struggle for civil equality, which he regarded as a "sacred duty."

Jacoby was a well-educated and positive Jew with a considerable knowledge of Hebrew. Like Riesser in Hamburg, he played an active role in the Jewish community of Königsberg during his early years, especially in developing a program for religious reform. His goal—which he believed could be fully attained only after emancipation—was a spiritual rebirth of Judaism that would go hand in hand with an improvement of the lot of the Jewish poor. Growing up in the city of Kant, and in philosophy and theology a man of the Enlightenment, Jacoby interpreted the Jewish religion as a rational, undogmatic ethical monotheism. Such a Judaism, he believed, was destined to develop into the religion of all humanity. His vigorous opposition to opportunistic conversion rested on religious as well as moral grounds. But, like Riesser, he also saw the Jewish religion as directed toward a universal goal, and that linked his Jewish identity with his political striving.

In the 1830s Jacoby stressed the particular plight of the Jews, to the point that a non-Jewish acquaintance thought he wanted to use the larger struggle for freedom only as a means for gaining Jewish emancipation. Like Riesser, Jacoby demanded equality for all Jews and without qualification, not as an act of grace but as a matter of justice. Yet he early recognized that the acquisition of Jewish rights was dependent on the success of the larger struggle for freedom in Germany and that the "ferment of the age" following the July revolution in France and the Polish rebellion could be used to advantage. He wrote to a Jewish friend, "Experience has taught that every *true* political advance also brings *us* closer to the fulfillment of our longing for a respectable status."[31]

From the beginning of his public career Jacoby was politically more radical than most of his fellow Jews and the distance between them widened. (On his political activities see chapters 7 and 8.) Although Jacoby had Jewish sympathizers, including the scholar Leopold Zunz, his political position in 1848 grieved his sisters and made friends in Königsberg believe him mad. In fact, Jacoby's political ideology developed in a direction contrary to that of most German Jews. While they entered the bourgeoisie and came to share its interests, he increasingly identified with the masses in Germany and elsewhere. From anger at the oppression of fellow Jews, his social conscience broadened to reach beyond them.

Although Ludwig Börne (1786–1837) was linked in his lifetime and thereafter with Heinrich Heine, he was not a poet but principally a political writer. If Heine, as a poet, chose his words for aesthetic effect, Börne believed that in order to fight his political battles effectively each word had to be a sword. However, like Heine, he was an apostate and, like him, he remained Jewish thereafter, both in the eyes of others and, in a much more limited and mostly negative sense, also in his own.

The matrix of Börne's relationship to Judaism lies in the Frankfurt ghetto where he was born and spent the first years of his life. It was a point of departure from which he escaped to university studies elsewhere and it presented the milieu that greeted him upon his return. As he surveyed it in 1807, after seven years spent away mostly among non-Jews, life on the old Jewish street seemed mildly ridiculous. He now felt outside and above it. The physical darkness of the ghetto, he thought, was paralleled by the benightedness of its spirit. Yet Börne noted much later that it was precisely this ghetto that determined his relationship to Germans and to Germany. In 1832, long after his conversion, he wrote that he was fortunate to be born both a German and a Jew, that, as a result, he had been able to take on German virtues but—because he had begun on the outside—also to avoid what he regarded as German faults. Born as a slave, he could better appreciate freedom; born without a fatherland, he desired one the more ardently. And, finally, "Because my birthplace was no larger than the Jewish ghetto and foreign territory, for me, began beyond its locked gate, therefore the city too does not suffice to be my fatherland, nor a region or a province, but only the entire large fatherland, as far as its language extends."[32] In his last published work Börne returned to the ghetto of his origins once more, this time raising it to the status of a metaphor that represented a politically backward and suffering Germany. "Is not Germany the ghetto of Europe?" he wrote in 1836. "Do not all Germans wear the yellow patch on their hats?"[33] Despite his cosmopolitanism, Börne spoke lovingly of his "unhappy fatherland." His attitude to the Jews, however, was more one of shared pain than of love.

Even before he returned from his studies to Frankfurt, Börne had written to his father that he would not emulate him as a Jew living out

29   Ludwig Börne, etching by T. S. Englehurt, based on
a painting by Moritz Oppenheim

his life within the Jewish community. He was uninterested in vying for
the favor of the Jewish street or thanking God if a Gentile errand boy
flattered him with "Baruch is not a bad guy; it's just a shame that he's a
Jew."[34] Börne's desire to make a name for himself in the larger world was
the principal motive for the decision in 1818, at the age of thirty-one, to
change his name from Baruch to Börne. He wanted to publish a periodical and thought that a Jewish name would prejudice potential subscribers against him. They would not believe that a Jew could express
opinions appropriate to the requirements of the age. His baptism a few

months later, although at first kept secret from friends and family, was similarly motivated.

Like Heine, Börne was unable to avoid the odium of his Jewish origins. Those who criticized his style or his views repeatedly ascribed them to his Jewishness; even friends referred to it. To their mind, the Protestant Ludwig Börne was no less a Jew than the son of the ghetto, Löb Baruch:

It is simply amazing! I have experienced it a thousand times and still it is always new. One group of people holds it against me that I am a Jew, a second forgives me for it, a third even praises me for it, but all think about it. It is as if they are caught up in this magic Jewish circle and no one can get out of it.[35]

This persistent attention to his Jewish origins angered Börne greatly, for it meant that not only were his readers unable to escape the "magic circle" but so was he: "For eighteen years I have been baptized and it doesn't help at all."[36] He objected to being called a "a friend of the Jews." "I am the friend of everyone,"[37] he insisted. Yet, in private correspondence with his confidante Jeanette Wohl, Börne was not averse to himself calling his rival Heine a yeshiva student and accusing him of the allegedly Jewish trait of employing witticisms for their own sake. Later Heine would return the compliment by placing Börne, as an alleged "Nazarene," in the camp of the Jews (and Christians) and not of the Hellenes.

Unlike Heine, Börne did not in any sense return to Judaism. In contrast to Riesser, after a few early articles, he avoided writing specifically on behalf of Jewish emancipation. During the last years of his life Börne became an adherent of the Catholic socialism preached by the abbé de Lamennais. "Everyone who loves is a Christian," he wrote at the time.[38] Yet he also wrote that he continued to feel the pain of persecuted Jews and was convinced that there could be no freedom in Germany without freedom for the Jews as well. At first Jews committed to the community rejected Börne as an apostate. A generation after his death, however, some as positive in their Jewish commitment as the philosopher Heymann Steinthal and the historian Heinrich Graetz enthusiastically laid claim to him. By then his championing of freedom and justice was sufficient for liberal and even conservative Jews to praise him as a Jew in spirit. That remarkable adoption of Börne as a Jew, of course, says less about Börne himself than about just how far beyond traditional understandings of Jewishness most German Jews by that time had traveled themselves.

Although the prominent socialist Ferdinand Lassalle (1825–1864) remained an unconverted Jew, for most of his brief life he did not positively affirm his Jewishness. Lassalle's father had been an active Jewish religious reformer in Breslau. As a youth his son also identified himself enthusiastically as a liberal Jew and regularly heard Abraham Geiger's sermons. However, like Jacoby, Lassalle was early drawn beyond Jewish concerns to advocacy of universal political and social aims. A Hegelian, he necessarily regarded Judaism as superseded; a social democrat, he held views that were shared by only that very small number of fellow Jews, who did not belong to the liberal bourgeoisie that Lassalle despised. His political associates were nearly all non-Jews and, in some cases, antisemites. Nonetheless, the right-wing *Kreuzzeitung* considered him representative of the prominent "revolutionary Jews," and he was the object of anti-Jewish epithets from the communists, Marx and Engels, who regarded him—with some justification—as a political compromiser. Lassalle himself thought that the Jewish people had degenerated from ancient times and soon wanted nothing to do with them as a group. There is no indication that he believed his mission on behalf of universal suffrage and social justice to be related to his heritage or identity as a Jew.

Among political thinkers of Jewish origin, Karl Marx (1818–1883) is both the most significant and the furthest removed from any positive relationship to Jews or Judaism. Baptized along with the rest of his family at the age of six, he soon became an atheist and a universalist who had contempt for all religion. In his unqualified cosmopolitanism he was the least German of the men discussed here, while in his understanding of Judaism he was the most denigrating. Yet he belongs in this group not only because, like the others, he was frequently regarded as a Jew but also because he represents the most obvious instance of a tendency that, to a lesser degree, was present also in Börne and in Lassalle: the association of Jewishness with precisely those qualities the individual finds most odious in order to establish a psychological distance from his origins.

In 1821 Börne had called the greed of the commercial world, which he detested, "Jewishness" and said it was a characteristic that could occur among Christians and Muslims as well as among Jews. He thus defined being Jewish as possessing just that quality of personality that, as an idealist, he rejected most strongly. However, Börne did not carry the matter any further. Marx did. In his *Zur Judenfrage* (On the Jewish Question, 1844), he presented a definition of Judaism that closely resembled that put forward by the enemies of Jewish emancipation. He reduced

Judaism as a whole to what he believed to be its worldly basis: selfishness, haggling, and the worship of money. According to Marx, this "Judaism" was the bane of contemporary society, which it held in subjugation. He therefore did not argue for the emancipation of the Jews but for the emancipation of society from Judaism. His mythical definition of Judaism has often and correctly been explained as the product of Jewish self-hate: he projected onto the Jews characteristics from which, unable to forget his own Jewish origins, he was seeking to liberate himself. In Marx we are therefore presented with an extreme result of integration into the non-Jewish milieu while continuing to feel the effects of the Jewish point of origin. Like the others, Marx, too, in a sense remained tied to his Jewishness, but in his case that tie consisted only of the compelling psychological need to brand as Judaism the values furthest removed from those to which he aspired.

5. Art and Music: Oppenheim and Meyerbeer

The artist Moritz Oppenheim (1800–1882), often called "the first Jewish painter," was remarkable in two important respects. First, his choice of vocation was extraordinary. Historically, Judaism did not encourage artistic creativity, which had long been closely associated with the church and was often, though not consistently, seen as a violation of the second commandment, which prohibited the making of graven images. Oppenheim was the only significant painter during the first part of the nineteenth century who was born and lived his entire life as a Jew. Second, unlike most later Jewish artists, Oppenheim chose Jewish subjects for much of his work, often with an intent that was Jewish as well as artistic. However, as an artist, his importance is limited. He was a highly competent representative of the Biedermeier romantic style but he was not an innovator. Art historians claim he was influenced by the Nazarene school of painters, one of whose leading representatives was the converted grandson of Moses Mendelssohn, Philipp Veit. Unlike Veit, however, Oppenheim gained his reputation mostly among Jews. His work is of particular interest because it so well reflects German Jewish ideals and emotions in the middle and later decades of the nineteenth century.

Oppenheim spent the first years of his life in the ghetto of Hanau, not far from Frankfurt. His parents were pious and observant Jews, but enlightened enough not to oppose their son's interest in painting. His quest for an artistic education led him first to Munich, then to Paris and Rome.

In Italy he ceased to keep the dietary laws meticulously, no longer wore a hat and beard, and painted some scenes from the New Testament, but he resisted frequent suggestions that he become a Christian. In fact, he later wrote in his memoirs that such attempts only made him a more committed Jew. For Jewish holidays he sought out the Roman ghetto, which evoked fond memories of his parental home. His Italian experience is the apparent basis for two pictures expressing Jewish anguish in the face of an intolerant Christianity. One, from the time of his stay in Rome, shows Roman Jews being forced to listen to Jesuit conversionary sermons, as was still the case when he lived there. A later painting recalls the Mortara affair of 1858, when a surreptitiously baptized Jewish child was claimed for the church in opposition to the will of its parents.

30   Moritz Oppenheim, self-portrait

Oppenheim settled permanently in Frankfurt in 1825 and quickly established a reputation among Jews and non-Jews as an excellent painter of individual and family portraits. His paintings of Börne and Heine became very well known. The Rothschilds gave him commissions to paint members of the family and engaged him to purchase art works on their behalf. Oppenheim pleased Goethe with his illustrations for *Hermann und Dorothea* and received the honorary title of "Professor of the Plastic Arts" from the grand duke of Weimar. In 1833 he created the first of his artistic works to possess symbolic value for German Jewry. Originally entitled *Homecoming of a Jewish Volunteer from the War of Liberation to His Traditionally Observant Family,* it depicts a young soldier in hussar uniform, who has returned home after helping to free his country from the French. His father carefully inspects the medal for valor that the young soldier wears on his chest while his mother looks lovingly at her handsome son, who sits hatless at the Sabbath table. The son here represents the Jewish future, the hope that German Jews will be entitled to equality because they are willing to fulfill the state's most dangerous demand upon them. In the artist's view it is a future that does not require breaking ties with the past. The son can still feel at home in the midst of his traditional family. He can link hands with his father and thereby symbolically link the generations. The new duties, Oppenheim suggests, can live within the context of the old; there need be no sharp break. With remarkable effect, Oppenheim combines two sacred emotions felt by most German Jews: reverence for the family and patriotism for the fatherland. Most appropriately, Baden Jews presented the portrait as a gift to Gabriel Riesser in appreciation of his efforts on behalf of their emancipation. It symbolized Riesser's own wish that "like father and son, so too should successive eras embrace, honor, and love one another."[39] Oppenheim, in fact, graphically depicted the essence of Riesser's political argument: the ability of Jews to become politically integrated Germans without uprooting themselves from the still cherished religious milieu of the families in whose midst they had grown up.

Much later, during the last decades of his life, Oppenheim created what would become his greatest popular success: a series of grisailles, eventually twenty in number, called *Portraits from Old Jewish Family Life.* In the style of genre pictures, long popular in Germany, they mostly depicted events in the Jewish life cycle and the celebration of Jewish holidays. If the earlier painting of the volunteer's return home expressed German Jews' political aspirations, these pictures appeal to the nostalgia of a

31   Moritz Oppenheim: *Homecoming of a Jewish Volunteer from the
War of Liberation to His Traditionally Observant Family*, oil, 1833

Jewish community that wants to preserve memories that are dear to it and
in danger of being lost. Like the ghetto stories (Oppenheim himself men-
tions Kompert in his memoirs), the pictures seek to convey the religious
life of traditional German Jews on the edge of modernity but only just
beginning to be touched by it or not yet touched at all. As Oppenheim
presents it, that life possesses a powerful beauty and integrity, which
appeal to the emotions of the viewer. Most of the scenes are set in Jewish
homes or synagogues where family occasions or the celebration of holidays bring the generations joyfully together. Unity and serenity reign;
religious piety and familial love are everywhere apparent. Oppenheim's
pictures convey seriousness and mild humor but never scorn or irony. In
none of these idealized scenes is there anguish or pain. There is no depiction of the sorrowful holiday of the Ninth of Av, which recalls the destruction of the Temple in Jerusalem, nor of a funeral scene. Nowhere is there

any indication of a hostile outside world. Even the ghetto dweller in one picture, whose job it is to sell goods in the village, seems without anxiety as he leaves home for the week in the company of his son, his own father bidding him farewell. The few Gentiles depicted all appear to be friendly, clearly in a happy relationship with Jews. The homes are mostly well furnished and the Jewish families well and neatly dressed. Viewers are drawn

32 Moritz Oppenheim: *The Village Peddler*

to the appealing human warmth. In the form of lithographs or pho-
tographs, the pictures were seldom absent from Orthodox Jewish homes,
where they gave artistic representation to practices mostly still observed
in a similar manner. But even for those Jews who were already two generations removed from the ghetto or who were wholly neglectful of religious observance, Oppenheim's scenes could give expression to the familial attachment that remained sacred among Jews otherwise alienated from
their faith. Through the power of emotion, Oppenheim's collective portraits bridged the intellectual gulf that separated secularized Jews from
the religious world of their recent ancestors.

     As Oppenheim is the only significant artist in early nineteenth-cen-
tury Germany who remained a Jew, Giacomo Meyerbeer (1791–1864) is
the only serious musical composer who falls into the same category.
However, Meyerbeer is more fundamentally analogous to Auerbach than
to Oppenheim in that his public, too, was the non-Jewish world and his
operas were not on Jewish themes. In his own eyes Meyerbeer was a
European composer, though when the Jewish writer Alexandre Weill
showed that three of the songs in his early opera *Robert le Diable* were
taken from synagogue music and one was musically identical with a popular Sabbath evening table hymn (*menuḥah ve-simḥah*) Meyerbeer
admitted that memories from his childhood had indeed been present in
his mind at the time of its composition. As in the case of Auerbach,
Meyerbeer did not try to hide his Jewishness, nor did the musical world
disregard it.

     Jakob Liebmann Meyer Beer, as he was originally called, was the old-
est brother of the playwright Michael Beer, whose *Der Paria* received our
attention earlier in this chapter. His wealthy family in Berlin could easily provide the best available instruction for its musically talented son. It
also supplied him with a tutor for Jewish studies, the radical enlightener
and Jewish educational reformer Aaron Wolfssohn, who was probably
responsible for the Deism his pupil adopted. But while Meyerbeer became a minimally observant Jew, who, like Auerbach, visited the synagogue only rarely, he did keep the vow, made to his pious mother after
the death of her father, that he would never change his religion. In 1815
he composed a Hallelujah chorus for the modernized Jewish services
Israel Jacobson began to conduct that year in Berlin. Many years later,
shortly before his death, he again considered the possibility of composing music for the synagogue, as the French Jewish operatic composer
Jacques Halévy had done, but he did not live long enough thereafter to

carry out the intent. His offspring became Christians, much to Meyer-beer's painful regret.

Giacomo Meyerbeer's international acclaim during the nineteenth century was immense. For decades he was the most renowned operatic composer in Europe. His *Les Huguenots* (1836) was the most successful opera produced during the first half of the nineteenth century and by 1900 had been performed a thousand times in Paris alone. Critics were divided

33 Giacomo Meyerbeer at age eleven, painting by Georg Weitsch, 1802

on Meyerbeer's musical accomplishments, but the general public throughout Europe loved his work. His grand operas, with their elaborate staging, large choral scenes, and use of the newest instruments, were visually and musically exciting even when they lacked spiritual depth. Neither his Jewishness nor his public image as a representative of French opera stood in the way when Frederick William IV, upon the prompting of Alexander von Humboldt, in 1842 appointed him director of music in Berlin, which was a Prussian state office. His one opera with a distinctly German theme, *Das Feldlager in Schlesien* (The Army Camp in Silesia, 1844), was frequently performed in Berlin on patriotic occasions.

For all of his fame, Meyerbeer remained acutely aware of his Jewishness and assumed that criticism of his work was motivated by an anti-Jewish bias shared by nearly all non-Jews. To Heine he wrote in 1839 that the effect of circumcision was permanent: "Whoever doesn't bleed to death from the operation by the ninth day will have it *continue* bleeding for the rest of his life, even after he's dead."[40] His immense wealth was both a blessing and a curse. It enabled him to live comfortably and to assist (and gain the gratitude of) worthy writers and musicians. But his affluence also bred animosity when he did not offer gifts or loans as freely as some desired or—as in the instances of Heine and Wagner—the recipients resented their dependence on him. For Heine, who during his later years loved to mock Meyerbeer in spite of the latter's frequently indicated high regard for him, the composer represented not only the wealth Heine envied but also living proof that an unbaptized Jew could make a recognized name for himself in European culture.

For Richard Wagner, writing his infamous essay "Judaism in Music," which first appeared anonymously in 1850, Meyerbeer—from whom he had learned musically and who had helped bring his first operas to the stage in Germany—possessed far darker symbolic significance. The "Jewish composer of our days who is known far and wide," as the author called him, refusing to mention his name, reminded Wagner unpleasantly of his earlier musical and financial dependence. Now he became the best example of the Jews' inherent inability to make a significant contribution to German culture. Even Felix Mendelssohn (1809–1847), the baptized grandson of Moses Mendelssohn and composer of Protestant church music who, Wagner admitted grudgingly, possessed talent, culture, and a sense of honor to the highest degree, was unable at any time "to evoke the profound heart and soul wrenching effect that we expect from art."[41] Having once praised Meyerbeer for his chaste sensibility, he now completely reversed his opinion, condemning the Jewish composer as a purveyor of false emotions whose popularity could best be explained by the degeneration of the public's taste in music. What was true for music was true as well for literature. It was no more possible for a Jew to be a German poet than a German composer. Heine, whom Wagner had also once befriended, now became for him a very talented poetic Jew, who skillfully employed scorn to uncover the lies of others but, in thinking himself a poet, had likewise become a liar. Of the four Jews to whom Wagner referred only Börne, he believed, had exceptionally eluded the curse of Jewishness not by his baptism but by the painful and liberating utter extirpation of the Jew within.

Wagner's article also laid out a broader charge about the Jews and German culture. They alone were ultimately responsible for its recent decay: the "*Verjudung* of modern art." He claimed that the German people felt an instinctual revulsion at a Jewish nature that, as it expressed itself in speech and in song, was fundamentally different from their own. Almost forty years after the first performance of *Unser Verkehr*, Wagner still held up allegedly indelible characteristics of language to prove that Jews must inevitably remain alien. Lacking roots in the German people, they could never address its emotional life except as outsiders. The cultivated Jew in this respect was no different from the Jew who lacked Bildung. Wagner's implied conclusion is that acculturation must necessarily fail, that Jew and German cannot be integrated within the spirit and emotion of any single individual. The thrust of this argument could not have been more devastating for the cultural hopes and aims of German Jewry. In 1869, still convinced of its truth, Wagner republished the essay in his own name, giving it wider currency.

It would be one-sided and misleading, however, to regard Wagner's virulent polemic as representative of German public opinion, in general, on the anticipated success or failure of Jewish acculturation at mid-century. The widespread fame enjoyed by the baptized Jews, Heine, Börne, and Mendelssohn, and by the unbaptized Jews, Auerbach and Meyerbeer, indicates that a broad range of Germans did not believe Jewish origin or conviction made a writer or composer unworthy of their attention. In 1848 non-Jews, who agreed with their political positions, supported Riesser and Jacoby regardless of their Jewishness. Yet popular acknowledgment was easier to attain than official recognition. Those Jews who sought to make a cultural contribution in fields located primarily in universities—in the humanities and the sciences—found that, in the absence of conversion, their path to a professorship was blocked. The most ambitious paid the necessary price. Others, some of them no less talented, were forced to do their work outside the university or to abandon it altogether. Even among those active in branches of culture not associated with universities— music, art, and literature—the pressure to convert remained strong. While few Christians at mid-century agreed with Wagner's proto-racism, German Jews had not succeeded in destroying the prevalent notion that acquisition of a perfected German Bildung also required—at least in name—the adoption of its religious foundation.

7 | From Subject to Citizen

T he increasing integration of German Jews in the cultural sphere took place parallel to similar developments in political and social life. The change in their identity from Jews living in the German states to German Jews or Jewish Germans was only possible on the basis of their greater participation in public and social life in general. However, as was the case with cultural developments, integration in this area remained incomplete. Although Jews had been wearing uniforms as soldiers of the German states since the beginning of the nineteenth century, and although many of them had achieved legal equality— some even entering the local parliaments as city councillors—they were nevertheless still excluded from state offices, numerous clubs, and dignitaries' associations. Even as the door to German society was being opened to them, Jews were stilled barred from entering its innermost chambers.

1. Loyalty and Patriotism

Motivated by a desire for acceptance within mainstream society, German Jews let it be known that their Judaism did not represent an obstacle to achieving that end. Jewish representatives firmly rejected the claim by opponents to their emancipation that Jews formed "a state within a state," emphasizing instead the purely religious character of Judaism. In addition to the traditional loyalty toward the sovereign, since the end of the eighteenth century public statements of gratitude, sermons, and textbooks

used in Jewish schools expressed a new identification, at first with individual German states and later with the German nation at large. Rabbis
and heads of Jewish communities stressed that Jewish religious law did
not stand in the way of fulfilling their newly won civic duties. Jews of
Austria, Prussia, and other German states demonstrated their love of the
fatherland on the battlefield during the Napoleonic Wars.

This redefinition of their relationship to the state was closely tied to
the granting of legal equality. In return for their emancipation, Jews had
to prove their loyalty as citizens. German Jews could follow the example
set by their coreligionists in neighboring France, who had been forced to
define their position vis-à-vis the state at an assembly of French Jewish
notables convened by Napoleon in 1806. The Jewish dignitaries emphasized that they viewed all Frenchmen as their brothers, unconditionally
recognized currently valid law in France, and were prepared to defend the
nation in armed conflict.

In the German states as well, where in contrast to France only partial
emancipation was granted, representatives of the Jewish communities
announced their willingness to subject themselves to the state and its
rulers. As soon as Frederick William III signed the Prussian Emancipation
Edict in March 1812, the elders of the Berlin Jewish community—including David Friedländer—issued the following statement to their monarch:

> Our ancestors have from time immemorial fulfilled their duties as
> *subjects* with unshakeable, never wavering loyalty. To this history
> has borne witness. How much the stronger and the more indissolu
> ble shall the bond be that ties the *citizens* to the sacred person of His
> Imperial Majesty and to the fatherland, since reverence and love
> have now been joined by the utmost gratitude.[1]

Similar letters by Jews of Breslau, Königsberg, and Potsdam followed a
short time later.

The change from subject to citizen was the determining force behind
the new sense of identity on the part of German Jews. The loyalty they
had declared as subjects toward their rulers, who were often hostile to
Jews, was usually based on utilitarian considerations intended to guarantee their security in a state regarded as foreign. As citizens or soon-to-be
citizens, on the other hand, they were truly in a position to identify themselves with the state in which they lived, considering it their fatherland.
As soon as the state accepted them as equals, or at least promised them
equality, they left no doubt as to their patriotism. German Jews increas-

ingly viewed themselves as part of a German state, and soon as part of the German nation, while their Jewish identity was relegated more and more to the private sphere of their religious beliefs.

This new sense of identity was expressed through numerous revised statutes and regulations of Jewish organizations and associations as well as in political statements by prominent Jewish representatives. Even a text such as the "Regulation for Burials in the Israelite Religious Community of Mainz" (1832), which hardly seems ideological, starts with a phrase denoting the new self-definition: "The national in us must diminish more and more. We form, thanks to the enlightened times, no longer a state within a state, no political corporation. Rather, we enjoy protection in our dissenting religion."[2] Only a few years later Gabriel Riesser could declare, without raising opposition, that "the nationality of the Jews lives only in our memories. . . . In reality, it has died."[3] When at the first assembly of Liberal rabbis in Germany, in 1844 in Brunswick, the question was posed whether German Jews should regard all people as their brothers, without any national distinctions, the preacher Naphtali Frankfurter of the Hamburg Temple responded as follows: "Recognizing human dignity is a cosmopolitan principle in Judaism. However, I strongly emphasize the love of one's [particular] nation and of its members. As people we love all people, but as Germans we love Germans as children of our fatherland. We are, and ought to be, patriots and not merely cosmopolitans."[4]

It was the responsibility of the intellectual elite within the communities to reinforce the new notion of Jews as German patriots. One of the most effective educational methods for strengthening patriotic attitudes were textbooks and catechisms intended to help Jewish students prepare for the newly created confirmation ceremony. These learning materials were especially important in the eastern parts of Austria, where they were used to "Germanize" the Yiddish-speaking Jewish populace. The impact of the catechisms of Herz Homberg (1749–1841), a former collaborator in Moses Mendelssohn's Bible translation and tutor of his sons, was unsurpassed in this regard. An essential element of his textbooks were lessons on love of one's fatherland and obedience to the laws of the monarch. It is therefore appropriate that the only prayer reprinted in *Bne-Zion* (Sons of Zion, 1812; see also chapter 3) is for the monarch. According to Homberg, the king reflects divine power on earth, and his commands must be obeyed entirely, since "everything that the regent of a nation orders regarding civil and political matters has the same power of law and holiness as if laid down by a king in Israel or the former highest court of the Israelites (the Sanhedrin)."[5]

Homberg's textbooks reflected the Austrian version of love of one's fatherland, which was largely shaped by Joseph von Sonnenfels, the baptized grandson of the rabbi of Brandenburg, in the final third of the eighteenth century. In contrast to the later form of Germanic-Christian nationalism that was influenced by Romanticism, this form of patriotism was based on rationalistic utilitarian principles. The well-being of the individual is very closely tied to the public welfare. For Sonnenfels love of the fatherland was a "manifestation of self-love. We seek that which is best for us by seeking that which is best for the fatherland; we love ourselves through our love for the fatherland." For Homberg love of the fatherland was first and foremost "valuing its constitution, laws, institutions, morals, and customs above all else, and supporting and reinforcing the common good in every possible way."[6] In a multinational state like Austria only such a supranational concept of love of fatherland was possible. Homberg's own biography provides ample proof of this. He was a native Bohemian Jew who became part of the circle surrounding Mendelssohn in Berlin. After leaving Berlin he spent the rest of his long life in Vienna, Trieste, Lemberg (L'viv), and Prague. Though they were all part of one fatherland, these cities later became centers of four different national movements.

Jews in Prussia and other German states, too, found the Austrian form of love of the fatherland more attractive than one based on a common "national spirit" (Volksgeist), which all too often excluded Jews from the outset. Only a few representatives of Orthodox Judaism still hesitated to declare themselves part of the German nation, though stressing their love for the fatherland and readiness to sacrifice for the sovereign. Among them was Rabbi Israel Deutsch (1800–1853) of Beuthen, who wrote, as late as the mid-nineteenth century: "We can come together and love one another as individuals, as citizens, and as cosmopolitans, but as a people we should and must remain outwardly separate until Providence shall choose to remove all differences of faith."[7] Even the followers of the Jewish Reform movement, however, clearly rejected the fanatical Germanness that was rooted in Romanticism. Saul Ascher, philosopher and champion of emancipation in Prussia, had already fiercely challenged it in his work Die Germanomanie (Germanomania, 1815). At a time when patriotism could mean both the welfare of each individual German state and an identification with the German nation as a whole, Jews were torn between the two concepts. On the one hand, they were asked to prove themselves loyal citizens of a state that refused to grant them full emancipation; on the other, they hoped national unification would ultimately bring legal equality, even though they were fully aware of the anti-Jewish sentiments expressed in the German national movement of the Vormärz, the period from 1815 until the March Revolution of 1848.

The loyalty shown by the Jewish population toward their rulers and the laws of the state was not a modern phenomenon. Prayers for the well-being of the respective ruler and the principle of obeying the laws of the state go back to late antiquity. The notion that non-Jewish state laws are to be obeyed to the same extent as are Jewish religious laws refers back to the dictum of the Babylonian scholar Rabbi Samuel from the third century. He declared that state law is also valid law for Jews (*dina de-malkhuta dina*). However, the interpretation of this sentence changed substantially during the period discussed here. Until the end of the eighteenth century the principle of dina de-malkhuta dina was applied only to certain areas defined in talmudic literature, essentially pertaining to laws regulating taxation of the Jewish communities. It was never used to justify the violation of Jewish religious laws.

In the age of emancipation Liberal rabbis expanded this talmudic principle to virtually all areas of social life. In order to facilitate the acceptance of Jews in society, they even modified essential aspects of Jewish religious law, such as observing the Sabbath and the dietary and marriage laws, whenever these conflicted with the demands of the modern state. Making reference to Rabbi Samuel's principle, a Liberal rabbi from Saxony-Meiningen declared in 1842 that Jewish schoolchildren were permitted to write on the Sabbath. A year later one of the leading reformers among German rabbis, Samuel Holdheim, referred to the same talmudic dictum in allowing government agencies to make legal decisions concerning marriage and divorce.

The question of reconciling Jewish religious law with civic duties was raised during this period specifically with respect to compulsory military service, which had been extended to apply to Jews for the first time. Within the scope of Austrian emperor Joseph II's reform politics, Jewish subjects were required to serve in the military starting in 1788. Between 1788 and 1815 at least 36,200 Jews served in the imperial army. In the German states controlled by Napoleon, especially the Kingdom of Westphalia, there was a large number of Jewish soldiers, some of whom gave their lives on the battlefields of Europe. The final breakthrough in Prussia

and other German states came during the Wars of Liberation against
Napoleon. Among Jews in Prussia alone the number of volunteers ran to
about 400 in 1813–1814, corresponding to 0.8 percent of the total Jewish
population, a ratio above the average participation among Prussians in
general. This is remarkable given the fact that only a few years earlier
Napoleon's troops had torn down the ghetto walls in European cities.

34   Wilhelm Devrient: *Jewish War Veteran*

The proportion of Jewish volunteers in some smaller states was even greater. Their percentage in Mecklenburg-Schwerin was three times that of the Christians who volunteered. The memoirs of Löser Cohen, a Jewish volunteer from Mecklenburg, convey the enthusiasm felt by Jewish soldiers:

> March 25, 1813, drew near, the day our ruler issued the call to volunteer for the two rifle corps to be formed. My heart pounded with joy; I was so thankful to be able to prove myself to ruler and fatherland. I approached my beloved parents with the words "The time has come when we Jews have the opportunity to faithfully serve the fatherland. I am committed to sacrifice myself for the beloved fatherland."[8]

Although his mother shed bitter tears, Cohen's father gave him his blessing. Others among the approximately eight hundred German-Jewish soldiers who fought in the Napoleonic Wars may have had similar experiences.

Among the volunteers there was also one woman. Louise Grafemus (Esther Manuel), a baptized Jew from Hanau, disguised herself as a man and served as an uhlan in the Prussian army, hoping to find her husband, who was serving in the allied Russian army. In a letter to the Prussian king she reported on her experiences as a female soldier and the two wounds she suffered. She also explained her motivation: "Although this is not a function of my sex, I was so overcome with patriotic zeal and devotion to the fatherland that I felt compelled to take this unusual step."[9] Her alleged attainment of the rank of sergeant and receipt of the Iron Cross is likely legendary, but it is documented that she received a pension from the Prussian state for the duration of her life. Another woman, Amalie Beer, mother of the composer Giacomo Meyerbeer, distinguished herself not on the battlefield but in a military hospital. She was the first Jew to receive the Medal of Louise (*Luisenorden,* named after the Prussian queen) for her care of the wounded.

Of course there were also those who sought to evade compulsory military service by paying a fee. Especially in the early phase of conscription in Austria, Joseph II received numerous petitions from Jewish communities in Galicia seeking to have Jews released from military service. Aside from common objections such as the long period of required service and the prevailing hygienic conditions in the army at that time, petitioners were also motivated by fear that they would be unable to observe Jewish religious laws. When military service was made compulsory for Jews in most German states during the nineteenth century, such attempts to gain release from service were made less frequently, though a few are known from the Deutsch-Krone region of West Prussia and from Heidelberg. Jews in the small Bavarian town of Floss expressed reservations, since they had still not been granted equal rights at the local level: "As certain as we are of the distinguished honor it is for every citizen to serve, so little do we feel obligated, since we do not enjoy the pleasure of having the status of citizen in Floss."[10]

The response of rabbis with respect to the new situation of compulsory military service varied. The earliest German-language blessing of Jewish soldiers by a rabbi was given in 1788 by Chief Rabbi Ezekiel Landau (1713–1793) of Prague. Despite his sense of duty to the emperor and fatherland as well as his hopes of an improved legal status to come, Landau expressed concerns about the fulfillment of all religious commandments:

My brothers, you who were my brothers, are still my brothers, and shall always be my brothers as long as you remain pious and upright! God and our most merciful emperor wish that you should be taken for military service. Go then to your destiny, follow without complaint, obey your superiors, be loyal and patient. But do not forget your religion. Do not be ashamed to be *yehudim* [i.e., Jews] among so many Christians. Pray to God daily upon rising, for service to God comes before all else. . . . You shall also be able to observe the Sabbath, as I have heard that you will usually rest on this day. Grease the wagons on Friday before evening falls, and anything at all that you can do the day before, do it then. . . . Refrain from all forbidden foods as long as possible. The emperor mercifully said that you shall never be forced to eat meat; you can always nourish yourselves from eggs, butter, cheese, and other permitted foods until you come to *yehudim*, where your benevolent comrades-in-arms and superiors will then allow you to join them.

During his speech Landau distributed *tsitsiyot* (fringes attached to the prayer shawl), tefilin (phylacteries), and prayer books to the twenty-five recruits. At the same time he urged that they prove themselves to be good soldiers "so that people will see that even our nation, oppressed until now, loves its rulers and governmental authorities and, if necessary, is willing to lay down lives. I hope that because of your efforts . . . these shackles that still loosely bind us will be fully removed."[11]

Landau was a man of the eighteenth century, but even in the nineteenth century Orthodox rabbis—predominantly in rural areas—expressed words of concern about whether the Jewish religious laws (Halacha) would be observed in the military. More and more, however, religious leaders articulated a new position that allowed for certain violations of the Halacha in times of war. In Breslau Rabbi Aaron Karfunkel advised Jewish volunteers during the Napoleonic Wars that in view of the "struggle for king and fatherland" religious duties were to be set aside. In times of war, according to Karfunkel, Jewish soldiers did not need to follow the dietary laws to the letter, nor were they required to recite all the prescribed prayers, for God "shall accept the service for the fatherland as a prayer." The assistant rabbi of Königsberg even spoke of a "holy war . . . for God, king, and fatherland"[12] when he delivered a sermon on the occasion of consecrating the local synagogue in 1815 and at the same time gave his blessing to fifteen enlistees.

Given the patriotic tenor of these rabbis, it should not be surprising that the catechisms of Herz Homberg, who was mentioned earlier as a radical reformer, called for absolute obedience to the state, even if it meant violating Jewish religious law. In his *Bne-Zion* Homberg had already declared that fighting for one's fatherland and monarch meant far more than merely fulfilling a duty, for "one cannot leave this world in a more noble manner than as a hero in battle for fellow citizens and liberty laid down in law." In his later catechism, *Ben Yakir* (Dear Son, 1814), the teacher asks the student whether in times of war "all duties of our religion [are to] be fulfilled." He answers:

It is true that on the battlefield one is not always in a position to satisfy all religious duties. In a war in which there is great danger, where the lives of many thousands of people are at stake, one need not strictly observe the religious requirements. The Talmud itself allows that one set aside the commandment to keep the Sabbath holy in order to save the life of even a single person.[13]

Declarations of patriotism were not limited to the military service of individual Jews; rather, they were clearly expressed in numerous official documents by rabbis and the heads of Jewish communities. They often made reference to traditional Jewish texts, especially the verse from Jeremiah (29:7): "Seek the welfare of the city to which I have exiled you, and pray to the Lord on its behalf; for in its prosperity you shall prosper."

Many communities, such as the one in Breslau, organized collections to benefit the war effort. Jewish merchants in Berlin, the Society of Friends, and other Jewish organizations and individuals worked enthusiastically to support the fund-raising efforts. In 1810, in the Franconian communities of Altenkunstadt and Burgkunstadt, the Jewish Education and Social Club paid a weekly allowance of one florin "to anyone without means who is serving as a defender of the fatherland and not avoiding this duty by finding a substitute." After the soldiers were discharged they received another three hundred florins.[14] And it was certainly no coincidence that the responsible parties chose as the date for the consecration of the new Israelite Temple in 1818 in Hamburg the fifth anniversary of the Battle of Leipzig in which the French forces met defeat.

By the end of the Napoleonic Wars, according to lists that were located decades later, over eighty Jewish soldiers in Prussian uniforms alone had been decorated and over forty had received promotions. However, with the end of hostilities, their careers as officers also came to an end. The hope that Rabbi Landau had explicitly expressed and to which other Jewish representatives doubtless gave silent assent turned out to be illusory. This was most obvious in Prussia, where Jewish officers and candidates for the officer corps were given no opportunity to continue their service. Prussian authorities justified this policy on the grounds of the king's own prescript that Jewish superiors should not be allowed to command Christian soldiers. Until World War I Jewish soldiers were allowed to become officers in the Prussian army only if they chose to convert.

The solitary exception to this rule was Meno Burg (1789–1853), who was promoted to the rank of a noncommissioned artillery officer in May 1813. In the winter of 1814–1815 he was hired as a mathematics teacher at the artillery brigade school in Berlin. The king made it perfectly clear that Burg would have to get baptized in order to continue his military career. Since he adamantly refused to convert, he was denied a promotion to the rank of artillery captain in 1830. When Burg was nonetheless promoted two years later, he was given a different uniform to distinguish him from Christian officers of the same rank. The fact that Burg was promoted at all, and even later received the title of major, can be traced back to his enjoying special favor from the head of the Prussian artillery, Prince August. Burg was well aware that he was the only Jew who had served during the Napoleonic Wars to be later raised to the rank of officer and that no other Jew had joined him in receiving such an honor.

Most other German states followed the restrictive policies of Prussia, but some proceeded in a more liberal fashion. Six Jews entered the officers' ranks in nineteenth-century Bavaria. Isidor Marx (1789–1862) was the first; he was promoted to the rank of lieutenant. Like Burg, Marx was

35 Meno Burg, the only Jewish officer in the Prussian army

forced to suffer numerous insults and setbacks. In his case he had to appear before the Ministry of War to protest his exclusion from serving on military courts because of his religious affiliation. In Austria there were Jewish officers as early as the first decade of the nineteenth century, but here, too, Jews were deferred during the reactionary period. Joseph Heinrich Singer (1797–1871), born in Lemberg, was an Austrian counterpart to Meno Burg. Though unbaptized, he served from 1831 as a captain in the Austrian army. In contrast to Burg, however, Singer enjoyed further promotions, becoming a colonel in 1847 and a major general only a year and a half later. Ironically, it was Singer—the first Jewish general in a European army—who, as commander of one of three brigades sent to Romagna in July 1849, recaptured the port of Ancona from Italian troops for the pope.

2. The Awakening of Political Consciousness

Jews residing in German states at the beginning of the nineteenth century received new rights along with their newly ordained duties. For the first time some were allowed to vote and hold office. Although still excluded from state posts and estates assemblies in the German states, they could distinguish themselves in the cities as politicians and dignitaries. In the decades before 1848 German Jews also entered the political limelight across regional boundaries as journalists and publishers.

Prerequisite for participation in local elections in Prussia, as laid down in the cities' ordinance of 1808, was acquisition of civic rights (*Bürgerrecht*) and a fixed minimum income. In principle both Jews and Christians were able to satisfy these requirements, although in most larger cities the proportion of those eligible to vote rarely exceeded 7 percent of the total population. In Berlin 275 Jews had attained civic rights by the April 1809 elections, in addition to twelve Jewish families that already had them since 1791. No figures are available regarding the exact number of Jews who, following the 1809 elections, were eligible to run for office or vote for the 102 representatives to the city assembly (*Stadtverordnete*) and fifteen unpaid city councillors (*Stadträte*). However, we know that two Jews were elected to these bodies of self-government. Banker Salomon Veit (1751–1827) was a city assemblyman; Moses Mendelssohn's student, David Friedländer (1750–1834), was elected a city councillor. Later, Ferdinand Moritz Delmar (Salomon Moses Levy), a baptized banker, also became a city councillor.

As early as 1793 Friedländer had expressed his ardent desire to be allowed to participate in local political affairs. "We are awaiting with childlike longing the moment of being appointed [to offices]; we are happy that we shall be allowed to participate and become more active for the good of the whole [society]."[15] Although he was pleased to be named "assessor of the Berlin manufactory and commercial collegium," after the election reform of 1808 he had to admit that Berlin Jewry was far from being allowed to participate in administrative affairs to a degree proportionate to its size. After Friedländer left office in 1814, and Veit in 1822, there were no elected Jewish representatives in the Berlin city administration until 1838. Since close relations between Jews and non-Jews were present only within the thin upper social stratum, Jewish representatives lacked sufficiently wide support to be elected. In the middle class, with its tight social network of guilds, church, lodges, and clubs, there was little contact between Christians and Jews. The fact that Jews were underrepresented among local politicians in major Prussian cities can thus not be traced to political disinterest, as some historians have assumed. The Jews in Berlin did their best to attain local civic rights and exercised their right to vote in disproportionately large numbers. The same was true in Königsberg, where Samuel Wulff Friedländer, a nephew of David Friedländer, sat on the city council beginning in 1809.

Legal discrepancies persisted in local bodies, even after the election of Jews. In Prussia, for example, only Christian members of the city councils were allowed to vote for members of the Prussian parliament. When a Jewish member of the city council in Königsberg, Moritz Wedel, was asked to step out during the election of representatives to parliament in 1840, he threatened to give up his mandate in protest. The president of the province, however, refused to accept it and reprimanded Wedel:

> Prussian Jewry was granted extensive rights by the Edict of 1812. But this by no means implied that Jews were thereafter free to demand all rights granted over the course of time to Christian citizens. . . . Consequently, it cannot be acknowledged that you have rightful cause to regard the continuation of your official duties on the city council as a violation of your personal or civic honor.[16]

Whereas Jews were long underrepresented in the local administrations of large cities in Prussia, the situation was different in the smaller towns of Upper Silesia, Posen, and to some extent West Prussia. The Jewish middle class in these areas was often more integrated in the towns' social life; even before the middle of the nineteenth century Jews here held important positions in commercial and cultural life. Two other factors contributed to Jews in these towns being elected to the local governments: first, their position as mediators between the German and Polish segments of the population; second, the considerable size of the Jewish population in these towns. In parts of Upper Silesia state the number of elected Jewish representatives was proportionately even higher than the relative size of the Jewish population. In Guttentag, where Jews made up 10 percent of the total population, they comprised half of the city council and one-quarter of the municipal assembly in 1815. Jews made up half the population in Zülz in 1827, but two-thirds of the city representatives.

The situation in the province of Posen differed on account of an official regulation that limited the number of Jewish members of the city council, usually to a maximum of one-fourth or one-third of all repre-

sentatives. Such restrictions sometimes produced a type of corporate representation, that is, Jewish voters elected a fixed contingent of Jewish representatives. In other places, however, Polish or German voters preferred
Jewish candidates, and Jewish voters Christian candidates. This sometimes
led to exceptional cases in which village or town mayors were Jewish, such
as in the village of Zawade in the 1840s and, after 1850, in the town of
Sarne, in the province of Posen. In some parts of Posen Jews even held the
paid position of financial officer in the municipal administration. In the
city of Posen itself, however, the first Jewish members of the city assembly were not elected until 1846, since until then the Jews had supported
non-Jewish German candidates.

Prussia was the first German state in which Jews were elected to local
offices. Although such election was theoretically possible in German
states that came briefly under French rule, Jews in Westphalia, Frankfurt, and the Hanseatic cities apparently showed little ambition to hold
office during this short period. Some exceptions were the banker Meyer
Amschel Rothschild, who became a member of the electoral assembly in
Frankfurt, and the physician Joseph Oppenheimer, who succeeded him
in 1812. When Jews were given local voting rights in 1813 in Bavaria
and a short time later in Hesse-Kassel, Hesse-Darmstadt, Württemberg,
and Baden, their active participation in local politics went forward
rather slowly. Not until the 1840s, when other states had begun granting Jews local civic rights, was there any significant increase in the number of Jewish local politicians, including village mayors, as was the case
in the Württemberg village of Unterschwandorf. Altogether, there were
300–320 Jews who were active members of city governments before
1848, half of them serving in the Prussian province of Posen and the
administrative district of Oppeln (in Upper Silesia) alone. As far as the
occupations of these Jewish local politicians can be reconstructed, a clear
majority of about 70 percent was active in commerce, banking, and industry, predominantly as merchants. Another 20 percent were independent professionals.

Political activity of Jews in public bodies was limited to the local level.
The estates assemblies of the German states were virtually closed to Jews.
Exceptional were the religious reformer Israel Jacobson and his brother,
both of whom had acquired an estate in Mecklenburg and were invited to
the representative body (*Landstände*) of this quite reactionary German
state. Bavarian court banker Joseph von Hirsch was elected to the Bavarian chamber of estates in 1845, but he could not assume the position be-

cause it required giving a Christian oath of allegiance. Representing Baden at the general German Exchange Conference (*Wechsel-Kongress*), Mannheim banker Joseph Hohenemser was the only unbaptized Jew serving in such an official capacity before 1848. Only two Jews became state civil servants in Prussia in this period: Meno Burg, who was already mentioned, and Solomon Sachs, the government building inspector.

The number of converted Jews with positions in the estates assemblies or as state civil servants was, however, far greater. Most prominent among them was Friedrich Julius Stahl (1802–1861), a specialist in canon law who was sent to the Bavarian chamber of estates from the University of Erlangen. Stahl, who was born in Catholic Bavaria and raised as an Orthodox Jew, served as a representative in the upper house of the Prussian parliament after 1848. As a politician he became a champion of the extremely conservative ideology of a Christian-Prussian state that would refuse Jews the same rights it extended to Christians (on Stahl see chapter 5).

Denied full access to political office, Jews could still exert influence on public opinion as journalists and publishers. As early as 1821 the antisemite Ludolf Holst complained that Jews attempted "to take over the editorial offices of a great many political newspapers and journals."[17] And Leopold Zunz, pioneer of the scholarly study of Judaism, could note as early as 1819 that forty more or less significant German writers were of Jewish descent. These included Zunz himself, as editor of the *Haude- und Spener'schen* newspaper in Berlin, as well as his colleague, author Lazarus Bendavid, and Gabriel Riesser, who wrote for the Hamburg *Börsenhalle*.

Yet despite the fact that some Jewish political writers appeared in the first third of the nineteenth century, a notable rise in Jews working in publishing and political journalism did not occur until the 1840s. Exemplary is Zacharias Löwenthal of Mannheim who, before his baptism in 1847, published the works of authors associated with the Young Germany literary movement. When he lost his right to publish in Mannheim for printing Gutzkow's controversial novel, *Wally, die Zweiflerin* (Wally, the Doubter), he moved to Frankfurt, where he published Marx and Engels's *Die heilige Familie* (The Holy Family). Together with Jakob Rütten (formerly Rindskopf), Löwenthal—who by this time had changed his name to Loening—founded the Rütten and Loening Literary Publishing House, which remained one of the most important institutions of its kind in Germany for almost a century. In Berlin Moritz Veit had published literature since 1834, a decade before being elected a member of the city council in 1846 and two years later a representative of the Liberals to the National Assembly in St. Paul's Church.

The participation of Jews in journalism was most obvious on the staff of the important opposition newspaper, the *Rheinische Zeitung*, in Cologne. In addition to founder Dagobert Oppenheim, Moses Hess, who later wrote the Zionist work *Rome and Jerusalem*, was also on the founding committee. Hess, along with Karl Marx and Heinrich Heine, was among the most active participants in the work of the newspaper. Even before the paper was founded in 1841, Hess had made a name for himself as a pioneer of scientific socialism through his books *Die Heilige Geschichte der Menschheit* (The Sacred History of Humanity, 1837) and *Die Europäische Triarchie* (The European Triarchy, 1841).

In contrast to Gabriel Riesser, whose political activities focused on the demand for the emancipation of the Jews, Johann Jacoby's most important political writings and statements dealt with Jewish issues either peripherally or not at all (on Riesser's and Jacoby's relations to Judaism see chapter 6). Jacoby's pamphlet, *Vier Fragen beantwortet von einem Ostpreussen* (Four Questions Answered by an East Prussian, 1841), summarized the political position of the liberal opposition in Prussia and urged Frederick William IV to keep the promise of his predecessor to approve a constitution. Contemporaries were well aware of the initial impact of this pamphlet and the central role that Jacoby played in the democratic movement in Germany. Historian Karl Biedermann wrote Jacoby: "You were the first to say the words that are certainly in the hearts and on the lips of thousands. You have given solid form to ideas that have since spread like wildfire throughout your fatherland. We in the rest of Germany likewise feel their effects vividly."[18]

Criminal prosecution did not keep Jacoby from continued political involvement. In 1842 he was sentenced to two and a half years in prison because of his work. When he appealed successfully it became a breakthrough for the legal recognition of political opposition. Jacoby continued his activities as a political writer with two pamphlets in 1845 explicitly demanding that a representative body of the entire nation be convened. The former scenario repeated itself; he initially received a strict sentence and was acquitted upon appeal.

Jewish concerns were not an issue in these writings, but Jacoby was aware of the close connection between the specific fate of German Jewry and the more comprehensive future of German society as a whole. In a letter he wrote:

> Just as I am *both* a Jew and a German, the Jew *in me* cannot become free without the German, and the German cannot be freed without the Jew. Just as I cannot divide myself, I also cannot separate in myself the freedom of one from the freedom of the other. We are languishing all together in a great prison. Whether that prison gets larger or smaller, the chains heavier or lighter, is but a small difference for those longing not for comfort but for liberty. This liberty cannot be granted to an individual. Only *all* of us together can attain it or *none* of us will. For it is by one and the same enemy and for the same reason that we are being held prisoner. Only the *destruction* of the prison can lead us to our goal.[19]

While Jacoby worked in "the provinces" prior to 1848, there were also Jews who were politically active in Berlin, the Prussian capital. In 1843 city councillor Daniel Alexander Benda declared in his *Katechismus für wahlberechtigte Bürger Preussens* (Catechism for Citizens of Prussia who are Eligible to Vote) that achieving political liberty was a prerequisite for German unification.

The fact that all the German Jews mentioned here were radical democrats or liberal-minded political activists by no means implies that these political views were common among the general Jewish population in the period leading up to the March 1848 revolution. Most Jewish politicians active at a local level represented the same bourgeois attitudes as their Christian colleagues and many of them, such as the Cologne banker Abraham Oppenheim, regarded themselves as conservatives. Although no reliable statistics are available, it can be assumed that most of the Jews living in German states had generally conservative views toward the existing system of rule and government. This included proponents of the Jewish Reform movement but even more so Orthodox Jews, who continued to dominate German Jewry until the middle of the century. They tended to interpret all criticism of the existing state by Jewish writers as a violation of the duty to remain loyal to the laws of the state. It is therefore necessary to distinguish the Jewish population at large, which in this period was mainly conservative and loyal to the monarchy, from the more radical liberal and democratic attitudes of the small number of politically active Jewish writers.

3. Professional and Social Progress

Professional and social integration of Jews in German-speaking Central Europe advanced only slowly during the first half of the nineteenth century. While considerable success was achieved in some areas, Jews remained excluded from others. Professional organizations, such as stock exchange corporations and chambers of commerce opened up to the Jews (see chapter 2), as did liberal clubs and associations. But Jews hoped in vain for a career at German universities. The height of persisting social barriers is evident in the difficulties experienced by successful Jewish bankers and businesspeople in receiving official recognition, in the continuing conflicts over equal rights for Jews at the local level, and in the resistance to their active participation in social clubs.

Not until 1834 was the title of privy commercial councillor, reserved for distinguished businessmen, awarded to a Jew, Nathan Rothschild. All in all, five Prussian Jews received the title of *Geheimer Kommerzienrat* by 1848, and eleven others were given the lower status of *Kommerzienrat*. However, in Prussia no Jew was raised to the nobility without previous conversion until the Gründerzeit, the period of rapid industrial expansion after 1871. This was very different from the situation in Austria. In contrast to the Prussian state, where guilds, courtly circles, bureaucrats, and officers kept their ranks closed until well into the nineteenth century, the Austrian government supported the social integration of Jewish bankers and merchants into the upper strata of the bourgeoisie. By 1872, when Bismarck's banker, Gerson Bleichröder, became the first unbaptized Prussian Jew to receive a title of hereditary nobility (Cologne banker Abraham Oppenheim had previously been ennobled, but he had no male heirs), this honor had long ceased to be a rarity in Austria. As early as 1797 business partners Bernhard Eskeles, Nathan Adam Arnstein, and Salomon Herz were all ennobled. Eskeles, who founded and directed the Austrian National Bank and his brother-in-law, Arnstein, were even named barons in 1822. The Arnstein-Eskeles company had proven its patriotism in 1813 by donating 155,000 florins to support the fatherland. By 1848 twenty-six Jewish families had received titles of nobility in Austria.

In some of the smaller German states, too, it was possible for Jews to be ennobled without converting to Christianity. The Bavarian banker Jacob Hirsch (1765–1840) purchased the Gereuth Manor in Lower Franconia in 1815, thus satisfying the formal prerequisite for a title of nobility. Three years later, as Jacob von Hirsch-Gereuth, he was the first Jew to become a major landowner in Germany who possessed patrimonial jurisdiction. His son Joseph von Hirsch (1805–1885), who was also a court banker in Munich, served as consul for Württemberg in 1840; and his grandson Moritz von Hirsch (1831–1896)—the addressee of the initial version of Herzl's *Judenstaat* (The Jews' State)—rose to fame during the second half of the century in banking and railroad construction in Belgium, Austria, and France. Like the Rothschilds in Frankfurt, the Hirschs in Munich remained faithful to Judaism, whereas other Bavarian Jewish families, like the Seligmann-Eichthals or the Pappenheimers, paid for their titles of nobility with baptism.

Social recognition of Jews varied according to their respective occupations. Among physicians, for example, there were individual Jews who at a very early time were treated as equals by their Christian colleagues. Although there were only two Jewish doctors practicing in Berlin in 1750, the number had risen to twelve by the turn of the century, representing nearly one-quarter of all practicing physicians. Even in smaller cities there was often a considerable number of Jewish doctors. In 1800 three of eleven doctors in Posen were Jewish, including the first city physician (*Stadtphysikus*). Some areas with a large Jewish population, such as Kempen in the province of Posen, at times had only Jewish doctors. Nevertheless, there were restrictions on Jewish physicians throughout the entire first half of the nineteenth century. Most states did not allow Jews to become military doctors, positions to which they had been welcomed during the Napoleonic Wars. In 1845 the Berlin city council still did not allow Jews to serve as physicians for the poor, explaining that this position often included functioning as pastor for a dying patient.

Jewish lawyers had considerably more difficulty. Only very few states— Württemberg, Baden, the two Hessian states, and Frankfurt am Main— allowed Jewish lawyers to practice in the first half of the nineteenth century. In Karlsruhe Veit Ettlinger (1796–1877) was the royal court attorney from 1824. In contrast to numerous Jewish jurists who converted to Christianity, Ettlinger was also active in the affairs of the Jewish community. There were ten Jews among ninety-four attorneys in Frankfurt am Main in 1837, most of whom were part of the upper social stratum of the community. The only options given Jews in most other states, especially Prussia, were baptism or working outside of their profession. Karl Marx's father Heinrich, for example, chose baptism in order to continue the career in law that he had started during the period of French rule in Trier. Samuel

Loeb Grünsfeld, who in 1834 became a royal advocate in the Bavarian city of Fürth, and Gabriel Riesser, who served as a notary in Hamburg starting in 1840, are exceptions that prove the rule.

Physicians and lawyers belonged to the growing class of Jews with a higher secular education. In fact, the proportion of Jewish students at many universities soon surpassed the percentage of Jews in the general population. In the first half of the nineteenth century, for example, Jews made up 2–3 percent of the student body in Heidelberg; in the 1840s, in Breslau, as much as 8–10 percent. Even disregarding the large number of foreign students who were Jewish, one can assume that in the period from 1815 to 1848 the proportion of Jewish students relative to the total Jewish population was twice the proportion of Christian students. However, a college diploma represented the end of the academic careers of almost all of the Jewish students; in seeking a position as professor they confronted barriers against the hiring of Jews in state civil service positions. Some managed in individual cases to become unpaid lecturers (*Privatdozenten*) in liberal states such as Baden, but even there it was impossible to receive a salaried position. The academic senate of the University of Heidelberg issued the following statement in 1815: "The status of an academic teacher must be regarded as too honorable to be violated by the intriguing nature, self-interest, and intrusiveness of a Jew. For daily experience shows that these attitudes predominate collectively among Jews."[20]

In Bavaria applicants received letters of rejection written in a similar tone, even for positions as Privatdozenten. Sigmund Julius Beer, who graduated with honors from the University of Heidelberg, spent seven years seeking a position as a lecturer in the department of medicine at the University of Würzburg, until a ministerial resolution of 1824 ultimately served as a final rejection. An earlier statement, made by the department, held that "only a Jew [could] be so shameless to claim that . . . the subjects of psychology, anthropology, and the theory of animal magnetism were covered either insufficiently . . . or not at all."[21]

Not a single Jew was hired as a full professor in Gemany prior to 1848, and even the number of unpaid Jewish university lecturers remained very small. Prussia had the most stringent restrictions, following a cabinet order of 1822 that prohibited Jews from acquiring the postdoctoral degree of *Habilitation*, a prerequisite to becoming a professor. An 1847 Prussian law finally allowed Jews access to an academic career at Prussian universities but restricted them to the areas of medicine, the natural sciences, geography, and languages. Yet even this limited prerogative met opposition from the academic senates of all universities, except Berlin and Bonn, which filed objections on the basis of the denominational wording of their statutes. Even in Hesse-Kassel, where Jews could serve in the civil service since 1833, there were no Jewish full professors before 1848.

The obstacles faced by mathematician Moritz Abraham Stern (1807–1894) serve to illustrate the difficulties often encountered by German Jews in their academic careers. He had received his doctorate from the most prominent German mathematician, Karl Friedrich Gauss, in Göttingen and started working there as a lecturer. A friend of Gabriel Riesser, he ardently supported his struggle for emancipation and was actively involved in founding the society for radical religious reform in Frankfurt am Main. Although well-qualified, Stern was not given a permanent position at the University of Göttingen, since he refused to convert. Even non-Jewish contemporaries saw this religious discrimination as cause for criticism. The *Hallesche Jahrbücher* wrote in 1842 that "Stern would have long been a professor if he were not a Jew."[22] He had to eke out his living through temporary contracts and private instruction and was forced to sell a gold medal he had been awarded in 1838 by the Brussels Academy of Science. Stern finally became an associate professor in 1848, and in 1859—thirty years after receiving his doctorate—he was the first Jew to be named full professor at a German university. Before 1848 there was only one case of a Jew becoming a full professor anywhere in the German-speaking realm. Physiologist and anatomist Gustav (Gabriel) Valentin held a position in Bern from 1836, but even in Switzerland he was deemed an exception at the time.

Outside the university, academic and cultural institutions and numerous—though by no means all—clubs and associations opened their doors to Jews during this period. The Academy of Fine Arts in Berlin accepted court medal engraver Abraham Abramson as a member in 1790. Prior to that a society of Jewish and Christian friends of music had formed, honoring the memory of Moses Mendelssohn with concerts and donating its proceeds to the poor of all religious denominations. Museum societies in Altona, Karlsruhe, and Stuttgart already had Jewish members in the early nineteenth century, although similar associations elsewhere still barred their doors to Jews.

Restriction of Jewish membership in the reading societies, which were formed in hundreds of cities starting in 1760, also varied from city to city. Progressive reading clubs, such as that in which Johann Jacoby played a central role in Königsberg, often formed the intellectual core of the liberal democratic movement and were open to Jews and non-Jews alike. Whereas Ludwig Börne's father and two Jewish physicians were already on the membership list of a reading society in Bonn in 1790, Börne himself complained that certain reading societies in Frankfurt am Main still did not accept Jewish members in 1819. There were indeed reading societies in the first half of the nineteenth century in Frankfurt as well as Berlin that accepted only Christians; exclusively Jewish societies also existed, as did those with both Christian and Jewish membership.

Remarkably, some of the clubs that regarded themselves as nationalistic had little difficulty accepting Jews as members. Jewish gymnasts were among the members of the Hamburg gymnastics club of 1816, the oldest of its kind in Germany. Contemporary sources confirm that this was not an exception in the early history of the gymnastics movement. An 1847 report of a gymnastics tournament in Mainz relates: "Not only are there many Jewish gymnasts who are participating actively, but also a great number of Jews are among the enthusiastic spectators."[23] The gymnastics clubs did not begin to discuss closing their membership to Jews until the 1880s. Singing clubs, which were part of the national movement in the period before the 1848 revolution, were also open to Jews. However, separate Jewish and Christian singing clubs began to form, since the standard repertoire included many Christian songs. Even the nationalistic student fraternities (*Burschenschaften*) before 1848 were not generally opposed to accepting Jews, despite some antisemitic tendencies. While the total number of Jewish members in the secret Burschenschaften is difficult to determine, some individuals are known by name. Johann Jacoby, for example, was a member of a fraternity in Königsberg in 1824. Ferdinand Lassalle was active in Breslau in 1845, and Moritz Jutrosinski, a Jewish medical student, even represented a Breslau group at a meeting of all Burschenschaften in Germany, in 1848 in Eisenach. The writer Berthold Auerbach spent several months in jail after being accused of a revolutionary conspiracy in connection with his membership in a Tübingen fraternity. In Erlangen David Morgenstern (1814–1882), who later became the first Jewish parliamentarian in Bavaria, was in the Germania Burschenschaft. Jews did, however, remain barred from some fraternities, especially those with Teutonic tendencies, such as the Schwarzen (Blacks) in Giessen, the Teutonen in Erlangen, and the Jena Burschenschaft.

Some Jewish men participated in the salons in Berlin and Vienna, but they were primarily a sphere belonging to Jewish women. Around the turn of the nineteenth century Jews made up about 20 percent of all women attending salons in Berlin. The ratio of Jews among those women who hosted salons in Berlin is much more dramatic. Of the twelve women who held social gatherings in their homes, nine were of Jewish descent. In Vienna, the house of Fanny von Arnstein (née Itzig) was an important social meeting place. During the Congress of Vienna in 1815 an illustrious group of aristocrats and diplomats regularly gathered in her salon on Tuesday evenings. Among the guests were Cardinal Severoli, the papal nuncio in Vienna, the Duke of Wellington, as well as Prussian state officials Prince Karl August von Hardenberg and Wilhelm von Humboldt. Fanny von Arnstein was raised in Prussia and attached great importance to celebrating Christmas according to Prussian custom, with a decorated tree—which was registered with dismay by the Austrian authorities. However, in contrast to the most prominent Berlin salonières—Henriette Herz, Rahel Varnhagen, and Mendelssohn's daughter Dorothea Veit—Arnstein refused throughout her lifetime to convert and she took up the concerns of her fellow Jews during the congress. Baron von Stägemann, the Prussian delegate at the congress, reported: "I spent yesterday evening at the Arnsteins, where I also supped.... Mrs. Ephraim released her flashes of inspiration and let them strike. Mrs. von Arnstein was particularly gracious to me, since I have prepared a favorable resolution for the Jewish communities in Hamburg, Lübeck, and Bremen."[24] The salon society of Berlin and Vienna at the close of the eighteenth century made it possible for the first time for women and men of different social status and religious affiliation to meet regularly and speak intensively in a private setting. But their social encounter was to end early in the new century. The Christian-Germanic identity that became prevalent within a small circle of writers and intellectuals in Prussia soon found its expression in the Christlich-Deutsche Tischgesellschaft, which did not accept even converted Jews into its ranks (see chapter 1). The free social interchange that characterized the salons came to an end without having exerted any lasting influence on the lives of German Jews.

Like the Christlich-Deutsche Tischgesellschaft, most of the exclusive dignitaries' associations remained closed to Jews throughout the first half of the nineteenth century. Simon Aron (Belmont), a merchant in Alzey and father of well-known American banker August Belmont, was active in starting the local carnival club, Narhalla, and led its shrovetide carnival meetings in 1844, but his efforts to become a member in the respected local elite club proved futile. Even possession of a title of nobility did not help the banker Joel Jakob von Hirsch gain membership in the Harmony Society, an elite social club in Würzburg in the 1830s. The response of Würzburg Jews was thereupon to form their own social club with similar goals. Only under exceptional circumstances were Jews accepted as members in dignitaries' associations. Alexander Haindorf (1782–1862) an (honorary) professor at the medical-surgical educational institution in Münster, for example, not only became a member of the Westphalian Association for History and Archeology but could even be president of the Art Association for the Rhineland and Westphalia. However, he remained the only Jew in Westphalia to obtain membership in such a society during the first half of the nineteenth century.

Tensions between the Christian and Jewish populations sometimes arose with respect to Jews participating in riflemen's societies and festive shooting matches (*Schützenfeste*). In some places Jews were allowed to join rifle clubs, while elsewhere they could participate in the festivities, but not as active riflemen. The riflemen's society in Werl rejected the membership of Levi Lazarus Hellwitz (1786–1860), a financial broker and staunch supporter of religious reform who served for a time as head of the Jewish community in Westphalia. In justification of the rejection it was explained that Jews were not full citizens, they were not allowed admission to any clubs, and they enjoyed no local civic rights. In addition, the explanation continued, the shooting matches opened with religious services and possessed a Christian character. Hellwitz and his supporters were not appeased. They countered with appeals for tolerance toward people of different faiths and arrived at the opening of the *Schützenfest* of 1825. In the rioting that ensued Hellwitz and his companions were chased from the fairgrounds. That same evening "a journeyman carpenter belonging to the party of Jews [was] beaten to death with a wagon stake during an altercation on the street."[25] Soon afterward Hellwitz left the town of Werl to settle elsewhere.

In extreme cases the Jewish population remained totally excluded from community affairs until the mid-nineteenth century, maintaining a separate corporate existence. In the Upper Palatinate town of Floss the local authorities successfully protested the dissolution of the independent Jewish community, as prescribed by the Bavarian government in 1819. The approximately four hundred Jews living there, who fought to no avail to be allowed to share municipal institutions, were forced to reestablish their own political community in 1824, electing their own mayor and Jewish delegates. They were permitted to share only the police authorities with the rest of the local inhabitants. Even after a fire in 1838 rendered Jews homeless, they were allowed to settle only temporarily outside of the Jewish quarter. A year later they were forced to leave the non-Jewish part of the town. The only other documented example—albeit less extreme— of separate Jewish existence is from the Thuringian town of Aschenhausen, where approximately thirty Jewish families had their own town administration.

Even in places where Jews lived as part of the local community, there was often considerable resistance to their being granted full equality. They continued to be denied essential rights of local residents, in particular access to so-called *Bürgernutzen*, or communal resources, which had great financial significance in many smaller communities. Whereas current law allowed both Jews and Christians to make use of such resources in the form of wood and grass, this did not coincide with the traditional way of thinking of the Christian village and town populace. In some cases conflicts over Jews using these public resources persisted into the twentieth century. In the Hessian town of Kirchhain, for example, the issue whether Jews should be included in the list of citizens authorized to use such public resources was finally settled by the Supreme Administrative Court of Berlin only in 1921.

Resistance to Jews' receiving equal rights at the local level sometimes manifested itself in violence. After Jews in the Hessian town of Windecken were promised access to communal firewood in accordance with new regulations, the homes of Jews were attacked in April 1835. Following the receipt of threatening letters, the windows and doors of sixteen homes were shattered and broken down with axes. Five years earlier in the same region, in the former county of Hanau, there had been massive anti-Jewish rioting, at that time, however, not the result of specific local events but part of a broader wave of similar actions throughout southern Germany and in Hamburg, spawned by the 1830 July Revolution in France.

Assessing the political and social integration of Jews in the German-speaking realm during the sixty years between Mendelssohn's death and the failed German revolution yields contradictory images. By 1848 German Jews had, without exception, left their ghetto and were on their way to becoming German citizens. But the high hopes of social integration among Mendelssohn's heirs were fulfilled only in part. In the first half of the nineteenth century there were instances at a local level in which Jews and Christians came together within an institutional framework, though that was limited largely to the upper social strata in the cities. Declarations of loyalty toward the authorities of individual German states and increasing identification with the German nation in the Vormärz period led neither to acceptance in state offices nor to election into the regional parliaments. A more far-reaching integration was now less dependent on specific regulations pertaining to the Jewish minority and more on comprehensive changes in society itself. The events of 1848 finally brought these changes within reach.

Part Two
1848–1871

8 | Between Revolution and Legal Equality

The years between the failed revolution and the founding of the Second German Empire were marked by significant political, demographic, and economic developments for Jews living in the German states. Although the legal equality that was attained in certain areas at the beginning of this period turned out to be just as short-lived as the related democratic achievements of the revolutionary years in general, this reactionary backlash did not prove lasting. After a number of smaller German states in the south finally granted their Jewish residents legal equality in the early 1860s, the establishment of a dual Habsburg monarchy and the founding of the North German Confederation, both in 1867, brought the emancipation process to an end in both Austria-Hungary and Prussia. The German-Jewish population also experienced unprecedented demographic changes between 1848 and 1871. Whereas before 1848 Jews in most of the German states lived largely in rural areas or small towns, rapid urbanization occurred in the second half of the century. Migration from the smaller communities was augmented by a significant wave of emigration to the United States. However, the changes during this period were most visible in the economic and social spheres. A large portion of the Jewish minority managed to climb from the lower social classes into the middle class, a development shared by no other population group. This economic rise brought with it increasing social acceptance, which, however, still remained far from complete even at the founding of the German Empire in 1871. Once full legal emancipation had been achieved, barriers still existed at the personal level, in local clubs, and with regard to acceptance into certain professions. This period also witnessed violent antisemitic riots, although these occurred mainly during the revolution itself. In general, the setbacks suffered by German Jewry from 1848 to 1871 could not dampen the general optimism instilled by a sense of economic and political advance.

1. 1848: A Year of Contradictions

No other population group experienced the unrest of the revolution of 1848–1849 in the German states with such mixed feelings as the Jewish minority. For the first time Jewish politicians entered the public limelight as elected representatives at the state level; legal barriers to their state and local civic rights finally fell. Yet while German Jews welcomed these developments, they were also outraged over the most violent anti-Jewish unrest since the "Hep Hep" riots of 1819.

Before German Jews could reap the benefits of the revolution, they were confronted with violence. As early as February 1848, as news spread of the revolutionary events in Paris and two Jews were appointed ministers in France, riots broke out against the Jewish communities in Alsace. After their homes were destroyed and their property pillaged, numerous Jewish refugees sought shelter and protection on the other side of the Rhine, in Baden, and also in Switzerland. But here, too, they became victims of violent attacks. In the first half of March physical assaults on Jews took place in Müllheim, Gailingen, Randegg, and other localities. In the Kraichgau and the Odenwald region, in particular, scarcely any Jewish communities were spared plunder, vandalism, and blackmail. In all, thirty-three anti-Jewish riots were registered during the March Revolution in Baden. Other centers of violence were Franconia, Württemberg, eastern Westphalia, and Upper Silesia, that is, rural areas with a relatively high proportion of Jews—as had also been the case during the anti-Jewish rioting of 1819 and 1830. A detailed description of the attacks is extant for the town of Baisingen in Württemberg. There, after violent actions in mid-March, during which ten Jewish homes were demolished, the Jewish community had begun to protect itself with hired guards. On Easter Monday, April 24, 1848,

> a gang of about forty Christian residents of the town formed . . . and began first and foremost to chase our hired Jewish and Christian

guards from the street. They smashed down the doors of most of the Jewish homes and broke the windows of the stores. They were armed with heavy stones, large and small clubs, axes, and cleavers. They threw [stones] through the shattered windows into the homes and yelled: "Money or death!"[1]

The anti-Jewish rioting was not the only violent unrest during the chaos of 1848. There was fighting at the barricades on the streets of the cities, and the rural population revolted against the authorities after crop failures in 1845 and 1846 had led to severe hardship in the agrarian communities. Sometimes not only Jews but pastors, teachers, or mayors were victims of the violence. However, anti-Jewish rioting was not always related to general acts of violence. One must assume that although the former cannot be strictly separated from the popular discontent, it was just as strongly fed by specifically anti-Jewish sentiment arising from traditional religious and economic motives and, in particular, from the local civic equality granted to the Jews. Precisely in the rural areas and in small towns, there was sometimes considerable resistance to the social mobility and increased social acceptance of Jews and to their new activity in politics. Finally, the role played by religious prejudices in the 1848 riots should not be underestimated: it was not by chance that the peak of the violence in many areas occurred on Good Friday and on Easter Monday.

In the Habsburg Empire anti-Jewish actions also occurred in larger cities. Although no violence against Jews took place in Vienna, there was massive rioting in Pressburg (Bratislava), Budapest, and Prague. Demands by Christian merchants to ban Jews from districts of the city outside the Jewish living area, which had already led to anti-Jewish unrest in Pressburg, marked the start of rioting shortly before Easter 1848 in Prague as well. There were subsequent demands to close the open-air flea market, followed soon after by violent actions. The incensed mob attacked a Jewish store in the Christian part of the city; Jewish traders at the open-air market were also physically assaulted and their stands looted. Although things stayed calm in Prague during the Easter holidays themselves, not least due to a public appeal by the archbishop, anti-Jewish actions resumed in late April. When the Jewish section was attacked in early May, a Jewish militia that had already been formed was generally successful in fighting off the attackers, keeping them from entering the homes and shops, though considerable material damage ensued through broken window panes and destruction of storerooms. Jews in other Bo-

36   Anti-Jewish riots in Pressburg (Bratislava), April 24, 1848

hemian and Moravian cities protected their property as members of the general militia. In Prossnitz, an industrial center in Moravia where many factories were run by Jews, they even formed a Jewish unit of two hundred men, which was successfully able to ward off the anti-Jewish aggressors. In some Hungarian cities citizens motivated by fear of competition were able to convince city authorities to ban Jews, but the central government intervened against such measures.

The growing number of anti-Jewish pamphlets during the revolution projected a contradictory image of Jews—one repeatedly propagated thereafter—as the group to blame either for the atrocities of the revolution or of the reactionaries, depending on the appropriate context. Jews appeared both as beneficiaries of the revolution, which would bring them emancipation, and as counterrevolutionaries.They were condemned by the left as police informers and agents of an alleged Rothschild conspiracy, while in the conservative press the revolution was soon regarded as a "Jewish conspiracy" and a "Red Jewish agitation." The conservative Berlin *Kreuzzeitung*, which had blamed "180 Jews and other boys, bankrupt craftsmen, and drunks" for starting the March Revolution in Berlin, at the same time accused Jews of cowardly hiding in attics. And immediately after the revolutionary actions, the *Kreuzzeitung* predicted, "God's judgment [will] respond to the treason and ingratitude of wayward Jews with persecution the likes of which the world has never known and which will then, without doubt, strike innocent Jews as well."[2]

However, it would be a distortion of the facts to limit an evaluation of the significance of the revolutionary years to the physical conflict in the streets and the anti-Jewish propaganda in broadsides and the press. These negative phenomena stand in remarkable contrast to political developments in the parliaments that formed during this period and to the revolutionary events themselves. A new age truly seemed to be dawning for German Jewry. Jews were welcomed by non-Jews as comrades-in-arms at the barricades; they were accepted as colleagues in parliamentary debates. Even on the local level violent riots like those in Baisingen could produce countervailing reconciliatory tones. For example, a newspaper from the neighboring town of Horb reported in April 1848 that "luckily, not all the towns in our district share the attitudes in Baisingen. This was pleasantly

37 Anti-Jewish leaflet from the year 1848

demonstrated in today's election of representatives to the National Assembly. When [citizens of]the three communities of Mühl, Nordstetten, and Rexingen came here today to exercise their right to vote, they arrived peacefully together with their Jewish citizens, drank together in the pubs, and returned home together in peace." A few days earlier the same provincial paper had printed a poem entitled "Christian or Jew" under the heading "You are all children of one Father." One of the verses, in rhymed rendition, went as follows:

> Christian or Jew!
> Whether it's to God or Jehovah we pray,
> Attend church or synagogue on Sabbath day,
> If only the person that's in us we'll see,
> Then the same Fatherland ours will be,
> Then the same blood will flow in us too
> Then it's all one,
> Whether Christian or Jew![3]

The names of approximately 130 Jews who participated in armed revolutionary struggles throughout Germany have been documented, though the actual figure is certainly higher. In Austria, where the revolution was generally more violent and the legal status of Jews generally worse than in most German states, Jewish participation was particularly striking. Of the five casualties in the street battles of the March Revolution in Vienna, two were Jews. They were of different social backgrounds: the polytechnic college student Karl Heinrich Spitzer and the weaver Bernhard Herschmann. Jewish and Christian clergy participated together in the funeral services that were held for them and for others who had fallen (see chapter 5). In Berlin, where the bourgeois press and representatives of the proletariat spoke out in articles and public statements for the emancipation of the Jews, and where individual Jews played a significant role in the democratic associations, the number of Jews lost in the March unrest comprised 4–5 percent of the total number of deaths, a higher percentage than that of Jews in the population as a whole. At the funeral services for those who died in the March Revolution in Berlin, Rabbi Michael Sachs spoke along with Christian members of the clergy.

During the final days of the revolution and its bloody suppression, Jews were again among the casualties. On November 23, 1849, in Vienna, Hermann Jellinek—whose brother Adolph would become the rabbi of Vienna eight years later—was executed because he had called for armed struggle against the reactionary forces and for support of social democracy. In the Rhineland and Westphalia as well, strong Jewish participation in the struggles has been documented. At the large public assembly in September 1848 in Düsseldorf, three of the speakers before the crowd of ten thousand democrats were Jews, including Ferdinand Lassalle. Among the delegates to the Westphalian Congress for the Affairs and Rights of the Prussian National Assembly and the Prussian People that convened in November 1848 were also two Jewish teachers and Rabbi David Rothschild of Hamm, all of whom had been sent by local associations and political clubs.

The impression that there was relatively high Jewish participation in revolutionary politics can be confirmed with respect to political bodies. Once again, Vienna played a significant role. The revolutionary mood was triggered there not least by the passionate appeal of the Hungarian Jewish physician Adolf Fischhof (1816–1893), on March 13, 1848, to overthrow the regime. The student committee formed at the end of March had a large number of Jewish members in addition to the chair, Joseph Goldmark. And Fischhof chaired the security committee that was convened in May, where Karl Freund, one of his two deputies, was also of the Jewish faith. Goldmark and Fischhof, as well as the preacher Isaac Noah Mannheimer of Vienna, and Rabbi Berusch Meisels of Cracow, were elected to the Reichstag in July of that year.

In 1848, for the first time, Jews were represented in the parliaments or constitutional assemblies in Prussia, Bavaria, Brunswick, Mecklenburg-Schwerin, Saxony-Anhalt, Hesse-Homburg, Frankfurt, and Lübeck. Fourteen of 188 representatives in Hamburg were Jews. The greatest symbolic significance, however, was accorded the five Jewish parliamentarians in the Preliminary Parliament (*Vorparlament*) in Frankfurt and the nine representatives in the National Assembly. Among the former was the writer Berthold Auerbach; among the latter, the soon-to-be National Liberal politician Ludwig Bamberger. The two most prominent Jewish politicians in the period from 1815 up to the March Revolution of 1848, Johann Jacoby and Gabriel Riesser, both served as representatives in the Preliminary Parliament and the National Assembly (on these two men see chapters 6 and 7). Jacoby, who had the more radical political views of the two, did not succeed in gaining election in his hometown of Königsberg; he was able to enter the Frankfurt National Assembly as a substitute in April 1849, after earlier winning a seat in the Prussian National Assembly in Berlin. He was part of the deputation that tried, in vain, to gain support

38   Johann Jacoby at the head of the delegation to
King Frederick William IV, 1848

from Frederick William IV for the interests of the parliament. During the
deputation he made his famous comment, that it is the bad luck of kings
that they do not wish to hear the truth. Jacoby, who became a progressive
member of the Prussian parliament in the 1860s, ended his career as a
social democrat.

Like Jacoby, Riesser, who served for a time as second vice president of
the National Assembly, also tied demands for the emancipation of the
Jews to more comprehensive social reform, opposing narrower views. His
remark was often cited: "If with one hand I am offered emancipation,
which answers all my most sincere wishes, and with the other the realization of the beautiful dream of Germany's political unity, together with
its political freedom, I would without any hesitation choose the latter, for
I am deeply and utterly convinced that it would include the former."[4]
After all the professional disadvantages he had experienced, which even
led him to make plans to emigrate, at the beginning of the 1840s he cherished the—illusory—hope of becoming the first Jewish parliamentarian
in Germany, as a representative in the Hesse-Kassel parliament. But since
he was denied state civic rights there, like Jacoby, he had to wait until the

revolutionary events of 1848 before serving as a representative. Although he failed election in his hometown of Hamburg, the constituency of Lauenburg—where Jews did not even have the right to settle—gave him a mandate to the National Assembly. Riesser reached the peak of his political career with the "Speech to the Emperor" that he gave during March 1849 in St. Paul's Church, in which he spoke out for a constitutional dynastic empire.

There were two Austrian-Jewish representatives in the National Assembly. One was Ignaz Kuranda (1812–1884), a publicist representing the Bohemian city of Teplitz, who founded the journal *Die Grenzboten* in 1841 while in exile in Belgium. The moderate liberal politics he expounded in the period leading up to the March 1848 Revolution had already thrown him into disfavor with Austrian and Prussian authorities. The other was Moritz Hartmann (1821–1872), a writer largely alienated from Judaism, who made a name for himself in the Czech national struggle. There was also a large number of baptized Jews in the Preliminary Parliament and the National Assembly, the most prominent of whom was Eduard Simson (1810–1899), who, as president of the National Assembly, led the delegation offering the imperial crown to the Prussian king in 1849.

Most of the Jewish representatives that assembled in St. Paul's Church were part of the political center-left or center-right. A few of them, including Jacoby, belonged to the left wing, and two of the baptized Jews considered themselves politically on the right. Like a majority of the non-Jewish parliamentarians, most of the Jews came from the free professions, while merchants and businessmen were generally not involved in the revolutionary actions and even opposed them. Estimates show a similar picture with respect to the political orientation of the Jewish population at large. It can be assumed that at least half of all German Jews were conservatives or loyalists who feared that the revolutionary events could threaten political and economic stability. Approximately one-third of the Jewish population could be considered liberals, and less than 15 percent radical democrats and socialists. Those Jews who supported the revolution were generally motivated by hopes for complete equality, while those who opposed it were prompted by fear for their economic subsistence.

Concerns that the revolutionary events could give rise to the ultimate dissolution of the traditional structure of the Jewish communities were hardly ever expressed any longer, even in Orthodox circles. On the eve of the revolution—and thus for the last time in German-Jewish history—the Orthodox newspaper *Der treue Zions-Wächter* (The Faithful Guardian of Zion) had warned of the undesirable consequences of complete emancipation. In reaction to the restrictive Prussian law of 1847 pertaining to the Jews, the newspaper wrote:

> From our standpoint, we cannot dispute the government's stated principle of [considering the Jews] a separate national entity; in fact, we must express explicit approval. We see in the laws, first, the securing of this national, and therefore religious, interest and we hold the firm conviction that to some extent we can and must do without even the acquisition of political rights if the prevalent forces require such a sacrifice.

One year later, even among Orthodox Jews like Rabbi Grünebaum of Ansbach, the predominant opinion was that participation in the elections to a "German Parliament" corresponded to the religious obligations of Orthodox Jews. Grünebaum agreed with numerous rabbis in declaring that participation in the elections was "not merely permissible from a religious point of view, but that it represented a sacred religious duty."[5]

If numerous Orthodox community leaders expressed praise for the revolution and emancipation, this was even more the case among their liberal colleagues, as demonstrated by the leading publicists Ludwig Philippson in the *Allgemeine Zeitung des Judenthums* and Julius Fürst in the *Orient*. According to Fürst, a Hebraist and representative in the Frankfurt Preliminary Parliament, the two elements were definitely interrelated:

> If the democratic principle triumphs . . . then the Jews will be guaranteed equality. The magnificent basic rights for all peoples of Germany . . . are also for you, Israel, in the midst of Germany! Be brave and determined, Israel, fight for Germany's well-being, for Germany's greatness and glory, dedicate your God-given strength to the fatherland that has now accepted you![6]

Yet even proponents of a political transformation, for the most part, spoke out against violent measures and supported a politics of law and order. Thus in 1850 the historian Isaac Marcus Jost summarized the years of the revolution as follows:

> With the exception of the truly *magnificent, lawful, and virtuous* uprising that brought admirable changes to our fatherland up until June 1848, from which the most beautiful blossom might have

grown, all that followed was only a sick swindle, in which most people did not participate and won't participate if it ever returns.[7]

Jost was not the only prominent representative from the founding generation of the Wissenschaft des Judentums (the scholarly study of Judaism)
who took up the cause of the revolution in 1848. Leopold Zunz, like Jost,
was active in numerous associations and assemblies and in March 1848
expressed enthusiasm for the political developments, even to the point of
giving them messianic interpretations. He wrote to his friend, Philipp
Ehrenberg, on March 5, 1848, that the "Day of the Lord approaches" and
a month later assured Ehrenberg of his conviction that he would "celebrate the redemption next Passover." He could not resist finding analogies
to the historic fate of the Jews, especially since the second day of the uprising in Berlin, March 19, was the day the Jews celebrated Purim, the festival commemorating salvation from threatening danger and the punishment of those politically responsible. "They have erected a gallows in
front of Metternich's residence in Vienna and have hung his coat of arms
upon it. This also corresponds to Purim," wrote Zunz in a letter of March
19, a few lines after allaying fears of continued anti-Jewish riots by referring to the punishment of the evil Haman (according to Jewish tradition,
a descendent of Amalek) in the Book of Esther: "The storming of the mob
against Jews in certain areas shall pass without a trace, like other mischief,
and peace shall remain. With these thoughts I will celebrate the memory
of Amalek tomorrow, and that of Haman the following day."[8] The Jewish
scholar Moritz Steinschneider commented in a letter to his fiancée, dated
March 20, 1848, "I do not believe that things looked any different on this
day in [ancient] Shushan than they look here." He added a description of
the street fighting: "You could also have seen me carrying stones and
rolling blocks. . . . In four weeks Prussia's Jews must be emancipated, for
the masses are already emancipating them now."[9]

Demands for emancipation met with no notable resistance, at least not
within the parliamentary framework. The only representative at the assembly in St. Paul's Church to speak out openly against legal equality for
Jews was the Württemberg radical Moritz Mohl, brother of the more
moderate finance minister Robert von Mohl. But even he had to admit
in his plea to limit Jewish rights that his proposal would cost him popularity. Indeed, his venture found little support, inspiring Jost to respond
with the following pun: "Mohl was truly sent packing and the same
thing will happen to many another Mohel [circumciser—here meaning

one who trims Jewish rights]."[10] In 1848–1849 there also seemed little need to discuss the emancipation of the Jews in most of the state parliaments. The Commission of the Baden People's Chamber, for example, which approved a bill in April 1848 providing equal political rights for Jewish citizens, passing it on to the representatives, added that a detailed justification was "a waste of time," for "the powerful call of time . . . has eliminated [all obstacles] at once."[11]

In light of such attitudes, it was consistent that in 1848–1849 the National Assembly as well as numerous state parliaments incorporated the emancipation of the Jews as an integral component of liberal and democratic politics. The small state of Hesse-Homburg led the way, granting its Jewish population equal legal status on March 6–7, 1848. In the same month Hesse-Nassau, Anhalt-Bernburg, and Anhalt-Dessau followed. However, not until the second reading of the German basic rights in St. Paul's Church in Frankfurt, on December 10, 1848—according to which "the enjoyment of civic and civil rights shall not be limited or restricted . . . on the basis of religious affiliation"—was there a final breakthrough in most German states. Some directly adopted this resolution within the framework of basic rights; others incorporated it in new, imposed constitutions, as was the case with Prussia in December 1848 and Austria in March 1849. Emancipation laws in the Free and Hanseatic cities were also not promulgated until 1849.

In some of the smaller states, including Mecklenburg-Strelitz and the Hohenzollern principalities, no comprehensive changes were implemented. Bavaria represented a special case. King Maximilian II, who had recently assumed the throne, had already promised Jews legal equality in March 1848; three months later a constitutional law granted Jews the right to vote and hold office in the state parliament. And in December 1849, with an overwhelming majority of ninety to forty-one votes, the Chamber of Representatives passed an emancipation law that had already been approved in the State Council. The law provided complete civil and political equality for Bavarian Jewry. But as soon as the Bavarian populace heard through the press of the intention to grant equal rights to Jews, a storm of local petitions ensued, protesting the measure. Complaints were filed in 1,753 communities—most of them in the same month or early January. They paraded a conglomeration of anti-Jewish stereotypes. One petition from the Upper Palatinate claimed that Jews hated Christians from the day they were born; one, from Middle Franconia, deemed them vampires who would suck the last drop of blood from the bodies of their Christian neighbors. Three Lower Franconian communities referred to Jews as "Asian cholera." The most frequent arguments were economically motivated, against Jews as "usurers." In Lower Franconia, in particular, the enraged public convened "people's assemblies," in order to halt the planned emancipation of the Jews. Both the Jewish communities and the government feared a renewed outbreak of the previous year's wave of the anti-Jewish violence. This atmosphere, especially in rural areas, provided the necessary pretext for the conservative Chamber of the Imperial Councils—scarcely friendly to emancipation to begin with—to refuse its approval of the entire legislation in February 1850. Instead, a new bill was passed the following year that granted Jews no more than civil equality with Christians.

2. The Last Step on the Road to Emancipation

Bavaria was not the only state that introduced reactionary policies in the early 1850s. The defeat of the revolutionary movement brought on a definite political backlash regarding emancipation of the Jews. The emancipatory legislation that was passed or at least attempted in 1848–1849 in twenty-six German states was actually instituted in only five small states (with a total Jewish population of twelve thousand people). For a majority of German Jewry the legal status obtained during the revolution had scarcely more impact than the "Basic Rights of the German People" did for the population at large.

Even some of the former revolutionaries now explicitly dissociated themselves from Jewish emancipation. One of them was Richard Wagner, who wrote in 1850:

> When we were fighting for the emancipation of the Jews, we were really fighting more for an abstract goal than for a concrete instance. Just as all of our liberalism was a luxurious intellectual game in which we disputed over the freedom of the people, without any knowledge of this people—even with an aversion to any real contact with it—so likewise the zealousness of our struggle for equal status for the Jews arose more from the inspiration of the mere thought than from any real sympathy. For all the talking and writing in support of emancipation of the Jews, in spite of ourselves, any actual contact with Jews repulsed us.[12]

The worsening legal status of Jews in the 1850s proved to have much more significant consequences, however, than the changed views of individual intellectuals, especially in the largest states, Prussia and Austria. Although article 12 of the Prussian constitution promised equal status to Jews and all religious minorities, it was in fact largely revoked through article 14 of the "revised" constitution of 1850, which stated: "The Christian religion shall be the prerequisite for [access to] all institutions of the state connected with religious observance." In practice this meant that, until the 1870s, Jews were once again excluded from any offices that required taking an oath as well as any positions in the areas of education and culture.

In Austria the reactionary 1850s brought about abolition of the rights attained in 1848–1849. The imperial patent of December 1851 repealed the constitutional regulations passed in 1849, and in October 1853 an imperial ordinance made all restrictions that existed prior to 1848 regarding Jewish property rights in all crown lands once again valid. Freedom of movement and access to state offices and certain professions were once again put into question "until a definitive regulation pertaining to the civil status of the Israelite population shall be made," as the Decree of 1853 emphasized.

In many smaller states, too, such as Hanover, Holstein, and Württemberg, the achievements of the revolution with respect to equality of the Jews were reversed in the reactionary period that followed. At the beginning of the 1850s a large majority of German Jewry was again subjected to much of the legal discrimination it had suffered in the period leading up to the revolution. In Hesse-Kassel Jews even lost all rights they had achieved in the period from 1815 up to 1848.

In the long run, however, it was not possible to continue a politics of legal segregation that relegated the Jewish population to second-class citizenship while, economically and culturally, they were simultaneously becoming more and more integrated. The liberal economic politics that started in the 1850s, as well as the unification efforts of the Nationalverein (German National Union) and the Greater German Reformverein (Reform Union), which aimed at fundamentally changing the political system, made legal restrictions placed on Jews seem anachronistic. The Liberal minister A. Lamey of Baden stressed this general social context in a letter of 1860 to Grand Duke Frederick: "The entire structure of our state can no longer tolerate that a class of subjects is excluded from a number of legal rights on account of so trivial a matter as their declared religious faith." Lamey argued that partial solutions were no longer acceptable; "total emancipation" must be achieved.[13] The liberal politics of the 1860s finally abandoned the principle that was prevalent in the German states since the Enlightenment, according to which the state had first to educate and then to examine the Jews in order to determine whether they were worthy of emancipation. The emancipation legislation that followed was not so much a reward for the level of acculturation Jews had attained as it was an expression of the principle of legal equality for all citizens.

In Baden the process of Jewish emancipation culminated in October 1862 with the Law on the Civic Equality of the Jews, signed by the Grand Duke, after political rights had already been granted in 1849. Elevation from the status of protected citizens to full citizens and the elimination of all differences in rights—together with earlier changes that had lifted all special regulations for Jews in the areas of freedom of movement and choice of profession—represented almost total emancipation of the Jews. The sole legal differences that remained during a ten-year interim period were claims to communal property (*Bürgernutzen*) and the assumption by the local municipality of the Jewish services for the poor.

Inspired by this success in a neighboring state, rapid progress toward legal equality was also made in Württemberg through independent efforts by both a Jewish "emancipation commission" and the government starting in 1861. Once again, the decisive argument for granting rights to the Jews was not the extension of any particular favor to them but the liberal principle of equal rights for all citizens. Thus Representative Scholt, for example, expressed little enthusiasm for Jewish emancipation but supported it as a necessity, indeed, a necessary evil. "The Jews are simply there, and no one . . . would suggest expelling them from the land; the only choice that exists is either to continue treating them as something foreign or to absorb them."[14] A December 1861 law already granted Jews in Württemberg the same state political rights as Christians, and with their attainment of local rights in 1864 the emancipation process was complete. There was no interim period here that prolonged the process for years, as was the case in Baden.

In Frankfurt am Main a public vote in 1864 resulted in an overwhelming majority of the population approving the removal of all remaining restrictions regarding political rights for Jews and for the rural population. And even in conservative Bavaria significant legal improvements were made in 1861, such as the removal of discriminatory professional restrictions and the repeal of *Matrikel* laws (see chapter 1), which had greatly restricted freedom of movement for Jews. Conditions for Bavarian Jews, however, were still less favorable than those in south-western Germany.

North of the Main River the emancipation process in the first half of the 1860s was sluggish at best. Although Hamburg's new constitution of 1860 provided for strict separation of church and state, thus removing any legitimation for a Christian state, the situation in Prussia—the most populous German state and most crucial with regard to the Jewish situation—was just the opposite. Here that legitimation was retained through article 14 of the Prussian constitution. The Prussian state could not bring itself to any form of consistent emancipation for the Jews. It was only possible for individual liberal-minded ministers to push through some practical improvements in their respective domains. A few months after he confirmed a paid Jewish city council member in Posen, Minister of the Interior Count Maximilian von Schwerin decreed in February 1860 that Jews would be allowed to exercise police authority in rural areas and become town mayors. The right of Jews to vote in local and provincial parliamentary elections was another achievement of the early 1860s. However, a comprehensive legal breakthrough would not come until almost a decade later, by which time it was not in the name of the Prussian state but in that of the new North German Confederation.

Just as German unification did not emerge from the street fighting of 1848 but from the military conflicts of the Prussian state between 1864 and 1871, the emancipation of the Jews in northern Germany was also a direct consequence, in the words of Bismarck, of a state born of "blood and iron." The Law of the Equality of Religions as Regards Common and State Civic Rights in the North German Confederation, which was established in the aftermath of the German War of 1866, was passed in July 1869. It was a clear statement opposing any connections between religious belief and civic rights. The legislation of the North German Confederation affected not only the Jews in the former Prussia but also those in the other states incorporated as a result of the War of 1866: Hanover, Holstein, Kassel, Nassau, and Frankfurt. It was then extended to apply to all of Germany when the Reich adopted it in 1871.

This reorganization of power in Central Europe as a result of Prussia's triumph over Austria also determined the fate of Austrian Jewry. Whereas the Prussia-dominated empire founded by Bismarck granted Jews equal rights in 1871, the Habsburg monarchy had already taken this step four years earlier, at the time of the Austro-Hungarian Compromise, when Jews in both halves of the Habsburg state gained full equality.

3. Demographic Developments

The political events of 1848 and the legal equality that German Jewry achieved in the 1860s were important steps on the way to full recognition as German citizens. But no less significant were long-term demographic and social changes. Although most German Jews still lived in towns and villages at the end of this era, a growing urban Jewish bourgeoisie was emerging.

The total number of Jews residing within the borders of what was to become the German Empire grew from about 400,000 at the beginning of the period to about 470,000 in 1867. Compared with the total population, this represented a constant proportion of 1.2 percent. In 1848 about half of German Jewry—218,750 persons—lived in Prussia, and after the annexation of lands in 1866 their numbers rose to 314,797, or 62 percent of all German Jews. Starting in 1861, however, when Jews comprised 1.38 percent of the total Prussian population, a steady decline in the relative proportion of Jews can be seen, despite an increase in absolute numbers. Demographic developments were by no means uniform throughout Prussia. Berlin, especially, and some other major cities experienced a considerable increase in their Jewish populations, whereas in Posen, the province most densely populated by Jews, both their absolute number and their proportion relative to the rest of the population decreased noticeably. The only state that showed similar developments was Bavaria, which had the second largest Jewish population. In 1844 62,830 Jews still lived in the kingdom, but by 1867 the figure had decreased to 49,840, representing a decline in proportion from 1.41 to 1.04 percent. In this case as well it is necessary to distinguish among various provinces. Regions with a considerable Jewish population—Franconia, Swabia, and the Palatinate—registered sharp decreases, whereas there was a marked growth in the Jewish population in Old Bavaria, especially Munich, where scarcely any Jews had lived before. The Grand Duchy of Hesse was a special case, as the Jewish population there comprised the highest percentage in any larger German state. At the beginning of the period—approximately the mid-1850s—the Jewish population in Hesse peaked at 3.44 percent of the total population. Similar to the situation in Posen and Bavaria, the absolute number of Jews in Hesse decreased starting in the 1860s, although to a much less drastic degree.

In most other German states, too, the beginning of the 1860s marked the peak in the relative proportion of the Jewish to the general population, but absolute figures, for the most part, continued to rise slightly. A substantial increase was registered thereafter only in the Kingdom of Saxony where drastic laws had strictly limited Jewish settlement before 1848. In the mid-1840s there were still less than 1,000 Jews living there; by the end of the 1860s the figure had risen to over 3,000. Jews were still prohibited from settling in some smaller states such as Bremen, Lübeck, the two states of Reuss, and Saxony-Altenburg until well into the 1850s and 1860s.

In order to understand the distinct chronological and geographical differences in demographic developments, both natural growth rates and migratory movements must be taken into account. In neither the 1850s nor the preceding decades could the percentage increase in the Jewish population be attributed to a higher birthrate compared with the total population. Instead, a lower mortality rate, particularly among infants and children, was the significant factor. With the drop in birthrate among Jews in the second half of the century, and a lowered mortality rate in the general population, a marked decline in the relative size of the Jewish population sets in.

Emigration contributed to a decrease in the absolute size of the Jewish population in certain regions. From 1848 to 1871 the German states experienced no significant Jewish influx. About 4,000–5,000 mostly Eastern European Jews settled in major cities, predominantly Berlin, Hamburg, and Leipzig. But for most Jews leaving Eastern Europe Germany represented merely a stopover on their way overseas. In addition to the transmigration of Eastern European Jews, there was an even more significant number of German Jews seeking to immigrate to the United States. They contributed to a disproportionately high level of German emigration in general during this period. According to varying estimates, the number of Jewish emigrants (not including the Habsburg Empire) for the period from 1845 to 1871 was between 70,000 and 113,000, with the higher figure the more probable. Approximately half the emigrants came from Prussia, especially the province of Posen, with the next largest group coming from Bavaria. In Württemberg, the only state with reliable statistics regarding Jewish emigration, records show that the ratio of Jews among all emigrants during this period was 2.1 percent, that is, about three times the share of Jews in the general population. Since the wave of emigration did not reach its peak in Württemberg until after the emancipation process was completed in the 1860s, it is not possible to attribute the high rate of emigration entirely to discrimination.

Nevertheless, as a motive for emigration the precarious legal status of Jews cannot be ignored. This was especially apparent in Bavaria, where the Matrikel laws, which remained in force until 1861, unquestionably contributed to the high figures. Approximately 20,000 to 25,000 Jews left the kingdom between 1840 and 1871. Efforts made by the Bavarian government beginning in 1852 to counter this emigration wave through more stringent passport and border controls produced a drastic decline in emigration (from 25,304 in 1854 to 6,906 one year later), but the already disproportionately high proportion of Jews among all emigrants continued to rise (from 3.6 to 4.8 percent).

The recollections of Isaak Bernstein, a grain dealer from the province of Posen, illustrate the desperation of those forced to emigrate. Bernstein, who was from a poor Jewish family, secretly went to the United States in 1852 after losing his hard-earned fortune:

> To escape my unbearable worries and poverty and shame, and not to be dependent on the goodwill of my family, I came to the decision to emigrate to America. My second wife and my children remained well cared for at home and in the business of her parents; I brought my oldest child to my parents. At first I told my wife in August 1852 that I was traveling to a region I knew well—Danzig, Marienwerder—to find a place where we could more easily support ourselves. I took with me only twenty-five talers as travel money and essential clothing, and I did not let my wife know of my [true] travel plans. I did not go to Danzig, but to Hamburg; with palpitating heart and bitter tears I had to abandon my wife and my two children in the cradle. My funds did not suffice for the sea voyage. I sold my silver watch and gold ring and for twenty-eight talers embarked in mid-September in the steerage of a sailing vessel. After forty-four agonizing days we landed in New York.[15]

Although Bernstein returned to his wife and children eight years later, most other emigrants sent for their families. Within a few decades large communities were reduced to a mere shadow existence or faced with total dissolution. The Württemberg town of Jebenhausen, for instance, still contained 537 Jews in 1838, making up about half of the total population. But by 1862 the number of Jews had declined to 392; in 1871 only 127 Jews were still living there, and by the end of the century only nine. By 1871 329 Jews from Jebenhausen had gone to the United States.

The example of Jebenhausen also illustrates the dual character of

Jewish rural emigration. In addition to those who went to the United States, many German Jews left rural villages and small towns to settle in larger towns and cities nearby. Neighboring cities, especially those with railroad connections that had helped them become economic centers, attracted rural German Jews. The favored destination of Jews from Jebenhausen was nearby Göppingen. By 1871 194 Jews from Jebenhausen had settled there and established a Jewish community. The two waves of emigration were distinct in that those who emigrated to America were generally poorer and left as early as the 1840s and 1850s, while those who moved to Göppingen were often more well-to-do members of the community who generally migrated in the 1860s and 1870s. Only a few of the older cattle dealers remained in Jebenhausen. Other village communities followed the same trend, which led the writer Berthold Auerbach to complain in the early 1870s:

> Dead! Emigrated! is what you hear constantly, when you ask about someone or other. The addiction to America has now been joined by freedom of migration within the land, and it is just like in private society: when one stands up to leave, the others stand up as well and become restless. Over in Schwandorf the synagogue is deserted and the Jewish cemetery has been abandoned. There are no Jews there anymore. I see it coming—maybe already in a decade—that the same will be true in Nordstetten.[16]

For centuries Jews had been totally barred from settling in many of the new centers, which finally opened their gates to them in the 1850s and 1860s. Aside from Göppingen, they were now able to settle in other Württemberg cities such as Heilbronn, Ulm, and Cannstadt. In Bavaria the same was true for Augsburg, Regensburg, and Schweinfurt. Once rural Jews in Baden were given freedom of migration in 1862, they began settling in Freiburg, Constance, and Offenburg. Freedom of migration also temporarily led to the establishment of rural communities, especially in the Rhineland, Posen, and Upper Silesia.

Taken as a whole, migration to urban centers overshadowed all other population trends. In Nuremberg, where before 1848 no Jews had permission to settle, the Jewish population grew from 74 in 1852 to 1,813 in 1871; in Munich during the same period the number of Jews increased from 1,252 to 2,884. The Jewish population in Stuttgart, which was only 234 in 1846, grew to over 2,000. The Leipzig Jewish community, which was not founded until after 1848, already had 2,531 members in 1875 (of whom 527 had been born in the city). The Jewish population in Cologne reached 3,172 by 1871. There were also many cities in the Ruhr that experienced a growth in their Jewish populations between 1848 and 1871, often analogous to increases in the total population, running between 200 and 300 percent. For example, the Dortmund Jewish community grew from 200 to 677 members; the increase in Duisburg was from 90 to 253; in Essen from 320 to 832, and in Elberfeld from 130 to 626. Numerous Jewish communities that already existed prior to 1848 doubled in size between 1852 and 1871. Breslau grew from about 7,500 members to about 14,000; in Frankfurt am Main the membership rose from about 5,000 to almost 10,000. The size of the Jewish community in Hamburg, which was the largest in Germany up to the middle of the nineteenth century, grew at a much slower rate, from 9,000 to 13,000.

Migration to the capital cities in Prussia and Austria was of a far greater magnitude. Whereas those moving to Vienna came from various regions of the Habsburg Empire, most of the Jews that moved to Berlin came from the province of Posen, often with a stopover in Breslau. In Berlin the Jewish population had increased from less than 10,000 in 1852 to over 36,000 in 1871. On the other hand, although it still had the third largest Jewish community in Prussia in 1871 (7,000), the city of Posen experienced a decline during this period. The decline in smaller cities such as Kempen (from 3,000 in 1852 to 2,500 in 1871), Lissa (from 3,000 to 1,900), Krotoschin (from 2,350 to 1,450), and Inowraclaw (from 2,100 to 1,600) is even more pronounced. Altogether, approximately 50,000 Jews left the province of Posen between 1834 and 1871, about half of them emigrating overseas and half settling in Berlin. In the fifteen years from 1856 to 1871 alone, 26,500 Jews left the province, comprising 63.2 percent of migration in general. Similar figures are also available for West Prussia, where the total Jewish population decreased between 1855 and 1871 from 25,000 to 14,000.

Migration to Vienna took on even more dramatic proportions. On the eve of the revolution there were only an estimated 2,000–4,000 Jews living there. According to official records, the number increased slightly by 1857, to 6,217, representing 1.3 percent of the total population. However, twelve years later there were already 40,000 Jews in Vienna, making up 6.6 percent of the total Viennese population. By that time, in terms of number of Jewish residents, Vienna had left the traditionally Jewish population centers of Prague, Krakow, and Lemberg far behind. By far the largest number of Jewish immigrants to Vienna during this period came from the Hungarian part of the empire, followed by Bohemia and Moravia. Also in this period Galician Jews started moving toward the metropolis on the Danube because of overpopulation, famine, and cholera epidemics in their homeland. However, the massive wave of refugees from Galicia arose only after it became clear in the 1870s that Jews were being forced out of economic life by a Polish nationalist campaign.

There were different migration patterns in Bohemia and Moravia during the 1850s and 1860s. While Jews from the densely populated quarters of smaller cities were moving to Vienna, Prague was likewise absorbing a considerable number. The Prague Jewish community doubled in size between 1848 and 1880, reaching a total of over 20,000. However, in comparison with both the general population growth of the city and increases in other major Jewish communities in Central Europe, this development was rather moderate. The ratio of Jews in the total population of Prague dropped from 9 to 6.5 percent during this time. Although Prague was the largest Jewish community in Central Europe around 1848, it stood in the shadow of the Berlin and Vienna communities at the beginning of the 1870s.

At least as significant as migration to Prague was the movement of Bohemian and Moravian Jews to small and mid-sized cities, often only a short distance from the settlements they were leaving. Within only three years after freedom of migration was granted in 1849, the number of localities with Jewish residents tripled, from about eight hundred to over two thousand. In the 1860s Jewish communities were then founded in the larger, mostly German-speaking towns that had prohibited Jews from settling there until the middle of the century, such as Eger (1862), Reichenberg (1863), Saaz (1864), and Carlsbad (1869). This migration from Czech-speaking regions to the German-speaking areas, which were rapidly becoming industrialized, was part of a general trend that was also widespread during the second half of the nineteenth century among the non-Jewish population. But whereas Czech factory workers in the German-speaking regions demanded rights as a national minority, the opposite was true for Jewish immigrants. Although they maintained their Jewish religion, they soon identified nationally and culturally with their German-speaking surroundings.

On the eve of the revolution Jews were still prohibited from settling in the province of Salzburg, in Styria, Carinthia, and Cariola, and there were less than one thousand Jews living in the Tirol and Vorarlberg regions. Even in subsequent decades there was no significant Jewish migration to cities in these areas, due to legal restrictions that still existed. Individual Jews settled in Salzburg and Innsbruck, but a major Jewish community was established only in Graz.

Except for the small states mentioned earlier, the only other place in the German-speaking realm that had similar restrictive policies with respect to Jewish settlement was Switzerland, where the 3,146 Jews living there in 1850 made up only 0.13 percent of the total population. The Liberals, who had triumphed there in 1848, continued to limit the rights of Jews to settle, triggering objections from foreign diplomats. In 1857 the United States ambassador to Switzerland filed a protest when an American citizen was denied a residence permit in Switzerland on the grounds of his being Jewish. Six years later the general consul of the Netherlands refused to sign a mutual immigration treaty, after Switzerland explicitly stipulated the exclusion of Jewish citizens from the privileges of the agreement. Although Jews in Aargau received emancipation in 1862, a negative vote in a popular referendum on the issue swiftly led to its repeal. Continued foreign pressure finally forced the Swiss to grant Jews the same freedom of migration and the same rights as Christian citizens in 1866. Yet even as legal equality was thus achieved at the state level, the struggle continued locally. Not until 1879 did Jewish residents of the village communities of Endingen and Lengnau receive equal rights, and even then they were still excluded from voting in local elections and forced to form their own separate local community. Freedom of migration, together with persisting legal restrictions in the villages where Jews resided, led to an urbanization process in Switzerland as well, with Jewish communities established in Zurich, Baden, Basel, St. Gallen, and Lucerne.

4. Economic Ascent

Within a generation German Jews rose socially and economically to an unprecedented degree. In 1848 about half of German Jewry was still poor and between one-third and one-quarter were in the lowest tax categories. Only 15–30 percent had entered the bourgeoisie with a secure standard of living and were counted in the middle or upper tax classes. By the time the German Empire was established, this picture had totally changed. Over 60 percent of all Jews had entered the middle or upper tax brackets, and those living in poverty or at the margins of society, depending on the region, made up only 5–25 percent of all German Jewry. For the majority

of German Jews the period from 1848 to 1871 was marked by economic
upswing and a rise in social position.

What caused this rapid economic ascent? Without a doubt, general
economic developments and liberal economic politics proved favorable to
the specific situation of the Jews. They were traditionally overrepresented
in those economic branches—brokerage and merchandising—that gained
importance alongside an expanding industry. On the other hand, the
occupations from which they had traditionally been excluded, such as
agriculture and skilled trades, suffered increasingly. This alone, however,
would not have enabled numerous marginally subsisting Jews without
capital and those in the lower middle classes to advance. A prerequisite for
such advancement was the acquisition of the necessary start-up capital. In
addition to support provided by family and relatives, Jewish loan associations and credit banks were very imporant in this regard. They offered
interest-free funds to craftsmen and petty merchants, often without a
surety. The collapse of the final legal barriers as well as the granting of
freedom of migration and subsequent urbanization contributed their
share as well. Finally, the lack of non-Jewish business initiatives as a result
of both the traditional mentality of the non-Jewish rural population and
the inflexible state bureaucracy also served to benefit enterprising Jewish
businessmen and bankers.

The relatively high concentration of Jews in the area of banking is as
apparent in this period as before 1848. After 1848 hundreds of mostly
small private banks were established in Germany, as they had been earlier in England. Documents show that in 1860 there were 157 banks in
Berlin. According to an antisemitic source, two-thirds of these were supposedly owned—at least in part—by persons of Jewish origin. More reliable statistics are available for 1871, when the number of banking firms
had already grown to 580. Of these 23 percent were exclusively Jewish-
owned and another 37 percent were joint Christian-Jewish enterprises.
Although there is an increase in the absolute figures here, a relative
decrease is already apparent in the number of private banks whose owners are of Jewish descent. This decline continued after the founding of the
empire, as the dominance of the major banking firms increased. Outside
Berlin, however, banks with owners of Jewish descent maintained their
leading position throughout this entire period almost without interruption. The most prominent Hamburg banking families were the Behrens,
Heines, and Warburgs; the Oppenheims were the most significant in

Cologne, the Kaskels and Arnholds in Dresden, the Ladenburgs in Mannheim, and the Heimanns in Breslau. The outstanding position of the Rothschilds of Frankfurt among German-Jewish bankers steadily diminished in the second half of the nineteenth century. Other bankers, many of whom first made a name for themselves while protégés of the Rothschilds, began outdistancing their mentors. The best example here is the Bleichröder banking firm, founded in 1828 by Samuel Bleichröder, who started his economic climb as an agent for the Rothschilds. In 1855, the year Samuel Bleichröder died, Amschel (Anselm) Meyer Rothschild, the oldest son of the founder of the dynasty and head of the parent company in Frankfurt, also passed away. His death and succession by his nephew Meyer Carl (1820–1886)— Amschel Meyer had no children of his own—marked the beginning of the last chapter of the parent company in Frankfurt, which was finally liquidated in 1901. On the other hand, the Bleichröder banking firm was taken over by Samuel's son Gerson (1822–1893) and entered its heyday. Gerson Bleichröder gained importance starting in 1859, when he began providing Bismarck with money and financial advice during his long struggle to unify Germany.

But even Bleichröder's extraordinary success, and that of the Rothschilds before him, were no guarantee of immediate recognition at the highest social levels. This can be seen in the practice of awarding titles. In 1852 Bismarck denied the Rothschilds' request to be given the title of court banker. When, a year later, Meyer Carl Rothschild did in fact receive the title, the Red Eagle Medal that was awarded on the occasion did not have its usual cruciform shape, but an oval one, for "non-Christians." Rothschild, who had no lack of medals and who particularly enjoyed wearing his Greek Medal of Redemption and the Spanish Medal of Isabella the Catholic, was deeply insulted. He refused to wear the Red Eagle Medal for non-Christians and, according to Bismarck, refrained from attending certain social functions to avoid having to display it.

Bleichröder received the Red Eagle Medal five years later, most likely in the same "non-Christian" form. He quickly rose from commercial councillor, a title conferred on distinguished businessmen, to privy commercial councillor in 1861, eventually becoming the first Jew in Prussia to receive, in 1872, a hereditary title of nobility. Yet, despite all his titles, the Christian aristocracy still maintained a clear social distance from the "Jewish parvenu." In Austria, on the other hand, the practice of ennobling

Jews, which had already begun prior to 1848, continued during this period. Whereas in Prussia Bleichröder's obtaining a title of nobility was a historic event, it would hardly have been worth mentioning in Austria where 161 Jewish families were raised to nobility between 1848 and 1884.

Both the Rothschilds and Gerson Bleichröder remained loyal to Judaism. The following description of Amschel Meyer Rothschild in a letter by Bismarck to his wife contains anti-Jewish stereotypes, but it also reflects the respect a Prussian Junker felt toward the Jewish banker who lived in a traditional manner: "I picked the enclosed tiny leaf for you in the garden of old Amschel Rothschild. I like him since he is a haggling Jew through and through and doesn't want to appear as anything else, yet he is also strictly an Orthodox Jew who doesn't touch anything at his dinner parties, and eats only kosher food."[17] Bleichröder was elected to the board of the Jewish community in Berlin in 1864; he observed some Jewish rituals and most holidays. It disheartened him that his children chose to be baptized as Protestants. Other Jewish bankers, however, encouraged their children's conversion; some even set the example themselves. Many families—the Mendelssohns for example—honored their family tradition but had long since dissociated themselves from the religion of their ancestors.

On the other hand, a small number of Jewish industrialists was strictly Orthodox. Of these, the best known was the Hirsch family, which was active in the copper trade. They set up a modest copper goods store, which they were able to expand greatly in 1863 by taking over a brassworks near Eberswalde, outside Berlin. By the end of the 1860s it had become one of the largest Prussian companies in the metalworks industry. In spite of this impressive economic ascent, the Hirsch family limited its social life to the small circle of Orthodox Jews in the communities in Halberstadt and Berlin. They educated their children in a traditional manner and made an effort to hire only Orthodox workers and apprentices. The latter enjoyed the rare opportunity of working in an industrial enterprise that strictly observed the Sabbath.

The rise of most bankers and industrialists in the nineteenth century was closely tied to finance of the expanding railroad network (see chapter 2). After 1848 there was no more enigmatic figure involved in building the German railroads than Bethel Henry Strousberg (1823–1884), an industrialist from East Prussia. After earning his fortune publishing magazines in England and having assured his entry into the upper social strata by converting to Christianity, Strousberg returned to Germany in 1855. As "general entrepreneur," that is, both the building contractor and largest shareholder, he obtained rights to construct a number of railroad lines in Prussia in the 1860s. Strousberg's brilliant career, however, came to an abrupt conclusion at the end of the decade. His gigantic project to build several railroad lines connecting Romania to the European railway network led to his ruin when the Romanian government reneged on the contract. Strousberg was the first diversified industrialist in Germany, owning engine works, iron- and steelworks, coal mines, and processing plants for foodstuffs. After his Romanian railroad project collapsed, he was accused of bearing the main responsibility for the ensuing industrial crisis and forced to experience bankruptcy, arrest, and public denunciation.

In addition to banking and credit, Jewish entrepreneurs also held prominent positions in the textile industry, above all in Berlin and Silesia but also in Bohemia and Moravia. There was relatively little Jewish participation in other branches of industry except in the production of food and luxury items and in newly developing fields such as the chemical and electrical industries. Jews rarely gained access to the almost totally closed circle of industrialists in heavy industries such as mining or iron- and steelworks. Exceptional were the Rothschild ironworks in Witkowitz in Moravia. A very different picture emerges with regard to medium-sized merchandising, which boomed as a result of urbanization in the decades

39   Baron Rothschild's ironworks in Witkowitz, around 1850

following 1848. As agriculture and the crafts were struck by a general long-term decline, the small number of Jews who had entered these fields waned after 1848. In 1861 only 0.9 percent of the working Jewish population in Prussia was involved in agriculture. A slight decline could also be observed in the areas of industrial labor and the crafts. In the free professions Jews had not been able to gain much of a footing before 1871, since the legal restrictions of the reactionary period, which affected academic career choices, continued to have an impact. Only in medicine were Jews, as in the past, strongly represented. However, after the first Jewish judicial trainees were appointed in Prussia in 1856, a positive trend could also be observed in the profession of law, which then emerged even more clearly beginning in the 1880s. In 1871 2.52 percent of all jurists in Prussia were Jewish, a figure fully proportionate to the Jewish population in the large cities. It included junior lawyers (*Referendare*, 7.6 percent) and judicial trainees (*Assessoren*, 6.6 percent), however hardly any judges (0.2 percent) and no state attorneys at all.

The most dramatic rise was in the traditional fields of trade and commerce. In 1843 approximately 48 percent of all Prussian Jews worked in these fields; by 1861 the ratio had risen to 57 percent. The high number of self-employed Jews serves to illustrate the large growth in the Jewish bourgeoisie. In 1861 two-thirds of the working Jewish population in Prussia were self-employed, a figure also corresponding approximately to the empire as a whole. It deviated greatly from statistics regarding the professions of the non-Jewish population. In 1871 in Berlin, 71.9 percent of the Jewish population was self-employed, compared with only 38 percent of non-Jews. A large portion of this category was comprised of small shopkeepers and family members who assisted them.

The diversity among Jewish merchants varied from region to region—sometimes considerably—and in particular between urban and rural settings. There were more wholesalers in urban centers, whereas rural areas were clearly dominated by small trade. Here, too, distinctions must be made among individual occupations. An analysis of occupational patterns in Lower Hesse shows that Jews clearly predominated in certain trade sectors, such as hides (92.4 percent), yard goods (83.4 percent), and cattle (82.8 percent). In some areas Jews were far less represented, such as tobacco (14.6 percent) and the sale of petty and junk items (18.2 percent). Jews were involved less and less in occupations regarded as "itinerant and usurious," which were branded as less honorable. In 1828 85 percent of all Jewish heads of household in Lower Hesse had worked in these areas, but

40   Wilhelm and Rebekka Kann and their son Adolf,
a merchant family from Eberswalde, 1851

the figure went down to 18 percent in 1852 and further to 13 percent in 1860. If the corresponding statistics for Hesse-Kassel after 1848 were considerably higher, this had less to do with actual occupational patterns than with the interpretation of various occupations as itinerant by officials who viewed Jews unfavorably. According to the Israelite Supreme Ecclesiastical Authority (*Israelitische Oberkirchenbehörde*) in Württemberg in 1846, Jewish peddlers in rural areas had adopted "a trade that deviated from the one they had practiced earlier." The authority noted:

A large portion of the more well-to-do among them, such as those from Buchau, Buttenhausen, and other towns, do not by any means go from house to house through the towns, carrying sacks offering a variety of articles, and accepting used clothing as payment, as had earlier been common among Jewish petty traders. . . . The peddlers carry more proper, sometimes even significant inventories of goods— admittedly mostly inexpensive fabrics—and they visit fairs and markets here and in foreign lands, where they offer their wares for sale in small shops.[18]

In Buttenhausen, where the Jewish population made up about half of the total residents throughout most of the nineteenth century, there was a drastic contrast between the social advancement of Jews and that of the general population. Still, in 1825, Jews here had paid only 25 percent of the property tax, but within forty years this figure rose to 84.4 percent. The Jewish share of the total taxes paid also increased considerably, though it never reached the same magnitude. The shrinking of the lower social strata was especially apparent in the province of Posen, which was known for its relatively high proportion of poor Jews up to 1848. In 1869 only 12 percent of the Jewish population was still registered as "poor," compared with 20 percent of the German-Protestant population and even 33 percent of the Polish Catholics. Developments in the cities were similar, as figures for Breslau in 1874 illustrate. Among Christians 80–90 percent of taxpayers there had an annual income of less than five hundred talers, whereas only slightly more than one-third of the Jewish population was in this income class. On the other hand, 15 percent of Jews compared with 2–3 percent of Christian residents earned over two thousand talers per year.

5. Incomplete Integration

After 1848 Jews made definite progress with respect to professional and social integration. For the first time there were at least a few Jewish parliamentarians, university professors, lawyers, and judges. On the local level contact between Jewish and Christian dignitaries as well as joint participation in liberal social clubs, choirs, and reading societies intensified. Nonetheless, one could hardly speak of full integration. The barriers separating Jews and Christians in everyday life were still far too visible. Jews and Christians coexisted parallel to one other rather than really living together, especially in villages and towns, and even in the cities only a small minority of Jews moved in Christian circles, with the exception of the public sphere.

In the politically reactionary decade following the failed revolution, Jews still appeared only rarely on the political stage beyond the local level. Only nine Jewish representatives had seats in state parliaments during those years. Remarkably, there were three in Lübeck—the highest in any one parliament—although Jews were not allowed to settle there at all before 1848. The legislative assemblies in Frankfurt and Bavaria each had two Jewish representatives. In Prussia Moritz Veit was the sole Jew in the parliament, serving for two years. These figures were certainly an improvement over the pre-1848 years, when Jews were totally excluded from the regional parliaments, but in comparison with the political activity of Jews during the revolution they showed a clear decline.

The liberal epoch that began in 1858 represented the final opening of the parliament gates to Jewish representation. This was apparent at the local level, where the number of Jews serving as representatives increased considerably. The number of city councillors who were Jewish rose from 190 during the reactionary period to over 300 in the subsequent decade. On the national level there was a disproportionately high number of at least 9 Jews among the approximately 190 founding members of the German National Union in 1859. Two of them, Gabriel Riesser and Moritz Veit, were also elected to its presiding body. The number of Jews at the founding assembly of the Greater German Reform Union was even larger, if proportionately less significant. In the 1858–1859 elections 19 Jews entered the regional parliaments, and by 1866 the number had risen to 70. However, these figures tend to blur regional differences. Most parliaments continued to lack any Jewish representatives, while Frankfurt and Hamburg each elected no less than 28 Jews. The only other state with a significant number of Jewish representatives was Prussia, with 8.

Some of the Jewish parliamentarians had fought for emancipation as Liberals, such as Fischel Arnheim in Bavaria and Rudolf Kusel in Baden. The most prominent Jewish politician of the period in Austria was Ignaz Kuranda, a publicist and long-standing leader of the Liberals. He also successfully defended Jewish rights in court against the notorious Viennese antisemite Sebastian Brunner, and served, from 1860, as a board member of the Jewish community in Vienna. Jewish politicians who had made names for themselves in general politics at the time in Prussia, by contrast, did not maintain close ties with the Jewish community or the Jewish religion.

The two leaders of the National Liberal Party stand out among the most prominent Jewish politicians of the liberal period. Eduard Lasker (1829–1884) and Ludwig Bamberger (1823–1899) came from very different backgrounds, yet they had similar political careers. Lasker grew up in Jarotschin, a town in Posen, and was Prussian through and through, whereas Bamberger came from Mainz and made no secret of his aversion to Prussian hegemony. Lasker was raised in a traditional Jewish environment and as a child had translated Friedrich Schiller's *Teilung der Erde* (The Division of the Earth) into Hebrew. He maintained a certain emotional bond with Judaism, although he rarely expressed it openly. Bamberger's Jewish education was rudimentary and he was more removed from his Jewish origins. Both men suffered professional discrimination as Jews. Lasker was the most senior judicial trainee in Prussia, since, resented by authorities, he was excluded from becoming a judge. Bamberger had also studied law and his Jewish origins, too, quickly robbed him of any hope of securing an appropriate post. Both men assumed radical positions in 1848. Lasker published a paper called *Der Sozialist* (The Socialist) and Bamberger, in addition to his journalistic activities, participated in the uprising in the Palatinate as part of the Rhine-Hessian auxiliary corps. He was later sentenced to death in absentia. Like many former radicals, they both became moderates in the 1860s, setting unification of the empire as their primary political goal. This made them important representatives of the National Liberal Party, which supported Bismarck's unification policy. Lasker was elected to the Prussian Parliament in 1865 as a member of the Progressive Party (*Fortschrittspartei*) and a year later drafted the party platform for the National Liberals. Bamberger spent almost twenty years in exile in France, where he succeeded in earning a considerable fortune as a banker. He returned to Mainz in 1868 and was immediately voted into the German Customs Parliament (*Zollparlament*) for the National Liberals. The political activities of these two nineteenth-century German-Jewish parliamentarians would evolve much further during the Kaiserreich after 1871.

Lasker's and Bamberger's moderate, liberal political attitudes were thoroughly representative of most German Jews at the time. About 85 percent tended to support the Progressive Party or the National Liberals during the liberal era before the founding of the empire. Most of the remainder was affiliated with the conservative camp, which in 1867 for the first time sent a Jew, Meyer Carl Baron von Rothschild, to the Prussian Upper Chamber.

Although only about 1 percent of the Jewish population associated itself with the socialist movement that was beginning to take shape at this time, its adherents included some of the most prominent politicians of the early labor movement, such as Karl Marx (who was baptized as a child) and Ferdinand Lassalle (1825–1864), who was raised in Breslau, where his father was a member of the city council. While Marx declared the necessity of class struggle as a prerequisite for revolution after 1848, Lassalle maintained his allegiance to the goals of 1848 even under the existing conditions. It was thus Lassalle and not Marx who attempted to implement the theoretical concept of a social democratic revolution. To this end he founded the first organized German labor movement in 1863, the

General German Workers' Association. Although he prepared the ground for organizing the German workforce, Lassalle was unable to reap the harvest of his toil. When he died, one year after founding the association, which he had led in rather autocractic fashion, it had only four thousand members. Lassalle's death was an expression of the many contradictions of a life caught up in a constant struggle between Jewish heritage, bourgeois society, and revolutionary action. He died from wounds suffered in a duel fought to restore his reputation after he was rejected by the family of his bride, Helene von Doenniges, on account of his Jewish background and political activities.

In the decade preceding the establishment of the German Empire, Jews began to be chosen—albeit hesitantly—for state office. Moritz Ellstätter (1827–1905), who became minister of finance in Baden in 1868, was the first Jewish minister in a German state—but he was also the only one until 1918. In Prussia, where unbaptized Jews were still barred from becoming military officers or attorneys, they were also, unsurprisingly, prohibited from seeking a career in government. Although Baden, Bavaria, and some other states began naming Jews as judges, following the example set by Hamburg where Gabriel Riesser became a high court judge in 1860, here too Prussia lagged far behind. The Prussian ministry of justice never took such a step, consistently and successfully opposing supportive statements by the Lower House and petitions by Jewish notables throughout the 1860s.

Jewish political acceptance appeared earlier in city-states that had important, well-established communities. This could be seen not only in numerous Jewish representatives being sent to the legislative bodies and Riesser's appointment to the Hamburg high court but in laws governing daily life. In 1849 the Hamburg constituent assembly eliminated a separate oath for Jews, replacing it with the common "So help me God." Two years later, for the first time, a law was passed permitting interfaith marriages between Jews and Christians, the introduction of civil marriages and civilian registry offices having removed the last formal barriers to them. After initial resistance most Hamburg guilds opened their doors to Jews in the 1850s, though by that time guilds had also lost much of their former importance.

Contact between Jewish and Christian dignitaries, which rarely existed in the period before 1848, and official meetings and distribution of honors on the local level increased starting in the late 1850s after temporarily waning during the reactionary period. Local choirs performed when a rabbi was installed and Jewish community members composed respectful verses on the occasion of a new pastor's investiture. When synagogues were consecrated Christian clergy and the city mayor provided edifying words of greeting. Wealthy Jews organized funding for major church construction projects and Christians helped with donations to build local synagogues. Interfaith charity organizations now frequently replaced those that were distinguished along religious lines. The desperate situation of Russian Jews at the end of the 1860s led to unprecedented Christian support of Jewish refugees, culminating in 1869 when the Prussian royal couple attended a concert to benefit the needy in the New Synagogue in Berlin.

These encounters within a formal institutional context should not blur the fact that social contact between Jews and Christians in everyday life was quite limited. Although Jews and Christians worked together and started spending more time together in clubs and political meetings, they usually remained apart in their private lives. Reporting on a trip to a spa in 1852, Ludwig Philippson, the publisher of the leading Jewish newspaper, noted "the strict separation . . . between Jewish and Christian visitors" and concluded that "it is indeed so: the Jews stay with the Jews, the Christians with the Christians. . . . It is as if each group feels comfortable and relaxed only among its own . . . despite isolated, rare exceptions." Similarly, an 1870 newspaper article in the *Breslauer Morgenzeitung* on the first joint ball of Christian and Jewish merchants in the city reported: "Our Christian and Jewish businesspeople here merchandised, discounted, dined, supped, flirted, and even intermarried with each other, but they have never danced together. Is that not very strange?"[19]

Similar reports came from the small towns and villages. Eduard Silbermann, a trader, described the coexistence of Christians and Jews in the Upper Franconian village of Bischberg (near Bamberg) as harmonious yet reserved:

> On the whole, the Jewish population has lived in peace with the Christians. In particular, the Jews have not been disturbed or harassed in the practice of their rituals and customs. At the time of the yearly church fair the Christian families sent "fritters and fair bread" to Jewish homes, while we reciprocated at Passover by sending matzos, which were much liked by the Christian population. . . . Naturally, there was no formal socializing in such a small place.[20]

Occasionally, however, violent incidents disrupted the harmony. The Würzburg riots of June 1866 were triggered by an increase in beer prices and Jews served as scapegoats for the popular outrage. First the windows were shattered in Rabbi Seligmann Baer Bamberger's house and then the mob of soldiers, workers, and apprentices systematically ransacked other Jewish homes. The familiar chant protesting "Jewish usurers" could be heard from the mob of mostly have-nots. Their "class struggle" was directed against well-to-do Jews but left wealthy Gentiles in peace. A year earlier, and again in May 1866, "hep hep" chants reminiscent of the rioting in 1819 had already rung out, combined with the destruction of Jewish property in the nearby villages of Laudenbach, Wiesenfeld, and Thüngen. Like the events in 1819 and 1848, the Würzburg beer riots of 1866 specifically targeted the Jews. But, unlike them, the violence of the 1860s remained scattered and localized.

The intensification of social contact now became apparent in associational life. It was definitely possible for a Jew to become the village's champion rifleman or for the rifle tournament to be postponed because of a Jewish holiday. Still, the fact that Jewish newspapers continued to find it newsworthy when elite clubs accepted Jewish members in the 1850s or when a Jew gave a talk before a non-Jewish audience points to the continuing limits of Jewish-Christian coexistence.

In the decades after 1848 German universities accepted a growing number of Jewish students. According to Jacob Toury's figures, in 1852 there were approximately 1,400 Jewish college students in Germany. Thirty years later there were over 3,000 Jews registered at German universities, comprising 8 percent of the student bodies. However, the number of Jews with full professorships increased only slowly. No breakthrough was possible in the first decade after the attempted revolution. Although physician Jacob Herz held anatomy lectures every semester at the University of Erlangen, they could not be listed in the course schedule. When in 1854, after teaching for thirteen years, Herz applied for the postdoctoral *Habilitation* degree required for full professor status, the response of the department of medicine was clearly negative: "By no means can we authorize and justify that just such a person with the abilities and education of Dr. Herz, who disdains becoming a Christian, should be able to function as a fully authorized teacher at an institution that imparts higher learning to a Christian society."[21] Not until fifteen years later, in 1869, was Herz named a full professor in Erlangen. The situation was similar in other states and other academic departments. Julius Fürst started teaching Middle Eastern studies in 1839 at the University of Leipzig, but he was not given the title of full professor until twenty-five years later, and even then he was restricted by not being allowed to vote either for the university rector or the parliamentary delegate. Gustav Weil, an Arabic studies specialist at the University of Heidelberg, could become an unpaid lecturer in 1836 only because he was also employed as an assistant librarian in the university library. He spent years fighting to receive the title of associate professor (*Extraordinarius*), which he eventually obtained in 1845, but without the corresponding salary. Not until he threatened to stop teaching was he named full professor (*Ordinarius*) in 1861. Two years earlier, at the University of Göttingen, mathematician Moritz Abraham Stern—as mentioned in the previous chapter—became the first Jew to receive the title of full professor in Germany. During this period there was not a single Jew who became a full professor in Prussia. In Austria Wolfgang Wessely (1801–1870), a specialist in jurisprudence and Middle Eastern studies, was the first unbaptized Jew to receive full professor status at the University of Prague in 1861, but an equivalent appointment at the University of Vienna did not take place until a decade later.

If a Jew wanted to earn academic laurels without converting, the only place in the German-speaking realm where this was possible without great difficulty was in Switzerland. Historian Max Büdinger was appointed full professor in Zurich in 1861. Two years earlier Moritz Lazarus (1824–1903) received an honorary professorship at the small university in Bern, where he worked (from 1862 as a full professor) with three other Jewish lecturers until he received a position at the War Academy in Berlin in 1867. In 1864 he even served as rector and dean of the University of Bern. Together with his brother-in-law, Heymann Steinthal (1823–1899), Lazarus established the field of ethnopsychology. The two men published the journal *Zeitschrift für Völkerpsychologie* starting in 1859. They both affirmed their Jewish heritage as well in their scientific studies as in their public pronouncements, forming part of the small but significant group of German-Jewish scholars who played a role in German culture while remaining active within the Jewish community. Another of these scholars was the archeologist Jacob Bernays (1824–1881), the oldest son of "Chacham" Isaac Bernays of Hamburg. In contrast to his younger brother, who adopted Christianity, Jacob remained faithful to Judaism and paid the price of having to face obstacles in his academic career. Although he was a lecturer at the University of Bonn from 1848 to 1853, he waited in vain for an advancement dependent only on his conversion. Bernays refused to take this step and joined the faculty of the Jewish Theological Seminary in Breslau.

He also belonged to the Professors' Circle there and was a friend of historian Theodor Mommsen. In 1866 he was finally given a position at his alma mater in Bonn, spending the rest of his life there as an associate professor and head librarian.

The two decades before the founding of the empire was a period in which Jews played a less significant role in Germany's cultural life than they did either earlier or later. The time had not yet come when the likes of a Hermann Cohen or Edmund Husserl would make their impact upon philosophy and a variety of Jewish scholars upon the natural sciences. There was no longer the equivalent of a Heinrich Heine or a Ludwig Börne in the area of literature and journalism, although Berthold Auerbach continued to write. Most Jewish authors and artists that came upon the scene during this period were soon forgotten.

Likewise, in the field of music the heyday for Jewish composers had ended by 1848, and it did not reemerge until much later. Felix Mendelssohn died in 1847 and Giacomo Meyerbeer was no longer very prolific because of a severe illness. Gustav Mahler and Arnold Schönberg belong to the following generation. Of German-Jewish composers active during this period, Jacques Offenbach (1819–1880) was the only one to receive lasting acclaim. Son of a cantor in Cologne, Offenbach wrote a variety of operas while in exile in France. There were, however, numerous Jewish performing musicians, both baptized and unbaptized, who became widely known. Violinist Joseph Joachim (1831–1907) of Hungary had already inspired Franz Liszt while still a child, before being influenced by Felix Mendelssohn and Robert Schumann in Leipzig. As concert master in Hanover, he became a good friend of Johannes Brahms. For years Brahms continued to send all his manuscripts from Vienna to Joachim for corrections. A year after being hired in Hanover and immediately after composing his "Hebrew Melodies" in 1855, Joachim converted to Protestantism. His significance for posterity lies in the widespread popularity that he won for Beethoven's chamber music. He performed his works in London for decades, helping to spread Beethoven's fame beyond the European continent. Joachim attained renown not only as an eminent violin virtuoso but as the greatest teacher for an entire generation of students of the instrument.

When Joachim became head of the newly established music academy in Berlin in 1866, there was one dissenting voice in the midst of the applause. Richard Wagner advised against choosing Joachim for the position, accusing him of lacking qualification as a conductor. By this time

Wagner's antisemitism was no longer a secret. Three years later he even republished his notorious, initially anonymous invective entitled *Das Judenthum in der Musik* (Judaism in Music; see chapter 6). Nevertheless, there were also Jewish musicians who worked actively with Wagner. Joseph Rubenstein, a young pianist from Russia, greatly admired the composer and lived for several months in Bayreuth. Wagner's tender treatment of his psychologically unstable student was due in no small measure to the fact that Rubenstein renounced his Jewish heritage and saw Villa Wahnfried as the proper environment for his "cure." Another pianist, Carl Tausig (1841–1871), dedicated himself totally to Wagner's works and performed on strenuous propaganda tours intended to help establish Bayreuth as a musical center. Wagner and Tausig developed a father-son relationship Wagner could reconcile with his antisemitic sentiments only by declaring Tausig's real father to be Christian. Hermann Levi (1839–1900)—court conductor in Munich after 1872—was musically closest to Wagner's work in Bayreuth. With the support of his patron, Ludwig II, Wagner requested that Levi be on the podium for the premiere of *Parsifal* in 1882 and later referred to his conducting as exemplary for all time. Although Levi was sometimes influenced by Wagner's negative attitudes toward Judaism, he resisted the latter's persistent efforts to convert him to Christianity. Instead, Levi, who in his youth had composed a work on the occasion of the consecration of the Mannheim synagogue as well as a new version of the Sabbath song *Veshamru* for the synagogue in his hometown of Giessen, offered his services as musical adviser to the Jewish community in Munich.

These personal contacts did not, however, lead to any changes in the anti-Jewish sentiment that reigned in Villa Wahnfried. Cosima and Richard Wagner shared a hatred of Jews, whether expressed in their pleasure over Jewish deaths in a fire at a Viennese theater or in their suspicions that a Jewish conspiracy was behind any untoward event. Even their joy over the Prussian troops triumphantly entering Berlin in 1871 after the war with France was diminished because the press account reporting the victory celebration stemmed from the pen of a Jewish author.

Wagner assisted in the emergence of a new type of anti-Judaism that deliberately made use of racist rather than religious argumentation. Wilhelm Marr, who launched the new term *antisemitism* in 1879, was a typical representative of this new movement. Like Wagner, Marr had dissociated himself from all organized religions and in 1848 identified himself with the radical revolutionaries. Whereas Wagner became a celebrated composer, however, Marr remained an obscure writer and political organizer for whom antisemitism became more and more his mission in life. After returning from exile in Costa Rica in 1859, he obtained a seat as a radical democrat in the Hamburg city council, where he soon confronted the liberal Gabriel Riesser head-on. Marr published his first major anti-Jewish work, *Judenspiegel* (Mirror of the Jews) in 1862. Although it was originally intended as an attack on Orthodox Judaism, Marr soon decided to wage a more general attack on Liberal and Orthodox Jews alike. Here he already made use of the concept of "the Jewish race," even though this did not imply that Jews were incapable of assimilation. Like Wagner, he represented the view that in the end, if they totally abandoned their Judaism—which meant more than mere baptism—the Jews could indeed be integrated into German society. His own biography provided ample proof of his conviction. Whereas Wagner had surrounded himself with a circle of Jewish musicians and admirers, Marr went even further, to the point of marrying women of Jewish descent.

Similar contradictions can be found in popular literature. Gustav Freytag, a liberal who publicly defended Jewish emancipation, also spread negative stereotypes about Jews. Like many liberals, he equated Jewish emancipation with the dissolution of Judaism. The Jewish character in his popular book *Soll und Haben* (Debit and Credit, 1855) is a symbol of rootlessness and lack of honor amidst the sturdy world of the German bourgeoisie. Another much-read novel of this period, Wilhelm Raabe's *Hungerpastor* (The Hunger Pastor, 1864), makes the contrast between the Christian hero and the Jewish villain even more obvious. According to Raabe, conversion to Catholicism did nothing to change the innately immoral character of Jews. Finally, although the conflict between the heroic Teuton and the cowardly, conspiratorial Jew in Felix Dahn's *Ein Kampf um Rom* (A Battle for Rome, 1867) was concealed in a historical plot, readers could easily transfer it to the present. The Jewish protagonists in all three novels reflect more or less the same stereotype of the profoundly immoral Jew who retains his dialect and is incapable of integration.

The internal contradictions of modern antisemitism, as it was developing during this era, became ever more apparent. On the one hand, Jews were asked to abandon their Jewishness and become fully assimilated as Germans. On the other hand, they were attacked as undesirable intruders who supposedly dominated culture and the business world. Jews were supposed to stop being Jews, but they could become real Germans only in exceptional cases. The prerequisites for acceptance into German society were never clearly spelled out.

As great as the resistance to social recognition of German Jews during the two decades from 1848 to 1871 might seem in retrospect, it was vastly overshadowed in the consciousness of German Jewry by their tremendous economic and social advance. Thus optimism, if not euphoria, prevailed among Jews at the end of this period. Wilhelm Marr and his colleagues had not yet founded antisemitic parties and scholars such as Heinrich von Treitschke were still reserved in their public statements. As long as anti-Jewish attacks were limited to the literary sphere, while social recognition in daily life made visible progress, there was little reason for concern. Two decades after 1848 German Jewry's at first short-lived achievements appeared finally to be irrevocably established. Firmly moored within German society and culture, Jews persisted in not fully relinquishing their Jewish identity. In fact, that identity now began to assume new forms of expression.

9 | Jewish Identity in the Decades After 1848

1. The Ongoing Process of Absorption

While he was still in the grasp of the messianic enthusiasm unleashed by the extraordinary events of 1848, the Jewish historian Isaac Marcus Jost had written to friends: "Jewish matters naturally fall into the background; they don't fit this world. Whenever I run into people from the synagogue, I think I'm seeing ghosts from the Middle Ages."[1] Even during the following decade of political reaction, and the more so during the 1860s as the drive toward full equality once again made rapid progress, the relegation of Judaism to the periphery of personal identity, if not to irrelevance, became ever more common among German Jews. What still mattered was the drive toward complete equality—and until 1871 that quest remained, as in the first half of the century, a principal component of Jewish solidarity. But observances that kept Jews separate, such as dietary laws and Sabbath observance, now became, in the words of one Bohemian Jew, the "ballast of an age gone by."[2] Liberalism appeared to many as the neutral ground upon which Jew and Gentile could meet. The shared hope of political progress replaced separate religious aspirations. As they moved from village to small town to city, from established communities to new ones where Jews had not previously settled, the migrants left their ancestral traditions behind. Contemporary memoirs portray families in which Jewish knowledge and Jewish practice have become minimal, displaced by general education and a bourgeois lifestyle fundamentally similar to that of German non-Jews of the same class. Whereas in most instances it was the husband, in others it was the wife who pushed forward the family's abandonment of tradition. Time and again rabbis complained of the prevalent Jewish "indifference." Although there were also significant countertrends that shaped the visible image of Judaism in these years—and we shall dwell on them here—the less apparent but dominant trend was toward a loss of Jewish distinctiveness. Secular interests increasingly displaced religious ones at a time when Jewishness was, at least in part for political reasons, defined officially in strictly religious terms. As the German sphere grew, for most Jewish families, the Jewish one was proportionately diminished.

It was in the area of social relationships that Jews still remained most obviously separate. Although they shared the education and cultural values of non-Jews, with few exceptions they continued to associate mainly with fellow Jews. Jewish societies brought coreligionists together regularly, sometimes for specifically Jewish purposes, but in many instances for secular ones, or simply for the sake of conviviality. Even converted Jews still socialized with Jewish family and acquaintances or with fellow converts; Jews and ex-Jews continued to feel more comfortable among their own. There were Jewish cafés, hotels, and restaurants that attracted a predominantly or exclusively Jewish clientele. For some they served as a regular place of Jewish meeting, fulfilling a function no longer served by the synagogue except for a minority. Yet during the liberal 1860s even social barriers were breaking down. Especially in the larger cities, among the more well-to-do and the intellectuals, regular social contacts across religious lines became more common. Although still prohibited in Prussia and most other German states, mixed marriages now occurred increasingly, reaching the largest dimensions in Hamburg, where over two hundred were registered between 1851 and 1868 in a community of about twelve thousand. Other Jews, desiring to cut ties with organized Judaism but without conversion to Christianity, were in a few places (Hamburg, Lübeck, Württemberg) allowed to withdraw from their local communities, thus avoiding payment of community taxes.

In certain regions, such as Posen, Jewish schools still flourished, and in Baden they now came under Jewish supervision. But elsewhere they were in decline. In communities too small to afford a Jewish school Jewish children attended Christian schools; in the cities many parents preferred the gentile school over the Jewish one. Advanced education occurred almost invariably in a Christian environment. Within such schools, Jewish children, for the most part, mingled socially with coreligionists, but it was frequently assumed that they would write on the Sabbath and, in some instances, even take part in Christian religious instruction in the lower grades. Children not attending a Jewish school received minimal Jewish religious instruction of two hours per week, generally not taken seriously and often only voluntary in the higher schools. Preparation for the Bar Mitzvah ceremony provided boys with only a modicum of Hebrew knowledge that was quickly forgotten; confirmation instruction usually gave both sexes little more than superficial knowledge of religious principles.

Whereas in the 1840s, in the flush of religious controversy, a variety of Jewish newspapers had come into being, in the following years they ceased publication, leaving, for a time, only the veteran *Allgemeine Zeitung des Judenthums* as the one strong link connecting the scattered Jewish communities. Except where certain governments had earlier created statewide Jewish religious institutions, communities in this period remained bereft of any organizational structure apart from the local one. In Prussia the authorities consistently opposed efforts to create a representative body. In Bohemia, where religious indifference was especially prevalent and Jewish education badly neglected, a representative conference, held in Prague in 1850, failed to establish a central organization, preferring instead to preserve local autonomy and to avoid the additional costs. Not until 1869 was it possible to call together lay and professional delegates from forty-eight German communities to an assembly in Leipzig, the first gathering of its kind. Representatives from the major Jewish communities were present, though none from Baden and Württemberg. The delegates established a loose organization, known as the Deutsch-Israelitische Gemeindebund (German-Israelite Alliance of Communities), which would concern itself principally with matters of community administration, philanthropy, and defense activities. Although it determined to exclude religious matters from its agenda, the DIGB did not become fully representative. The Orthodox mistrusted it, and their communities would not join.

In the two decades after 1848 German Jewry remained essentially divided—as did Germany. Religious and educational institutions continued to vary from state to state and from community to community, as did the rate of acculturation. As for the divisions in religious ideology, which emerged earlier, they now crystallized more clearly and assumed permanent institutional forms.

2. Orthodoxy and Reform

Unlike the agitated 1840s, the years of political reaction were not conducive to ideologically motivated religious reform. The lay radicalism and
the rabbinical conferences had called wide attention to religious issues
and stimulated lively discussion. Now that the storm had passed, all was
quiet; a "weary indifference" reigned.[3] In part this was a reflection of the
situation within Christianity, which had absorbed the conservatism of the
political atmosphere. As Protestantism became an ideological support of
the political status quo, official German Catholicism linked itself more
closely with Rome and thus to the papacy of Pius IX, which consistently
opposed both religious and political liberalism. Dissatisfied Christians
scornfully left the church; intellectuals and scholars did not seek to
reform it. In the absence of an alliance with organized Christianity, political liberalism appeared to Jews, as to Christians, not as an extension of
their religious faith but as a secular substitute for it. If earlier Jewish reformers had been able to derive inspiration from trends in Christianity
for their own activity, its current position seemed more in accord with
Jewish Orthodoxy. Likewise, to the dismay of the Jewish Reformers, philosophical radicalism, soon appearing in the form of materialism, could no
longer be harmonized with religion, as had been possible when Kant and
Hegel were the dominant influences. It is noteworthy that these years
produced no new Jewish theological systems or ideologies; the doctrines
formulated earlier were simply repeated and elaborated. Nor did a new
intellectual leadership emerge. The principal figures of the earlier period,
now in middle age, overshadowed the younger generation. More than before, rabbis became subservient to the laity.

If earlier some German states had stimulated and occasionally even
compelled religious reform, now, as in Prussia under Frederick William
III, they generally found it politically undesirable. Since most Jewish religious reformers had supported the 1848 Revolution, in the years of reaction they were considered untrustworthy. Governments in the following
years preferred to forge alliances with the traditionalists and pressed for
the appointment of Orthodox rabbis. In Berlin the Reform Congregation
was, for a time, even placed under police supervision. In the Habsburg
Empire the effect of political reaction on religious progress was still more
severe. There the government suppressed all efforts at religious reform
and supported the Orthodox as the true Austrian patriots.

In the small towns, where most German Jews still lived at mid-century, the desire to avoid controversy generally led to the rejection of religious reforms or to moderate compromise, especially as religious progressives moved away to the cities, allowing unity to be restored. But in the larger communities the lines of division opened up earlier could no longer be erased. The loose coalitions clustered around Reform and traditionalism developed further into permanent factions, which competed with each other in community elections. Arrangements for separate liberal and traditional services within a larger community united for social welfare purposes, first instituted in Breslau, became the common pattern. Increasingly, the religious liberals were successful in gaining the leadership positions in community organizations. In Berlin moderate progressives took control in 1854 and maintained it consistently thereafter for the rest of the century.

Although the 1850s and 1860s were not a period of theoretical or practical innovation, they do witness the institutionalization of doctrines and practices advocated first by individuals and then collectively during the rabbinical conferences. Following 1848 local initiatives replace collective ones. Whereas in the earlier period extensive liturgical reform was limited to separatist Reform congregations in Berlin and Hamburg, now non-Orthodox prayerbooks are composed for nearly a dozen community synagogues, including Breslau, Mannheim, Königsberg, Frankfurt am Main, Leipzig, and Berlin. In most cases it is the construction of a new synagogue that prompts the creation of an appropriate new liturgy. In some instances a new prayerbook wins broader acceptance, as in Baden, where the Mannheim prayerbook is quickly adopted in the new communities of Freiburg, Offenburg, and Konstanz. The tendency of the prayerbooks is to shorten the service, introduce a few German prayers and hymns, and eliminate references to a desired return to Zion. Sometimes the Hebrew text remains more traditional than the translation or the worshipper is offered the choice of either the customary or an altered Hebrew prayer. Invariably, there are compromises to please as wide a segment of the non-Orthodox community as possible. In Abraham Geiger's words: "Let the prayerbook be, like the synagogue, a place of peaceful getting together for communal edification, not a site of frenzied combat."[4]

It was indeed not changes in the liturgy that caused the greatest religious controversy within the larger German communities but the trend toward instituting organ accompaniment of the service. The old halachic arguments were again brought forth as one community after another, especially when it was building a new synagogue, considered whether or not to make use of the instrument. But, for most, the issue of legal permissibility had become secondary. More prominent was the question whether adoption of the organ in the synagogue was intrinsically objectionable as an importation from Christianity that had no place in Jewish worship. The moderate traditionalist Manuel Joël in Breslau did not believe the organ was necessarily linked to another faith, but Isaac Noah Mannheimer in Vienna, who was liberal in other respects, rejected its use for that very reason. The writer and community secretary in Vienna, Ludwig August Frankl, argued that it was as much an imitation of Christianity to employ an organ as it would be to build a synagogue in the Gothic cruciform pattern. The organ, he held, was "Christianity in sound, Gothic architecture Christianity in brick."[5] Yet, despite opposition by traditionalists and by some liberals, the organ was widely adopted for the liberal service in the larger communities. By 1870 it was ten times as common as twenty years earlier. The presence of the organ, more than the nature of the liturgy, became the distinguishing characteristic of liberal, as opposed to traditional, Jewish worship.

Even in synagogues with organs, however, women continued to sit separately from men and to play no role in religious leadership. An exceptional example of female religious activism occurred in Baden in 1855 when women in the Mannheim community directed a petition to the Supreme Jewish Council in defense of the reforming activity of their rabbi, Moses Präger. They expressed outrage that the prayer in which the man thanks God for not having created him a woman should, at the behest of the council, be reintroduced into the service and they gave thanks to God "that that time lies behind us when Jewish married and unmarried women were excluded from the general worship and forced into patient silence behind walls and lattices, when they were scarcely found worthy of worshipping the Creator equally together with their husbands and children."[6] The women noted that they felt no less obligated to pray than the men and that the service should be no less edifying for them.

In the sphere of religion it was, however, a more traditionally oriented woman who gained the most attention. Fanny Neuda (1819–1894), the young widow of the rabbi in Loschitz in Moravia, in 1855 published a book of original prayers and devotions, most them from her own pen, entitled *Stunden der Andacht* (Hours of Devotion). Earlier Ashkenazi women had composed such devotions in Yiddish (known as *tehines*) and more recently rabbis and educators had written modern versions in German. But Neuda was the first woman to compose such a work entirely in

German—in fact without any Yiddish terms at all and also without the
angels and demons that appeared frequently in the teḥines. Because it was
the work of a woman and included devotions for special occasions in the
woman's life cycle, the author hoped it would "be the more likely to res-
onate in women's hearts."[7] In an added "word to the noble mothers and
women in Israel," Neuda urged mothers to provide for the religious education of their daughters along with instruction in languages and the arts.
Very quickly her work became immensely popular. Wolf Pascheles, the
veteran Prague Jewish publisher and distributor of Hebrew and German
Jewish books, issued a deluxe edition, an edition in Hebrew letters, and
one bound together with a traditional prayerbook. The book was reprinted at least twenty-eight times and enjoyed a large readership in
English translation as well.

As religious reform spread within the German communities, a portion
of the Orthodox came to the conclusion that they could no longer rely
upon the community's institutions and that, in order to preserve the
Jewish faith in unadulterated form, they would have to establish an independent religious and educational structure. The Orthodox separatist
movement began in Frankfurt am Main when a group of about three
dozen men founded the Israelitische Religionsgesellschaft (Israelite Religious Society) there in 1850. The earliest members, who included the local
Rothschilds and other well-to-do Frankfurt bankers, declared their intention to continue supporting, as well, the institutions of the general community and thus were able to receive approval from a sympathetic government to engage their own rabbi. A few months later Samson Raphael
Hirsch (their second choice after the Berlin rabbi Michael Sachs) arrived
from Nikolsburg in Moravia to assume spiritual leadership of the group.
By 1853 the size of the IRG had grown to 180 families and it could boast
its own newly constructed synagogue as well as a school with 84 students.
Its religious service, though conducted with a traditional prayerbook and
without organ, was no less decorous than that of any liberal synagogue.
Its school, though devoting a considerable portion of the curriculum to
Jewish subjects, prided itself on supplying students with a complete
German education.

Similar separatist Orthodox groups, largely inspired by the IRG, were
formed in Mainz, Darmstadt, Wiesbaden, and Karlsruhe. The largest of
these, Adass Jisroel in Berlin, was established in 1869, after the community leadership had repeatedly given evidence of a liberal thrust. It chose
Esriel Hildesheimer, then rabbi of Eisenstadt in Hungary, to be its spir-

itual leader. The learned Hildesheimer, who possessed both a yeshiva education and a German doctorate, was more open to the discipline of Wissenschaft des Judentums than Samson Raphael Hirsch. In 1873 he founded the Rabbinerseminar für das orthodoxe Judentum in Berlin, which produced the spiritual leadership of German Orthodoxy for the following generations.

With the establishment of Hirsch's monthly periodical *Jeschurun* in 1855 and Marcus Lehmann's weekly *Israelit* five years later, separatist Orthodoxy was able to give encouragement to observant Jews who, in view of their shrinking numbers, despaired of Orthodoxy's ability to sustain itself, claiming that "nothing is going to help." The response given by Hirsch and Lehmann was a new militant defense of Orthodox interests, colorfully expressed by Hirsch: "Only if, as in the days of our ancestors, we gird ourselves with swords can we today, on a rubble-covered field with enemies lurking all around, hope to advance the building of our sanctuary."[8] The new Orthodox party organs were intended to replace for Orthodox Jews Philippson's allegedly nonpartisan but in fact liberal *Allgemeine Zeitung*. They preached separation as the only salvation wherever reformers controlled a community and urged parents to steer their children away from marriage into non-Orthodox families. Although the separatist societies were everywhere much smaller than the general community, their existence served to slow the pace of reform, as local leaders sought to inhibit their creation or the expansion of their membership by avoiding any measure that might be considered radical.

Toward the end of our period, more than two decades after the rabbinical conferences of the 1840s, the German religious reformers once more gathered sufficient energy to meet together for collective deliberations. This time, however, the meetings were in the form of synods, convened in Leipzig in 1869 and again, two years later, in Augsburg. The first, held in conjunction with the assembly of communities and presided over by the prominent Jewish intellectual Moritz Lazarus, brought together rabbis, scholars, and lay leaders from sixty communities in Germany, Austria, and elsewhere in Europe and America. Although it gave sanction to certain religious reforms, such as use of the organ, it defeated more radical proposals and reaffirmed the importance of Hebrew in Jewish education and prayer. The second synod, less well attended, bore a more distinctly reformist complexion, concerning itself especially with improving the status of women in Jewish marital law and custom. Although the leadership planned continuation of the synods, the impulse to convene further gath-

Präsidium

der ersten israelitischen Synode zu Leipzig.

II. Vicepräsident	Präsident	I. Vicepräsident
Ritter v. Wertheimer	Prof. Dr. M. Lazarus	Dr. A. Geiger
aus Wien.	aus Berlin.	aus Frankfurt a/M.

41   The presiding committee of the first Israelite synod in Leipzig, 1869:
Josef von Wertheimer, Moritz Lazarus, and Rabbi Abraham Geiger

erings proved insufficient. By 1871 religious liberalism had gained its objectives in the local communities and there were no new theoretical or practical issues to discuss. Indeed, the controversies over theology and religious practice had begun to seem a bit stale. Attention had long been diverted to building institutions that would reflect the new economic status and the new religious needs of German Jewry.

3. Synagogues and Seminaries

As German Jews gained in prosperity and as their numbers grew in the larger towns and cities, they sought to give tangible expression to their improved situation. They established new Jewish hospitals and other charitable institutions. But, most visibly, they built impressive synagogues that could compete in opulence and modern technical innovations with any Christian church. Scores of new structures now arose all over German-speaking Europe. Among the most lavish were those in Leipzig (1855), Mannheim (1855), Vienna (1858), Frankfurt am Main (1860), Stuttgart (1861), Berlin (1866), and Breslau (1872). Contemporaries fully recognized the symbolic message of these imposing new buildings. The synagogues of earlier times, one writer imagined, had reflected the condition of an unemancipated Jewry. In them "everything, even the gables of the roof, bowed deeply, everything was cramped and constrained—just like the people who prayed in them."[9] The new synagogues, by contrast, were high ceilinged and well lighted. They stood proudly on a principal street of the city where they could be admired by Christian and Jew alike. Although the architects were mostly Christian, it was not unusual for Jewish contractors and craftsmen to participate in the construction—a point of pride especially noted by Jewish writers. The increased attendance of women at the services was reflected in the larger percentage—sometimes even half—of the seats allotted to them in some of the new structures. Contemporaries called the grandest synagogues "monumental." They were indeed massive testimonies in stone to the self-perceived Jewish advance from pariahdom to *Bürgertum*. They reflected both the Jews' economic achievement and their continuing political aspiration. A non-Jewish editor commented in 1854 that the cornerstone just laid for the new synagogue in Leipzig was symbolically the cornerstone of full Jewish equality in Saxony. When completed, the building would be "a new bond between fellow citizens separated only by religious denomination."[10] Similarly in Frankfurt, the new synagogue, standing at the end of the old Judengasse emblematic of earlier prejudice and persecution, represented the "proud monument to a more civilized and humane era."[11]

It is remarkable that at a time when monumental churches were also being built the Christian structures, except for their dimensions, should exercise a decreasing influence on synagogue architecture. Whereas synagogue construction earlier in the century had leaned heavily on the Romanesque style, the forms of architecture for the two religions in these decades diverged, as Jews devised their own sacral style. Communities building new synagogues now often sought to give them a distinctively Jewish character that would contrast with their Christian counterparts. It was the Moorish or Syrian-Arabic style, drawn from Islam, that was employed for the most resplendent new synagogues built in the larger Jewish communities beginning in 1855. The most outstanding examples were in Leipzig, Vienna, Stuttgart, and Berlin. While they were being built, and after their completion, the Moorish synagogues invariably drew widespread admiration.

That Jewish communities should increasingly choose this style is no doubt due in part to their veneration for the Sephardi heritage, which the Jewish Enlightenment had already praised for its openness to secular disciplines like philosophy and poetry and which had long served as a model for Jewish modernization. It was also a result of the desire to establish a distinctive style of synagogue construction in the absence of an indigenous tradition of Jewish architecture. And it reflected a new interest in Jewish history. But, most fundamentally, the choice of an Eastern model was intended to convey a second message, alongside that of economic success: though integrated into the Occident, the Jews were not ashamed of their Oriental heritage, and they now felt sufficiently secure to display that relationship to the world. Not surprisingly, use of the Moorish style declines with the rise of antisemitism. It is abandoned in the last decades of the century, lest it strengthen further the arguments of those who had by then already begun to claim the Moorish structures as further evidence that the Jews in Germany—despite their emancipation—remained foreigners.

The new synagogues were remarkable not alone for their architectural magnificence but also for the sacred music that was heard within their walls. In 1825 the Vienna community, intent on creating a decorous, aesthetically pleasing but basically traditional service, had called the young Isaac Noah Mannheimer from Denmark to be its preacher along with a promising, equally young musician from Hohenems, Salomon Sulzer, to

42 Consecration of the New Synagogue in Berlin,
Oranienburger Strasse, 1866

be its cantor. Sulzer (1804–1891) was not only an outstanding singer but also a talented composer, the pioneer of modern synagogue music. In 1840 he published the first volume of his *Schir Zion*, consisting mostly of his own compositions, many of which were speedily adopted throughout German-speaking Europe and also in some American and Eastern European synagogues. Although Sulzer himself continued to sing mostly in the older Seitenstettengasse temple, his choral compositions were heard regularly, as well, in the magnificent new Leopoldstadt synagogue, completed six years after the Vienna community finally gained official recognition in 1852.

Sulzer's music, though essentially giving ordered form to traditional Jewish motifs, was significantly influenced by the Viennese environment and by the music of the Catholic Church. The second of the great German synagogue composers, Louis Lewandowski (1821–1894), who was chief choir master of the Jewish community in Berlin, resisted the incorporation of Protestant elements into his music but was strongly drawn to the German folk song, which gave his melodies great emotional appeal. Whereas Sulzer was a classicist, Lewandowski was a romantic, ironically much influenced by the music of Moses Mendelssohn's converted grandson Felix. Although not himself a proponent of the organ, Lewandowski created for the new Berlin synagogue, for the first time, a complete worship service attuned to the use of that instrument. His compositions rapidly became more popular than Sulzer's, especially in northern Germany. German Jews, whether they attended synagogues with an organ or without one, whether the music was sung by a choir or by the congregation, came to feel that Lewandowski's melodies were an indispensable element of the religious service. According to Leopold Zunz, his music allowed the ancient liturgy to become once more the "the possession of the community."[12]

The rabbis who preached in the new synagogues were men who had not had the benefit of ordered theological study. Some had studied in yeshivot of the old style, others with private instructors. They had gained their secular knowledge following their Jewish education and not in conjunction with it. Already in the 1830s Abraham Geiger and Ludwig Philippson had sought to remedy this situation by calling for the establishment of a Jewish theological faculty at a German university. But the project could not be carried out for lack of sufficient funds from Jewish communities and because no German institution of higher learning was ready to accept such a faculty. It was not until two decades later, when a wealthy Breslau Jew, Jonas Fränckel, left a sizable legacy to establish an institution of higher Jewish learning, that the prospect of systematic training for rabbis came into view.

Although Abraham Geiger was then serving as rabbi in Breslau and seems to have been the donor's choice to head the institution, the executors of Fränckel's will selected the more conservative Zacharias Frankel, believing that students graduating from a seminary under his supervision would more readily gain acceptance in German communities. In addition, Frankel possessed a fundamentally different and more fitting approach to rabbinical training. Whereas Geiger expressed the opinion that modern rabbis needed to receive their advanced Jewish education within the critical ambience of the university, Frankel was of the opinion that only an independent Jewish institution could do justice to the particular character of Jewish theological study. The potential conflict between Jewish tradition and critical *Wissenschaft* could only be avoided, he believed, when studies were conducted under the guidance of a "wise master" and within a Jewish environment where only a single spirit prevailed.

The Jüdisch-theologisches Seminar opened in Breslau in 1854 with seventeen students from Germany and one from Austria. During the first two decades about half the students came from Prussia, especially from the more traditional environments of Posen and Silesia. Like that of a yeshiva, its curriculum focused on the Jewish legal corpus, but it paid relatively more attention to Bible and it introduced the study of Jewish history. Its faculty, which was mandated to be fully observant in personal religious practice, included, besides Frankel, the historian Heinrich Graetz and the classical philologist Jacob Bernays. Like Frankel, its graduates occupied a middle position between Orthodoxy and Reform, sometimes finding employment in German communities as liberal rabbis, sometimes as conservatives.

The new seminary very quickly came under attack from the Orthodox, who did not consider its graduates acceptable; although religiously observant, they had not unequivocally been taught the wholly divine origin of the Oral Law. The Breslau institution, Hildesheimer believed, simply did with silk gloves what the radicals undertook with hammer and truncheon. Yet the Reformer Abraham Geiger was equally dissatisfied with the rabbinical training received in Breslau. To his mind the intensive study of the minutiae of Jewish law and the failure to fully confront the challenge of critical scholarship made the seminary's curriculum inappropriate and inadequate for the modern rabbi. Geiger was therefore among those who urged the establishment of a new institution of higher Jewish learning, founded upon unhampered free inquiry and dedicated as much to the advancement of Jewish scholarship as to the training of rabbis. Plans for such an institution, the Hochschule für die Wissenschaft des Judentums (see volume 3), were advanced at the Leipzig synod but could be carried out only after the Franco-Prussian War.

4. Popular Culture

Although German Jews required the new synagogues, reformed prayer-books, organs, and professional choirs to mark their new status and satisfy their aesthetic sensibility in the realm of religion, none of these innovations arrested the process of secularization. Except for the fully orthodox, German Jews visited their synagogues only occasionally. A generation earlier, the edifying sermons and religious reforms had returned alienated Jews to the religious service. But their novelty had now worn off and their significance declined. "In those days public discourse had only *one* abode, the pulpit; today the sermon has to withstand competition from political speeches and from informative, entertaining lectures of all kinds," complained one unhappy rabbi.[13]

As long as the Jewish home continued to transmit Jewish identity, the declining role of public worship and even the contraction of Jewish education might not have seemed crucial. However, by the second half of the century the bourgeois Jewish home was frequently little different from its Christian counterpart in the customs, values, and knowledge that it transmitted from one generation to the next. Increasingly, it appeared that for the preservation of Judaism in Germany not the rarely visited synagogue but the home required attention. Hence the outpouring during these decades of books and periodicals intended to reintroduce matters of Jewish interest into the circle of the family.

In an age when bourgeois families sat together to read popular sentimental periodicals "for young and old, for everyone with a warm heart inside his ribs ... far from all argumentative politics and all differences of opinion in religion and other matters,"[14] there seemed to be a need as well for Jewish equivalents that would present similar entertaining stories and heartwarming poetry—except that their content and message would be specifically Jewish. Weary of religious controversy, which could only divide, rabbis and Jewish educators turned in these years to the creation of a popular culture, a unifying Judaism of the heart that drew upon classical sources, but with the distinct intention of adapting them to the bourgeois taste of the average German Jew. By 1858 Rabbi Leopold Löw could note from Szeged in Hungary that Jewish literature, especially in Germany, was experiencing "an unprecedented and very hopeful upswing."[15]

Ludwig Philippson's *Jüdisches Volksblatt*, begun in 1853, and Leopold Stein's *Der Freitagabend*, launched six years later, had similar goals: to teach informally and to entertain. Like Christian family periodicals, they tried to address the entire family, scrupulously avoided controversial issues, and reached out to the common folk, who were little interested in theological debates or details of the emancipation process—matters that were still focal in the *Allgemeine Zeitung des Judenthums*. Reading them, the nonintellectual Jew could "again and again for a short while be transported to the isle of his religion, his history, his life, there to rest and gather strength to keep from losing his way."[16] The home, the refuge of the family, it was hoped, would also become the refuge for Judaism. No longer did it seem necessary to stress the importance of German *Bildung*, but rather to assure that, at least in the home, German culture would not entirely displace the Jewish heritage. Philippson now began to write *gebildet* in quotation marks. He noted that it was time the Jew overcame the self-denial that flowed in the wake of acculturation and "return to the Jew within." Leopold Stein called his weekly newspaper *Freitagabend* because that word was redolent with cherished memories of the family gathered around the table for the Friday evening Sabbath meal. As among Christians, so among Jews religion in these decades was not held to the criterion of reason but judged by its capacity to sustain an atmosphere of warmth and togetherness within the family. In the home religious ceremonies or even merely the reading of a Jewish family newspaper might perhaps slow the process of erosion. Since such family literature was deemed an appropriate sphere for the creativity of women as well as men, Stein welcomed a talented young woman poet, Minna Cohen from the town of Elmshorn in Holstein, as one of his regular contributors. Although they did not attain the circulation hoped for by their founders, the two periodicals enjoyed a modicum of success, with Philippson's reaching a few thousand readers and lasting for a dozen years before it was absorbed into his *Allgemeine Zeitung des Judenthums* in 1866.

Popular Jewish culture began to flourish in other forms as well: in illustrated monthlies and, especially, in the increasing number of Jewish calendars and literary annuals. The first successful combinations of the older genre of the Jewish calendar with the newer one of the yearbook appeared in Brieg, near Breslau (1841), and in Vienna (1842). Others fol-

lowed in Prague (1852) and Berlin (1857). Although they differed in some
respects, their similarities were basic. The calendar-yearbooks were
printed in a small format so that the husband might easily take them
along in his pocket on business trips, referring when necessary to the
commercial information provided in the calendar section on such matters
as trade fairs, currency exchange, and operating railroads, and dipping
into the literary selections of the yearbook when a free hour became
available. The calendar section of these volumes was composed of both a
general and a Jewish calendar, the latter with the traditional Jewish scriptural readings and sometimes information about the proper observance of
Jewish holidays. The yearbook section might include a review of the most
significant Jewish events of the preceding year, translations into German
of selections from medieval Jewish literature, stories, poetry, descriptions
of Jewish life in exotic lands and, almost invariably, short biographies of
outstanding Jews of the past and present. It did not matter whether the
contributors were traditionalists or radical reformers. A single volume
could contain an article on Maimonides by the Orthodox Rabbi David
Deutsch, who had led the protest against Abraham Geiger's selection as
rabbi of Breslau, along with one by Geiger himself on Jewish defense
against Christian accusations during the Renaissance. For amusement
there might be selected anecdotes from the pen of the apostate Moritz
Saphir. These popular—and in some cases long-lived—calendar-yearbooks reached Jews all over German-speaking Europe, fostering a non-
ideological, at least minimal Jewish awareness.

In 1855 the indefatigable Ludwig Philippson, already engaged in editing two weekly periodicals in addition to his rabbinical duties in Magdeburg, launched a new project, likewise intended to reintroduce a Jewish
ambience into the home via the written word. Few Jewish books were
then appearing and even these seldom enjoyed a broad readership. Publishers were reluctant to issue works on which they could not expect to
recoup their investment. Philippson's response was to create an Institute
for the Advancement of Jewish Literature, a kind of book club to which
subscribers could belong by paying a modest annual fee and receive, in
turn, all of the books published by the institute during that year. Members were promised that the books would not be recondite scholarly works
and that they would not contain politics or polemics. Instead, like the popular periodicals, they would be able "to captivate the interest of the
masses and provide them with entertainment and instruction."[17] Within
three months Philippson obtained twelve hundred subscribers and put

together an editorial board, composed initially of himself along with the historian Isaac Marcus Jost and the preacher and scholar of Midrash and Kabbalah Adolph Jellinek. During the nearly twenty years of its existence the institute published some eighty works by forty-eight authors, or an average of more than four books per year in virtually every field of Jewish literature, especially history, biography, and belles lettres. Like those represented in the yearbooks, the institute's authors likewise ranged widely in religious orientation, though the strictly Orthodox and some purist scholars would have nothing to do with Philippson's initiative. By 1865 Philippson could claim to have distributed 182,000 volumes; at its height the list of subscribers reached 3,600. Membership appealed especially to Jews in middle-sized and smaller communities, while those in the major cities that had been the early centers of the Haskalah and the Reform movement showed relatively little interest. Although the institute still had 1,400 members at the end of its existence in 1874, membership declined steeply during its second decade, a process Philippson attributed to its novelty having worn off, a younger generation absorbed in secular newspapers and novels, and the lack of promising new manuscripts.

5. Wissenschaft des Judentums

The most important work published by Philippson's institute lay in the border area between popular literature and pure scholarship. Seven of the eleven volumes of Heinrich Graetz's *Geschichte der Juden* (History of the Jews, 1853–1876) appeared under its auspices. Unlike his predecessor, Isaac Marcus Jost, who had been concerned above all with presenting the Jews in a favorable light to non-Jews, Graetz (1817–1891) wrote Jewish history especially for Jews, with the clear intention of using awareness of the past to broaden and deepen Jewish self-consciousness in the present. Through his work Graetz was determined to recreate the historical memory of his Jewish readers, to enable Jews to repossess a past from which acculturation had detached them.

Just as general historiography in Germany had come increasingly to center upon the German legacy and to act as a force for German unity, so did Graetz approach study of the Jewish past as the most effective vehicle for shoring up a sense of Jewish unity in a community divided by religious strife and diminished in Jewish awareness. At a time when religious belief and halachic practice were declining, the saga of Jewish history would instill a sense of ethnic pride and a desire for Jewish perseverance.

43   The historian Heinrich Graetz

Graetz portrayed the Jewish experience as twofold: an external history of suffering and martyrdom together with an inner history of spiritual creativity. Both were important for his purpose. Jewish readers would identify the more strongly with a people that had suffered so grievously yet, despite the suffering, contributed richly to Western civilization.

Graetz had early come to the conclusion that Judaism could not be fully understood by such philosophical constructions as had been popular in the 1830s and 1840s, since they necessarily presented Judaism only selectively and hence only in part. History alone could encompass Judaism in its totality. It could reveal the essence of Judaism, which Graetz claimed to find in the elaboration of its transcendent God idea. His own multivolume work focused upon the Jews as a people that cradled and developed that idea. Graetz was neither a theologian like Geiger, interested primarily in the history of Judaism as a religion, nor a historian who focused primarily on the social and economic history of the Jews. It was the people as creator of an ongoing religious culture—its peculiar religious *Volksgeist*—that interested him above all.

Though committed to the principles of scientific research, Graetz wrote passionately and not always objectively. His lively narrative was an almost novelistic account of the struggle between good and evil. His heroes were biblical prophets, rabbis, philosophers, poets, and non-Jewish friends of the Jews; his villains were the kabbalists, Hasidic rabbis, the unbending orthodox, Christianizing reformers, and antisemites. Invariably, he judged major figures—popes, kings, and philosophers—by how they treated Jews and Judaism. He was contemptuous of apostates, especially when they become enemies of their former coreligionists. His attitude to Germany was ambivalent. Graetz identified strongly with the humanistic tradition of the German Enlightenment but was fearful of German Romanticism, which he believed to be inimical to Jewish interests. Yet there was no question at all about his high regard and high hopes for German Jewry. Unlike the Eastern European Jews, for whom Graetz had little respect and much disdain, the German Jews, beginning with Moses Mendelssohn, had brought about a rebirth of Judaism in modern guise. They had contributed—and would continue to contribute—to European culture as Jews. Not surprisingly, two-thirds of his last volume, covering the period from 1750 to 1848, dealt with the Jews of Germany, although they constituted a relatively small minority of world Jewry. They were the special object of Graetz's historical and contemporary interest.

A more strictly scholarly literature likewise blossomed in the decades following 1848. In part this surge of significant works was due to the widely held belief that the decline in Jewish religious interest could most effectively be reversed by giving more intense attention to Wissenschaft des Judentums. According to Zacharias Frankel, it seemed the "most effective lever to set wearied souls back into motion and awaken renewed concern for higher things."[18]

In 1851 Frankel founded the *Monatsschrift für Geschichte und Wissenschaft des Judentums* (Monthly Journal for History and the Scholarly Study of Judaism), a periodical mainly devoted to scholarship but one that also commented on contemporary Jewish life. As the organ of the seminary in Breslau, its orientation lay between Orthodoxy and Reform. It affirmed critical analysis of talmudic sources but scrupulously excluded Pentateuch criticism from its pages. Because it was associated with an institution and not a single individual, it was able to maintain itself through a succession of editors for eighty-three volumes during nearly ninety years, even through most of the Nazi period, until 1939. The same combination of detailed study of the past together with reflection and comment on the present also characterized Abraham Geiger's more personal *Jüdische Zeitschrift für Wissenschaft und Leben* (Jewish Journal for Scholarship and Life, 1862–1873), though here historical criticism was applied without restraint.

Frankel and Geiger both produced their most important monographs during this period. Frankel's *Darkhe ha-mishnah* (The Paths of the Mishnah, 1859) grew out of class lectures at the Breslau seminary in which he sought to place the ancient rabbis, known to students from their dicta in the Talmud, within their time and place, thus providing a historical context for the study of Jewish law. Frankel here historicized the talmudic traditions and attributed a high degree of legal initiative to the ancient rabbis, understanding them not as mere vessels of the Halacha, in line with the traditional understanding, but, to a degree, as its creators. Responsive to new challenges, "they instituted ordinances in accordance with the condition of the state and of human society in their days."[19] Each generation, therefore, was not merely an inheritor but built upon its predecessors, continually expanding the structure of Jewish law.

Abraham Geiger's *Urschrift und Übersetzungen der Bibel in ihrer Abhängigkeit von der innern Entwicklung des Judentums* (The Original Text and Translations of the Bible in Their Dependency on the Inner Development of Judaism, 1857), as the title suggests, was considerably more radical than Frankel's *Darkhe ha-mishnah*. Geiger here humanized even the Written Law, showing that it had changed in response to historical developments. A textual comparison of versions revealed a struggle between democratic Pharisees and aristocratic Sadducees, which left its imprint on the received Masoretic text and laid bare the transition from biblical to rabbinic Judaism. Geiger thus demonstrated clearly for the first time the interdependence between the history of the text and the history of the Jewish religion. His favorable view of Pharisaism also marked a departure from the widespread negative view based on the New Testament. During these years Geiger likewise produced his most comprehensive work, a series of forty-three popular lectures entitled *Das Judentum und seine Geschichte* (Judaism and Its History, 1864–1871). Like Graetz, Geiger here did not hesitate to be judgmental of the past, praising those currents in Judaism that were universalistic and open to reason while finding value in the Kabbalah only as an antidote to talmudic legalism. His lectures were not a history of the Jews themselves but of their religious literature as the most accurate reflection of the Jewish spirit. For Geiger, who believed that Jewish identity in Germany was to be defined almost exclusively in religious terms, Jewish scholarship was necessarily the historical study of the Jewish religion.

Frankel and Geiger continued to be the most eminent leaders of the conservative and liberal schools within German Judaism. Thus their scholarly writings unsurprisingly reflected their religious points of view. Other scholars, however, now purposely removed themselves from the struggle over the future religious orientation of German Jewry and tried to establish Wissenschaft des Judentums as a realm apart from ideological polemics. Leopold Zunz wrote sarcastically of the tree of "religious scholarship" that had sprung up in Breslau and later would have nothing to do with the liberal seminary in Berlin despite repeated attempts to draw him into its orbit. He preferred to live independently, if modestly, on the small pension granted him by the Berlin community since 1850. Though he identified strongly with the subjects about which he wrote, Zunz had little regard for scholarly popularization. He thought mammoth projects like Graetz's history premature and unreliable, while Graetz, in turn, considered Zunz's work mired in detail. However, Zunz complained most when his work was ignored by Christian scholars, for he still believed, as in his youth, that the place of Wissenschaft des Judentums was in the larger world of academic research.

For Zunz, as for Graetz, Jewish history was composed of suffering and spiritual creativity. In his most important work of this period, three volumes devoted to the poetry of the synagogue, Zunz showed how external oppression had sometimes been the stimulus to exquisite religious expression. His painstaking scholarship brought to light forgotten liturgical poems that he discovered hidden away in the manuscripts of libraries he visited in Germany, England, France, and Italy. His philological descriptions elucidated the texts; his translations made them once more accessible. He created a new respect for Jewish liturgical creativity, though his lack of synthetic talent made him fall short of producing a connected, easily readable history. Zunz was now regarded as the "doyen" of Jewish scholarship, the man who more than any other exemplified the ongoing tradition of intensive Jewish learning as it continued in a new form, transposed from Jewish law to Jewish literature. It was also Zunz who most clearly symbolized the central role of German Jewry in Jewish scholarship, a position it would continue to enjoy into the twentieth century.

Zunz's younger contemporary and friend, Moritz Steinschneider (1816–1907), exceeded even the master in his fierce determination to practice Wissenschaft des Judentums free of any institutional constraint. Still today considered the greatest of Jewish bibliographers, the immensely erudite Steinschneider is best known for the catalogues of Hebrew manuscripts that he compiled for major European libraries and for editing a series of bibliographical periodicals, beginning in 1858. Conceptually, Steinschneider's greatest contribution was to expand the field of Jewish literary scholarship beyond the realms of religion and spiritual creativity. Medieval Jews as scientists and transmitters of Islamic science were one of his special interests. In concluding a very lengthy and learned historical survey of Jewish literature, Steinschneider had complained of "widespread and uncontrolled dilettantism, which may well redound to the honor of the Jews' culture but can only damage their scholarship."[20] He yearned in vain for an elite professional Jewish scholarship that would be carried out in German universities. Like Zunz, he thought little of Graetz's work and likewise refused an offer to teach at the new liberal Jewish institution of higher learning in Berlin. That school he called the "new ghetto for Jewish Wissenschaft."[21] Although he grudgingly recognized the legitimacy of the study of Jewish history and literature within a Jewish context, it was its recognition as "part and parcel of history and cultural history in general" that mattered to him most.[22]

6. Nostalgia and Thoughts of National Revival

Both the popular Jewish periodicals and yearbooks and some of the more serious works of Jewish scholarship directed the reader's attention beyond party division to the collective heritage of the Jewish people. During these years of political quiet, when tradition was once more elevated above innovation in Germany, Jews were more receptive than previously to reopening a connection with earlier periods of Jewish history that were still free of the fragmentation caused by modernity. A romanticism emerged within German Jewry that parallels similar currents in general culture. Though seen by more radical religious ideologues as a retreat from the need to grapple with contemporary problems, it was, in essence, a new form of collective Jewish self-expression. We have already noted in an earlier chapter the increasing popularity of ghetto stories and the portraits of the Jewish family executed by Moritz Oppenheim. To these must be added the recovery and adaptation of the medieval Jewish poetic heritage and the creation of modern poetry filled with nostalgia for Israel's earlier glory. If during the preceding decades German Jews looked resolutely forward, seeking to distance themselves from the premodern past, some now looked longingly backward at what they had lost.

Michael Sachs (1808–1864), the religious conservative who served as rabbi and preacher in the Berlin community from 1844 until his death twenty years later, devoted his literary efforts to bridging the gulf between classical Jewish literature and contemporary taste. Heinrich Graetz very perceptively characterized Sachs by contrasting him with his colleague in Berlin, Samuel Holdheim. Whereas the rabbi of the Reform congregation was a torn personality, sharply analytic and prosaic, a modernized version of the Polish talmudist, Sachs was harmonious, romantic, and poetic, incarnating the spirit of medieval Spain. As community rabbi, Sachs was a centrist, favoring only cosmetic reforms and disregarding theological issues; politically, he was a royalist. As a scholar and poet he was neither daring nor a great literary artist. But he was a master of sympathetic understanding and poetic adaptation, able to read rabbinic and medieval Jewish literature with an eye to what could still address the emotions of Jews in the present. The major results were a more appreciative than scholarly book on the religious poetry of Spanish Jewry and a popular "book for the home" entitled *Stimmen vom Jordan und Euphrat* (Voices from the Jordan and Euphrates, 1853). In both works Sachs played the self-assigned role of "interpreter," translating freely into German what he felt to be the best literary creations, giving them a form that appealed to contemporary aesthetic sensibility, and making possible their integration into contemporary culture. Talmudic law and medieval Jewish philosophy remained closed realms for most German Jews, but ancient midrash and Spanish poetry could address them collectively. In keeping with the religious spirit after 1848, their special appeal was less to the mind than to the heart.

As German Jews reread their classical literature, Germanized and Europeanized through translation and adaptation, they could not remain unaware of its Oriental origins. Indeed, Max Letteris (1804–1871), one of the most prominent mediators between Hebrew and German literary culture in the Habsburg Empire, specifically entitled his own poetic renditions of talmudic legends *Sagen aus dem Orient* (Fables from the Orient, 1847). As Jews became ever more Westernized, they not only—

as we have seen—built "Eastern" synagogues to set their worship apart, they were also less reluctant to relate poetically to the land of their origins, though not without considerable ambivalence. Minna Cohen's first poem in *Der Freitagabend* was a nostalgic reflection upon ancient Jerusalem, represented by the Temple's only surviving wall, but it was also a clear affirmation that the Jewish future lay in the West. The very title of Ludwig Wihl's book of poems, *West-östliche Schwalben* (West-Eastern Swallows, 1847), revealed a felt duality. The sunny, pious, and happy Levant is the object of the poet's nostalgia. But it is only his inspiration and point of origin, not his home. Jerusalem lives within him, he says, but—tellingly—he calls Palestine "ancestral land" (*Väter Land*), not "Fatherland" (*Vaterland*). His Jewish consciousness has its roots in the East, but its branches are in the West. Similarly, when Ludwig August Frankl visited Palestine in 1856, in order to establish a school there, he wrote a popular romanticized account of his journey entitled *Nach Jerusalem!* (To Jerusalem!) and brought back a rock hewn from Mount Zion to be used as a keystone for the new temple in Vienna. But for Frankl, too, the ancient land of Israel had played out its role in Jewish history. Its patrimony could regain expression only spiritually and in the larger world. "The work of Israel on this soil seems to be complete," he wrote from Jerusalem, "and what has been called a curse is in fact its blessing: to be dispersed over the earth, an entire people of apostles."[23] Displaced from their land, the Jews had assumed a universal mission. German Jews looked back toward it nostalgically, to remind themselves of their origins but not as their hope for the future.

Few and isolated were the voices in Germany of this period that actively propagated the idea of a large-scale return of the Jews to their land. In the view of the Orthodox, massive immigration was inextricable from the messianic redemption and hence in God's hands alone. They and liberal Jews alike looked forward to the completion of their emancipation on German soil. Despite setbacks and disappointments, they remained hopeful of their ultimate acceptance. When in 1858 the Mortara affair in Italy (the forced and declared irreversible baptism and abduction of a Jewish child) showed that even in a Western country religious prejudice still prevailed, more than three hundred German communities joined in a petition that called on the Prussian monarch to intervene. The petitioners were certain of his sympathy for their cause.

Yet, paradoxically, it was just this certainty regarding their status in a state of law that served as a principal argument in one of two remarkable

44   The writer Ludwig August Frankl in Jerusalem,
obtaining a keystone for the new temple in Vienna

proto-Zionist writings that appear in this period. Zevi Hirsch Kalischer
(1795–1874) was an Orthodox rabbinic scholar living in Thorn near the
Prussian border with Russian-controlled Poland. As early as 1836 he had
broken with the prevalent Jewish conception that the redemption could
only be initiated by divine intervention. Twenty-six years later, in 1862,
he elaborated his views in a Hebrew book called *Derishat tsiyon* (Seeking

Zion), which, shortly thereafter, appeared also in German. Here he argued, using prooftexts from Jewish sources, that resettlement of the land and even reinstitution of the sacrificial service could be undertaken in advance of the miraculous advent of the messiah. Moreover, the events of recent history were the best indication that the time was ripe for such initiatives. As never before, God had bestowed favor upon the Jews in Western and Central Europe. Their wealthy men—Moses Montefiore and the Rothschilds, for example—enjoyed the trust of kings and princes. The Jews had already achieved, or would soon attain, complete equality. These developments, Kalischer argued, had to be interpreted as the dawn

45   Rabbi Zevi Hirsch Kalischer

of redemption and, in practical terms, they also made concerted action possible. It was now incumbent upon Jews, reading the signs of renewed divine concern for Israel, to initiate the regeneration of Jewish life in Palestine, preparing the way for the messiah and the final redemption for Israel and all humanity.

Not surprisingly, these radical views did not find wide approval, even among the Orthodox. Samson Raphael Hirsch and Esriel Hildesheimer both found reasons for objection. But Kalischer was not entirely isolated. His work received the explicit approval of a few Orthodox rabbis in Germany, and even the conservative Michael Sachs promised support. A second Hebrew edition appeared four years after the first and another before his death. In 1860 the mystic Chaim Lorje had founded a society for the colonization of Palestine in Frankfurt an der Oder, which established branches in other German cities and held a conference in Berlin in 1863. It published Kalischer's book and supported his views. Although the society lasted for only four years, others, founded about the same time in Germany, gathered wider support for more limited objectives, especially the economic productivization of the Jews then living in Palestine. Liberals too felt a special obligation to support coreligionists who had chosen to live in the "holy land of our great past."[24] A large number of German Jews, about seventeen hundred, joined the French-initiated Alliance Israélite Universelle, founded in 1860, which acted to defend Jewish rights and established schools in Palestine and elsewhere in the East.

Among Kalischer's arguments for colonizing the Land of Israel was the visible determination of other nationalities in Europe, like Italy, Poland, and Hungary, to assert their cultural and political independence. How could the Jews not follow their example? These instances of nationalist revival were likewise a principal influence on a second Zionist tract that appeared the same year, Moses Hess's *Rome and Jerusalem*. Hess (1812–1875) had gained recognition earlier as a neo-Hegelian and ethical socialist. He had, for a time, adopted Feuerbach's view of Judaism as egoism and been a close associate of Karl Marx, though he did not share Marx's dialectical materialism. Whereas he once favored the disappearance of Judaism through mixed marriage, he had now come to believe that complete assimilation was impossible. Dislike of the Jews ran too deep: "The Germans hate the Jews' religion less than their race, their peculiar faith less than their peculiar noses."[25] Neither could Jewish noses be "reformed" nor dark curls baptized into straight blond hair. The German

46   Moses Hess, socialist and precursor of the
Zionist movement

people and the Jewish people, according to Hess, existed in a unique relationship of mutual attraction and repulsion that made harmonious existence impossible. The only solution for the Jews was to follow the successful example of the Italians and reconstitute themselves once more as
an independent nation. The ghetto novels, the poetry, and the works of
history, were, Hess believed, signs that a popular national revival was already underway.

Like Kalischer, whose work he had read, Hess found some support for his views. Heinrich Graetz, who carried on a long correspondence with him, believed that his book "must become a new ferment in a rotten state of affairs"[26] and he sought to gain readers for it. But, in an age of growing emancipation, Hess's deep pessimism ran counter to the buoyant mood of German Jewry. Kalischer was able to draw upon messianic sentiments still alive among Orthodox Jews. Hess's essentially secular argument did not have the same appeal. Liberals like Abraham Geiger explicitly rejected it. Mostly, his tract was simply ignored, not to be rediscovered until the birth of political Zionism toward the end of the century.

Conclusion

The year 1871, when Germany at long last achieved unification, was a watershed for the German Jews as well. Their political emancipation, which had first been seriously proposed by Christian Wilhelm Dohm in 1781 and received royal sanction, to a degree, with the Toleration Edicts of Joseph II shortly thereafter, had finally come to complete fruition. Austrian Jews gained equality in 1867; Jews in the North German Confederation in 1869 and then in the entire newly founded Reich two years later. It had been a long and difficult process, with advances followed by reverses. With the exception of the old Orthodox, German Jews during these ninety years had made the securing of emancipation their chief collective passion. They had followed its progress from state to state, cheering every success, bemoaning every setback. Now they rejoiced that at long last they had attained their objective; they looked forward confidently to the future. And indeed nearly a decade would pass, until toward the end of the 1870s public opinion about the role of the Jews in the German state would once again shift, both in certain influential circles and more broadly among the populace, making the Jews aware that perhaps they were not regarded as fully equal after all.

German Jewry was now very different from what it had been ninety years earlier. Despite emigration, it had greatly increased, more than doubling in Germany from about two hundred thousand to more than half a million, with similar growth in the German-speaking portions of the Habsburg Empire. Urbanization had turned a mostly small-town and village

Jewry into one that was increasingly concentrated in the bigger cities. Berlin, which had only about three thousand Jews in 1800, contained close to forty thousand in 1871; Viennese Jewry, with less than a thousand at the beginning of the century, was even slightly larger than Berlin Jewry seven decades later; both communities had by far surpassed Prague which, in the eighteenth century, had boasted the largest number of Ashkenazi Jews. The process of population flow to the larger cities, especially to the capitals, would continue with even greater magnitude during the following decades in Germany and in Austria, as it did also in England and France, where London and Paris became the dominating centers of Jewish population.

The embourgoisement of German Jewry was almost complete. At the top of the economic hierarchy were a few very wealthy Jews: members of the Rothschild family and Gerson Bleichröder, for example, whose fortunes gave them political influence. At the bottom of the scale remained relatively few poor Jews, who served as objects of an extensive array of Jewish charitable institutions. But Jewish charity was increasingly channeled abroad, to Jews in Eastern Europe and Palestine. Most German Jews were engaged in solid bourgeois occupations, many of them in retail trade. Increasingly, they were also attending universities, although the entry of Jews into the professions in highly disproportionate numbers would come only later. Excluded from state service, they played an active role in professional organizations and were elected to local assemblies, regional and national legislatures.

Perhaps most remarkable was the success of Jewish acculturation. Moses Mendelssohn's Pentateuch translation had been a symbolic beginning. His disciples' efforts to create a modern Hebrew culture had proven only episodic. The main thrust from Mendelssohn onward was clearly toward the German language and German culture. The path toward attaining *Bildung* was rocky for the first generation that emerged from the ghetto. But their children, educated in modern Jewish schools or in general ones, usually acquired German language and culture with little difficulty. Not only did Jews become disproportionate consumers of German culture, they contributed to it significantly. Among the leading writers, Heinrich Heine and Ludwig Börne thought they could be influential in Germany only if they joined the camp of the majority by converting nominally to Christianity; Berthold Auerbach, in remaining Jewish, proved them wrong.

Already, in the Wars of Liberation in the second decade of the century, Jews in Prussia had sought to demonstrate their new loyalty not only to a monarch but to the new conception of the liberal state. They became patriots, sharply differentiating their ongoing religious separation from their being at one with non-Jews in their national pride. No one expressed such sentiments as eloquently as Gabriel Riesser, the champion of Jewish equality, who, more than any other single individual in this period, was admired by his coreligionists. That Christians accepted the Jews' aspirations only with great hesitation is apparent not only from the legal setbacks, the anti-Jewish writings, and occasional outbreaks of violence, such as the "Hep Hep" riots of 1819, but also from the distance that they still kept from Jews. Despite the progress of emancipation, social separation remained the rule. For some German Jews, by the end of the period covered by this volume, such social separation was their chief expression of Jewishness. Jewish content had become peripheral to their lives, but they mingled with and married fellow Jews.

Yet, in various forms, many of them new, Judaism remained a living force. The Jewish community was no longer the organic entity it had been earlier. It lacked authority over the lives of individual Jews; its judicial functions had been ceded to the state. But, as a religious and charitable entity, the community remained viable. Even the most highly acculturated Jews continued to be associated with it and participated at least occasionally in organized Jewish religious life. In the countryside the old ways lived on throughout our period. In the cities new forms of Judaism emerged: the modern Orthodoxy of Samson Raphael Hirsch, the Reform of Abraham Geiger and Samuel Holdheim, the middle position of Zacharias Frankel. The rise of Wissenschaft des Judentums demonstrated that Jews could dissect their own tradition with the same tools of historical criticism employed by Christian scholars. Under pressure of Christian prejudices a cadre of Jewish thinkers set out to prove that Judaism was not superseded either by Christianity or by modern philosophy.

In the process German Judaism became factionalized as new groups emerged within it. At first there were the maskilim, the Jewish enlighteners, with their goal of expanding the intellectual horizon of their fellow Jews. Then came the religious reformers, who sought to bring Judaism up-to-date by aestheticizing the worship service, introducing sermons and decorum, but also to Germanize Judaism by divesting it of its political dimensions, especially the desire for the reestablishment of Jewish sovereignty in the Land of Israel. By 1871 the great majority of the German Jews were no longer observant of Jewish ritual law in its totality. Ethical monotheism, based on the Hebrew prophets, had become the foundation of their Jewishness. Within the urban communities, which now boasted lavish new synagogues and attractive liturgical music, some Jews continued to worship in the old manner but most attended synagogues that installed elaborate organs and used a modified liturgy. Religious lines emerged ever more clearly, institutionalized through liberal and traditionalist parties that competed in community elections and by the extreme positions of the independent Reform Congregation in Berlin and neo-Orthodox communities in various cities that set up their own institutions.

Although political Zionism, which would later divide German Jewry, had not yet appeared, the last decades of our period do witness some isolated expressions of Jewish national feeling and, more broadly, a sense of nostalgia for the old milieu that had disappeared and could be revived only through literature such as the popular ghetto stories. Heinrich Graetz's major history of the Jews provided them with the first comprehensive history of their past that actively engaged their sympathies, laying a new basis for collective memory.

In sum, it seems accurate to say that, at the beginning of our period, there were Jews and Jewish communities in Germany, but there were not yet German Jews. Then, over the course of almost a century, being German came to be at least as essential to the identity of nearly all Jews in German-speaking Europe as was their being Jewish. Duly recognizing their Oriental origins, Jews clearly saw themselves as Westerners, participants in shaping the new Europe and patriots of the countries in which they lived. In this respect German Jews were not different from English or French ones. But for them, unlike their coreligionists further to the west, emancipation had been a protracted, difficult struggle and their acculturation, to the minds of some non-Jews such as Wagner, seemed, even after two generations, still incomplete.

The year 1871, then, represents a pinnacle, a hopeful moment, a seeming completion. Yet the German Jews' relation to their fellow Germans had by no means been fully resolved. What followed not long thereafter proved once again the vicissitudes of living as a Jew in Germany.

Abbreviations

AIGK	*Akten des VII. Internationalen Germanisten-Kongresses* (Göttingen, 1985)
AZJ	*Allgemeine Zeitung des Judenthums*
BLBI	*Bulletin des Leo Baeck Instituts*
Frankel	Jonathan Frankel and Steven J. Zipperstein, eds, *Assimilation and Community: The Jews in Nineteenth-Century Europe* (Cambridge, 1992)
Freund	Ismar Freund, *Die Emanzipation der Juden in Preussen*, 2 vols. (Berlin, 1912)
Glatzer	Nahum N. Glatzer, ed., *Leopold Zunz. Jude-Deutscher-Europäer* (Tübingen, 1964)
Grab	Walter Grab and Julius H. Schoeps, eds., *Juden im Vormärz und in der Revolution von 1848* (Stuttgart, 1983)
HSA	Nationale Forschungs- und Gedenkstätte der klassischen deutschen Literatur and the Centre National de la Recherche Scientifique, eds., *Heinrich Heine Säkularausgabe* (Weimar and Paris, 1970–)
HUCA	*Hebrew Union College Annual*
Jeggle	Utz Jeggle, *Judendörfer in Württemberg* (Stuttgart, 1969)
JIDG	*Jahrbuch des Instituts für Deutsche Geschichte*
JSS	*Jewish Social Studies*
LBIYB	Leo Baeck Institute Year Book
Liebeschütz	Hans Liebeschütz and Arnold Paucker, eds., *Das Judentum in der deutschen Umwelt 1800–1850* (Tübingen, 1977)
MGWJ	*Monatsschrift für Geschichte und Wissenschaft des Judentums*
Mosse	Werner E. Mosse, Arnold Paucker, Reinhard Rürup, eds., *Revolu-*

tion and Evolution: 1848 in German-Jewish History (Tübingen, 1981)

Richarz   Monika Richarz, ed., *Jüdisches Leben in Deutschland. Selbstzeugnisse zur Sozialgeschichte 1780–1871* (Stuttgart, 1976)

Rönne   Ludwig von Rönne and Heinrich Simon, *Die früheren und gegenwärtigen Verhältnisse der Juden in den sämmtlichen Landestheilen des Preussischen Staates* (Breslau, 1843)

WZJT   *Wissenschaftliche Zeitschrift für jüdische Theologie*

ZRIJ   *Zeitschrift für die religiösen Interessen des Judenthums*

Notes

1. Legal Status and Emancipation

1. Cited in A. Heppner and J. Herzberg, *Aus Vergangenheit und Gegenwart der Juden und der jüdischen Gemeinden in den Posener Landen* (Koschmin-Bromberg, 1909), 17–18.

2. Cited in Gerhard Hentsch, *Gewerbeordnung und Emanzipation der Juden im Kurfürstentum Hessen* (Wiesbaden, 1979), 18.

3. Christian Wilhelm Dohm, *Über die bürgerliche Verbesserung der Juden*, part 1 (Berlin and Stettin, 1781), 130.

4. Ibid., 34.

5. Ibid., 26–28.

6. Johann Georg Krünitz, *Ökonomische Encyklopädie* . . . , part 31 (Berlin, 1784), 566.

7. Johann David Michaelis, *Beurteilung der ersten Dohmschen Schrift "Über die bürgerliche Verbesserung der Juden,"* repr. C. W. Dohm, *Über die bürgerliche Verbesserung der Juden*, part 2 (Berlin and Stettin, 1783), 61.

8. Ibid., 71.

9. Cited in Freund, 1:90.

10. David Friedländer, *Akten-Stücke die Reform der jüdischen Kolonieen in den Preussischen Staaten betreffend* (Berlin, 1793), 182.

11. J. G. Fichte, *Sämtliche Werke* (Berlin, 1845), 6:149–50.

12. Reprinted in Ludwig Geiger, *Geschichte der Juden in Berlin* (Berlin, 1871 [Leipzig, 1988]), 2:312–13.

13. Reprinted in Freund, 2:271.

14. Ibid., 276.

15. Rönne, 264–65.

16. E. R. Huber, ed., *Dokumente zur deutschen Verfassungsgeschichte,* 2d ed. (Stuttgart, 1961), 1:80.

17. Rönne, 39.

18. Ernst Moritz Arndt, *Blick aus der Zeit auf die Zeit* (Germania [Frankfurt], 1814), 195, 197.

19. Cited from the subheading to his work.

20. Ibid., 64.

21. Ludwig Börne, "Der ewige Jude," in Ludwig Börne, *Sämtliche Schriften* (Düsseldorf, 1964), 2:522.

22. Michael Hess, *Freimüthige Prüfung der Schrift des Herrn Professor Rühs, über die Ansprüche der Juden an das deutsche Bürgerrecht* (Frankfurt am Main, 1816), 82.

23. Cited in Isaak Markus Jost, *Neuere Geschichte der Israeliten von 1815 bis 1845,* part 1 (Berlin, 1846), 227.

24. Rönne, 281.

25. Ibid., 284.

26. Ibid., 282–83.

27. J. D. F. Rumpf, *Landtagsverhandlungen der Provinzialstände in der Preussischen Monarchie,* 1st issue (Berlin, 1826), 77.

28. Karl Streckfuss, *Über das Verhältnis der Juden zu den christlichen Staaten* (Halle, 1833), 22–27.

29. Gabriel Riesser, *Vertheidigung der bürgerlichen Gleichstellung der Juden gegen die Einwürfe des Herrn Dr. H. E. G. Paulus. Den gesetzgebenden Versammlungen Deutschlands gewidmet* (Altona, 1831), repr. M. Isler, ed., *G. Riesser's Gesammelte Schriften* (Frankfurt am Main and Leipzig, 1867), 2:181–82.

30. Johann Jacoby, *Über das Verhältnis des Königl. Preuss. Ober-Regierungsraths Herrn Streckfuss zur Emanzipation der Juden* (Hamburg, 1833), repr. *Gesammelte Schriften und Reden von Dr. Johann Jacoby,* 2d ed., part 1 (Hamburg, 1877), 42.

31. *G. Riesser's Gesammelte Schriften,* 3:299.

32. Hessisches Staatsarchiv Marburg, Lahn 9a Min. d. Ausw., no. 1431.

33. Geheimes Staatsarchiv Preussischer Kulturbesitz, Justizministerium, Rep. 84a, no. 11951, sh. 121.

34. AZJ 6(1842):200–01.

35. *Vollständige Verhandlungen des Ersten Vereinigten Preußischen Landtags über die Emancipationsfrage der Juden* (Berlin, 1847), 224–25.

2. Population Shifts and Occupational Structure

1. Cited in A. Heppner and J. Herzberg, *Aus Vergangenheit und Gegenwart der Juden und der jüdischen Gemeinden in den Posener Landen* (Koschmin-Bromberg, 1909), 193.

2. Ludwigsburg State Archives, E 146/1193 (O. A. Künzelsau, 1818), cited in Jeggle, 55–56.

3. Statements made by Senator I. A. Günther in *Genius der Zeit* (1800), cited in Helga Krohn, *Die Juden in Hamburg 1800–1850* (Frankfurt am Main, 1967), 90, n. 23.

4. Cited in Jacob Toury, "Der Eintritt der Juden ins deutsche Bürgertum," in Liebeschütz, 219–20.

5. J. G. Hoffmann, *Sammlung kleiner Schriften staatswissenschaftlichen Inhalts* (Berlin, 1843), 387.

3. Jewish Communities in Transition

1. Cited in M. Brann, "Die schlesische Judenheit vor und nach dem Edikt vom 11. März 1812," in *Jahresbericht des jüdisch-theologischen Seminars Fraenckel'scher Stiftung für das Jahr 1912* (Breslau, 1913), 26 n.

2. Reproduced in Claudia Prestel, *Jüdisches Schul- und Erziehungswesen in Bayern 1804–1933* (Göttingen, 1989), 391.

3. Cited in Adolf Lewin, *Geschichte der Badischen Juden seit der Regierung Karl Friedrichs (1738–1909)* (Karlsruhe, 1909), 257.

4. *Sulamith* 1/2(1807):138.

5. J. M. Lilienfeld, *Patriotische Gedanken eines Israeliten über jüdische Religion, Sitten und Erziehung* (Frankfurt am Main, 1812), vi–vii.

6. Cited in Mordechai Yaffe, "Moritz Jaffe. Das Lebensbild eines jüdischen Lehrers in der Provinz Posen in der ersten Hälfte des 19. Jahrhunderts," BLBI 31(1965):211.

4. Jewish Self-Understanding

1. N. N. Glatzer, ed., *Leopold Zunz. Jude—Deutscher—Europäer* (Tübingen, 1964), 103.

2. Salman Rubaschoff, "Erstlinge der Entjudung" (Drei Reden von Eduard Gans im Kulturverein), *Der jüdische Wille* 1(1918):195–96.

3. *Entwurf von Statuten des Vereins für Cultur und Wissenschaft der Juden* (Berlin, 1822), Introduction, 1.

4. *Gesammelte Schriften* (Berlin, 1875), 1:4.

5. Ibid., 5.

6. *Zur Geschichte und Literatur* (Berlin, 1845), 21.

7. "Über die in den hebräisch-jüdischen Schriften vorkommenden hispanischen Ortnamen," *Zeitschrift für die Wissenschaft des Judenthums* 1(1822/23): 115.

8. "Beitrag zur jüdischen Geschichte und Bibliographie," WZJT 1(1835):358.

9. "Jüdische Geschichte," ibid., 172.

10. *Geschichte der Juden* (Leipzig, 1870), 11:449.

11. Letter to Joseph Muhr, Jan. 26, 1842, AZJ 62(1898):438.

12. *Igrot tsafun* (Altona, 1836), 80.

13. *Antrittspredigt . . . bei dessen Einführung in sein Amt als Rabbiner und Prediger der Genossenschaft für Reform im Judenthum zu Berlin* (Berlin, 1847), 8.

14. WZJT 4(1839):9.

15. ZRIJ 2(1845):15

16. *Gesammelte Schriften* (Frankfurt am Main, 1902–12), 6: 393.

17. Ibid., 2: 422.

18. ZRIJ 1(1844):16

19. WZJT 1(1835):287.

20. *Nachgelassene Schriften* (Berlin, 1875–78), 5:181.

21. WZJT, 4(1839):10.

22. *Zur Judenfrage* 2(1844):417.

23. *Die fünf Bücher Mose* (Frankfurt am Main, 1831), ix.

24. Moritz Veit Collection, Central Archives for the History of the Jewish People, Jerusalem, P47/1.

25. AZJ 9(1845):235.

5. Judaism and Christianity

1. "Ideen zur Philosophie der Geschichte der Menschheit," in B. Suphan, ed., *Herders Sämmtliche Werke* (Berlin, 1909), 14:67.

2. "Die Religion innerhalb der Grenzen der blossen Vernunft," in K. Rosenkranz and F. W. Schubert, eds., *Immanuel Kant's Sämmtliche Werke* (Leipzig, 1838), 10:152–53.

3. Kant, "Der Streit der Facultäten," ibid, 308.

4. Friedrich Schleiermacher, *Der christliche Glaube,* 2d ed., 2 vols. (Berlin, 1830–31), 1:86.

5. "Die Positivität der christlichen Religion," in H. Nohl, ed., *Hegels theologische Jugendschriften* (Tübingen, 1907), 148.

6. Ludwig Feuerbach, *Das Wesen des Christenthums* (Leipzig, 1843), 450.

7. *Allgemeine Encyklopädie der Wissenschaften und Künste,* 2d series, 27 (Leipzig, 1850), 347.

8. Heinrich Ewald, *Geschichte des Volkes Israel bis Christus,* 3/2 (Göttingen, 1852), 564.

9. Cited in S. Maybaum, "Die Wissenschaft des Judentums," MGWJ 51(1907):655.

10. Franz Delitzsch, *Wissenschaft, Kunst, Judenthum* (Grimma, 1838), 8.

11. Cited in AZJ 54(1890):136.

12. Hannah Adams, *Die Geschichte der Juden von der Zerstörung Jerusalems an bis auf die gegenwärtigen Zeiten* (Leipzig, 1820), 2:353.

13. S. Hensel, ed., *Die Familie Mendelssohn 1729–1847* (Berlin, 1879), 86.

14. J. M. Raich, ed., *Dorothea v. Schlegel geb. Mendelssohn und deren Söhne Johannes und Philipp Veit. Briefwechsel* (Mainz, 1881), 1:437–38.

15. Friedrich Julius Stahl, *Der christliche Staat und sein Verhältniss zu Deismus und Judenthum* (Berlin, 1847), 53.

16. Salomon Ludwig Steinheim, *Die Offenbarung nach dem Lehrbegriffe der Synagoge, ein Schiboleth*, part 1 (Frankfurt am Main, 1835), 359.

17. Salomon Formstecher, *Die Religion des Geistes, eine wissenschaftliche Darstellung des Judenthums* (Frankfurt am Main, 1841), 13

18. Samuel Hirsch, *Die Religionsphilosophie der Juden oder das Prinzip der jüdischen Religionsanschauung und sein Verhältniss zum Heidenthum, Christenthum und zur absoluten Philosophie* (Leipzig, 1842), 98, n. 1.

19. Ibid., 870.

20. AZJ 60(1896):166.

21. Abraham Geiger, *Das Judenthum und seine Geschichte* (Breslau, 1871), 3:198.

22. A. Rebenstein [Aron Bernstein] in *Zur Judenfrage in Deutschland* 2 (1844): 12.

23. Letter of April 11, 1799, *Jahrbuch für Israeliten*, 1865–66, 52.

24. I. M. Jost, *Geschichte der Israeliten*, 10/3 (Berlin, 1847), 207.

25. *Unparteiische Universal-Kirchenzeitung für die Geistlichkeit und die gebildete Weltklasse des protestantischen, katholischen, und israelitischen Deutschlands* (1837), 1:14–15.

26. Joseph Levin Saalschütz, *Zur Versöhnung der Confessionen, oder Judenthum und Christenthum, in ihrem Streit und Einklang* (Königsberg, 1844).

27. Carl Scholl, *Drei Vorträge, gehalten vor der deutschkatholischen Gemeinde Mannheim* (Darmstadt, 1846), 9, 10.

28. *Protocolle der ersten Rabbiner-Versammlung abgehalten zu Braunschweig* (Brunswick, 1844), 73.

29. Samuel Holdheim, *Einsegnung einer gemischten Ehe zwischen einem Juden und einer Christin in Leipzig* (Berlin, 1849), 7.

6. Becoming German, Remaining Jewish

1. *Zeitung für die elegante Welt*, 1801, Nr. 75, Sp. 603 f., cited by Ulrike Schmidt, "Jüdische Bibliotheken in Frankfurt am Main," *Archiv für Geschichte des Buchwesens* 29(1987):244.

2. Ludwig Börne, *Sämtliche Schriften*, ed. I. and P. Rippmann (Düsseldorf, 1964–68), 1:10.

3. AZJ 23(1859):651.

4. *Unser Verkehr. Posse in einem Aufzuge*, 8th ed. (Berlin, n.d.), 11.

5. *Goethe's Werke* (Berlin, 1881), 28:201.

6. Michael Beer, *Der Paria. Trauerspiel in einem Aufzuge* (Stuttgart und Tübingen, 1829), 11–12.

7. Golo Mann, *Deutsche Geschichte des 19. und 20. Jahrhunderts* (Frankfurt am Main, 1958), 166.

8. Letter to Moser, August 23, 1823, HSA, 20:107. (References are given only for longer prose citations from Heine. The poetic works are available in numerous editions.)

9. Letter to Moser, April 23, 1826, HSA, 20:240.

10. Letter to Moser, June 25, 1824, HSA, 20:167.

11. "Berichtigung" (1849), in Heinrich Heine, *Sämtliche Schriften*, ed. K. Briegleb et al. (Darmstadt, 1968–76), 5:109.

12. "Shakespeares Mädchen und Frauen" (1838), ibid., 4:257.

13. Letter to Moser, January 9, 1824, HSA, 20:133.

14. M. Isler, ed., *Gabriel Riessers Gesammelte Schriften*, 4 vols. (Frankfurt am Main and Leipzig, 1867–68), 4:87.

15. Cited from N. Lazarus and A. Leicht, eds., *Moritz Lazarus' Lebenserinnerungen* (Berlin, 1906), 46.

16. Cited from Ludwig Geiger, *Die deutsche Literatur und die Juden* (Berlin, 1910), 243.

17. Berthold Auerbach, *Briefe an seinen Freund Jakob Auerbach* (Frankfurt am Main, 1884), 1:248.

18. Heine letter to Heinrich Laube, April 5, 1847, HSA, 22:246.

19. Auerbach, *Briefe*, 1:324.

20. "Gratulations-Schreiben an meine Freundin Sara Levi zum Tode ihres einzigen 12jährigen Sohnes" (1832) in *M. G. Saphir's Schriften* (Brünn, Vienna, and Leipzig, 1880), 5:72–75.

21. "Literatur-Briefe" (1834) in ibid., 26:21–22.

22. Introduction, Leopold Kompert, *Aus dem Ghetto*, 2d ed. (Leipzig, 1850), xiv.

23. AZJ 12(1848):512–13.

24. AZJ 14(1850):3.

25. Gabriel Riesser, "Ein Wort des Dankes an die israelitischen Bürger Badens" (1835), in *Gesammelte Schriften*, 4:717.

26. Gabriel Riesser, "Über die Stellung der Bekenner des Mosaischen Glaubens in Deutschland" (1831), in ibid, 2:89 (emphasis in citations here and elsewhere is in original).

27. Gabriel Riesser, "Vertheidigung der bürgerlichen Gleichstellung der Juden gegen Einwürfe des Herrn Dr. H. E. G. Paulus" (1831), in ibid., 2:183–84.

28. WZJT 4(1839):291.

29. Gabriel Riesser, "Jüdische Briefe," in *Gesammelte Schriften*, 4: 90.

30. Cited in M. Veit, "Gabriel Riesser," *Preussische Jahrbücher* 11(1863):4.

31. Johann Jacoby, *Briefwechsel*, ed. E. Silberner (Hanover, 1974), 121.

32. Ludwig Börne, *Sämtliche Schriften*, 3:511.

33. Ibid., 3:889.

34. Ibid., 5:606.

35. Ibid., 3:510.

36. Ibid., 3:419.

37. Ibid., 1:1032.

38. Ibid., 2:895.

39. Riesser, "Ein Wort des Dankes," 4:720.

40. Giacomo Meyerbeer, *Briefwechsel und Tagebücher*, ed. H. Becker and G. Becker (Berlin, 1975), 3:196.

41. Richard Wagner, *Das Judenthum in der Musik* (Leipzig, 1869), 25.

7. From Subject to Citizen

1. Cited in Ludwig Geiger, *Geschichte der Juden in Berlin* (Berlin, 1871), 144.

2. Central Archives for the History of the Jewish People (Jerusalem), Darmstadt Collection, 4th series, no. 62.

3. M. Isler, ed., *Gabriel Riessers Gesammelte Schriften*, 3 (Frankfurt am Main and Leipzig, 1867), 366–67.

4. *Protocolle der ersten Rabbiner-Versammlung abgehalten zu Braunschweig* (Brunswick, 1844), 75.

5. Herz Homberg, *Bne-Zion. Ein religiös-moralisches Lehrbuch für die Jugend israelitischer Nation* (Augsburg, 1812), 177.

6. Joseph von Sonnenfels, *Über die Liebe des Vaterlandes* (Vienna, 1771), 15; Homberg, *Bne-Zion*, 175.

7. Cited in Jacob Toury, "'Deutsche Juden' im Vormärz," BLBI 29(1965):69.

8. E. Lindner, ed., *Memoiren des Freiwilligen Jägers Löser Cohen* (Berlin, 1993), 18.

9. Reprinted in Moritz Stern, *Aus der Zeit der deutschen Befreiungskriege* (Berlin, 1935), 2:8.

10. Cited in Jacob Toury, "Der Eintritt der Juden ins deutsche Bürgertum," in Liebeschütz, 173.

11. The German original, written using the Hebrew alphabet, can be found in *Ha-Me'asef* (1789), 252; repr. Ruth Kestenberg-Gladstein, *Neuere Geschichte der Juden in den böhmischen Ländern* (Tübingen, 1968), 38.

12. Both quotations can be found in Horst Fischer, *Judentum, Staat und Heer in Preussen im frühen 19. Jahrhundert* (Tübingen, 1968), 38.

13. Herz Homberg, *Bne-Zion*, 175–76; *Ben Jakir*, 2d rev. ed. (Prague, 1826), 78–79.

14. *Sulamith* 3/1(1810):34.

15. Cited in Stefi Wenzel, *Jüdische Bürger und kommunale Selbstverwaltung in Preussischen Städten 1808–1848* (Berlin, 1967), 38.

16. GstA Berlin-Dahlem, XXth H.A., Rep 2, Tit 16, No 4.

17. Cited in Jacob Toury, *Die politischen Orientierungen der Juden in Deutschland. Von Jena bis Weimar* (Tübingen, 1966), 6.

18. E. Silberner, ed., *Johann Jacoby Briefwechsel (1816–49)* (Hanover, 1974), 181–82.

19. Ibid., 56–57.

20. Cited in Monika Richarz, *Der Eintritt der Juden in die akademischen Berufe* (Tübingen, 1974), 171.

21. Ursula Gehring-Münzel, *Vom Schutzjuden zum Staatsbürger. Die gesellschaftliche Integration der Würzbürger Juden 1803–1871* (Würzburg, 1992), 282.

22. Cited in Richarz, 412.

23. Cited in Henry Wassermann, "Jews, Bourgeoisie, und Bourgeois Society in a Liberal Epoch, 1840–1880" (Hebr. diss.) (Jerusalem, 1979), 56.

24. Cited in Hilde Spiel, *Fanny Arnstein oder die Emanzipation. Ein Frauenleben an der Zeitenwende, 1758–1818* (Frankfurt am Main, 1962), 436.

25. Cited in Stefan Rohrbacher, *Gewalt im Biedermeier. Antijüdische Ausschreitungen in Vormärz und Revolution (1815–1848/49)* (Frankfurt am Main, 1993), 252.

8. Between Revolution and Legal Equality

1. Cited in Stefan Rohrbacher, *Gewalt im Biedermeier. Antijüdische Ausschreitungen in Vormärz und Revolution (1815–1848/49)* (Frankfurt am Main, 1993), 208–9.

2. All newspaper citations can be found in Eleonore Sterling, *Judenhass. Die Anfänge des politischen Antisemitismus in Deutschland (1815–1850)* (Frankfurt am Main, 1969), 140–41.

3. Both citations can be found in Jeggle, 174–76.

4. *Der Jude* 1(1835):100–1.

5. Cited in Jacob Toury, "Die Revolution von 1848 als innerjüdischer Wendepunkt," in Liebeschütz, 363–64.

6. Cited in Walter Grab, "Aspekte der Judenemanzipation in Tagesliteratur und Publizistik 1848–1869," in *Der deutsche Weg der Judenemanzipation 1789–1938* (Munich, 1991), 112.

7. Jost to S. M. Ehrenberg, December 4, 1850, in Jost's unpublished correspondence with Samuel Mayer Ehrenberg and Philipp Ehrenberg, Jost Collection, Leo Baeck Institute Archives, New York, 746.

8. Glatzer, 263–73.

9. Reprinted in Adolf Kober, "Jews in the Revolution of 1848 in Germany," JSS 10(1948):163–64.

10. Jost to S. M. Ehrenberg, September 8, 1848, 685.

11. Cited in Reinhard Rürup, "Die Judenemanzipation in Baden," in *Emanzipation und Antisemitismus* (Göttingen, 1975), 66.

12. Original edition of *Das Judenthum in der Musik* (1850) in Richard Wagner, *Gesammelte Schriften*, ed. J. Kapp (Leipzig, n.d.), 13:8–9.

13. Rürup, "Die Judenemanzipation in Baden," 70.

14. Cited in Jacob Toury, *Soziale und politische Geschichte der Juden in Deutschland 1847–1871* (Düsseldorf, 1977), 328.

15. Richarz, 472–73.

16. Berthold Auerbach, *Briefe an seinen Freund Jakob Auerbach* (Frankfurt am Main, 1884), 2:165–66.

17. Cited in Egon Caesar Conte Corti, *Das Haus Rothschild in der Zeit seiner Blüte, 1830–1871* (Leipzig, 1928), 337.

18. Jeggle, 184.

19. Both citations in Jacob Toury, *Soziale und politische Geschichte*, 122, 128.

20. Richarz, 83.

21. Monika Richarz, *Der Eintritt der Juden in die akademischen Berufe* (Tübingen, 1974), 212.

9. Jewish Identity in the Decades After 1848

1. Jost to S. M. and Philipp Ehrenberg, March 15, 1849, Jost Collection, Leo Baeck Institute Archives, New York.

2. Cited in W. Iggers, ed., *Die Juden in Böhmen und Mähren. Ein historisches Lesebuch* (Munich, 1986), 160.

3. Philipp Ehrenberg to Leopold Zunz, October 4, 1849, in N. N. Glatzer, ed., *Leopold Zunz and Adelheid Zunz: An Account in Letters, 1815–1885* (London, 1958), 223.

4. *Israelitisches Gebetbuch* (Breslau, 1854), viii.

5. "Die Orgel in der Synagoge," *Ben Chananja* 4(1861):215.

6. Cited in Adolf Lewin, *Geschichte der badischen Juden* (Karlsruhe, 1909), 331.

7. *Stunden der Andacht. Ein Gebet- und Erbauungsbuch für Israels Frauen und Jungfrauen, zur öffentlichen und häuslichen Andacht, so wie für alle Verhältnisse des weiblichen Lebens* (Prag, 1855), x.

8. *Jeschurun*, Prospectus (October, 1854):[2].

9. *Illustrirtes Unterhaltungs-Buch für Israeliten* (Pest, 1866), 1:2

10. *Die Gartenlaube* 2(1854):478.

11. From the widely circulated German periodical *Didaskalia*, cited in *Der Freitagabend* 2(1860):50.

12. *Festrede zur Jubelfeier des Herrn L. Lewandowski* (Berlin, 1865), 12.

13. MGWJ 18(1869):165 n.

14. *Die Gartenlaube* 1(1853):1.

15. *Ben Chananja* 1(1858):8–9.

16. *Jüdisches Volksblatt* 1(1853):1.

17. AZJ 19(1855):238.

18. MGWJ 1(1852):3.

19. *Darkhe ha-mishnah* (Leipzig, 1859), 3.

20. J. S. Ersch and J. G. Gruber, *Allgemeine Encyklopädie der Wissenschaften und Künste* 2/27 (Leipzig, 1850), 471.

21. *Hebraeische Bibliographie* 14(1874):117.

22. Ibid. 9(1869):78.

23. Ludwig August Frankl, *Nach Jerusalem!*, part 2: *Palästina* (Leipzig, 1858), 2.

24. Salomon Herxheimer, *Sabbath-, Fest- und Gelegenheits-Predigten* (Leipzig, 1857), 394.

25. H. Lademacher, ed., *Ausgewählte Schriften* (Cologne, 1962), 235.

26. R. Michael, ed., *Heinrich Graetz-Tagebuch und Briefe* (Tübingen, 1977), 212.

Bibliographical Essay

Two recent works dealing with the entire period covered in this volume (and more) are especially worthy of recommendation. Trude Maurer's *Die Entwicklung der jüdischen Minderheit in Deutschland (1780–1933)* (1992) provides a critical analysis of recent literature on the subject; and *Die Juden in Deutschland 1780–1918* (1994), by Shulamit Volkov, offers a brief yet informative summary.

1. Legal Status and Emancipation

There is, to date, no detailed presentation of the changing legal status of Jews in the individual German states and other territories. The most precise documentation exists regarding developments in Prussia. A recent in-depth analysis, based on original sources, is Annegret Brammer's published doctoral dissertation, *Judenpolitik und Judengesetzgebung in Preussen, 1812 bis 1847, mit einem Ausblick auf das Gleichberechtigungsgesetz des Norddeutschen Bundes von 1869* (1987). Nevertheless, older studies are still indispensable, such as those by Rönne and Freund. The four volumes published by the state archives of Rhineland-Palatinate, *Rheinland-Pfalz: Dokumente zur Geschichte der jüdischen Bevölkerung 1800–1945* (1972–1982) are an important source for Prussia's western territories. An impressive evaluation and interpretation of extant printed sources and secondary literature for the early phase of emancipation can be found in Albert A. Bruer, *Geschichte der Juden in Preussen (1750–1820)* (1991).

The Conditions of "Protection" and Reforms of the Late Enlightenment

The aforementioned works by Annegret Brammer and Albert A. Bruer are also basic for this subject. A systematic presentation is offered in Jacob Toury, "Der

Eintritt der Juden ins deutsche Bürgertum," in Liebeschütz, 139–242; and in the following symposium proceedings: W. Grab, ed., *Deutsche Aufklärung und Judenemanzipation* (1980); and M. Awerbuch and S. Jersch-Wenzel, eds., *Bild und Selbstbild der Juden Berlins zwischen Aufklärung und Romantik* (1992). For the period up to 1786, an indispensable work is Selma Stern's *Der preussische Staat und die Juden,* part 3: *Die Zeit Friedrichs des Grossen* (1971). Jacob Katz provides a synthesis in *Out of the Ghetto: The Social Background of the Jewish Emancipation, 1770–1870* (1973).

Reform-Oriented Policies in the Habsburg Empire

The most detailed study on this topic is Josef Karniel, *Die Toleranzpolitik Kaiser Josephs II* (1985); a basic work on Bohemia is Ruth Kestenberg-Gladstein's *Neuere Geschichte der Juden in den böhmischen Ländern,* part 1: *Das Zeitalter der Aufklärung 1780–1830* (1969). Another work dealing with Bohemia is the volume published by the Collegium Carolinum: F. Seibt, ed., *Die Juden in den böhmischen Ländern* (1983), in which the most relevant essays are Anna M. Drabek, "Die Juden in den böhmischen Ländern zur Zeit des Landesfürstlichen Absolutismus," 123–43; and Eila Hassenpflug-Elzholz, "Toleranzedikt und Emanzipation," 145–59. An older yet still essential reference work is A. F. Pribram, *Urkunden und Akten zur Geschichte der Juden in Wien 1526–1847,* 2 vols. (1918). Likewise still of value in the earlier literature is Ludwig Singer, "Zur Geschichte der Toleranzpatente in den Sudetenländern," in *Jahrbuch der Gesellschaft für Geschichte der Juden in der Čechoslovakischen Republik* 5 (1933), 231–311. The essay by Klaus Lohrmann, Wilhelm Wadl, and Markus Wenninger, "Die Entwicklung des Judenrechtes in Österreich und seinen Nachbarländern," in K. Lohrmann, ed., *1000 Jahre österreichisches Judentum* (1982), 25–53, goes back much further in time but deals with this subject as well.

Policies in German Territories Under French Influence

On individual German territories see the following: Arno Herzig, *Judentum und Emanzipation in Westfalen* (1973); Reinhard Rürup, "Die Emanzipation der Juden in Baden," in his *Emanzipation und Antisemitismus. Studien zur "Judenfrage" der bürgerlichen Gesellschaft* (1975), 37–73; Stefan Schwarz, *Die Juden in Bayern im Wandel der Zeiten* (1963); Gerhard Hentsch, *Gewerbeordnung und Emanzipation der Juden im kurfürstlichen Hessen* (1979); Helga Krohn, *Die Juden in Hamburg 1800–1850* (1967); Bernhard Post, *Judentoleranz und Judenemanzipation in Kurmainz 1774–1813* (1985); Paul Arnsberg, *Die jüdischen Gemeinden in Hessen,* 2 vols. (1972); Rachel Heuberger and Helga Krohn, *Hinaus aus dem Ghetto. Juden in Frankfurt am Main 1800–1950* (1988). On the grand duchy of Warsaw founded under Napoleon, which later became the Prussian province of Posen, absence of more recent literature requires reference to the older work of A. Heppner and J. Herzberg, *Aus Vergangenheit und Gegenwart der jüdischen Gemeinden in den Posener Landen* (1909).

Reform Efforts, Restoration, Reaction

Almost all of the references listed above have information on this subject as well. In addition, the following are worthy of mention: Jacob Toury, *Soziale und politische Geschichte der Juden in Deutschland 1847–1871* (1977), which refers all the way back to the early nineteenth century; Helmut D. Schmidt, "The Terms of Emancipation 1781–1812," in LBIYB 1(1956):28–47; Herbert A. Strauss, "Preemancipation Prussian Policies Toward the Jews," in LBIYB 11(1966):107–36; Alwin Müller, *Die Geschichte der Juden in Köln von der Wiederzulassung 1798 bis um 1850. Ein Beitrag zur Sozialgeschichte einer Minderheit* (1984); Hendrikje Kilian, *Die jüdische Gemeinde in München 1813–1871. Eine Grossstadtgemeinde im Zeitalter der Emanzipation* (1989). The following works deal specifically with the expression of anti-Jewish sentiments and anti-Jewish riots: Jacob Katz, *Die Hep-Hep Verfolgungen des Jahres 1819* (1994); Stefan Rohrbacher, *Gewalt im Biedermeier. Antijüdische Ausschreitungen in Vormärz und Revolution (1815–1848/49)* (1993); Rainer Erb and Werner Bergmann, *Die Nachtseite der Judenemanzipation. Der Widerstand gegen die Integration der Juden in Deutschland 1780–1860* (1989); Herbert A. Strauss, "Die preussische Bürokratie und die antijüdischen Unruhen im Jahre 1834," in H. A. Strauss and K. R. Grossmann, eds., *Gegenwart im Rückblick* (1970), 27–55; Eleonore Sterling, *Judenhass. Die Anfänge des politischen Antisemitismus in Deutschland (1815–1850)* (1969).

Conflicts During the Years Before 1848

On this subject as well, Jacob Toury's standard work must be mentioned as a primary reference, *Soziale und politische Geschichte der Juden in Deutschland 1847–1871*. Another significant study is Toury's essay "Die Revolution von 1848 als innerjüdischer Wendepunkt," in Liebeschütz, 359–76. For a critical analysis of the attitudes of the non-Jewish population to the granting of civil equality to Jews, see Reinhard Rürup, "Judenemanzipation und bürgerliche Gesellschaft in Deutschland," in his *Emanzipation und Antisemitismus*, 11–36. The debate on emancipation of Prussian Jews directly prior to the 1848 revolution is documented in detail in E. Bleich, ed., *Der Erste Vereinigte Landtag in Berlin 1847* (1847, repr. 1977). Annegret Brammer's dissertation, mentioned above, and Anton Maria Keim's *Die Judenfrage im Landtag des Grossherzogtums Hessen 1820–1849* (1983) both draw upon the Bleich volume. Barbara Strenge, *Juden im preussischen Justizdienst 1812–1918* (1995) examines the problems faced by Jews in gaining access to legal careers in government service.

2. Population Shifts and Occupational Structure

Demography

Demographic developments among Jews in Germany for the end of the eighteenth and the beginning of the nineteenth centuries can only be pieced together from a number of sources. Some of these are monographs for individual cities or territories, including those listed above for chapter 1. Another source consists of contemporary official data that were recorded for legal and taxation purposes. Documentation is more reliable for the first half of the nineteenth century, although still based on the same type of sources. The most outstanding work for Prussia is Heinrich Silbergleit's *Die Bevölkerungs- und Berufsverhältnisse der Juden im Deutschen Reich*, vol. 1: *Preussen* (1930). More detailed, though limited to one year are the tables and other official data edited by C. F. W. Dieterici, *Tabellen und amtliche Nachrichten über den Preussischen Staat für das Jahr 1849* (1851); unfortunately, this work is available only in major libraries. Likewise relatively rare but important is S. Neumann, *Statistik der Juden in Preussen von 1816–1880* (1884). Jacob Toury analyzes the developments in individual German states, sometimes going back to the 1820s, in the aforementioned *Soziale und politische Geschichte der Juden in Deutschland 1847–1871*. The following works are devoted to the problem of migration: Avraham Barkai, "German-Jewish Migration in the Nineteenth Century, 1830–1910," LBIYB 30(1985):301–18; Rudolf Glanz, "The German-Jewish Mass Migration 1820–1880," in *American Jewish Archives* 22(1970):49–66; and Eugen von Bergmann, *Zur Geschichte und Entwicklung deutscher, polnischer und jüdischer Bevölkerung in der Provinz Posen seit 1824* (1883). To date there is no statistical work available specifically on Jews in the Habsburg Empire.

Economic Activities Around 1800

Analogous to the situation regarding information on demographic developments, data on the economic activities of Jews at the end of the eighteenth century can only be gathered from scattered diverse sources. The most detailed data in this area, too, are those for Prussia, particularly the records for individual provinces at the end of the reign of Frederick II as printed in Selma Stern, *Der preussische Staat und die Juden*, vol. 3.2.2 (1977). Statistics on a number of diverse communities can be found in Jacob Toury, "Der Eintritt der Juden ins deutsche Bürgertum," in Liebeschütz, 139–242. On the activities of the court factors and their descendants, extensive information—though tinged with antisemitism—can be found in the study by Heinrich Schnee, *Die Hoffinanz und der moderne Staat*, 6 vols. (1953–1967). On individual cities, regions, or states, in addition to works mentioned for chapter 1, the following are worthy of consultation: Hugo Rachel and Paul Wallich, *Berliner Grosskaufleute und Kapitalisten*, vol. 2: *Die Zeit des Merkantilismus 1648–1806* (1938); Hugo Rachel, "Die Juden im Berliner Wirtschaftsleben zur Zeit des Merkantilismus," *Zeitschrift für die Geschichte der Juden in Deutschland* 2(1930):175 ff.; Hans-Jürgen Krüger, *Die Judenschaft von Königsberg 1700–1812* (1966); Max Aschkewitz, *Zur Geschichte der Juden in Westpreussen* (1967); Gustav Otruba, "Der Anteil der Juden am Wirtschaftsleben der böhmischen Länder seit dem Beginn der Industrialisierung," in F. Seibt, ed., *Die Juden in den böhmischen Ländern* (1983), 209–68.

Areas of Enterprise Between 1815 and 1848

The literature dealing specifically with this period is both richer in detail and more systematic. Once again Jacob Toury provides both an overview and detailed information in his *Soziale und politische Geschichte der Juden in Deutschland 1847– 1871.* Arthur Prinz, *Juden im deutschen Wirtschaftsleben. Soziale und wirtschaftliche Struktur im Wandel 1850–1914,* ed. A. Barkai, (1984) is also very informative. The statistics and interpretation presented in Avraham Barkai, "The German Jews at the Start of Industrialisation: Structural Change and Mobility, 1835–1860," in Mosse, 123–49, are precise and of great value. Werner E. Mosse specifically treats the topic of Jewish entrepreneurs in trade and industry in his two works, *Jews in the German Economy: The German-Jewish Economic Elite, 1820–1935* (1987), and *The German-Jewish Economic Elite, 1820–1935: A Sociocultural Profile* (1989), as well as in the volume he edited along with Hans Pohl, *Jüdische Unternehmer in Deutschland im 19. und 20. Jahrhundert* (1992). Kurt Grunwald has focused on the banking trade in *Studies in the History of the German Jews in Global Banking* (1980). In his essay "Europe's Railways and Jewish Enterprise. German Jews as Pioneers of Railway Promotion," in LBIYB 12(1967): 163–209, he also goes into depth on capital investments made by Jews in infrastructure. The history of rural Jewry, a long-neglected subject of historical research, is examined for this period by Monika Richarz in "Emancipation and Continuity—German Jews in the Rural Economy," in Mosse, 95–114. See also most recently M. Richarz and R. Rürup, eds., *Juden auf dem Lande* (1997).

3. Jewish Communities in Transition

The Persistence of Tradition

The most comprehensive treatment of the premodern Jewish community remains Salo W. Baron, *The Jewish Community: Its History and Structure to the American Revolution,* 3 vols. (1942). A brief overview with considerable attention to Germany is the article "Gemeinde" in the German *Encyclopedia Judaica.* Relatively little has been written specifically on the old-style traditionalism of the German countryside. Some of the memoirs in M. Richarz, ed., *Jüdisches Leben in Deutschland. Selbstzeugnisse zur Sozialgeschichte 1780–1871* (1976) contain relevant material. An uncritical but nonetheless interesting article on this subject is Yeshayahu Wolfsberg, "Popular Orthodoxy," LBIYB 1(1956):237–54. The persistence of traditional elements was first emphasized in the important essay by Jacob Toury, " 'Deutsche Juden' im Vormärz," LBIYB 29(1965):65–82; see also Steven M. Lowenstein, "The Pace of Modernization of German Jewry in the Nineteenth Century," LBIYB 21(1976):41–56; and, especially for the rural communities, Utz Jeggle, *Judendörfer in Württemberg* (1969). With regard to Yiddish, Peter Freimark, "Sprachverhalten und Assimilation. Die Situation der Juden in Norddeutschland in der 1. Hälfte des 19. Jahrhunderts," *Saeculum* 31(1980):240–61; and

Jacob Toury, "Die Sprache als Problem der jüdischen Einordnung im deutschen Kulturraum," JIDG 4(1983):75–96, are especially noteworthy. Max Weinreich's "Holekrash: A Jewish Rite of Passage," in D. K. Wilgers, ed., *Folklore International* (1967), 243–53, explores the background of this ceremony.

External Pressure and Internal Division

For the breakdown of the medieval structure see especially Azriel Shohet, *Im ḥilufe tekufot* (Beginnings of the Haskalah among German Jewry, 1960) and Jacob Katz, *Tradition and Crisis* (1961). Katz presents a concrete example in "R. Raphael Kohen, the Rival of Moses Mendelssohn" (Hebr.), *Tarbiz* 56(1987):243–64. For the breakdown of communal authority in Berlin see Steven M. Lowenstein, *The Berlin Jewish Community: Enlightenment, Family and Crisis, 1770–1830* (1994); and Michael A. Meyer, "The Orthodox and the Enlightened—An Unpublished Contemporary Analysis of Berlin Jewry's Spiritual Condition in the Early Nineteenth Century," LBIYB 25(1980):101–30.

New Forms of Jewish Community Organization

Although most of the hundreds of regional and community histories that have appeared in recent years do not focus on the first half of the nineteenth century, a few of them give it substantial treatment. There are also some older works that are still useful. Especially worth noting among the earlier studies are Ludwig Geiger, *Geschichte der Juden in Berlin* (2 vols., 1871; repr. 1988); A. Heppner and J. Herzberg, *Aus Vergangenheit und Gegenwart der Juden und der jüd. Gemeinden in den Posener Landen* (1904); M. Brann, "Die schlesische Judenheit vor und nach dem Edikt vom 11 März 1812," in *Jahres-Bericht des jüdisch-theologischen Seminars für das Jahr 1912* (1913), 3–44; Adolf Lewin, *Geschichte der badischen Juden seit der Regierung Karl Friedrichs (1738–1909)* (1909); and Aaron Tänzer, *Die Geschichte der Juden in Württemberg* (1937). A sampling of postwar literature includes Arno Herzig, *Judentum und Emanzipation in Westfalen* (1973); Paul Arnsberg, *Die Geschichte der Frankfurter Juden seit der Französischen Revolution*, 3 vols. (1983); Alwin Müller, *Die Geschichte der Juden in Köln von der Wiederzulassung 1798 bis um 1850* (1984); M. Treml et al., eds., *Geschichte und Kultur der Juden in Bayern*, 2 vols. (1988); P. Freimark and A. Herzig, eds., *Die Hamburger Juden in der Emanzipationsphase 1780–1870* (1989); and Franz D. Lucas and Margret Heitmann, *Stadt des Glaubens. Geschichte und Kultur der Juden in Glogau* (1991). See also the generalizations and relevant sources in Jacob Toury, *Der Eintritt der Juden ins deutsche Bürgertum. Eine Dokumentation* (1972).

The Transformation of Jewish Education

The most comprehensive work on Jewish education in Germany during this period remains Mordechai Eliav, *Ha-ḥinukh ha-yehudi be-germaniyah bime ha-haskalah ve-ha-imantsipatsyah* (Jewish Education in Germany in the Period of Enlightenment and Emancipation, 1960). See also his brief German summary in BLBI 11(1960):207–15. Most regional and communal histories devote some attention to education. The only recent book-length regional study is Claudia Prestel,

Jüdisches Schul- und Erziehungswesen in Bayern 1804–1933 (1989). For the Habsburg Empire see the relevant sections in Ruth Kestenberg-Gladstein, *Neuere Geschichte der Juden in den böhmischen Ländern* (1969); and Hillel Kieval, "Caution's Progress: The Modernization of Jewish Life in Prague, 1780–1830," in J. Katz, ed., *Toward Modernity: The European Jewish Model* (1987). The history of the Philanthropin was recounted in great detail by H. Baerwald and S. Adler in *Festschrift zur Jahrhundertfeier der Realschule der israelitischen Gemeinde (Philanthropin)* (1904); and more recently summarized in Inge Schlotzhauer, *Das Philanthropin 1804–1942* (1990). On the Jewish catechism see Jakob J. Petuchowski, "Manuals and Catechisms of the Jewish Religion in the Early Period of Emancipation," in A. Altmann, ed., *Studies in Nineteenth-Century Jewish Intellectual History* (1964).

The First Religious Reforms

The most recent comprehensive work is Michael A. Meyer, *Response to Modernity: A History of the Reform Movement in Judaism* (1988). Earlier literature includes Simon Bernfeld, *Toledot ha-reformatsyon ha-datit be-yisrael* (History of the Religious Reformation in Israel, 1900); David Philipson, *The Reform Movement in Judaism* (1931 [1907]); Caesar Seligmann, *Geschichte der jüdischen Reformbewegung* (1922); and, specifically on reform of the liturgy, Jakob J. Petuchowski, *Prayerbook Reform in Europe* (1968).

4. Jewish Self-Understanding

General Works

Four works that deal broadly with the subject matter of this chapter are Max Wiener, *Jüdische Religion im Zeitalter der Emanzipation* (1933); Heinz Mosche Graupe, *The Rise of Modern Judaism*, trans. John Robinson (1978); Eliezer Schweid, *Toledot ha-hagut ha-yehudit ba-et ha-ḥadashah* (A History of Jewish Thought in Modern Times, 1977); and Michael A. Meyer, *Response to Modernity: A History of the Reform Movement in Judaism* (1988).

History

Although it devotes relatively little attention to modern Germany, Yosef Hayim Yerushalmi, *Zakhor: Jewish History and Memory* (1982) is important for understanding the history of Jewish historical consciousness and its problematics in modern times. Selections from the reflective writings of Jewish historians through the ages are contained in M. A. Meyer, ed., *Ideas of Jewish History* (1974); and selections from the literature of Wissenschaft des Judentums in P. Mendes-Flohr, ed., *ḥokhmat yisrael: hebetim historiyim ufilosofiyim* (Modern Jewish Studies: Historical and Philosophical Perspectives, 1979). Michael A. Meyer, "The Emergence of Modern Jewish Historiography: Motives and Motifs," *History and Theory*, 27(1988):160–75) discusses the first examples of modern Jewish historical writing. Ismar Schorsch has gathered together his important studies on various aspects of Wissenschaft des Judentums in *From Text to Context: The Turn to History in Modern Judaism* (1994). The most comprehensive analysis of the historiography of Isaac Marcus Jost is Reuven Michael, Y. M. *Yost: avi ha-historiografiyah ha-yehudit ha-modernit* (I. M. Jost: The Father of Modern Jewish Historiography, 1983), with an earlier, briefer treatment in BLBI, 12(1960):239–58.

Religious Ideology

Although reviewers have taken issue with some of its interpretations, Noah H. Rosenbloom's *Tradition in an Age of Reform: The Religious Philosophy of Samson Raphael Hirsch* (1976) is important as the only full-length biography of the founder of neo-Orthodoxy. There are many shorter studies of Hirsch's thought. Among the more recent and significant are Pinchas E. Rosenblüth, "Samson Raphael Hirsch—Sein Denken und Wirken," in Liebeschütz, 293–324; the section on Hirsch in Mordechai Breuer, *Modernity Within Tradition: The Social History of Orthodox Jewry in Imperial Germany*, trans. Elizabeth Petuchowski (1992), 55–79; and Jacob Katz, "Rabbi Samson Raphael Hirsch to the Right and to the Left" (Hebr.), in *Torah im derekh erets* (1987), 13–31. The literature on Zacharias Frankel is much sparser; there is no critical biography. A selection of his writings in Hebrew translation with an introduction by Rivka Horwitz appeared as *Zacharias Frankel ve-reshit ha-yahadut ha-pozitivit historit* (Zacharias Frankel and the Beginnings of Positive-Historical Judaism, 1984). Horwitz, in "The Influence of Romanticism on Jewish Scholarship" (Hebr.), *Proceedings of the Eighth World Congress of Jewish Studies*, division B (1982), 107–14; and Ismar Schorsch, in "Zacharias Frankel and the European Origins of Conservative Judaism," in his abovementioned *From Text to Context*, 255–65, both argue for the influence of Friedrich Karl von Savigny upon Frankel. For Abraham Geiger we have a bibliography of secondary literature in J. J. Petuchowski, ed., *New Perspectives on Abraham Geiger: An HUC-JIR Symposium* (1975), 55–58. There is a selection of Geiger's works in English translation with a fine biographical introduction by Max Wiener: *Abraham Geiger and Liberal Judaism: The Challenge of the Nineteenth Century* (1981 [1962]) and a selection in Hebrew: *Avraham Geiger: Mivḥar ketavav al ha-tikunim ba-dat* (Abraham Geiger: Selected Writings on Religious Reform, 1979). The only consequential recent article on Samuel Holdheim is Jakob J. Petuchowski, "Abraham Geiger and Samuel Holdheim: Their Differences in Germany and Repercussions in America," LBIYB, 22(1977):139–59. Apart from the treatments in general volumes, one must therefore resort to the prejudiced but still valuable biography of his disciple and successor at the Berlin Reformgemeinde: Immanuel Heinrich Ritter, *Samuel Holdheim. Sein Leben und seine Werke* (1865), and Ritter's article, "Samuel Holdheim: The Jewish Reformer," *Jewish Quarterly Review* 1(1889):202–15.

Practice

Two important broadly and sociologically based studies are Ismar Schorsch, "Emancipation and the Crisis of Religious Authority: The Emergence of the

Modern Rabbinate," in Mosse, pp. 205–47 (also in Schorsch, *Text and Context*, 9–50); and Steven M. Lowenstein, "The 1840s and the Creation of the German-Jewish Religious Reform Movement," in Mosse, pp. 255–297. Thomas Rahe presents a brief balanced overview in his "Religionsreform und jüdisches Selbstbewusstsein im deutschen Judentum des 19. Jahrhunderts," *Menora*, 1(1990): 89–121. For Ludwig Philippson and the orientation of his newspaper, the best study is Johanna Philippson, "Ludwig Philippson und die Allgemeine Zeitung des Judentums," in Liebeschütz, 243–91. More narrowly focused is Mordechai Eliav, "Philippson's Algemeine Zeitung des Judentums und Erez Israel," BLBI, 46–47(1969):155–82. For an analysis of *Der treue Zions-Wächter* see Judith Bleich, "The Emergence of an Orthodox Press in Nineteenth-Century Germany," JSS, 42(1980):323–44. Robert Liberles focuses on communal politics in his *Religious Conflict in Social Context: The Resurgence of Orthodoxy in Frankfurt am Main, 1838–1877* (1985). Michael A. Meyer, "Alienated Intellectuals in the Camp of Religious Reform: The Frankfurt Reformfreunde, 1842–1845," *AJS Review*, 6(1981):61–86, is the most comprehensive treatment of its subject. There is no recent study devoted specifically to the Berlin Reform Congregation. However, Holdheim himself published a necessarily partial *Geschichte der Entstehung und Entwickelung der jüdischen Reformgemeinde in Berlin* (1857). Aside from the general works above, the rabbinical assemblies are treated in detail, with excerpts from the protocols, in David Philipson, *The Reform Movement in Judaism* (1931 [1907]). An introduction and excerpts in Hebrew appear in M. A. Meyer, ed., *Ve'idot ha-rabanim be'germaniyah ba-shanim 1844–1846* (The Rabbinical Assemblies in Germany in the Years 1844–1846, 1984).

5. Judaism and Christianity

General Works
To date, there is no comprehensive study that embraces perceptions and relations from both the Christian and the Jewish side in nineteenth-century Germany. It is a significant desideratum. Meanwhile, see the brief chapter "Judaism and Christianity Against the Background of Modern Secularism," in Jacob Katz, *Jewish Emancipation and Self-Emancipation* (1986), 34–48.

Christianity Against Judaism
Albert Lewkowitz discusses all of the major German thinkers in relation to Judaism in his *Das Judentum und die geistigen Strömungen des 19. Jahrhunderts* (1935). Nathan Rotenstreich has analyzed in detail the relevant texts in the writings of Kant and Hegel in his *The Recurrent Pattern: Studies in Anti-Judaism in Modern Thought* (1963). He has cast his net more widely in *Jews and German Philosophy: The Polemics of Emancipation* (1982). Two articles that deal with Kant's relation both to Judaism and to Jews are Heinz Mosche Graupe, "Kant und das Judentum," *Zeitschrift für Religions- und Geistesgeschichte* 13(1961):308–

33; and Jacob Katz, "Kant and Judaism: The Historical Connection" (Hebr.), *Tarbiz* 41(1972):219–37. Hegel and the Hegelians receive further attention in Hans Liebeschütz, *Das Judentum im deutschen Geschichtsbild von Hegel bis Max Weber* (1967). Liebeschütz also presents a broad overview of Christian thinkers' views on Judaism and of their influence on Jewish figures like Geiger and Frankel in his "Judentum und deutsche Umwelt im Zeitalter der Restauration," in Liebeschütz, 1–54. More specifically, see also Joseph W. Pickle, "Schleiermacher on Judaism," *The Journal of Religion* 60(1980):115–37. On Bruno Bauer and Jewish responses to his essay see Nathan Rotenstreich, "For and Against Emancipation: The Bruno Bauer Controversy," LBIYB 4(1959):3–36. Christhard Hoffmann analyzes in detail the views of ancient Judaism held by various Christian scholars in his *Juden und Judentum im Werk deutscher Althistoriker des 19. und 20. Jahrhunderts* (1988). For the popular view see Klaus Müller-Salget, "Das Bild des Juden im protestantischen Volksschrifttum des 19. Jahrhunderts," in H. O. Horch and H. Denkler, eds., *Conditio Judaica* (1988), 259–70. Finally, Alfred Low, *Jews in the Eyes of the Germans from the Enlightenment to Imperial Germany* (1979) is a broad popular, but apologetic, treatment that includes philosophers, theologians, and literary figures.

An early study of the mission to the Jews in Germany during this period is by one of its active leaders: Johann F. A. de le Roi, *Die evangelische Christenheit und die Juden unter dem Gesichtspunke der Mission geschichtlich betrachtet*, 2 (Berlin, 1891). Horst Fischer includes a brief treatment of the Berlin Society for Promoting Christianity Among the Jews as well as the subject of government policy on conversion from and to Judaism in his *Judentum, Staat und Heer in Preussen im frühen 19. Jahrhundert* (1968), 89–95. The most recent and extensive study is Christopher M. Clark, *The Politics of Conversion. Missionary Protestantism and the Jews in Prussia, 1728–1941* (1995).

Jews as Christians

There is no study devoted collectively to German Jews who converted from Judaism to Christianity that focuses on their relation to their faith of origin and their faith of adoption. Some relevant primary sources are excerpted in F. Kobler, ed., *Juden und Judentum aus drei Jahrhunderten* (1935). For Stahl we have Hans-Joachim Schoeps, "Friedrich Julius Stahl und das Judentum," in H. Lamm, ed., *Von Juden in München—Ein Gedenkbuch* (1958), 99–103; and Robert A. Kann, "Friedrich Julius Stahl: A Reexamination of His Conservatism," LBIYB 12(1967): 55–74.

Judaism Against Christianity

See the general works listed for chapter 4, which deal, in part, with this subject. Also Julius Guttmann, *Philosophies of Judaism*, trans. R. J. Z. Werblowsky (1964), 304–49. More specifically on this subject, there are treatments of Formstecher, Samuel Hirsch, Steinheim, and Geiger in Jacob Fleischmann, *Be'ayat ha-natsrut ba-maḥshavah ha-yehudit mi-Mendelssohn ad Rosenzweig* (The Problem of

Christianity in Modern Jewish Thought from Mendelssohn to Rosenzweig, 1964); and in Walter Jacob, *Christianity Through Jewish Eyes: The Quest for Common Gound* (1974). There has been a renewal of interest in Steinheim. See most recently the essays in J. H. Schoeps et al., eds., *"Philo des 19. Jahrhunderts"* (1993). The only article devoted to Formstecher's thought is Bernard Bamberger, "Formstecher's History of Judaism," HUCA 23(1950/51):1–35. Bettina Kratz-Ritter, *Salomon Formstecher. Ein deutscher Reformrabbiner* (1991) focuses on Formstecher's nontheological writings. Among a number of articles on Samuel Hirsch, most relevant to our topic is Emil L. Fackenheim, "Samuel Hirsch and Hegel," in A. Altmann, ed., *Studies in Nineteenth-Century Jewish Intellectual History* (1964), 171–201; and Gershon Greenberg, "Samuel Hirsch: Jewish Hegelian," *Revue des études juives* 129(1970):205–15. For Geiger see Michael A. Meyer, "Universalism and Jewish Unity in the Thought of Abraham Geiger," in J. Katz, ed., *The Role of Religion in Modern Jewish History* (1975), 91–104; for praxis, Meyer, "Christian Influence on Early German Reform Judaism," in C. Berlin, ed., *Studies in Jewish Bibliography, History and Literature* (1971), 289–303.

Between Jews and Christians

For Jewish relations with Christians in the countryside see especially Utz Jeggle, *Judendörfer in Württemberg* (1969), 169–73; on Orthodox attitudes for this period as well as later in the century, Mordechai Breuer, *Modernity Within Tradition*, 85–89, 311–14. The instance of the Munich physician is taken from Hendrikje Kilian, "Die Anfänge der Emanzipation am Beispiel der Münchner jüdischen Gemeinde," in M. Treml et al., eds., *Geschichte und Kultur der Juden in Bayern. Aufsätze* (1988), 272. The account of the Jews and Freemasonry is heavily indebted to Jacob Katz, *Jews and Freemasons in Europe, 1723–1939*, trans. Leonard Oschry (1970). See also his earlier "The Fight for Admission to Masonic Lodges," LBIYB 11(1966):171–209. Eugen Mayer's "An Ecumenical Experiment," LBIYB 13(1968): 135–41 is devoted to the *Unparteiische Universal-Kirchenzeitung*. On Jewish and Christian religious radicals, see Michael A. Meyer, "Alienated Intellectuals in the Camp of Religious Reform: The Frankfurt Reformfreunde, 1842–1845," *AJS Review* 6(1981):79–86, and the literature cited there. Hermann Lange, "Die christlich-jüdische Ehe. Ein deutscher Streit im 19. Jahrhundert," *Menora* 2(1991):47–80, is the first larger treatment of its subject.

6. Becoming German, Remaining Jewish

General Works

The standard work for the participation of Jews in the various branches of German culture continues to be the massive collection of articles edited by Siegmund Kaznelson, *Juden im deutschen Kulturbereich* (1959). In recent years academic symposia have yielded volumes that contain articles devoted to a number of the subjects discussed in this chapter. The most relevant volumes are W. Grab and J.

H. Schoeps, eds., *Juden im Vormärz und in der Revolution von 1848* (1983)—on Heine, Börne, Bohemian writers, Saphir, Beck, Marx, Rahel Varnhagen, and Lassalle; J. Reinharz and W. Schatzberg, eds., *The Jewish Response to German Culture. From the Enlightenment to the Second World War* (1985)—especially for the process of acculturation; and H. O. Horch and H. Denkler, eds., *Conditio Judaica. Judentum, Antisemitismus und deutschsprachige Literatur vom 18. Jahrhundert bis zum Ersten Weltkrieg*, 2 vols. (1988–89), containing about a dozen articles on various aspects of Jewish cultural history during this period.

The Problematic Acquisition of German Culture

The Jewish quest for *Bildung* and its ramifications are explored in George L. Mosse, *German Jews Beyond Judaism* (1985); and in David Sorkin, *The Transformation of German Jewry, 1780–1840* (1987). More specific studies of relevance include Jacob Toury, "Jüdische Buchhändler und Verleger in Deutschland vor 1860," BLBI 9(1960):58–69; Ulrike Schmidt, "Jüdische Bibliotheken in Frankfurt am Main. Vom Anfang des 19. Jahrhunderts bis 1938," *Archiv für Geschichte des Buchwesens* 29(1987):236–67; Gunnar Och, "Jüdische Leser und jüdisches Lesepublikum im 18. Jahrhundert. Ein Beitrag zur Akkulturationsgeschichte des deutschen Judentums," *Menora* 2(1991):298–336. On important German writers and the Jews see especially Wilfried Barner, "Jüdische Goethe-Verehrung vor 1933," in S. Moses and A. Schöne, eds., *Juden in der deutschen Literatur* (1986), 127–51. Important for the role of language in Jewish acculturation are Jacob Toury, "Die Sprache als Problem der jüdischen Einordnung im deutschen Kulturraum," in W. Grab, ed., *Gegenseitige Einflüsse deutscher und jüdischer Kultur von der Epoche der Aufklärung bis zur Weimarer Republik* (1982), 75–96; and Sander L. Gilman, *Jewish Self-Hatred: Anti-Semitism and the Hidden Language of the Jews* (1986). For the treatment of Jews in German plays and novels see the published dissertation by Charlene A. Lea, *Emancipation, Assimilation and Stereotype. The Image of the Jew in German and Austrian Drama (1800–1850)* (1978); Mark H. Gelber, "Wandlungen im Bild des 'gebildeten Juden' in der deutschen Literatur," JIDG 13(1984):165–78; Ruth K. Angress, "Wunsch- und Angstbilder. Jüdische Gestalten aus der deutschen Literatur des neunzehnten Jahrhunderts," AIGK 1:84–96. On Michael Beer see Lothar Kahn, "Michael Beer (1800–1833)," LBIYB 12(1967):149–60; Jürgen Stenzel, "Das Opfer als Autor. Poetische Assimilation in Michael Beers 'Der Paria' (1823)," AIGK 1:122–28.

Jewish Poets and Writers of Fiction

This is a subject that has spawned a large literature. Of the older general works, still worth noting is Ludwig Geiger, *Die Deutsche Literatur und die Juden* (1910). Marcel Reich-Ranicki presents an original and insightful analysis of the Jewish contribution in his *Über Ruhestörer. Juden in der deutschen Literatur* (1989). For an analysis of the internally directed moralistic and ghetto story genres see Hans Otto Horch, "Jüdische Literaturdebatten im 19. Jahrhundert am Beispiel der 'Allgemeinen Zeitung des Judentums'," AIGK 5:107–12. For the same subject as well as the reception of Jewish and non-Jewish writers among Jews, we have Horch's thorough and helpfully indexed study, *Auf der Suche nach der jüdischen Erzählliteratur. Die Literaturkritik der "Allgemeinen Zeitung des Judentums" (1837–1922)* (1985). For a survey of the non-Jewish reception of Jewish writers, see Jacob Katz, "Rezeption jüdischer Autoren durch deutsche Kritik und deutsches Publikum," BLBI 75(1986): 41–53. Within the huge literature on Heine these larger works have been especially helpful: Hartmut Kircher, *Heinrich Heine und das Judentum* (1973); Jeffrey L. Sammons, *Heinrich Heine: A Modern Biography* (1979); and S. S. Prawer, *Heine's Jewish Comedy: A Study of his Portraits of Jews and Judaism* (1983). For the recent state of the field in Heine studies see Jeffrey L. Sammons, *Heinrich Heine* (1991). Hillel J. Kieval compares six Jewish writers in his "The Social Vision of Bohemian Jews: Intellectuals and Community in the 1840s," in Frankel, 246–83. For Kapper, Kompert, and Hartmann see Margarita Pazi, "Jüdisch-deutsche Schriftsteller in Böhmen im 19. Jahrhundert," in Grab, ed., *Gegenseitige Einflüsse*, 203–58. On individual writers see Pazi, "Berthold Auerbach and Moritz Hartmann—Two Jewish Writers of the Nineteenth Century," LBIYB 18(1973):201–18; Jacob Katz, "Berthold Auerbach's Anticipation of the German-Jewish Tragedy," HUCA 53(1982):215–40; Jeffrey L. Sammons, "Observations on Berthold Auerbach's Jewish Novels," in his *Imagination and History* (1988), 177–91; Yomtov Ludwig Bato, "Moritz Gottlieb Saphir, 1795–1858," BLBI 5(1958):27–33; Lothar Kahn, "Moritz Gottlieb Saphir," LBIYB 20(1975):247–57; Wilma A. Iggers, "Leopold Kompert, Romancier of the Bohemian Ghetto," *Austrian Literature* 6(1973):117–38; Lothar Kahn, "Tradition and Modernity in the German Ghetto Novel" (on Kompert and Franzos), *Judaism* 28(1979):31–41; Ruth Kestenberg-Gladstein, "Karl Beck—Identitätsprobleme der ersten Assimilationsgeneration in deutscher Sprache," BLBI 60(1981):51–66.

Political Writers

Indispensable for this subject are the relevant sections in Jacob Toury's definitive work *Die politischen Orientierungen der Juden in Deutschland von Jena bis Weimar* (1966). The various ways in which Jews during this period responded to the persistence of their exclusion are discussed by Gilman, *Jewish Self-Hatred*; and by Eleonore Sterling, "Jewish Reaction to Jew-Hatred in the First Half of the Nineteenth Century," LBIYB 3(1958):103–21; and for certain prominent individuals in Paul Lawrence Rose, *Revolutionary Antisemitism in Germany from Kant to Wagner* (1990). Recent studies on individual political activists include Moshe Rinott, "Gabriel Riesser: Fighter for Jewish Emancipation," LBIYB 7(1962):11–38; Gad Arnsberg, "Gabriel Riesser als deutsch-jüdischer Intellektueller und liberaler Ideologe," *Menora* 2(1991):81–104; Edmund Silberner, *Johann Jacoby, Politiker und Mensch* (1976); Walter Grab, "Johann Jacobys Briefwechsel im Vormärz und in der Revolution von 1848/49," in P. von der Osten-Sacken, ed., *Juden in Deutschland* (1980), 149–68. For Börne there is a stimulating but in some respects questionable study by Orlando Figes, "Ludwig Börne and the Formation of a Radical Critique of Judaism," LBIYB 29(1984):351–82. More balanced are Lothar Kahn, "Ludwig Börne: First Jewish Champion of Democracy,"

Judaism 25(1976):420–34; the articles on Börne in relation to Judaism by Joseph H. Kruse and Georg Heuberger in A. Estermann, ed., *Ludwig Börne 1786–1837* (1986); and the popular biography by Willi Jasper, *Keinem Vaterland Geboren* (1989). For Lassalle we have Edmund Silberner, "Ferdinand Lassalle: From Maccabeism to Jewish Anti-Semitism," HUCA 24(1952/53):151–86; and the massive biography by Shlomo Na'aman, *Lassalle* (1970).

Art and Music

On Moritz Oppenheim see the important articles by Elisheva Cohen and Ismar Schorsch in the catalogue of the Oppenheim exhibition held at the Israel Museum, *Moritz Oppenheim: The First Jewish Painter* (1983); also Rudolf M. Heilbrunn, "Leben und Werk des Malers Moritz Oppenheim," BLBI 36(1966): 285–301; Elisheva Cohen, "Moritz Daniel Oppenheim," BLBI 53/54(1977/78): 42–74. For Meyerbeer see Heinz and Gudrun Becker, *Giacomo Meyerbeer. A Life in Letters* (1983). For Wagner and the Jews there is a detailed treatment by Jacob Katz, *The Darker Side of Genius: Richard Wagner's Antisemitism* (1986).

7. From Subject to Citizen

General Works

Most general works mention only briefly the new position of Jews in state and society. The volume edited by Hans Liebeschütz and Arnold Paucker, *Das Judentum in der deutschen Umwelt 1800–1850* (1977) is devoted specifically to this subject. Changes within Jewish society are the focus of the following significant works: Jacob Katz, *Out of the Ghetto* (1973); Michael A. Meyer, *The Origins of the Modern Jew: Jewish Identity and European Culture in Germany, 1749–1824* (1967); David Sorkin, *The Transformation of German Jewry, 1780–1840* (1987); and Steven L. Lowenstein, *The Berlin Jewish Community: Enlightenment, Family, and Crisis, 1770–1830* (1994). The following surveys include the social integration of Jews within the two major German states: William O. McCagg, Jr., *A History of Habsburg Jews, 1670–1918* (1989); and Albert A. Bruer, *Geschichte der Juden in Preussen (1750–1820)* (1991).

Loyalty and Patriotism

On the patriotism of German Jews in the first half of the nineteenth century we now have the published dissertation of Erik Lindner, *Patriotismus deutscher Juden von der napoleonischen Ära bis zum Kaiserreich* (1997). Benno Offenburg, *Das Erwachen des deutschen Nationalbewusstseins in der preussischen Judenheit* (1933), discusses the subject within the broader scope of intellectual history. Gil Graff, *Separation of Church and State. Dina de-Malkhuta Dina in Jewish Law, 1750–1848* (1985) provides an interpretation of the Jewish religious attitude toward the state in the age of emancipation. Grete Klingenstein's essay "Sonnenfels als Patriot," in *Judentum im Zeitalter der Aufklärung. Wolfenbüt-*

teler Studien zur Aufklärung (1977), 6:211–228, analyzes Joseph von Sonnen-fels's understanding of patriotism. On Herz Homberg's central role in the pro-cess of Germanization of Galician Jews, see Majer Balaban, "Herz Homberg in Galizien," in *Jahrbuch für jüdische Geschichte und Literatur* (1916), 19:189–221. On Homberg's catechisms see Joseph Walk, " 'Bne Zion' by Herz Homberg" (Hebr.), in *Annual of Bar-Ilan University—Studies in Judaica and the Humani-ties* 14/15(1977):218–32.

There are several works dealing with the subject of Jews and military service in Prussia and Austria. The most comprehensive of these is Horst Fischer, *Juden-tum, Staat und Heer in Preussen im frühen 19. Jahrhundert* (1968). The story of Meno Burg's life, based on his autobiography, is presented in popular form in Eugen Wolbe, *Major Burg. Lebensbild eines jüdischen Offiziers* (1907). This work has an apologetic ring to it, as does the collection by Moritz Stern, *Aus der Zeit der deutschen Befreiungskriege 1813–1815*, 5 vols. (1918, 1935–1938), which is more interesting from a scholarly point of view. A more recent work on Burg is Renatus Rieger, *Major Meno Burg. Ein preussischer Offizier jüdischen Glaubens* (1992). The period prior to 1848 is dealt with only briefly in Erwin A. Schmidl, *Juden in der k. (u.) k. Armee 1788–1918* (1989). The same is true for István Deák's short essay, *Jewish Soldiers in Austro-Hungarian Society*, Leo Baeck Memorial Lecture 34 (1990). Wolfgang von Heisl's *Juden in der österreichischen und öster-reichisch-ungarischen Armee* (1971) is written in a partly academic and partly anecdotal style. Ezekiel Landau's views on military service are analyzed in Ruth Kestenberg-Gladstein, *Neuere Geschichte der Juden in den böhmischen Ländern. Das Zeitalter der Aufklärung, 1780–1830* (1969). Only isolated research findings are available for other German states, including the introductory and concluding remarks on Mecklenburg-Schwerin in E. Lindner, ed., *Memoiren des Freiwilligen Jägers Löser Cohen. Kriegserlebnisse 1813/1814* (1993). On Bavaria see Rainer Braun's "Juden in der Armee," in *Bayern und seine Armee* (1987), 47–54. Marc Saperstein analyzes the sermons of rabbis in Prussia and Austria between the Seven Years War and the Napoleonic Wars in his article, "War and Patriotism in Sermons to Central European Jews," LBIYB 38(1993):3–14. Examples of Jewish patriotism at a local level can be found in Ludwig Geiger, *Geschichte der Juden in Berlin* (1871); Moshe Zimmermann, *Hamburgischer Patriotismus und deutscher Nationalismus. Die Emanzipation der Juden in Hamburg, 1830–1865* (1979); and Hendrikje Kilian, *Die Jüdische Gemeinde in München 1813–1871* (1989).

The Awakening of Political Consciousness

Jacob Toury has done the most extensive research on the integration of Jews into nineteenth-century bourgeois society. The following are the most relevant among his numerous publications: *Die politischen Orientierungen der Juden in Deutsch-land. Von Jena bis Weimar* (1966); "Der Eintritt der Juden ins deutsche Bürger-tum," in Liebeschütz, 139–242, "Jüdische Bürgerrechtskämpfer im vormärzlichen Königsberg," *Jahrbuch für die Geschichte Mittel- und Ostdeutschlands* 32(1983):

175–216, "'Deutsche Juden' im Vormärz," BLBI 29(1965):65–82, "Der Anteil der Juden an der städtischen Selbstverwaltung im vormärzlichen Deutschland," BLBI 23(1963):265–86, and the discussion on this subject between Toury and Jacob Jacobson in BLBI 26(1964):172–82. The standard work on Jews in German city government is Stefi Wenzel, *Jüdische Bürger und kommunale Selbstverwaltung in preussischen Städten 1808–1848* (1967). On individual political writers see the references for chapter 6.

Professional and Social Progress

On the integration of Jews at the state level, see the introductory passages in Peter Pulzer, *Jews and the German State. The Political History of a Minority, 1848–1933* (1992). A sociohistorical analysis of the Jewish salon culture in Berlin is provided in Deborah Hertz, *Jewish High Society in Old Regime Berlin* (1988). The most significant Jewish salon in Vienna is the subject of the biography written by Hilde Spiel, *Fanny Arnstein: A Daughter of the Enlightenment, 1758–1818*, trans. Christine Shuttleworth (1991). Indispensable for study of the acculturation process during the first half of the nineteenth century is Monika Richarz, *Der Eintritt der Juden in die akademischen Berufe. Jüdische Studenten und Akademiker in Deutschland 1878–1848* (1974). Statistics on Jewish titles of nobility in Austria can be found in William O. McCagg, "Austria's Jewish Nobles, 1740–1918," LBIYB 34(1989):163–83. Obstacles to integration at a local level are impressively illustrated in Stefan Rohrbacher's *Gewalt im Biedermeier. Antijüdische Ausschreitungen in Vormärz und Revolution (1815–1848/49)* (1993). Eleonore Sterling, *Judenhass. Die Anfänge des politischen Antisemitismus in Deutschland (1815–1850)* (1969) provides a general background to this subject. Attitudes in the towns of Floss and Aschenhausen are described in Stefan Schwarz, *Die Juden in Bayern im Wandel der Zeiten* (1963) and Jacob Toury, "Probleme jüdischer Gleichberechtigung auf lokaler Ebene," JIDG 2(1973):267–86.

The first chapter of Henry Wassermann's dissertation, "Jews, *Bürgertum*, and *bürgerliche Gesellschaft* in a Liberal Age (1840–1880)" (Hebr., 1979), provides the only systemic treatment of Jewish associational life in Germany during these years. Most studies of local Jewish history have concentrated on inner Jewish life and changes in the legal status of Jews. Some exceptions to this are Stefi Jersch-Wenzel, "Die Juden im gesellschaftlichen Gefüge Berlins um 1800," in M. Awerbuch and S. Jersch-Wenzel, eds., *Bild und Selbstbild der Juden Berlins zwischen Aufklärung und Romantik* (1992), 139–54; Arno Herzig, *Judentum und Emanzipation in Westfalen* (1973); as well as relevant essays in A. Herzig and S. Rohde, eds., *Die Juden in Hamburg 1590–1990* (1991); and M. Treml, ed., *Geschichte und Kultur der Juden in Bayern. Lebensläufe* (1988). With respect to a more rural area, see Dieter Hoffmann, *". . . wir sind doch Deutsche." Zu Geschichte und Schicksal der Landjuden in Rheinhessen* (1992). On the nationalistic German associations and their relationship to Judaism, see Hartmut Becker, *Antisemitismus in der Deutschen Turnerschaft* (1980); and Dieter Düring, *Organisierter gesellschaftlicher Nationalismus in Deutschland (1808–1847)* (1984).

8. Between Revolution and Legal Equality

General works

No other epoch of German-Jewish history has a standard work comparable to that for the period from 1848 to 1871. Jacob Toury's *Soziale und politische Geschichte der Juden in Deutschland 1847–1871* provides a detailed treatment of demographic and socioeconomic developments, issues of integration and acculturation, Jewish organizational structure, and emancipation legislation for these years.

1848: A Year of Contradictions

Jacob Toury provides definitive research on the anti-Jewish actions during the revolutionary period in his Hebrew work, *Mehumah umevukhah bemahapekhat 1848* (Riot and Confusion in the 1848 Revolution, 1968). Whereas Stefan Rohrbacher's earlier mentioned *Gewalt im Biedermeier* emphasizes the specifically anti-Jewish causes, the older study by Eleonore Sterling, *Judenhass*, viewed the Jews as a lightning rod for social protest in general. This explanation is also used by Rainer Wirtz in *"Widersetzlichkeiten, Excesse, Crawalle, Tumulte und Skandale." Soziale Bewegung und gewalthafter sozialer Protest in Baden 1815–1848* (1981). Valuable studies on specific regions include Michael A. Riff, "The Anti-Jewish Aspect of the Revolutionary Unrest of 1848 in Baden and Its Impact on Emancipation," LBIYB 21(1976):27–40; and Daniel Gerson, "Die Ausschreitungen gegen die Juden in Elsass," BLBI 87(1990):29–44. On the Jewish response, see Eleonore Sterling, "Jewish Reaction to Jew-Hatred in the First Half of the 19th Century," LBIYB 3(1958):103–21.

On Jewish participation in the revolution and in political life after 1848, see the aforementioned standard work by Jacob Toury, *Die politischen Orientierungen der Juden in Deutschland*; and the works by Ernest Hamburger, *Juden im öffentlichen Leben Deutschlands* (1968); and Adolf Kober, "Jews in the Revolution of 1848 in Germany," JSS 10(1948):135–64. Part 1 of Peter Pulzer's *Jews and the German State* is relevant for this period. A detailed study with respect to Berlin is provided by Rüdiger Hachtmann, "Berliner Juden und die Revolution von 1848," in R. Rürup, ed., *Jüdische Geschichte in Berlin. Essays und Studien* (1995), 53–84. On Austria, see *Studia Judaica Austriaca 1: Das Judentum im Revolutionsjahr 1848* (1974). A particularly informative article in this volume is Wolfgang Häusler, "Konfessionelle Probleme in der Wiener Revolution von 1848," 64–77. Essays on individual Jews who participated in the revolution can be found in Grab, for example, Arno Herzig, "Politische Zielvorstellungen jüdischer Intellektueller aus dem Rheinland und aus Westfalen im Vormärz und in der Revolution von 1848," 272–311; and Walter Grab, "Der deutsch-jüdische Freiheitskämpfer Johann Jacoby," 352–74.

The Last Step on the Road to Emancipation

The aftermath of the revolution of 1848 and its impact on the legal situation of German Jews is comprehensively described in Reinhard Rürup, "The European

Revolution of 1848 and Jewish Emancipation," in Mosse, 1–53; and Werner E. Mosse, "The Revolution of 1848—Jewish Emancipation in Germany and its Limits," in ibid., 389–401. On this subject see also Rürup's "Judenemanzipation und bürgerliche Gesellschaft in Deutschland," in his *Emanzipation und Antisemitismus. Studien zur "Judenfrage" in der bürgerlichen Gesellschaft* (1975), 11–36. On Bavaria, see, in addition to the aforementioned work by Stefan Schwarz, *Die Juden in Bayern im Wandel der Zeiten*, the study by James F. Harris, *The People Speak! Anti-Semitism and Emancipation in Nineteenth-Century Bavaria* (1994), which focuses on anti-Jewish petitions against emancipation of the Jews in 1849–1850. Rainer Erb and Werner Bergmann also dealt with resistance to Jewish emancipation in *Die Nachtseite der Judenemanzipation. Der Widerstand gegen die Integration der Juden in Deutschland 1780–1860* (1989). The reception of emancipation in the media is examined in Walter Grab's essay, "Aspekte der Judenemanzipation in Tagesliteratur und Publizistik 1848–1869," in his *Der deutsche Weg der Judenemanzipation 1789–1938* (1991), 108–33.

Demographic Developments

Standard works in this area include Usiel O. Schmelz, "Die demographische Entwicklung der Juden in Deutschland von der Mitte des 19. Jahrhunderts bis 1933," *Zeitschrift für Bevölkerungswissenschaft* 7(1982):31–72; and Avraham Barkai, *Branching Out: German-Jewish Immigration to the United States, 1820–1914* (1994), and his "German-Jewish Migration in the Nineteenth Century, 1830–1910," LBIYB 30(1985):301–18. On emigration see also Jacob Toury, "Jewish Manual Labour and Emigration. Records from some Bavarian Districts, 1830–1857," LBIYB 16(1971):45–62; as well as several articles by Rudolf Glanz, in particular, "The German-Jewish Mass Emigration 1820–1880," *American Jewish Archives* 22(1970):49–66. Specifically on Jewish emigration from Württemberg, see Stefan Rohrbacher, "From Württemberg to America: A Nineteenth-Century German-Jewish Village on Its Way to the New World," *American Jewish Archives* 41(1989):143–71; and Adolf Kober, "Jewish Emigration from Wuerttemberg to the United States of America (1848–1855)," *Publications of the American Jewish Historical Society* 41(1952):225–273.

On the migration of German Jews within Germany, see, in addition to Barkai, Steven M. Lowenstein, "Rural Community and the Urbanization of German Jewry," *Central European History* 13(1980):218–36. Summaries of migration to Vienna can be found in the introductory chapters in Robert S. Wistrich, *The Jews of Vienna in the Age of Franz Joseph* (1989); and in Marsha Rozenblit, *The Jews of Vienna, 1867–1914: Assimilation and Identity* (1983). The statistical data in Anson G. Rabinbach's "The Migration of Galician Jews to Vienna, 1857–1880," *Austrian History Yearbook* 11(1975):42–54, are not totally reliable. On Bohemia and Moravia, see the essay by Ruth Kestenberg-Gladstein, "The Jews between Czechs and Germans in the Historic Lands, 1848–1918," in *The Jews of Czechoslovakia: Historical Studies and Surveys* (1968), 1:21–71.

Economic Ascent

The fundamental works on this subject are those by Avraham Barkai, the most important of which are "The German Jews at the Start of Industrialization— Structural Change and Mobility, 1835–1860," in Mosse, 123–50 (including statistics on emigration), "Sozialgeschichtliche Aspekte der deutschen Judenheit in der Zeit der Industrialisierung," JIDG 11(1982):237–60, and *Jüdische Minderheit und Industrialisierung. Demographie, Berufe und Einkommen der Juden in Westdeutschland 1850–1914* (1988). Barkai was also the editor of the posthumously published work by Arthur Prinz, *Juden im deutschen Wirtschaftsleben 1850– 1914* (1984). The history of the economic upper class is described in detail in the earlier mentioned two-volume work by Werner E. Mosse, *Jews in the German Economy: The German-Jewish Economic Elite 1820–1935* (1987) and *The German-Jewish Economic Elite, 1820–1935: A Sociocultural Profile* (1989). Mosse also wrote an article on the metalworks of the Hirsch family: "Integration Through Apartheid: The Hirschs of Halberstadt, 1780–1930," LBIYB 35(1990):133–150. For Strousberg's biography, see Joachim Borchart, *Der europäische Eisenbahnkönig Bethel Henry Strousberg* (1991). On the Rothschilds see the recent collection of articles: G. Heuberger, ed., *The Rothschilds: Essays on the History of a European Family* (1994). On Bleichröder see the groundbreaking study by Fritz Stern, *Gold and Iron: Bismarck, Bleichröder, and the Building of the German Empire* (1977).

Incomplete Integration

Other than the work by Jacob Toury that was mentioned under general works, there are no comprehensive studies on the integration of Jews in German society during this period. There are, however, a number of significant regional studies, including the following: Helga Krohn, *Die Juden in Hamburg. Die politische, soziale und kulturelle Entwicklung einer jüdischen Grossstadtgemeinde nach der Emanzipation 1848–1918* (1974); on a smaller town, see Ursula Gehring-Münzel, *Vom Schutzjuden zum Staatsbürger. Die gesellschaftliche Integration der Würzburger Juden 1803–1871* (1992). Utz Jeggle's *Judendörfer in Württemberg* (1969) provides a good presentation of the everyday experiences of rural Jewry and its relationship to the non-Jewish environment. There is as yet no fundamental examination of the situation in Austria. A fragmentary survey is supplied by Wolfgang Duchkowitsch, " 'Aber ich vergieße darüber keine Tränen.' Journalisten, Kultur- und Gesellschaftskritiker jüdischer Herkunft. Von der 'Aufklärung' über die Revolution zur Resignation," *Österreichisch-jüdisches Geistes- und Kulturleben* 2(1988):62–104. On Switzerland see Uri Robert Kaufmann, "Swiss Jewry: From the 'Jewish Village' to the City, 1780–1930," LBIYB 30(1985):283–99.

Political integration is discussed in the already mentioned monographs by Hamburger, Pulzer, and Toury. In addition, especially the works by Shlomo Na'aman deserve mention, including his essay, "Jewish Participation in the Deutscher Nationalverein, 1859–1867," LBIYB 34(1989):81–93, and his biography, *Ferdinand Lassalle. Deutscher und Jude* (1968). On the early developments of

Jews as instructors at German universities, the standard work is the abovementioned Monika Richarz, *Der Eintritt der Juden in die akademischen Berufe*. Bio-
graphic accounts on this subject are Hans I. Bach, *Jacob Bernays. Ein Beitrag zur
Emanzipationsgeschichte der Juden und zur Geschichte des deutschen Geistes im
neunzehnten Jahrhundert* (1974); and Norbert Kampe and Heinz-Dieter Schmie-
debach, "Robert Remak (1815–1865). A Case Study in Jewish Emancipation in the
Mid-Nineteenth-Century German Scientific Community," LBIYB 34(1989):95–
129. On Hermann Levi's position regarding Judaism, see the—somewhat one-
sided—essay by Peter Gay, "Hermann Levi: A Study in Service and Self-Hatred,"
in his *Freud, Jews, and Other Germans* (1978), 189–230. On representatives of a
resurgence of antisemitism, see the biographies by Jacob Katz, *The Darker Side of
Genius: Richard Wagner's Anti-Semitism* (1986); and Moshe Zimmermann, *William Marr. The Patriarch of Anti-Semitism* (1986). The relevant chapters in Jacob
Katz, *From Prejudice to Destruction: Anti-Semitism, 1700–1933* (1980) provide
the best survey of the transformation in anti-Jewish ideology during this period.

9. Jewish Identity in the Decades after 1848

General Works
Although it does not focus on religious and cultural developments, Jacob Toury's
Soziale und politische Geschichte der Juden in Deutschland 1847–1871 (1977)
contains much valuable material also for these aspects of the period and has influenced the treatment here.

Orthodoxy and Reform
A work of broader interest than its title suggests for the religious conflicts of this
period is Robert Liberles, *Religious Conflict in Social Context: The Resurgence of
Orthodox Judaism in Frankfurt am Main, 1838–1877* (1985). For the course of
Reform, see the general works noted for chapter 4. Although it focuses on the following period, much of Mordechai Breuer's *Modernity Within Tradition* is relevant for this period as well. David Ellenson's *Rabbi Esriel Hildesheimer and the
Creation of a Modern Jewish Orthodoxy* (1990) is the first full-length biography
of this important figure.

Synagogues and Seminaries
Invaluable for details on the construction and social significance of modern
German synagogues is Harold Hammer-Schenk, *Synagogen in Deutschland.
Geschichte einer Baugattung im 19. und 20. Jahrhundert* (1981). On liturgical
music see, most recently, H. Avenary, ed., *Kantor Salomon Sulzer und seine Zeit.
Eine Dokumentation* (1985); and Andreas Nachama/Susanne Stähr, "Die verges-
sene Revolution. Der lange Weg des Louis Lewandowski," *Menora* 3(1992):241–
55. *Das Breslauer Seminar. Jüdisch-Theologisches Seminar (Fraenckelscher
Stiftung) in Breslau 1854–1938* (1963) gathers earlier pertinent articles, while statistical information can be found in Hugo Weczerka, "Die Herkunft der Studie-

renden des Jüdisch-Theologischen Seminars zu Breslau 1854–1938," *Zeitschrift für Ostforschung* 35(1986):88–138. On the Liberal Seminary in Berlin we have Heinz-Hermann Völker, "Die Gründung und Entwicklung der Hochschule für die Wissenschaft des Judentums 1869–1900," *Trumah* 2(1990):24–46.

Popular Culture

Especially valuable in this area, and influential for the writing of this section, is the Hebrew doctoral dissertation of Henry Wassermann, "Jews, *Bürgertum*, and *bürgerliche Gesellschaft* in a Liberal Era (1840–1880)," Ph.D. diss., Hebrew University (Hebr., 1979). A portion serves as the basis for his "Jews and Judaism in the Gartenlaube," LBIYB 23(1978):47–60. Shulamit Volkov argues for continued broad Jewish differentiation in her important "Die Erfindung einer Tradition. Zur Entstehung des modernen Judentums in Deutschland," *Historische Zeitschrift* 253(1991):603–28, which deals, in part, with this period. Philippson's institute receives extensive treatment in Hans Otto Horch, *Auf der Suche nach der jüdischen Erzählliteratur* (1985), 153–64.

Wissenschaft des Judentums

There is no study of the subject that focuses exclusively on this period. An evaluation of the historical significance of Heinrich Graetz and a listing of earlier secondary literature on him are to be found in Heinrich Graetz, *The Structure of Jewish History and Other Essays*, ed. I. Schorsch (1975). For Steinschneider the most comprehensive treatment is still that contained in Alexander Marx, *Essays in Jewish Biography* (1947), 112–84.

Nostalgia and Thoughts of National Revival

Broadly important for this subject and influential for the treatment here is Richard I. Cohen, "Nostalgia and 'Return to the Ghetto': A Cultural Phenomenon in Western and Central Europe," in Frankel, 130–55. Franz D. Lucas and Heike Frank, *Michael Sachs. Der konservative Mittelweg* (1992) contains some new archival material and a helpful primary and secondary bibliography. Much has been written on Kalischer and Hess. Recent treatments, listing earlier literature, are Jody Elizabeth Myers, "Zevi Hirsch Kalischer and the Origins of Religious Zionism," in F. Malino and D. Sorkin, eds., *From East and West: Jews in a Changing Europe 1750–1870* (1990), 267–94; and Shlomo Avineri, *Moses Hess: Prophet of Communism and Zionism* (1985). Not listed by Avineri is the important Hebrew article by Michael Graetz, "On the Return of Moses Hess to Judaism—the Background to *Rome and Jerusalem*," *Zion* 45(1980):133–53.

Chronology

1818	Leopold Zunz's programmatic work *Etwas über die rabbinische Littera-tur* (On Rabbinic Literature)
1819	"Hep Hep" riots
1819	Association for Culture and the Scholarly Study of the Jews founded in Berlin
1820	Shalom Cohen founds the Hebrew journal *Bikure Ha-itim* in Vienna
1820	First volume of Isaac Marcus Jost's *Geschichte der Israeliten* (History of the Israelites)
1825	Heinrich Heine converts to Protestantism
1825	The Association for the Training of Elementary Teachers and Promotion of the Crafts Among Jews is founded in Münster
1828	The Israelite Supreme Ecclesiastical Authority (*Oberkirchenbehörde*) of Württemberg is established
1833	Moritz Oppenheim's painting, *Homecoming of a Jewish Volunteer from the War of Liberation to His Traditionally Observant Family*
1833	Preliminary Ordinance Pertaining to the Jews in the Grand Duchy of Posen is enacted
1836	Samson Raphael Hirsch's *Igrot tsafun* (Nineteen Letters on Judaism)
1837	Ludwig Philippson's *Allgemeine Zeitung des Judenthums*
1838	Start of the Geiger-Titkin dispute between traditionalists and reformers in Breslau
1843	First volume of Berthold Auerbach's *Schwarzwälder Dorfgeschichten* (Village Stories from the Black Forest) is published
1844	Karl Marx publishes his essay *Zur Judenfrage* (On the Jewish Question)
1844	First rabbinical assembly is held in Brunswick
1845	Reform congregation founded in Berlin
1847	A new law serves to standardize the legal status of Jews in Prussia
1848	Numerous anti-Jewish riots during the revolution
1848	Jewish representatives participate in the Frankfurt National Assembly
1848	Leopold Kompert's *Aus dem Ghetto* (From the Ghetto)
1850	Orthodox Israelite Religious Society secedes from the community in Frankfurt
1850	Richard Wagner's antisemitic pamphlet *Das Judenthum in der Musik* (Judaism in Music) is published anonymously
1851	Zacharias Frankel's *Darkhe ha-mishnah* (The Paths of the Mishnah)
1853	Heinrich Graetz publishes the first volume of his *Geschichte der Juden* (History of the Jews)
1854	The Jewish Theological Seminary, the first rabbinical seminary in Germany, is founded in Breslau
1855	Samson Raphael Hirsch founds the journal *Jeschurun*
1857	Geiger's *Urschrift and Übersetzungen der Bibel* (The Original Text and Translations of the Bible)

1859   Mathematician Moritz Abraham Stern is the first Jew to become a full professor (*Ordinarius*) at a German university

1860   In Hamburg Gabriel Riesser becomes the first German Jew to be named a judge

1860   The Orthodox weekly, *Der Israelit* (The Israelite), in Mainz

1862   Wilhelm Marr's first major antisemitic work, *Judenspiegel* (Mirror of the Jews)

1862   Zevi Hirsch Kalischer's *Derishat Zion*

1862   Moses Hess's *Rom und Jerusalem* (Rome and Jerusalem)

1862   With the Law on the Civil Equality of the Jews, Baden is the first German state to grant complete emancipation

1863   Ferdinand Lassalle founds the General German Workers' Association

1866   Jews in Switzerland are granted freedom of residence

1867   Jews in the Habsburg Empire are emancipated with the Austro-Hungarian Compromise

1867   Meyer Carl Baron von Rothschild is the first unbaptized Jew to enter the Prussian Upper Chamber

1868   Moritz Elstätter becomes Baden's minister of finance—the only Jew to hold a ministerial position in Germany before the First World War

1869   All religious denominations are granted equal status in the newly established North German Confederation

Sources of Illustrations

Index

Index

395

29, 41–42, 99, 290, 293; political participation in, 264, 265, 309, 311; prayerbooks for synagogues of, 323; protected Jews in, 10; rabbis and rabbinate in, 109; settlement policy in, 69

Bäder von Lucca, Die (The Baths of Lucca) (Heine), 214–15

Baisingen, anti-Jewish rioting in, 280–81, 283

Bamberger, Ludwig, 285, 309–10

Bamberger, Seligmann Baer, 98, 313

Banet, Mordecai, 113

Bankers, Jews as, 75–76, 80, 82–85, 268, 302–4

Baptisms, *see* Conversions to Christianity

Bar Mitzvah, preparation for, 321

Baruch, Löb (Börne), 239

Basel, 301

Bauer, Bruno, 172

Bavaria: anti-Jewish rioting in, 36; community administration in, 106; economic life in, 69–71, 78, 79, 87; Edict of 1813, 29, 47–48; education in, 114, 116, 117; emigration from, 59, 296, 297; German Confederation and, 28; German sermon and, 122; "Hep Hep" riots in, 37; Jewish population in, 53, 54, 58, 295; Jews excluded from university positions in, 270; judicial functions in, 101; legal status of Jews in, 11, 24, 29, 38, 47–48, 99, 294–94; *Matrikel* and, 24, 29, 47–48, 50, 293, 297; migration to, 298; military service in, 260–61; nobility to Jews of, 268–69; political participation in, 264–65, 285, 308, 309, 311; rabbis and rabbinate in, 106, 158–59; reactionary policies in

1850s and, 290–91; settlement policy in, 50, 69, 79; taxation in, 102

Bavarian Medical Widows' and Orphans' Pension Society, 193

Beck, Karl, 225–26

Beer, Amalie, 257

Beer, Jacob Herz, 68, 125

Beer, Michael, 68, 207–8, 246

Beer, Peter, 130, 138

Beer, Sigmund Julius, 270

Beer, Wilhelm, 68

Beer family, 62

Beggar Jews, 10, 63

Behren family, 302

Bellermann, J. J., 173

Belmont, August, 273

Belmont, Simon, *see* Aron, Simon

Benda, Daniel Alexander, 267

Bendavid, Lazarus, 265

Berg, 23

Berlin, 26, 350; Association for Reform in Judaism and, 144, 162–63, *163*, 196, 322, 352; calendar-yearbooks in, 335; conversions to Christianity in, 177; economic life in, 67–68, 75, 81, 84, 86, 87, 269, 302, 305, 306; education in, 113, 126; emigration to, 296, 299, 300; Enlightenment thinkers in, 12–15; Hebrew printing press of, 94; Jewish Enlightenment and, 90; Jewish population in, 55, *56*, 57, 58, 295; Jews excluded from university positions in, 271; legal status of Jews in, 1, 19–20, 39, 40–41; loyalty to monarch in Jews of, 252; military service in, 259; Orthodox separatist groups in, 325–26; political participation in, 262–63, 267; prayerbooks for synagogues of, 323; publishing houses in, 265–66;

practice in, 103; religious reform
in, 323; synagogue in, 328
Breweries, Jews involved with, 63, 64,
65, 69
Brieg, 334
Brokers, Jews as, 68, 80, 302
Brünn (Brno), 73, *85*
Brunner, Sebastian, 309
Brunswick: legal status of Jews in, 29;
political participation in, 285; rab-
binical assembly in, 163, 165–67;
rabbis and rabbinate in, 159
Budapest, 281
Büdinger, Max, 314
Burg, Meno, 260, *261*, 265
Burgkunstadt, 26
Burschenschaften, 272
Butcher guilds, 45
Buttenhausen: economic life in,
307–8; Jewish population in, *56*,
57–58

Calendars, popular Jewish culture in,
334–35
Calico cloth industry, Jews involved
in, 74, 76, 86–87
Calman family, 62
Cannstadt: economic life in, 87; emi-
gration to, 298
Cantor, for synagogues, 329, 331
Capitalism, 22, 77, 80, 81
Carinthia: lack of Jews in, 51; settle-
ment policy in, 300–1
Cariola, 300–1
Carlsbad, emigration to, 300
Carlsbad Decrees, 38
Carniola, 51
Cassel, David, 182
Cassel, Paulus (Selig), 182
Catholicism: civil equality of
Westphalian Jews and, 23;
German-Catholic movement and,

161, 162; Protestantism and,
196–97, 322
Cattle dealers, *see* Livestock trading
Chambers of commerce, Jews involved
in, 82, 268
Charity, 153, 312
Chemical industry, Jews involved in,
87, 305
Christianity, 30; Germanocentrism
and, 35; intellectuals on, 31–32, 33;
as state religion, 30, 31, 34; *see also*
Catholicism; Christian-Jewish relations; Conversions to Christianity;
Protestantism
Christian-Jewish relations, 1, 168–98,
351; Christianity against Judaism
and, 169–77; dignitaries and,
311–12; economic life and, 7, 10,
61, 69–71, 81–82, 88, 192; between
1848 and 1871, 320; Judaism
against Christianity and, 184–91;
mixed funerals and, 198, *198*, 284;
social contact and, 191–98; *see also*
Conversions to Christianity;
Guilds
Christian minorities, toleration for
those in Habsburg Empire, 16
Christian schools, 91, 116–17, 320–21
Christlich-Deutsche Tischgesellschaft,
30–31, 273
Christlich-Germanische
Tischgesellschaft, 31
Circumcision: Baden and, 41; Friends
of Reform and, 161–62
Cities: Christian-Jewish contact in,
192; economic life in, 305–7; emigration to, 296, 298–301, 350;
Jewish population in, 54–55, *56*,
56–57, 58; Jews expelled from, 54;
urbanization and, 349–50; *see also*
specific cities
Citizens, Jews as, 251–76; compatibil-

Society of Friends, 259

Sofer, Moses, 126

Sonnenfels, Joseph von, 254

South and New East Prussia, 8

Spinoza, Baruch, 170

Spitzer, Karl Heinrich, 284

Stägemann, Baron von, 273

Stahl, Friedrich Julius, 182–84, *183*, 189, 265

State bankers, Jews as, 74

Stein, Leopold, 127, 165, 334

Steinheim, Salomon Ludwig, 185–86, 187, 188

Steinschneider, Moritz, 194–95, 289, 341

Steinthal, Heymann, 239, 314

Stern, Moritz Abraham, 271, 314

Stern, Sigismund, 162, 196

Stöcker, Adolf, 182

Stock exchanges, Jews involved in, 68, 75, 82, 84, 268

Strauss, David Friedrich, 149, 188, 195

Streckfuss, Karl, 42–43, 173–74

Strousberg, Bethel Henry, 304–5

Stuttgart: economic life in, 71, 87; education in, 116; emigration to, 298; society-Jewish relations in, 271; synagogue in, 328, 329

Styria: lack of Jews in, 51; settlement policy in, 300–1

Sulamith, 117, 134, 153

Sulzbach, 11

Sulzer, Salomon, 198, *198*, 329, 331

Supreme Ecclesiastical Authority (Württemberg), 110

Supreme Jewish Council (Baden), 109

Surveyors, restrictions on Jews being, 39

Swabia, 295

Switzerland: anti-Jewish rioting in, 280; Jews in university positions in, 314; settlement policy in, 301

Synagogues: in Berlin, *330*, 331; cantor in, 329, 331; Christians involved with, 312; construction of impressive, 190, 328–29, *330*, 342–43; decorum in, 120; German sermon in, 120–22; Hebrew language in, 95; Moorish influence on, 190, 328–29, *330*, 342–43; non-Orthodox prayerbooks for, 323; organ in, 123, 166, 191, 323–24, 326, 331; preacher and, 120–21, 158; Reform movement and, 152, 190; regulations in, 120; rulers celebrated in, 99; in Seesen, 190; teachers as prayer leaders in, 96; in Vienna, *344*; Westphalia and, 108; women in, 324, 328; in Württemberg, 110; *see also* Rabbis and rabbinate

Synods, 326, 327, 328, 333

Tailors, Jews as, 87

Talmud: Baden and, 41; study of, 92

Tanneries, Jews involved in, 73

Tausig, Carl, 316

Taxation, 10; body tax, 8; communities levying, 100, 101, 102; Habsburg Empire and, 16; Prussia and, 19; withdrawal from community and, 320

Teachers, 78–79, 95–96, 115–16; universities excluding Jews as, 210, 268, 270–71, 306, 313–15

Temple Association (Hamburg), 126, 160

Territorial states (*Flächenstaaten*), legal status of Jews in late Enlightenment in, 7–11

Testimony, oaths when giving, 165

Teutonen (Erlangen), 272